MILTON STUDIES
XLIII

MILTON
STUDIES

XLIII ❧ Edited by
Albert C. Labriola

UNIVERSITY OF PITTSBURGH PRESS

MILTON STUDIES

is published annually by the University of Pittsburgh Press as a forum for Milton scholarship and criticism. Articles submitted for publication may be biographical; they may interpret some aspect of Milton's writings; or they may define literary, intellectual, or historical contexts—by studying the work of his contemporaries, the traditions which affected his thought and art, contemporary political and religious movements, his influence on other writers, or the history of critical response to his work.

Manuscripts should be upwards of 3,000 words in length and should conform to *The Chicago Manual of Style.* Manuscripts and editorial correspondence should be addressed to Albert C. Labriola, Department of English, Duquesne University, Pittsburgh, Pa., 15282–1703. Manuscripts should be accompanied by a self-addressed envelope and sufficient unattached postage.

Milton Studies does not review books.

Within the United States, *Milton Studies* may be ordered from the University of Pittsburgh Press, c/o Chicago Distribution Center, 11030 South Langley Avenue, Chicago, Ill., 60628, 1-800-621-2736.

Published by the University of Pittsburgh Press, Pittsburgh, Pa. 15260

Manufactured in the United States of America

Printed on acid-free paper

10 9 8 7 6 5 4 3 2 1

ISBN 0-8229-4216-X

ISSN 0076-8820

CONTENTS

MILTON STUDIES

XLIII

THE TALENTED MR. MILTON:
A PARABOLIC LABORER AND HIS IDENTITY

David V. Urban

IN HIS 1994 BOOK *Milton's Burden of Interpretation,* Dayton Haskin
notes that while a fair amount of Milton criticism has discussed the poet's
fascination with the parable of the talents (Matt. 25:14–30; cf. Luke 19:11–
27), surprisingly little has addressed his proclivity "to think of himself as a
version" of the "unprofitable servant" of Matthew's parable.[1] Having been
entrusted by his master with a talent of money, the servant in this parable
fearfully buries his talent, unlike his two fellow servants, who busily put their
talents to work and double their money. When the master returns, he chas-
tises the servant for his lack of industry, pronounces him "wicked and slothful" and has him "cast . . . into outer darkness." Haskin does much to explain
Milton's "uneasy" relationship to the parable and his tendency to identify
himself with the unprofitable servant. As valuable as Haskin's study is, he
does relatively little to analyze Milton's connection to the unprofitable servant in light of his comparable self-identification with the last-chosen laborers of the parable of the laborers in the vineyard (Matt. 20:1–16).[2] These
parabolic figures, unlike the unprofitable servant, receive God's grace and
reward in spite of their limited work in their master's vineyard. Very significantly, Milton makes use of this parable in a number of the same works in
which his identification with the parable of the talents appears so promi-
nently, including the early *Sonnet 7* and its companion letter "To a Friend," as
well as *Sonnet 19.* In these works, Milton employs the parable of the laborers
as a mitigating factor, offering the hope of God's favor amid his failures.
Although we cannot assert finally that Milton's autobiographical speakers—or
Milton himself—ever completely escape the horrible fear of being judged
"unprofitable" by God, the parable of the laborers serves, even if only temporarily, to assuage such spiritual anguish.

It is generally agreed that Milton's *Sonnet 7* ("How Soon Hath Time")
was written for the occasion of his twenty-fourth birthday, 8 December 1632.[3]
A few months later he included the sonnet in a letter "To a Friend." (The
recipient of this poem is unknown, although his former tutor, Thomas Young,
is often suggested.[4]) It is helpful to read *Sonnet 7* in relation to this letter, and
particularly so to acquire a greater understanding of Milton's lifelong identi-

fication with both the parable of the talents and the parable of the laborers. The letter was elicited by a conversation from the previous day in which its recipient had, it seems, "admonish[ed]" Milton for not yet having "credible employment" and reminded him "that the howres of the night passe on . . . & that the day w^{th}me is at hand wherin Christ com̄ands all to Labour while there is light." Furthermore, the friend has charged that Milton has "too much love of Learning" and that he has "given up [himself] to dreame away [his] Yeares in the armes of studious retirement like Endymion w^{th}the Moone."[5] We may assume that this well-intentioned friend was concerned that although Milton had earned a master's degree from Cambridge and already had attained the age required for taking Holy Orders (twenty-four), he was not yet pursuing ordination but instead was engaging in further preparation.

In his letter, which makes no reference to his ambitions to be a poet and implies that he eventually will enter the ministry, Milton acknowledges that his life is "as yet obscure, & unserviceable to mankind"; and, given his friend's sincere concern for his welfare, the young writer considers himself "bound though unask't, to give you account, as oft as occasion is, of this my tardie moving; according to the precept of my conscience, wch I firmly trust is not w^{th}out god."[6] What follows is a forthright explanation of his "conscien[tious]" decision to forego immediate employment. About halfway through the letter, the parable of the talents is named explicitly, as Milton asserts his "due & tymely obedience to that com̄and in the gospell set out by the terrible seasing of him that hid the talent" (YP 1:320). He goes on to explain that "this very consideration of that great com̄andment does not presse forward as soone as may be to underg[o] but keeps off w^{th}a sacred reverence & religious advisement how best to undergoe[,] not taking thought of beeing late so it give advantage to being more fit" (320; brackets in YP). Here, Milton demonstrates an intense self-awareness of the parable, but also distances himself from the hapless servant who hid his single talent. A tension within Milton seems evident here, one that betrays his "uneasy" relation to this parable. It is the third, unfaithful servant that he explicitly mentions, aware that others may well associate him with that "slothful" figure; at the same time, however, he seeks to identify not with that servant, but rather with the faithful ones, since he sees extensive preparation as the prerequisite for the faithful service the parable demands.

We may see from his letter that Milton's implicit connection between further preparation and true obedience to the parable is closely related to the idea of "conscience." As Margo Swiss explains, "Conscience is itself the essential justification for Milton's procrastination from . . . clerical commitment." Swiss notes that Milton's "scrupulous attention to conscience" reflects the influence of Puritan divines such as William Perkins.[7] Perkins, also a

Cambridge graduate, emphasized the need for a man's conscience to be settled fully before accepting a particular calling into God's service. In *How to Live and That Well* (1596), Perkins writes, "Againe, faith is required, whereby every man must beleeve that the calling in which hee is, is the particular calling, in which god will bee served of him. For unlesse the conscience be settled in this, no good worke can be done in any calling."[8]

Connecting Perkins's assertion with Milton's statement on conscience, we may speculate that, to a large degree, Milton's delay resulted from a lack of a "settled conscience" about the particular calling of the Anglican ministry. Relating Milton's scruples of conscience to his desire to obey the "commandment" of the parable of the talents, we see that Milton hoped to avoid the judgment of the unprofitable servant by not prematurely entering a ministerial vocation.

To be sure, Milton's lack of certainty about his calling was based essentially on his conviction that, despite his Cambridge education, he was neither intellectually nor spiritually prepared for such a weighty undertaking. Again, Milton's acute sensitivity to the grave spiritual responsibility of the ministry placed him firmly in line with the dominant Puritan attitudes of his day. As Swiss notes, the words of William Whately would have resonated profoundly with the young Milton. In *The New Birth* (1618), Whately exhorts ministers to "study day and night, and by continuall paines, putting forth thy selfe to all laboriousnesse. . . . Consider what a waighty duty, what a great honour it is to bee Gods instrument for the regenerating of others."[9]

Whately's message contains two major points that closely parallel two of Milton's most important concerns. The first is the need for ministers to apply themselves with ceaseless diligence to pious study, a pattern reflected by Milton both in his Cambridge years and in his periods at Hammersmith and Horton. The second is an admonition to soberly ponder the immense responsibility placed on those who would be shepherds of Christ's flock. Along with such a calling would come a grave reckoning at the end of the minister's life, one in which he would have to give an account for his faithfulness—or lack thereof—before God. The Bible itself is clear that such a reckoning would be even stricter for church leaders, to which this warning from the epistle of James attests: "My brethren, be not many of you masters, knowing that we shall receive the greater condemnation" (3:1).

John Owen's 1673 sermon "Ministerial Endowments the Work of the Spirit"—a message preached at an ordination service—speaks to the issues of conscience, judgment, and the ministerial call in direct relation to the parable of the talents. In an exposition of the parable pertinent to Milton's own vocational uncertainty, Owen warns against taking orders when one lacks the spiritual gifts requisite to such an audience:

For men to take upon them to serve Christ as officers in the work of his house, who have received none of these spiritual abilities to work with, is a high presumption, and casts reflection of dishonour on Jesus Christ, as if he called to work, and gave no strength; as if he called to trade, and gave no stock; or required spiritual duties, and gave no spiritual abilities. Christ will say to such on the last day, "How came ye in hither?"[10]

We may recognize in Owen's warning Milton's own concerns. To be sure, Milton recognized that he was a gifted individual. Were his talents, however, those that would make him a suitable overseer of people's souls? It would be better to wait for certainty than to enter into the ministry presumptuously, only to recognize that he had misunderstood his own talents. Such a situation would be doubly woeful, for he would not only find himself unable to carry out the priestly office, he also would be trapped in this office and unable to discharge his true vocation, whatever it may be.

In light of such teaching, Milton's scruples of conscience concerning ordination may be understood all the more clearly, and so may, for that matter, his connection with the parable of the talents in the letter "To a Friend." Since Milton believed that a stricter judgment awaited those in church leadership, a conscientious delay was entirely appropriate for one who feared rushing headlong into a decision like that which befell the un-faithful servant. Thus, although his "Love of Learning" might appear to some as the kind of "emptie & fantastick chase of shadows and notions" (YP 1:320) that might characterize the "wicked and slothful servant" (Matt. 25:26), Milton here may be characterized better as one who deems a prolonged period of diligent, albeit ostensibly unproductive, preparatory study a far better—and safer—use of his talents than premature entrance into the high and awesome calling of the priesthood.

Milton's reference to the parable of the talents is followed immediately by his hopeful connection with the parable of the laborers. Defending his choice to delay employment and endeavor "to be more fit," he offers the following explanation: "for those that were latest lost nothing when the maister of the vinyard came to give each one his hire" (320). By associating himself with the last hired laborers in this parable, Milton seeks to articulate a confidence before the judgment of God that is quite unlike the fearful atti-tude of the unprofitable servant. As he tries to convince his friend of the rightness of his own deferment from active service, Milton depicts a God who fully understands the young graduate's decisions, a God who is ready to reward Milton equally with those who have begun laboring in the Lord's vineyard earlier than he.

Milton's skillful juxtaposition of the two parables merits further analysis. We may speculate that Milton's friend earlier had mentioned the parable of the talents and admonished, however gently, young Milton "to Labour while there is light" (319) in order to avoid the fate of the unprofitable servant. If Milton's friend was, in fact, Young, the possibility of such a warning seems all the more likely, as we may assume that his former tutor used various biblical admonitions to exhort his students to diligent labor. Even if this friend did not himself ever introduce the subject of the parable, we still may identify the parable as a biblical "place" that resonated strongly not only with Milton but with many other Christians throughout early modern England.[11] That the parable already had become part of young Milton's consciousness is evident from his allusion to it in *Sonnet 7,* composed a little while before. Indeed, we may recognize that, given his situation in life, the parable of the talents would be a natural scriptural place for the sensitive young man to ponder. But it is Milton's interplay between the parable of the talents and the parable of the laborers that makes both this letter and *Sonnet 7* so intriguing in regard to Milton's personality and development, for we can see that Milton uses his identification with the latter parable to mitigate his identification with the former. By employing the parable of the laborers, Milton is able to place himself in relationship to the laborers who, though having worked only the last hour of the work day, have been rewarded by the owner of the vineyard with a full day's wages. By making this connection, he can invert his inclination to associate himself with the "slothful and unprofitable servant" and instead associate himself with the servants who made industrious use of the talents given them.

Shortly after his juxtaposition of these two parables, Milton includes *Sonnet 7* in the text of his letter. The letter "To a Friend" greatly aids our understanding of the poem, whose message closely parallels the overall thrust of the larger epistle. We also see in the sonnet Milton's skillful use of the two parables. Its octave reveals the autobiographical speaker's awareness of his coming of age and the meager degree of accomplishment and personal maturity that he can show for his years:

> How soon hath Time, the subtle thief of youth,
> Stol'n on his wing my three and twentieth year!
> My hasting days fly on with full career,
> But my late spring no bud or blossom show'th.
> Perhaps my semblance might deceive the truth,
> That I to manhood am arriv'd so near,
> And inward ripeness doth much less appear,
> That some more timely-happy spirits endu'th.   (1–8)

The octave also mentions the comparative productivity and maturity of any number of Milton's peers, the "more timely-happy spirits" of line 8.

These "spirits" often have been identified as poets who have accomplished more than the young Milton at this time. It seems more appropriate, however, in light of the sonnet's probable connection with the matter of ordination, to identify them as those Cambridge graduates who already have been ordained into the Anglican ministry at the usual age of twenty-three.[12] In any event, the speaker's modest output and humble station in life are magnified by the advanced position of his fellows, a juxtaposition that sets up the sestet's explicit allusion to the parable of the talents. The octave also demonstrates a tone of anxiety and shame that contrasts sharply with the hopeful attitude of the sestet:

> Yet be it less or more, or soon or slow,
> It shall be still in strictest measure ev'n
> To that same lot, however mean or high,
> Toward which Time leads me, and the will of Heav'n;
> All is, if I have grace to use it so,
> As ever in my great task-Master's eye. (9–14)

This striking expression of resolution mixed with peace may be understood largely in the context of the sestet's combining the parable of the talents and the parable of the laborers. Each accented word of the opening line of the sestet, as Anna Nardo points out, "deliberate[ly] echoes" the "anxious phrases" of the octave.[13] "Yet be it *less* or *more,* or *soon* or *slow*" reflects "much *less* appear," "*more* timely-happy spirits," "how *soon* hath Time," and "my *late* spring" (emphases mine). There is a redemptive use of the language of the octave, transforming the pessimistic tone of those phrases into the hopeful paradigm of the parable of the laborers. This transformation becomes complete as the sestet unfolds. Stephen Booth and Jordan Flyer point out "the leveling implications of 'All is . . . As ever' "; they also note that the use of the word "grace" in line 13, in relation to the divine "task-Master," portrays a God "indifferent to distinctions begun early and service begun late." The allusion to the parable of the laborers "assists in and justifies the assertion that all the distinctions that have previously been the poem's topics do not matter."[14]

At least on the surface, such divine equity in judgment has a profound effect on the young writer. By identifying himself with the late-chosen laborers of the parable, he gains a freedom that allows him to wait and prepare apart from the fear of being judged an unprofitable servant. At the same time, this freedom enables him to employ all the more diligently those gifts entrusted to him. As in the letter, in *Sonnet 7* the parable of the laborers is the vehicle that transforms Milton's potentially fearful identification with the parable of the talents into a positive association. Booth and Flyer note that the declaration of line 13—"All is, if I have grace to use it so"—allows for the paradoxical juxtaposition of the theology of "earned rewards" of the parable of the talents and the "metaphysical supra-logical justice that prevails in the divine economy" of the parable of the laborers. Lines 13 and 14 also display a paradoxical softening of the language describing God. On one hand, as Haskin points out, the title "task-Master" calls to mind Exodus 1:11, which tells of the "taskmasters" set over the Israelites "to afflict them with their burdens." Left by itself, this title evokes, in the context of this poem, a fearful image of the master of the parable of the talents, whose terrifying judgment awaits the unprofitable servant. And yet, this "task-Master" is one who, the speaker hopes, gives him "grace" to "use" his talents in a manner proper to both his calling and to the divinely orchestrated time frame in which that calling fully reveals itself. Thus, the young Milton may have a more peaceful relationship to the parable, one in which he may view himself as a "good and faithful servant" (Matt. 25:21, 23) because he is permitted, by the grace of his "great task-Master," to labor earnestly in the preparation necessary for his eventual call to active service. In saying this, we may agree with Nardo's paraphrase of the sonnet's final two lines: "All that I do, if I have grace to employ my inward ripeness thus, is done as ever conscious of being in God's sight and having God's guidance." Nardo observes that this ending "reasserts the central concern of sonnet and letter alike: that Milton believes his action and inaction are in obedience with God's will." In his "conscientious" obedience to the will of God in what he does and does not do, young Milton reflects one whose identification with the two parables has brought about a kind of spiritual tranquility in the face of potentially devastating circumstances.[15]

Despite this, we may recognize that the optimism Milton displays in *Sonnet 7* is colored with a certain tentativeness. The possession of grace he speaks of is unmistakably conditional: "*if* I have grace to use it so" (13, emphasis mine). Milton's tone indicates that he views whatever grace he may be granted as, ultimately, still dependent on the faithful exercise of his talents. In no way can he take God's reprieve as license for sloth. Such an outlook is consistent with John Calvin's reading of the parable of the laborers. Warning against interpreting the parable to mean that all will have "equality of . . . heavenly glory," Calvin asserts that "[w]e know that slackness is nearly always the fruit of over-confidence. That is why many sit down in the middle of the race as if they had got to the end."[16] Calvin maintains that the parable teaches God's freedom to call whomever he wishes at whatever time he wishes, without obligation to anyone. But he also stresses that

if anyone infers from this [parable] that men were created for activity and that each has his divinely appointed station, so that he shall not sink into laziness, he will not be twisting Christ's words. We may also gather that our whole life is useless and we are justly condemned of laziness until we frame our life to the command and calling of God. From this it follows that they labour in vain who thoughtlessly take up this or that kind of life and do not wait for God's calling.

Not surprisingly, Calvin's exegesis of this parable finally echoes his comment on the parable of the talents: that "Christ . . . means that there is no excuse for the slackness of those who both suppress God's gifts and consume their age in idleness." We also may see a distinct similarity between Calvin's words on God's calling and Owen's discussion of that subject and the parable of the talents. In the end, both parables offer the same basic admonition to their readers: Listen carefully for the call of God in your life and labor tirelessly in the particular vineyard to which God has directed.[17]

Thus, it is fitting that whatever solace the parable of the laborers offers the young Milton in the letter "To a Friend" and *Sonnet 7* is temporary and does not undo the hold that the parable of the talents has upon his consciousness. Indeed, it would be wrong to think that Milton intended it to do so. For Milton at this time in his life, the parable of the laborers softens the severity of the parable of the talents even as it reinforces its message of diligent labor in the light of God's call. The Milton of the early 1630s, with youth yet on his side, can, for a time, seek solace in the notion that he is working faithfully even as he awaits a final clarity of vocation. The parable of the talents, however, remains within his psyche, tamed for a season, but present throughout.

Our understanding of Milton's relationship to the parable of the talents during this period can be informed further by an examination of *Ad Patrem,* his Latin verse epistle to his father, probably written in 1634. A close inspection of *Ad Patrem* sheds important light upon not only Milton's relationship with John Milton Sr., but also how that relationship affected his lifelong preoccupation with that parable. Although *Ad Patrem* assumes that Milton's future career will be among the clergy, the occasion for the poem is a conflict between the writer and his father concerning the subject of poetry.[18] Milton's epistle reveals that his father "despise[d]" (17) poetry, that he had "contempt" (56) for it and considered it "futile [*venas*] and worthless [*puta*]" (57; "idle and unprofitable" in the Flannagan/Columbia translation[19]); in fact, he "hate[d]" poetry (67). Young John goes on, however, to write that he does not believe his father really hates poetry, for otherwise he would not have provided his son with an expensive education without pressuring him to enter the law or some other more lucrative profession (67–76). Milton thanks his father for his costly gift even as he attempts to convince John Sr. that poetry is genuinely compatible with his education and presumed ministerial career. The epistle's tone exhibits a kind of bashful playfulness; Milton is all too aware of his audience's previous generosity toward him even as he seems cautiously confident that his father will indulge him yet again. At the same time, the young writer displays an earnest ambition in his lines. He does not want to be perceived as a freeloader, but rather a wise investment. Although his words are couched in an appropriate humility, Milton expresses his clear intention to achieve greatness in his art, a greatness that will serve as a lasting recompense for his father.

The influence of the parable of the talents is evident at various points in *Ad Patrem,* beginning with those lines that describe the elder Milton's attitude toward poetry. We may notice that the words "idle" and "unprofitable" echo the master's condemnation of the "wicked and slothful" servant, specifically called "unprofitable" in Matthew 25:30. Milton's language also reflects the parable's in the need he feels to pay back his father what he has been given: "I do not know what gifts of mine could more aptly repay yours— though my greatest gifts could never repay yours" (lines 8–10); and "no requital equal to your desert and no deeds equal to your gifts are within my power" (111–12). The writer's acute awareness of his inability to repay his father, however, is coupled with an implicit desire to repay him through poetic achievement. Milton writes, "however humble my present place in the company of learned men, I shall sit with the ivy and laurel of a victor" (101–2). Significantly, this declaration of confidence closely precedes the above statement in lines 111–12; this juxtaposition seems to say, in effect, "Of course I can't ever repay what you've given me, but just you watch—after you see how successful I become, you'll consider yourself recompensed indeed." Therefore, on one level Milton seeks to flatter his father by proclaiming that the gift of his education is genuinely matchless; on another level, however, Milton clearly intends to repay his father with interest.

Two other factors link *Ad Patrem* and the parable. The first is an implicit connection between Milton's father and God the Father. John Shawcross observes two such parallels. In the first, Milton asks, "What greater gift could come from a father, or from Jove himself if he had given everything, with the single exception of heaven?" (95–96). The notion that his father's gift is, in essence, equivalent to the greatest earthly gift of the supreme God certainly lends credence to an analogy between the letter and the parable. In the second parallel, which concludes the letter, Milton addresses his "juvenile verses" (115) and declares, "perhaps you will preserve these praises and the name of the father / sung again and again, as an example to a future generation" (119–20, Shawcross's translation). Shawcross notes that we may see a connection with God the Father here because "his manifestation through the Son is constant example to future generations."[20]

The other factor that connects *Ad Patrem* (and John Milton Sr.) to the parable of the talents is the fact that the elder Milton was by trade a scrivener whose income largely consisted of lending money "at eight to ten percent interest."[21] We know that he largely financed his son's education through the interest from such loans, and that he was hardly a pushover when it came to collecting from lackluster borrowers. J. Milton French observes that he went to considerable lengths to recover money owed him, even if his original debtors were deceased.[22] These points are not made to dispute the affectionate relationship that Milton reportedly enjoyed with his father. Nonetheless, it seems highly plausible that his awareness of his father's sternness toward debtors somehow influenced Milton when, in *Ad Patrem,* he wrote of his inability to "repay" his father's generosity. Similarly, it seems equally plausible that the scrivener's position as a moneylender significantly informed young Milton's relationship to the parable, specifically to the master who berated the "wicked and slothful servant" who failed even to "put [his] money to the exchangers" so that his master would have received it back "with usury" (Matt. 25:26–27).

Assuming that *Ad Patrem* was enough to change his father's mind about the value of poetry, Milton still would have to bring forth a body of work to justify John Sr.'s continuing investment. The quick production of such poetry would not have been the immediate concern of young Milton, who very much saw his current situation as one of continued preparation, and who, as his playfully brash prediction in *Ad Patrem* indicates, foresaw literary success in the not-too-distant future. However, in light of the passage of time and Milton's modest early poetic achievement, the burden of such an unfulfilled boast would have grown increasingly heavy. And, while Milton's promise that he would "sit with the ivy and laurel of a victor" falls short of being a sacred oath, we still may recognize, in light of the almost divine status he assigns his father in *Ad Patrem,* the severe obligation under which Milton believed the speaker of an oath placed himself. In *De Doctrina Christiana* Milton writes, "An oath which involves a promise must be kept, even if we lose by it, so long as we have not promised something unlawful" (YP 6:685). Years later, with his promise to his father largely unfulfilled, we see Milton's relationship to the parable of the talents become progressively uneasy, a discomfort finally mitigated only by a renewed dependence on the parable of the laborers, whose absence is conspicuous in both *Ad Patrem* and *The Reason of Church Government* of 1642.

Though we shall discuss it only in passing, *Reason* is noteworthy to our analysis of Milton's relationship to the parables in question. In this tract the mature Milton presents himself as a divinely inspired prophetic spokesman for the Puritan cause. This "calling" has replaced his earlier intention to join the Anglican ministry, and he connects the office of the inspired prophet to that of the poet (YP 1:816). That Milton's career is now established and that he no longer can delay his active service to God influence his disturbing use of the parable of the talents in the introduction to *Reason*'s second book. Exhibiting a heightened degree of self-importance, Milton again identifies with the unprofitable servant. Noting "that God even to a strictnesse requires the improvement of these his entrusted gifts" (801), he claims that were he to neglect his prophetic gifts and fail to defend the Church, he would certainly be judged "timorous and ungratefull" and "slothfull" (804). In no other work does Milton demonstrate such a thoroughly negative use of the parable, a use bereft of the softening effects of the parable of the laborers seen in *Sonnet 7* and the letter "To a Friend." Having completed his time of extended preparation, he does not appeal to that parable to gain another reprieve from God. Rather, the Milton of *Reason* seems wholly dependent upon his own efforts to appease his heavenly Father and escape the fate of the unprofitable servant.

Roughly a decade later, however, when Milton in *Sonnet 19* ("When I Consider How My Light Is Spent") again identifies with the unprofitable servant in his most famous reference to the parable of the talents, he reintroduces the parable of the laborers.[23] This reintroduction is used at first to expose a weakened, discouraged Milton whose desire to serve God as a prophet/poet ironically manifests itself in bitterness toward God himself; by the end of the poem, however, the parable of the laborers is a vehicle of grace to teach the self-important, self-condemning Milton that his service to God is under the authority of a sovereign Lord who will accomplish his perfect plan with or without Milton's heroics.

The sonnet's octave is characterized by Milton's autobiographical speaker's discouragement and bitterness, something that his combined use of both parables works to accomplish. When the parable of the talents is referred to explicitly in line 3, we see its connection with all that precedes and follows in the poem. There has been plentiful speculation concerning exactly what the "one Talent which is death to hide, / Lodged with me useless" (3–4) really is. Traditional scholarly consensus holds that the "Talent" in question is Milton's poetic gift, and that his "light" that has been "spent" is his eyesight.[24] These designations, while not wrong, are too limited. As Haskin points out, Milton's notion of "talent" in the sonnet includes his poetic gift but encompasses a broader gifting.[25] It is better to recognize his poetic gift in conjunction with the prophetic office with which he has been entrusted, even as it is more appropriate to view Milton's vocation as a poet in conjunction with his calling as a prophet.

In the same way, the "light" of *Sonnet 19* on one level is certainly Milton's eyesight. However, as with "talent," Milton moves beyond a limited interpretation of such a potent word. In the context of the poem, "light" encompasses the spiritual enlightenment and direction given to believers, as well as the responsibility of the believer to shine forth God's glory and goodness before the world. These aspects of "light" are especially pertinent to Milton's prophetic "office." We may understand his anxiety in relation to his perceived failures as a prophet of God, one whose prophetic energies, for the past decade or more, have been dedicated inordinately to political pamphleteering. Milton's self-doubt here includes his dissatisfaction with his poetic output, but only as his role as a poet is viewed within the larger context of his prophetic office. Indeed, in retrospect we may see the occasion of *Sonnet 19* as a turning point of sorts in Milton's prophetic career, one in which he seems to eschew the parochialism of his prophetic role within the Puritan political cause in favor of a more universal prophetic office that is conducted properly through the vehicle of poetry. This vehicle finds its apex in *Paradise Lost,* but it is displayed with immense power in this very sonnet, a sonnet that has impacted countless readers in a way that Milton's political prose—the vehicle through which so much of his "light" had already been "spent"—has never done.

Early in the poem, then, we see a discouraged, disconsolate prophet, one whose blindness exacerbates his situation with a stinging and seemingly perpetual irony. We also may note the speaker's sincere desire to labor for God in spite of his crippled condition. Although his "Talent" is "Lodg'd with me useless," he announces that "my Soul [is] more bent / To serve there with my Maker, and present / My true account" (4–6). His desire to serve, however, is not based on genuine New Covenant faith, but rather is a response to his own fear of the unfair, even malicious God he perceives. The sonnet continues: "lest he returning chide; / Doth God exact day-labor, light denied, / I fondly ask" (6–8). That Milton's speaker is thinking wrongly about God here is evidenced by the resolution of the sestet, and Michael Lieb correctly notes the absence of Christian sentiment in the octave.[26] Indeed, the speaker here demonstrates a misunderstanding of the parable, even as he misunderstands God himself. In his resolution "[t]o serve," the speaker is not demonstrating "a right will" (contra Roger Slakey) nor, for that matter, right reason.[27] He is falling into the same error as the unprofitable servant, whose misperception of his lord as "an hard man" (Matt. 25:24) inspired him to hide his single talent in the ground.[28] In the case of the speaker, his misperception of the parable and God drive him to try to earn God's favor apart from recognizing his grace, and the result of such self-justifying efforts is further frustration and bitterness.[29]

This bitterness is particularly evident when Milton's speaker rejects his once beloved parable of the laborers. We see that the question "Doth God exact day-labor, light denied," contains a scornful allusion to the parable.[30] It is ironic that this parable, the very text that acted as Milton's "rescuer" from his struggles with the parable of the talents in the 1630s, should now reappear in the "fond murmur" of line 7. Clearly the grace that was received appreciatively by a late-blooming priest in training is less than satisfactory for a middle-aged prophet/poet mired in depression. Indeed, his spurning of the parable here demonstrates a frightening degree of hubris which transcends even the self-importance of *The Reason of Church Government*. The speaker, in essence, has transferred his own self-loathing to God himself; that is, because the speaker experiences such disgust toward himself, he portrays God, through the vehicle of the parable of the talents, as effectively rejecting him. What is more, the speaker has turned that perceived divine rejection into an accusation against the character of God. Milton is, in fact, "playing God" on two levels, for he simultaneously pronounces God's judgment upon himself even as he pronounces judgment on God.

The speaker's rejection of the parable of the laborers manifests itself through his distortion of its message of grace. In the parable, the lord of the vineyard exemplifies God's grace by granting a full day's wage to those laborers he hired only for the final hour of the workday. The speaker's "fond murmur"—which echoes the complaint of the discontented workers in the parable of the laborers, who "murmured against" the lord of the vineyard (Matt. 20:11)—turns this idea on its head. Milton's speaker insinuates that, unlike the generous lord of the parable, God would expect a full day's work from one who lacks the ability to work in the first place. Given the occasion for Milton's poem, we rightly may see in this line the image of a blind man groping helplessly to perform a task that requires sight, or perhaps that of laborers struggling to harvest their crop in the dark of a starless night. At the same time, we can imagine our prophet/poet striving to serve the very God who has withheld blessing from him. In all this, the speaker displays a marked self-righteousness, and to the reader familiar with Milton's earlier affection for the parable of the laborers, this self-righteous striving is particularly noteworthy. Indeed, here Milton has lapsed even further away from a focus on God's mercy than in *Reason*. There, Milton's public spiritual anxiety strikes us as odd, but it reflects the feelings of a man who, having completed his extensive preparation, earnestly desires to prove himself useful. In *Sonnet 19*, however, Milton's speaker actually belittles the parable he formerly cherished, rejecting its message of grace. And although Milton's blindness and the obvious sadness expressed in the octave give us genuine sympathy for the speaker, we still may recognize on his part a certain spiritual betrayal even as he accuses God of betraying him.

The speaker's words end at this point. *Sonnet 19*'s remarkable turn takes place in the middle of line 8, introducing the character "Patience," whose rebuttal of the speaker's murmur makes up the sestet. The speaker's silence is highly revealing. For what had been the active complaint of an achievement-consumed individual is replaced by his passive reception of Patience's words. We do not get the impression that Milton's speaker willingly steps aside from his posture of active complaint; rather, we see that he has been moved by a higher power—a messenger of the very God he has been accusing. And we sense that there is something at the same time irresistibly strong and disarmingly gentle about this displacement. To be sure, on one level there is great force behind Patience's words; for the speaker to attempt a rebuttal would be not only foolish, but also impossible. And yet, as he hears Patience speak, he recognizes that the God he has distrusted has, indisputably, the best interests of his cantankerous servant in mind.[31]

Even as Patience's words demonstrate God's compassion toward Milton's speaker, they also reveal a justification of God's character and a clear articulation of the speaker's relationship to him. God's absolute sovereignty is seen throughout Patience's speech, and the need for the speaker to accept this humbly is reinforced by the biblical allusions in the sestet. The words, "God doth not need / Either man's work or his own gifts," call to mind Psalm 50, in which God rebukes the Israelites for thinking that he somehow is dependent on their sacrifices. God declares, "I will take no bullock out of thy house, nor he-goats out of thy folds. For every beast of the forest is mine, and the cattle upon a thousand hills. . . . If I were hungry, I would not tell thee; for the world is mine, and all the fullness thereof" (50:9–10, 12).

In both *Sonnet 19* and Psalm 50, those who receive God's rebuke are chastised for thinking that they can act in a way that somehow will enhance God's position. In Psalm 50, those individuals are commanded, "call upon me in the day of trouble; I will deliver thee, and thou shalt glorify me" (15). God does offer them a chance to glorify him, but only through their dependence upon him. Having been rebuffed in their attempts to add to his glory, they are told in no uncertain terms that they are the needy ones, and that their most acceptable service to God is a humble display of such need.

A second, and oft-mentioned allusion appears in Patience's statement, "who best / Bear his mild yoke, they serve him best" (10–11). As many have noted, the words "mild yoke" echo Jesus' words in Matthew 11:29–30, where Jesus tells his listeners to take his "easy" yoke upon them. For purposes of our discussion of *Sonnet 19*, however, Matthew 11:25–26 is also pertinent: "At that time Jesus answered and said, I thank thee, O Father, Lord of heaven and earth, because thou hast hidden these things from the wise and prudent, and hast revealed them unto babes. . . . Come unto me, all ye that labor and are heavy laden, and I will give you rest. Take my yoke upon you, and learn from me; for I am meek and lowly in heart, and ye shall find rest unto your souls. For my yoke is easy, and my burden is light" (11:25–26, 29–30).

Jesus' opening statement declares that God's wisdom and blessings are not given to those commonly considered wise, but to the humble. This statement is followed by an invitation to the hurting to place themselves in a relationship of total reliance upon Jesus himself. Again, this biblical passage parallels the message of *Sonnet 19*, especially if we expand our understanding of "light" to include the spiritual inspiration offered to our author. Because of his own pride, he finds himself in a state of spiritual deprivation. We see in Jesus' words that the invitation to take up his yoke is also an invitation to learn from him. This dual invitation, however, is predicated upon a faith in him that exhibits complete dependence on him, imitating the humility of the one who describes himself as "meek and lowly in heart" (11:29). For our exhausted prophet/poet, the admonishment to "Bear his mild yoke" is, ultimately, the gateway to restored spiritual light, a light that is superior to that previously expended, for it is purified by the humble obedience of one who better serves a humble master.

These two biblical allusions set the stage for the allusion to the parable of the laborers in the concluding line: "They also serve who only stand and wait." These words, Patience's final utterance, reinforce the emphasis on humble dependence on God and the true service rendered by such an attitude. This line recalls the situation of the laborers who have been "standing idle in the marketplace" (Matt. 20:3) for the first eleven hours of the workday, waiting to be hired. Having been hired by the lord of the vineyard at the eleventh hour, they work a single hour and are given a full day's wages equal to those workers who were hired early in the morning. Noting the connection between the parable and line 14, E. A. J. Honigmann points out that Milton uses "wait" to mean "stay in expectation"[32]; the "idle" workers, by virtue of their willingness to wait to be chosen, demonstrate their total dependence on the call of the vineyard's lord to be made useful. When they finally are called, they are rewarded as much for their patient waiting as for their actual service rendered.

Clearly this kind of "service" is hardly the sort that Milton the prophet/ poet, the busy, experienced veteran of the pamphlet wars, would value for himself or anyone else. Indeed, the early hired laborers, who scornfully "murmured against" the lord of the vineyard for granting the others an equal wage (20:11), have essentially the same attitude as that of the speaker earlier in the poem: an attitude that disdains the grace of God in favor of calling attention to their own strenuous efforts. As with Milton's speaker, these murmuring laborers are silenced. Reminding them of their agreement to work for "a penny" for the day, the lord instructs them, "Take what is thine, and go thy way; I will give unto this last, even as unto thee" (20:14). In a word, these laborers have no right to complain, for they have not been cheated. Ultimately, what they are angry about is the lord's generosity—and the preposterous notion that eleven hours of useless waiting combined with one hour of work should be of equal value in his sight to their twelve hours of hard labor. Yet it is this very same absurd notion that the speaker is forced to accept by the final line of *Sonnet 19:* God's economy, quite simply, is not that of humankind, not even that of a prophet-poet who has considered all his previous labor as service unto God. As with the early hired laborers, such an idea is offensive to the speaker. It is in the end, however, the very thing that can rescue him, both from his self-hatred and from anger toward God.

In light of the struggles of the octave, and in light of the struggles of Milton's life, we may surmise that the resolution of line 14 is hardly an easy one for Milton's speaker, or Milton himself, to accept. While he finally must be thankful for this resolution, we sense that he accepts it not because it is palatable to him, but because it is a divine decree that he has not the strength to fight; furthermore, we recognize that the demons that torment the speaker in the octave of *Sonnet 19* have not been vanquished permanently; they shall return often enough to plague him. Nonetheless, we see here again that the parable of the laborers has acted to relieve Milton from himself and his burdensome relationship to the parable of the talents. Clearly, as the years have elapsed and as his battles, his accomplishments, and his disappointments have accumulated, it becomes increasingly difficult for him to accept the grace of God exemplified by the parable of the laborers. At the same time, here in his blindness, his exhaustion, his despair, he recognizes that he ultimately has no other recourse than to receive the very grace that so much of him wishes he did not need. This acceptance of grace also demonstrates a maturing in Milton's relationship to the parable of the laborers. Whereas in the letter "To a Friend" and *Sonnet 7* that parable serves to stave off his self-condemning tendencies while he prepares for active service, in *Sonnet 19,* with Milton having more of life to look back on than to look forward to, the parable does much more than enable him to bide his time. It offers a divine perspective that transcends the self-focused concerns of his autobiographical speaker. By turning Milton's attention away from his own situation and onto God's transcendent power, the parable is a vehicle of grace that offers relief from past failures and divine hope for an uncertain future.

Calvin College

NOTES

1. Dayton Haskin, *Milton's Burden of Interpretation* (Philadelphia, 1994), 33.

2. Haskin, ibid., does address the relationship between these two parables briefly with reference to *Samson Agonistes* (169–70). He does so in response to John Guillory's discussion of the two parables in "The Father's House: *Samson Agonistes* in Its Historical Moment," in *Remembering Milton*, ed. Mary Nyquist and Margaret W. Ferguson (New York, 1987), 158–59. For a more extended discussion of the tension—and eventual resolution—between the two parables in *Samson*, see David Urban, "The Parabolic Milton: The Self and the Bible in John Milton's Writings" (Ph.D. diss., University of Illinois at Chicago, 2001), 60–84.

3. This date was established by William R. Parker in "Some Problems in the Chronology of Milton's Early Poems," *Review of English Studies* 11 (1935): 276–83. Until Parker's article, December 1631 was generally held as the time of composition. William B. Hunter offers a more recent argument for the older view in "The Date of Milton's Sonnet 7," *English Language Notes* 13 (1975): 10–14.

4. Parker discusses the likelihood of Young in "Milton's Unknown Friend," *London Times Literary Supplement*, 16 May 1936, 420.

5. *Complete Prose Works of John Milton*, 8 vols., gen. ed. Don M. Wolfe (New Haven, Conn., 1953–82), 1:319. All references to Milton's prose are from this collection, hereafter cited in text as YP. References to Milton's poetry are from *John Milton: Complete Poetry and Major Prose*, ed. Merritt Y. Hughes (New York, 1957), except as noted. Biblical texts are from the Authorized Version.

6. William Riley Parker, *Milton: A Biography*, 2d ed., 2 vols., ed. Gordon Campbell (Oxford, 1996), 1.122. John Spencer Hill, *John Milton Poet, Prophet, Priest. A Study of Divine Vocation in Milton's Poetry and Prose* (London, 1979), 27–49, argues that Milton did not finally abandon his youthful aspiration to be an Anglican priest until after Laud's *Constitutions and Canons Ecclesiasticall* were passed by the Convocation in June 1640. See also Jameela Lares, *Milton and the Preaching Arts* (Pittsburgh, 2001), 16–29.

7. Margo Swiss, "Crisis of Conscience: A Theological Context for Milton's 'How Soon Hath Time,'" *MQ* 20 (1986): 98.

8. William Perkins, *How to Live and That Well* (London, 1596), 41.

9. Swiss, "Crisis of Conscience," 99; William Whately, *The New Birth* (London, 1618), 158–59.

10. John Owen, "Ministerial Endowments the Work of the Spirit," in *The Works of John Owen*, ed. Thomas Russell (London, 1826), 17:46–59.

11. Haskin, *Milton's Burden of Interpretation*, discusses this identification of the parable of the talents on the part of John Bunyan and John Donne (28–31).

12. Hunter, "The Date of Milton's Sonnet 7," 12.

13. Anna Nardo, *Milton's Sonnets and the Ideal Community* (Lincoln, Neb., 1979), 141.

14. Stephen Booth and Jordan Flyer, "Milton's 'How Soon Hath Time': A Colossus in a Cherrystone," *ELH* 49 (1982): 454.

15. See ibid., 455; Haskin, *Milton's Burden of Interpretation*, 114; and Nardo, *Milton's Sonnets and the Ideal Community*, 143.

16. John Calvin, *A Harmony of the Gospels: Matthew, Mark and Luke*, vol. 2, trans. T. H. L. Parker, ed. David W. Torrance and Thomas F. Torrance (Grand Rapids, Mich., 1979), 264–65.

17. Calvin, *A Harmony of the Gospels*, 265–66, 289.

18. Parker, *Milton*, 2:788–89, 1:126. Barbara K. Lewalski, *The Life of John Milton* (Oxford, 2000), 71, suggests late 1637 or early 1638.

19. *The Riverside Milton*, ed. Roy C. Flannagan (New York, 1998).

20. John T. Shawcross, *John Milton: The Self and the World* (Lexington, Ky., 1993), 87, 310.

21. Parker, *Milton*, 1:17.

22. J. Milton French, *Milton in Chancery: New Chapters in the Lives of the Poet and His Father* (New York, 1939), 62–67.

23. Most commentators argue that *Sonnet 19* was written between 1651 and 1655.

24. Parker, *Milton*, demonstrates the consensus position when he writes: " 'That one talent' must have seemed to him his long-felt, God-given capacity for composing a truly great poem—a capacity which, in the analogy of the parable, might have been taken from him as his failure to use it" (1:470).

25. Haskin, *Milton's Burden of Interpretation*, 96.

26. Michael Lieb, "Talents," in *A Milton Encyclopedia*, vol. 8, gen. ed. William B. Hunter (Lewisburg, Pa., 1980), 49.

27. Roger L. Slakey, "Milton's Sonnet 'On His Blindness,' " *ELH* 27 (1960): 122–30.

28. Calvin states that the unprofitable servant's perception of his lord ought not to be seen as the parable's endorsement of such a view of Christ, whom the lord represents: "This hardness [see Matt. 25:24] is not part of the essence of the parable, and they are philosophizing irreverently who here dispute how God acts towards his people. . . . Christ only means that there is no excuse for the slackness of those who both suppress God's gift and consume their age in idleness. From this we also gather that no form of life is more praiseworthy before God than that which yields usefulness to human society" (*A Harmony of the Gospels*, 289).

29. Here I find myself in agreement with Dixon Fiske's analysis in "Milton in the Middle of Life: Sonnet XIX," *ELH* 41 (1974). Fiske writes, "The sonnet does not criticize the implications of the parable of the talents, but rather the speaker who sees the wrong implications" (45).

30. Fiske notes, but does not elaborate on, this allusion (46).

31. The similarity between *Sonnet 19* and Herbert's "The Collar" comes to mind here. We recognize that for Herbert's speaker, the simple call "Child" is enough to quiet his discontented ranting and bring him to a state of humble worship (35–36). Milton's speaker requires a polemic of sorts to bring him to silent submission, and this contrast may testify to the degree to which he has convinced himself of God's cosmic injustice.

32. E. A. J. Honigmann, ed., *Milton's Sonnets* (London, 1966), 176.

BODILY METAPHOR AND MORAL AGENCY IN A *MASQUE:* A COGNITIVE APPROACH

Beth Bradburn

ONGOING DEBATE OVER the status of the Lady's claim to moral agency in *A Masque Presented at Ludlow Castle* seems to have been taken up into a larger critical project: the effort to counter new historicist skepticism about early modern subjects' sense of inwardness. Recent interpretations of the masque have emphasized the way in which Milton's text, by dramatizing the Lady's interiority, supports her insistence on freedom from "this corporal rind" (663).[1] The Lady's paralysis, often read by earlier critics as a symptom of Milton's moral ambivalence, becomes, instead, productive of inwardness.[2] In this essay I would like to reconsider the relationship between embodiment and moral agency in *A Masque.* Milton's exploration of the moral significance of corporeal experience diffuses into multiple bodily metaphors, of which "inwardness" is only one. The masque does uphold the Lady's claim to moral agency; it defines that agency, however, through a network of bodily metaphors rather than as a unitary concept, precluding any interpretation of moral agency as either wholly disembodied or wholly identified with interiority. My argument makes use of recent work in cognitive science to trace significant bodily metaphors in the masque and to situate these metaphors within seventeenth-century physiological theory.

Cognitive science is a complex interdisciplinary endeavor, comprising theories and methodologies from psychology, computer science, linguistics, neuroscience, and philosophy. Here I would like to draw on a basic idea that informs the work of cognitive theorists in several different areas. The idea is that mental concepts, including both the concepts used in abstract reasoning and those that unconsciously shape our understanding of basic subjective experiences such as time, communication, and agency, are structured by metaphors derived from concrete bodily experiences. George Lakoff and Mark Johnson call these "conceptual metaphors."[3] Our embodiment ensures, for example, that we will repeatedly experience the difference between up and down as we hold ourselves upright against the pull of gravity and observe correlations between increases in volume and in height. The brain organizes this pattern of perceptual and kinesthetic experiences into a "verticality schema," an analog representation whose very structure provides

19

meaning for abstract notions such as relative amount, value, or moral goodness. Expressions such as "rising prices," "higher education," or being "above
that kind of behavior," far from being isolated figures of speech, all participate in a single conceptual metaphor, "more is up."[4]

Conceptual metaphor theory not only seeks to explain the mechanisms
by which bodily experience shapes subjectivity but also points to the diversity
of bodily experiences that do so; the verticality schema is only one of many.
Another is the containment schema, derived from a pattern of experiences
such as eating and evacuation, moving in and out of bounded spaces, and
putting objects into containers. The containment schema enables us to conceptualize the logical notion of categorization, as well as the psychological one
of "inwardness." The psychologist Jean Mandler has argued that the basic
concept of agency derives in part from a schema of animacy, distinguishing
animate motion, which is irregular and self-instigated, from inanimate motion, which follows a linear path and is initiated by an external force.[5] The
linguist Eve Sweetser has traced polysemy and historical meaning-change in
Indo-European languages, attributing patterns in both to a schema of sensory
perception that uses visual metaphors for objective and intellectual processes,
and tactile metaphors for subjective and emotional perceptions. Sweetser also
points out that the metaphor "the mind is a body" structures our understanding of linguistic communication, in that we conceptualize language as an
object to be manipulated by the mind.[6] I will use all these schemas to trace
bodily metaphors in the masque.

If bodily experience is not unitary, neither is it independent of historical
forces. Various cultures construe and interpret corporeality differently. To
take an example with significant implications for the voluntarily chaste author
of *A Masque:* the containment schema gives rise to a conceptual metaphor
analogizing imaginative invention to conception and birth. In modern conversation, a speaker who referred to a book as a child, or to writing difficulties
as labor pains, would be instantly understood because of this metaphor, with
an added layer of irony, but no lack of comprehension, if the book's author
were male.[7] The same conceptual metaphor underlies Milton's remark in
Areopagitica that until the Inquisition, "books were ever as freely admitted
into the World as any other birth; the issue of the brain was no more stifl'd
than the issue of the womb."[8] For an early modern writer, however, the
analogy between brain and womb also evokes, as Mary Thomas Crane has
pointed out, the more literal domain of physiology. Early modern physicians,
such Helkiah Crooke, posited an anatomical "consent" between the two
organs, as well as a chemical relationship between the generative "seed" and
the "animal spirits" that were thought to carry out brain activity.[9] My discus-

sion of bodily metaphors in *A Masque* will show how thoroughly early modern physiology informs Milton's language and imagery.

An investigation of bodily experience in the masque must begin by acknowledging that its main character baldly asserts the moral and material independence of the mind from the body. When Comus threatens magically to paralyze the Lady if she does not accept his offer of refreshment, she retorts,

> Fool do not boast,
> Thou canst not touch the freedom of my mind
> With all thy charms, although this corporal rind
> Thou hast immanacled. (661–64)

Much appears to rest on this claim, and later events in the masque can be interpreted as undercutting it. Comus does carry out his threat, and although his spell is eventually reversed by Sabrina, the Lady does not speak again after she is "thawed" (852), and thus never confirms her uninterrupted mental freedom. Moreover, as Sabrina frees the Lady, she remarks that the chair in which she was restrained is "smeared with gums of glutinous heat" (916), a mysterious but undoubtedly corporeal image that has provoked heated debate over the Lady's possible complicity with Comus.[10]

I will argue that the masque affirms the Lady's moral agency while failing to uphold the precise terms of her claim. Her response to Comus implies that she sees no moral threat in his paralyzing spell because of her mind's material independence from her body. The truth is just the opposite: imposed stasis is no threat because mobility is only one node in a network of metaphors defining her agency—but all these metaphors depend on the body to organize and give meaning to psychological experience. The Lady's statement itself is underwritten by several such metaphors. When she refers to her "corporal rind," she evokes the containment schema, conceptualizing her mind as contained by her body. When she contrasts her mental freedom with the threatened physical restriction, she evokes the "mind as body" metaphor, analogizing freedom to mobility. And when she says that Comus cannot "touch" her freedom, she evokes a schema of sensory perception that links touch with carnal desire and vision with spiritual faith. I will trace the network of which these metaphors are a part, showing four ways in which the masque demonstrates the mind's dependence on bodily metaphors without compromising the Lady's moral agency.

The first of these four ways lies in Milton's treatment of the conceptual metaphor "the mind is a womb." The Lady's reference to her "corporal rind" echoes earlier remarks by the Elder Brother, who calls the body "the outward shape, / The unpolluted temple of the mind" (459–60). At least the chaste body is unpolluted. "When lust," on the other hand, "Lets in defilement to the inward parts, / The soul grows clotted by contagion" (465–66). As a negative image of impregnation, this passage highlights the moral dilemma presented by the conceptual metaphor that figures the brain as a womb, and creativity as fertility. Whatever moral implications are attached to sexuality can potentially cross over to the processes of imagination as well. Milton resolves the problem by generating multiple corporeal metaphors that signify, paradoxically, both fertility and chastity. This set of paradoxical metaphors underscores the impossibility of denying the analogy between the mind and the womb, but at the same time it transfers the suggestion of fertility to other parts of the body and affirms the Lady's chastity.

The masque is preoccupied with chaste feet. Comus senses the Lady's "chaste footing" (146) before he even sees her. She worries about directing her "unacquainted feet" (179) toward the sound of "wanton" (175) dancing and later implies that her own feet are not "well-practised" (309) in comparison with Comus's. The virginal Sabrina walks with "printless feet / O'er the cowslip's velvet head, / That bends not as I tread" (896–98). Pedal chastity confers mobility. The chaste woman, says the Elder Brother, "is clad in complete steel, / And like a quivered nymph with arrows keen / May trace huge forests, and unharboured heaths" (420–22). As with the body, so with the mind. Threatening thoughts "may startle well, but not astound / The virtuous mind, that ever walks attended / by a strong siding champion Conscience" (209–11).

This interest in chaste feet derives, I suggest, from the Petrarchan topos *bel piede* linking Laura's footsteps with an animating power over "some herbal form of nature," a source of both inspiration and virtue for the poet.[11] Sabrina walks across growing plants, making direct contact with fertile land. The Lady's chaste footsteps through Comus's "leafy labyrinth" (277) indirectly prove to be fertile. The "labour of [her] thoughts" (191), tracing in imagination the two brothers' "wand'ring steps" (192) becomes, in the masque's epilogue, Psyche's "wandering labours long" (1005) that culminate in the birth of "blissful twins" (1009). Mary Thomas Crane has pointed out that the topos *bel piede* operates in Robert Herrick's *Hesperides* as "a fantasy of fertility without penetration," and I would argue that it works similarly in *A Masque*.[12] By converting the brain-as-womb metaphor to the recurring image of chaste but fertile feet, Milton finds a bodily metaphor that affirms the generative power of thought while avoiding the taint of sex.

Milton provocatively symbolizes his imaginative fertility through two invented parentages. Psyche's blissful twins have no literary precedent. Other writers agree in assigning her a single offspring, Pleasure.[13] Similarly, Comus's birth is Milton's own conception; no source has been found for the Attendant Spirit's account of a union between Bacchus and Circe (50–58).[14] Because these literary offspring recall the problematic brain-as-womb metaphor, it is crucial that they also provide a way to represent chastity. In the case of Psyche, chastity appears as the "fair unspotted side" (1008) through which she delivers the twins. The Lady's side represents her chastity as well. When Comus finds the Lady alone in the woods, he asks how it is that her companions have "left [her] fair side all unguarded" (282). Fortunately, she is protected in the form of "a strong siding champion Conscience" (211). The OED cites this line as the first to use "siding" in this sense, implying, I would argue, a deliberate choice of wording in the passage.

The case of Comus is more complex. Circe passes on her "mighty art" (63) to him, but Milton also provides Comus with a twist on his mother's power. Whereas Circe's "charmed cup" causes the partaker to lose "his upright shape / And downward [fall] into a grovelling swine" (51–53), Comus's potion works only on the face, changing the "human countenance" into "some brutish form" (68–70). In the temptation scene, the Lady's face comes to represent her body in its potential for pleasure. "Course complexions," Comus tells her,

> And cheeks of sorry grain will serve to ply
> The sampler, and to tease the housewife's wool.
> What need a vermeil-tinctured lip for that
> Love-darting eyes, or tresses like the morn?
> There was another meaning in these gifts.   (748–53)

Facial expressions, however, can enact chastity. The Lady "frowns" (665) at Comus, recalling the "frown" with which, according to the Elder Brother, the chaste Diana repels those who would have her virginity (444–45). And although the Lady's song evokes a pleasurable "smile" for Comus (251), he acknowledges the song's "sacredness" and "sobriety," which are contrasted with the sensuality of Siren music (259–62).

The feet, the face, and the side all signify chaste fertility, and each represents in turn the Lady's moral agency. These synecdochic images are diverse, but not disconnected: they are all parts of the Lady's body. The masque links moral agency with embodiment, however various the latter may be. Moreover, moral agency does not wholly coincide with "inwardness." Each of these images joins the containment schema along some paths and departs from it along others. The side is linked with both pregnancy and the body's exterior surface. The face represents internal feelings and outer expression. The feet may be transmuted into a protective steel casing, but they simultaneously provide unbounded mobility.

The second way in which the masque insists on the corporeality of moral agency lies in its treatment of linguistic agency. Not even language can be construed as disembodied. As I explain above, cognitive linguists hold that we habitually think of language as an object propelled by the mind, and this conceptual metaphor generates a complex intertwining of corporeal and linguistic themes in the masque, linked through imagery of movement. In order to trace this pattern, I would like to look in detail at two parallel scenes, both moments at which the Lady's speech or song produces a strong emotional response in Comus. One is the scene in which the Lady speaks her mind to the enchanter about the "sage / And serious doctrine of virginity" (785–86).

Metaphorically, her speech extends and expresses the mental freedom she claims when Comus threatens to paralyze her: "Thou art not fit to hear thyself convinced," she tells him,

> Yet should I try, the uncontrolled worth
> Of this pure cause would kindle my rapt spirits
> To such a flame of sacred vehemence,
> That dumb things would be moved to sympathize,
> And the brute Earth would lend her nerves, and shake,
> Till all thy magic structures reared so high,
> Were shattered into heaps o'er thy false head. (791–98)

The words "spirits," "flame," and "nerves" all have physiological connotations. Early modern physicians held that the nerves were conduits for the animal spirits, which were responsible for movement.[15] Francis Bacon noted that the explosiveness of this chemical combination, the same as that in gunpowder, gave the spirits the necessary power to "move the whole body (which is of so great mass), both with so great force, as in wrestling, leaping, and with so great swiftness, as in playing division upon the lute."[16] The Lady's explosive speech incorporates the language of the physiology of movement, and in that sense it is a response to Comus's threat of paralysis; for he has said, with anatomical precision, that "if I but wave this wand, / Your nerves are all chained up in alabaster" (658–59).

The Lady appears to be right about the moral power of her speech because Comus responds with physical fear:

> She fables not, I feel that I do fear
> Her words set off by some superior power;
> And though not mortal, yet a cold shuddering dew
> Dips me all o'er. (799–802)

Ultimately, however, he persists with the offer of his cup. He recovers his resolve by continuing the bodily metaphor she has used, revising it to suit his own diagnosis of the situation:

> I must not suffer this, yet 'tis but the lees
> And settlings of a melancholy blood;
> But this will cure all straight, one sip of this
> Will bathe the drooping spirits in delight
> Beyond the bliss of dreams.   (808–12)

At this moment the two brothers and the Attendant Spirit break in, Comus freezes the Lady before he vanishes, and the full potential of the Lady's speech remains unexplored. The entire scene does serve, however, to link moral agency with both language and movement.

This scene is prefigured by the earlier scene in which the Lady invokes Echo. Lost in the woods, but heartened by the sight of a cloud's silver lining, the Lady appears to undergo a version of the physiological transformation, by means of "kindled spirits," that marks her motivation to speak in the later passage: "Such noise as I can make to be heard farthest / I'll venture, for my new-enlivened spirits / Prompt me" (226–28). Although she intends her song for Echo, it is heard instead by Comus, who responds strongly, as in the later passage, to the "sober certainty" (262) of its moral power:

> Can any mortal mixture of earth's mould
> Breathe such divine enchanting ravishment?
> Sure something holy lodges in that breast,
> And with these raptures moves the vocal air
> To testify his hidden residence.   (243–47)

Just as with the Lady's later speech, Comus is momentarily stunned by the song, but ultimately it strengthens his resolve to approach her: "I'll speak to her / And she shall be my queen" (264–65).

Here, too, Comus responds to and revises the Lady's image of her song as a form of movement. The Lady closes her invocation to Echo by calling her "Sweet queen of parley," saying: "So mayst thou be translated to the skies, / And give resounding grace to all heaven's harmonics" (240–42). "Translated" has a double meaning here; it refers both to linguistic expression (reinforced by the reference to the "queen of parley") and to upward movement. This is exactly the sort of polysemy that Sweetser would explain with reference to the conceptual metaphor that figures language as a moving object propelled by the speaker.[17] In this passage the metaphor has a certain entailment: because translation is an inanimate movement, one in which the moving force comes from an external agent, the Lady implies that her song is a passive object. Comus, however, attributes animate movement to the song, figuring it as a bird in flight,

> float[ing] upon the wings
> Of silence, through the empty-vaulted night
> At every fall smoothing the raven down
> Of darkness till it smiled.   (248–51)

The bird's "falls," presumably a series of downward swoops, describe the irregularity that distinguishes animate motion from inanimate.[18]

Sometimes, Milton intimates, language does not behave like an inanimate object, moving only according to the speaker's intentions. Rather, it exercises a capacity for self-movement, going places of its own accord. The Lady means for her song to reach Echo, but Echo never appears in the masque. Instead, the song evokes a response from Comus, who is exactly the sort of audience that the Lady has been "loth / To meet" (176–77). The song's diversion neither morally compromises the Lady nor signifies an unconscious complicity with Comus. It does, however, suggest that linguistic agency cannot be entirely disembodied, depending as it does upon a network of metaphors based on perceptual and motor experience.

Related to this construction of language is a third way in which the masque insists on the embodiedness of moral agency: by means of the verticality schema. The masque maps moral goodness onto a vertical scale; moral agency does not mean just moving voluntarily, but also moving up— climbing. The Attendant Spirit tells us at the outset that his errand of assistance is to help those "that by due steps aspire / To lay their just hands on that golden key / That opes the palace of eternity" (12–14). The steps must be upward steps, as virtue teaches mortals "how to climb / Higher than the sphery chime" (1019–20). Other language in the masque implicitly evokes this metaphor, as when the Lady refers to Comus as "base" (697) or when Comus's victims descend "to roll with pleasure in a sensual sty" (77). Indeed, the Christian metaphor that figures moral loss as a fall reflects this conceptual metaphor as well.

Vertical orientation and voluntary motion are, however, separate metaphors, though both are corporeal. What would be the moral status of someone who moved upward involuntarily, fell up, so to speak? Milton plays with just this question in an early epigram on the gunpowder plot. The speaker of that epigram says to Fawkes that he should have used the gunpowder instead to "blow up to heaven your filthy monks, because unless you give each of them an upward shove by this means or some other, not one will have an easy climb up the heavenly path" (7–10).[19] This passage plays on the diversity and separability of bodily metaphors that allow us to conceptualize abstractions such as morality and agency.

In fact, a similar joke in another gunpowder epigram may help further complicate the Lady's use of the word "translation." "Translation" also has a religious meaning: the transport of a human being directly up to heaven without the intervention of death, as in the case of Elijah.[20] This sense of "translation" is linked with the word's more literal meaning: it figures heaven and earth as disparate locations, and translation as the movement between them. Furthermore, translation entails the idea of movement by an external force since God is the only one who can translate someone. Milton plays with this notion, too, comparing Fawkes's attempt to blow up King James to the biblical translation of Elijah by a fiery chariot; Milton asks Fawkes whether he intended a kind of "evil piety" by blasting James up to heaven.[21] This poem also externalizes the explosive physiology of movement.

When Comus revises the Lady's figure of translation, not only does he convert it to voluntary movement, but he also reverses its direction from up to down, analogizing the song to the controlled movement of downward flight.[22] This serves, as does the gunpowder epigram, to tease apart the bodily metaphors in Milton's concept of moral agency: direction of motion is separable from degree of volition. Flight is not a human bodily experience, of course, but controlled downward movement is. We may descend a staircase, or run down a hill, as the Attendant Spirit does when he hears the Lady's song and realizes the danger surrounding her (567).

The Attendant Spirit begins his remedy of the situation by revising Comus's revision. For if the Lady's song moves in a direction she did not intend, attracting Comus as an audience, it also moves toward a benevolent, though equally unintended, hearer. Like Comus, the Spirit overhears the song and is struck by its beauty. Like Comus, he figures the song as a form of movement: "At last a soft and solemn-breathing sound / Rose like a steam of rich distilled perfumes" (554–55). Here the Spirit reinstates the upward movement of the song, metaphorically restoring the Lady's moral agency. He can do so because his intervention represents a corresponding downward movement from a source higher on the moral hierarchy. As the Spirit says in the masque's closing lines, "if Virtue feeble were, / Heaven itself would stoop to her" (1021–22).

This corporeal image makes an appropriate conclusion, for stooping entails volition of movement; a stooping body differs from a falling body exactly in the control that it has over its motion. The word has another early modern sense as well; it can refer to the downward movement of a bird in flight, the physical image that Comus has offered for the Lady's song.[23] Thus the Attendant Spirit, the agent through which heaven "stoops" to assist the virtuous Lady, rescues her from Comus metaphorically as well as literally. The metaphorical sense of "stoop," used of heaven's attention to the mortal world, is linked to its more physical senses through conceptual metaphor, the

schema of vertical orientation.[24] Although the Lady equates moral agency
with linguistic agency, the masque reveals the extent to which the latter is
underwritten by bodily experience.

Finally, the masque's fourth way of demonstrating the mind's dependence on the body involves the five external senses. Much has to occur
between the moment the Spirit hears the Lady's song and the happy conclusion in which he presents her safely to her parents. Even as the Spirit appears
to restore the Lady's moral agency in his revision of Comus's response to the
song, he also points to another bodily metaphor in the masque's network. By
analogizing the Lady's song to a perfume, the Spirit calls attention to the
corporeality of linguistic production, for early modern physicians understood
air to be the medium both of odors (inhaled through the nose) and of vocal-
ization, the organs of speech manipulating the breath in order to produce
sound.[25] Indeed, the masque itself has called attention to the physiology of
speech in other places, such as when Comus points out that the Lady's song
occurs through "mov[ing] the vocal air" (246); later, the Lady refers to "un-
locking" her "lips" in order to make her inspired speech (755).[26]

Even more importantly, however, the perfume metaphor participates in
a schematic understanding of the senses as arranged along a spectrum from
immaterial to material that structures the masque's language and imagery, a
frame of reference related to the Lady's eventual release. Crooke writes that
"the Sight and Touch be the extremes because they are most distant one from
another, by reason that the object of Touch is corporeall and materiall, and
the object of the Sight incorporall and spirituall."[27] An example of the
masque's use of this schema arises in the Elder Brother's account of the
respective effects of chastity and sin. He says that

> when a soul is found sincerely [chaste],
> A thousand liveried angels lackey her,
> Driving far off each thing of sin and guilt,
> And in clear dream, and solemn vision
> Tell her of things that no gross ear can hear.   (453–57)

When the body is unchaste, by contrast, "the soul grows clotted by contagion" (466), a tactile metaphor suggested both by the sensory image of
clotting and the etymology of "contagion."

As the Elder Brother's language implies, the sense of hearing lies one
step further toward the material end of the spectrum than sight does; its
relative "grossness" can be morally superseded by "solemn vision." The
masque attends to all five senses, meticulously matching each sense to its
place on the spectrum of materiality.[28] The metaphor of sensory perception is
thus not just one bodily metaphor, but five; it exemplifies the multiplicity of

metaphors through which the masque's investigation of the moral meaning of the body is diffused. Significantly, Sabrina, arguably the most important moral agent in the masque since she actually rescues the Lady, has herself become powerfully immortal through the reviving action of Nereus's ambrosial oil dropped in "through the porch and inlet of each sense" (838).[29]

Each sense has its place. Sight and touch are the extremes, "Hearing and Tasting are lesse distant one from another, and the Smell is equally affected to all, and therfore by good right challenges the middle place."[30] Hearing has almost the virtue of sight; when the Lady cannot see her way in the woods, she turns to hearing as an alternative means of navigation, "my best guide now" (170). Similarly, taste has almost the carnality of an "ill-greeting touch" (405) from the "rash hand of bold Incontinence" (396). Comus is linked with the sense of taste; the word "taste" occurs six times in the masque in reference to the consumption of Comus's potion; its only other synonyms in the masque, "drink" and "sip," occur once apiece.[31] The difference between tasting and touching emerges insofar as touch is more clearly a metaphor in the masque for sexual contact, whereas the "tasting" of the potion urged on the Lady by Comus is clearly bad, but not clearly a euphemism for sex. This distinction allows for the masque's discourse on temperance, which seems to include restraint in eating and drinking as well as sexual chastity.

As the middle term on the sensory spectrum, smell can go either way, toward the virtuous or toward the carnal. Comus is associated with bad smells: "rank vapours" (17), "mildew" (639), "vomit" (654), and "scum" (594), a fetid accumulation on the surface of stagnant water. The Attendant Spirit, by contrast, hails from "happy climes" (976) where "west winds, with musky wing / About the cedarn alleys fling / Nard, and cassia's balmy smells" (988–90), and where Iris "waters the odorous banks that blow / Flowers" (992–93). The very ambiguity of smell makes it an appropriate medium for moral deception. Thus, Comus's evil potion "dances in his crystal bounds / With spirits of balm, and fragrant syrups mixed" (672–73). Undeceived, the Lady rejects Comus's potion in spite of its pleasant fragrance, calling it a "liquorish bait" (699). "Liquorish" means pleasant-tasting; as the Lady has not actually tasted the potion, she must be able to imagine its taste from the smell. As Crooke observes, although taste and smell are distinct, they usually have "a mutuall consent."[32]

It is not enough for the Lady merely to decline Comus's temptations, however; he does, as subsequent events show, still have the power to paralyze her. Metaphorically, her own ability to generate a fragrance indirectly results in her eventual freedom. The song she has sung earlier, when she first recognized her danger, has been analogized to a "steam of rich distilled perfumes" by the hearer who knows how to help her. He will assist the brothers in dispatching Comus, and then call on Sabrina to perform the final rites that will reverse the enchanter's spell and free the Lady. Significantly, early modern physicians used fragrances as healing agents. Robert Burton prescribed them as a treatment for some forms of melancholy, the illness that Comus attributes to the Lady. And among the conditions that Burton's predecessor, Marsilio Ficino, lists as responsive to odors is loss of motion.[33]

Metaphorically, then, the Lady generates the smell that eventually heals her. Odd as this idea may seem, I would like to pursue it by way of conclusion, offering a reading of the notorious gums of glutinous heat.[34] That the Lady's body both generates smells and takes them in calls attention to the multiplicity of bodily experiences that underwrite the masque's idea of moral agency. We might begin by noticing that a likely meaning for "gums" indicates both that they have a pleasant odor and that they have been exuded from the Lady's body. "Gum" could refer to tree resin that was burned for its attractive fragrance. Milton's Eden, for instance, is filled with "groves whose rich Trees wept odorous Gums and Balm."[35] The Lady herself is like a tree: when Comus threatens to immobilize her, he says that she will be "as Daphne was / Root-bound, that fled Apollo" (660–61). As Comus does manage to paralyze her, the gums may be read as a kind of human resin, a fragrant secretion of the Lady's body.

The gums might be interpreted as tears; Milton's use of "wept" in the *Paradise Lost* passage would support this reading, as would Othello's remark that his eyes "drop tears as fast as the Arabian trees / Their medicinable gum."[36] But a consideration of the adjective "glutinous" points toward a different kind of bodily secretion. Burton informs his readers that the human body contains an innate or "radical" humor that seems to have three phases or forms: *cambium, ros,* and *gluten*.[37] This radical humor, as A. B. Chambers notes, could also be referred to as moisture, sap, humidity, or even heat.[38] In *The Reason of Church Government,* Milton uses the radical moisture as a metaphor for the "esteem, whereby men bear an inward reverence toward their own persons":

[I]f the love of God as a fire sent from heaven to be ever kept alive upon the altar of our hearts, be the first principle of all godly and vertuous actions in men, this pious and just honouring of our selves is the second, and may be thought as the radical moisture and fountain head, whence every laudable and worthy enterprize issues forth. And although I have giv'n it the name of a liquid thing, yet is it not incontinent to bound it self, as humid things are, but hath in it a most restraining and powerfull abstinence to start back, and glob it self upward from the mixture of any ungenerous and unbeseeming motion, or any soile wherewith it may peril to stain it self.[39]

Milton's language here directly expresses the theme of the masque, the Lady's "restraining and powerful" abstinence. In the prose passage, Milton reuses a metaphor from his masque; the glutinous gums are a form of the radical moisture.[40]

I can offer some further support for this reading. Chambers, investigating the word "gluten" in connection with a textual crux in a poem by Marvell, concludes that two phases of the radical moisture, *gluten* and *ros,* are associated respectively with the words "glue" and "dew."[41] "Dew" is the masque's name for whatever Comus secretes when the Lady delivers her vehement speech. The immediate context implies that he sweats in fear, but given that "gluten" appears later in the masque, I propose that both Comus and the Lady exude a form of the radical humor. The Lady, being virtuous and therefore bearing an "inward reverence toward her own person," does not allow this humor to mix with anything that may soil it. Instead, the gums mix with the "moisture" of Sabrina's "chaste palms" (917), breaking the enchanter's spell and freeing the Lady from her paralysis. The glutinous gums, then, should not be read as sign of the Lady's complicity with Comus, but neither should they be read, as Debora Shuger has claimed, as a "morally inconsequential" bodily experience.[42] The gums represent an active, positive chastity. They reveal the corporeality of moral agency, qualifying without negating the Lady's verbal claim to an "untouchable mind."

The Reason of Church Government recalls the containment schema, talking of "inward reverence" and "continence." However, it is clear from the passage itself that Milton does not find the metaphor of inwardness sufficient to express his notion of moral agency; he turns also, quite consciously, to a "liquid" metaphor. In *A Masque,* moisture and inwardness occupy only two nodes in the network of bodily metaphors I have traced. This network is diffuse, but that diffusion should neither be mistaken for moral ambivalence nor reduced to a single metaphor. The diversity of embodiment, far from undermining virtue, generates a complex representation of moral agency. The purpose of Milton's masque is not to devalue bodily experience, but rather to trace its complexity.

Wake Forest University

NOTES

I wish to thank Dayton Haskin, James Dougal Fleming, Mary Thomas Crane, Tony Jackson, and especially Amy Boesky for their generous help with this essay.

1. Milton's poetry, except *Paradise Lost*, is cited parenthetically from *John Milton: Complete Shorter Poems*, 2d ed., ed. John Carey (London, 1957).

2. On Milton's moral ambivalence, see, for example, Hugh M. Richmond, *The Christian Revolutionary: John Milton* (Berkeley and Los Angeles, 1974). He writes that the Lady's "paralysis might even be described in modern psychiatric terms as a neurotic dysfunction resulting from fear of repressed sensuality" (72). Christopher Kendrick, "Milton and Sexuality: A Symptomatic Reading of *Comus*," in *Re-membering Milton: Essays on the Texts and Traditions,* ed. Mary Nyquist and Margaret W. Ferguson (New York, 1987), also regards the Lady's immobility as "symptomatic" (50). Along similar lines, William Kerrigan, *The Sacred Complex: On the Psychogenesis of "Paradise Lost"* (Cambridge, Mass., 1983), reads the "root-bound" Lady's virtue as a "reaction formation to oedipal temptation" (55). On the Lady's paralysis as productive of inwardness, see Katherine E. Maus, *Inwardness and Theater in the English Renaissance* (Chicago, 1995), who reads Milton's masque as an example of Renaissance inwardness: "versions of the Lady's body, a perfectly enclosed, strictly delimited interior space, pervade the masque" (200). Similarly, Debora Shuger, " 'Gums of Glutinous Heat' and the Stream of Consciousness: The Theology of Milton's *Maske*," *Representations* 60 (1997), argues that the masque "complicates the poetics of self-fashioning" (17) through investigation of bodily experiences that produce inwardness. Michael Schoenfeldt, *Bodies and Selves in Early Modern England: Physiology and Inwardness in Spenser, Shakespeare, Herbert, and Milton* (Cambridge, 1999), shows how humoral theory provided an "organic account of inwardness" (8) for early modern subjects. Schoenfeldt discusses the masque only briefly, but argues that its focus on eating exemplifies Milton's preoccupation with the physiology of inwardness (132, 149).

3. An overview of conceptual metaphor theory may be found in George Lakoff and Mark Johnson, *Philosophy in the Flesh: The Embodied Mind and Its Challenge to Western Thought* (New York, 1999).

4. Mark Johnson, *The Body in the Mind: The Bodily Basis of Meaning, Imagination and Reason* (Chicago, 1987), discusses the metaphor "more is up" (xv).

5. Jean M. Mandler, "How to Build a Baby: II. Conceptual Primitives," *Psychological Review* 99 (1992): 596.

6. Eve E. Sweetser, *From Etymology to Pragmatics: Metaphorical and Cultural Aspects of Semantic Structure* (Cambridge, 1990), 38, 20. See also Michael J. Reddy, "The Conduit Metaphor: A Case of Frame Conflict in Our Language about Language," in *Metaphor and Thought,* 2d ed., ed. Andrew Ortony (Cambridge, 1993), 164–201.

7. For a discussion of this conceptual metaphor from a cognitive perspective, see Mark Turner, *The Literary Mind* (Oxford, 1996), 52–56.

8. John Milton, *Areopagitica*, in *Complete Prose Works of John Milton*, 7 vols., ed. Douglas Bush et al. (New Haven, Conn., 1959), 2:505.

9. Mary Thomas Crane, *Shakespeare's Brain: Reading with Cognitive Theory* (Princeton, 2001), 162; see also Crane's discussion of the word "pregnant" (162). Jay L. Halio, "The Metaphor of Conception and Elizabethan Theories of the Imagination," *Neophilologus* 50 (1966): 454–61. Helkiah Crooke, *Microcosmographia: A Description of the Body of Man* (London, 1615), 202, 252. Crooke's comprehensive anatomy was reprinted throughout the seventeenth century.

10. See John Leonard, "Saying 'No' to Freud: Milton's *A Mask* and Sexual Assault," *MQ* 25 (1991): 129–40; William Kerrigan, "The Politically Correct *Comus*: A Reply to John Leonard," *MQ* 27 (1993): 149–55; and Leonard, " 'Good Things': A Reply to William Kerrigan," *MQ* 30 (1996): 117–27.

11. James Villas, "The Petrarchan Topos *Bel Piede*: Generative Footsteps," *Romance Notes* 11 (1969): 167.

12. Mary Thomas Crane, "Herrick's Cultural Materialism," *George Herbert Journal* 14 (1990–1991): 34.

13. Carey, *Complete Shorter Poems,* 232, mentions Apuleis, Boccacio, and Spenser as examples.

14. For example, Ben Jonson's *Pleasure Reconciled to Virtue,* in *Works,* vol. 7, ed. C. H. Herford and Percy and Evelyn Simpson (Oxford, 1941), 479, introduces Comus only as "ye god of *cheere,* or ye *belly.*"

15. "The *Animal spirits* formed of the *Vitall,* brought up to the Braine, and diffused by the Nerves, to the subordinate Members, give sense and motion to them all." Robert Burton, *The Anatomy of Melancholy* (Oxford, 1628), pt. 1, sec. 1, member 2, subsection 2.

16. Francis Bacon, *Sylva Sylvarum; or, A Natural History in Ten Centuries* (1627; reprint, London, 1996), 352. Crooke, *Microcosmographia,* notes as well that the spirits "have in them a kinde of nimble violence and impetious motion" (172), although he compares them to lightning (824) rather than to gunpowder. The passage from Bacon was brought to my attention by Gail Kern Paster, "Nervous Tension," in *The Body in Parts: Fantasies of Corporeality in Early Modern Europe* (New York, 1997), 107–25, who discusses the importance of spirits in understanding early modern somatic experiences.

17. See Sweetser, *From Etymology to Pragmatics,* 20, for some other examples. Judith Anderson, "Translating Investments: The Metaphoricity of Language, 2 *Henry IV,* and *Hamlet,*" *Texas Studies in Literature and Language* 40 (1998), points out that for early modern writers, the term "translation" both exemplified and referred to "the figurality and cultural embeddedness of language" (232).

18. "Falls" has a second, musical sense in this passage as well.

19. "Sic potius foedos in caelum pelle cucullos, / Et quot habet brutos Roma profana deos, / Namque hac aut alia nisi quemque adiuveris arte, / Crede mihi caeli vix bene scandet iter." The translation is from Carey, *Complete Shorter Poems.*

20. See 2 Kings 2:11.

21. *In Proditionem Bombardicam,* 4. For a discussion of translation in this epigram and elsewhere in Milton's work, see William Kerrigan, "The Heretical Milton: From Assumption to Mortalism," *English Literary Renaissance* 5 (1975): 125–66.

22. Clive Hart has discussed the use of flight, and in particular downward flight, to represent interiority and volition in Western art and literature, in *Images of Flight* (Berkeley and Los Angeles, 1988).

23. In a much-quoted passage, for example, Burton compares himself to a hawk that, from the full height of its soaring, "comes downe amain, and stoopes upon a sudden" (2.2.3). See also *Paradise Lost* 3.73.

24. The OED cites several uses of "stoop" in this sense. "Stoop" is also a masquing term, referring to the lowering of a masque character on a cloud machine. See John Demaray, *Milton and the Masque Tradition: The Early Poems, "Arcades," and "Comus"* (Cambridge, Mass., 1968), 104, 136. Milton plays on the common physical metaphor in all these meanings.

25. Crooke, *Microcosmographia,* 645.

26. Jean E. Graham, "Virgin Ears: Silence, Deafness, and Chastity in Milton's *Maske,*" in *Milton Studies,* vol. 36, ed. Albert C. Labriola (Pittsburgh, 1998), 1–17, discusses the gender politics of the Lady's speeches and silences.

27. Crooke, *Microcosmographia,* 662.

28. Raymond Schoen, "The Hierarchy of the Senses in A Mask," *MQ* 7 (1973): 32–37, identifies a hierarchy of three senses (sight, hearing, and touch) in the masque, but does not discuss smell or taste. Donald M. Friedman, "*Comus* and the Truth of the Ear," in *The Muses Common-Weale: Poetry and Politics in the Seventeenth Century,* ed. Claude J. Summers and

Ted-Larry Pebworth (Columbia, Mo., 1988), 119–34, argues that Milton privileges hearing in the masque.

29. The Spirit's response to the song prefigures the story of Sabrina's revival. He "takes in," as smell and sound simultaneously, "strains that might create a soul / Under the ribs of death" (560–61).

30. Crooke, *Microcosmographia,* 662.

31. "Taste" is used at lines 51, 65, 66, 700, 714, and 812; "drink" at 516; "sip" at 810.

32. Crooke, *Microcosmographia,* 617.

33. Burton, *Anatomy of Melancholy,* 2.5.1.5; Marsilio Ficino, *De Vita,* vol. 2, ed. and trans. Carol V. Kaske and John R. Clark (Binghamton, N.Y., 1989), 225.

34. The possible sexual implications of the gums are discussed by J. W. Flosdorf, " 'Gums of Glutinous Heat': A Query," *MQ* 7 (1973): 4–5; John T. Shawcross, "Two Comments," *MQ* 7 (1973): 98; and Edward Le Comte, *Milton and Sex* (London, 1978), 1–2. Stanley Archer, " 'Glutinous Heat': A Note on *Comus,* l. 917," *MQ* 7 (1973): 99, linking the gums with birdlime, denies any sexual content. Shuger, " 'Gums of Glutinous Heat,' " however, argues that the birdlime signifies wet dreams (4). Margaret Hoffman Kale, "Milton's 'Gums of Glutinous Heat': A Renaissance Theory of Movement," *MQ* 29 (1995), connects the gums with a Dionysian "life force" (89).

35. Milton, *Paradise Lost,* ed. Merritt Y. Hughes (Indianapolis, 1962), 4:248.

36. William Shakespeare, *The Tragedy of Othello, the Moor of Venice,* in *The Riverside Shakespeare,* 2d ed., ed. G. Blakemore Evans (Boston, 1997), 5.2.350–51.

37. Burton, *Anatomy of Melancholy,* 1.1.2.2.

38. A. B. Chambers, *Andrew Marvell and Edmund Waller: Seventeenth-Century Praise and Restoration Satire* (University Park, Pa., 1991), 23.

39. Milton, *The Reason of Church Government,* in *Complete Prose Works,* 1:841–42.

40. John Rogers, *The Matter of Revolution: Science, Poetry and Politics in the Age of Milton* (Ithaca, N.Y., 1996), 103, situates the imagery of self-moving matter in Milton's later work in the context of midcentury vitalism, arguing that *A Masque* is more concerned with bodily integrity than with self-movement. If the gums of glutinous heat do anticipate the metaphor of radical moisture in *The Reason of Church Government,* however, then early modern humoral physiology, as well as vitalism, may inform Milton's imagery of self-moving matter.

41. Chambers, *Andrew Marvell,* 24. Chambers concludes that the problematic word "glew" should stand in "To His Coy Mistress," arguing that it connotes a complex transitional state between body and mind. Similar connotations may arise in Donne's poetry. For example, in "An Anatomy of the World," the dead Elizabeth Drury is said to have been "The Cyment which did faithfully compact / And glue all vertues" (49–50). The hands of the lovers in "The Extasie" are "firmely cimented / With a fast balme" (5–6). Donne's poetry is cited from *John Donne: Poetry and Prose,* ed. Frank J. Warnke (New York, 1967).

42. Shuger, " 'Gums of Glutinous Heat,' " 8.

REPAIRING THE RUINS:
MILTON AS READER AND EDUCATOR

Thomas Festa

MILTON, LIKE OTHER TEACHERS of literature, understood that education is essentially communal—not something that happens in isolation, but rather at the intersection of several minds, a collective endeavor. As Ben Jonson said, "hee that was onely taught by himselfe, had a foole to his Master." Reading, too, involves not only a single reader, but a community, especially when it serves as the primary medium of an educational process, and is therefore like education at once expressive and constitutive of community. While recent formulations of this concept, such as Stanley Fish's "interpretive communities" and Roger Chartier's "communities of readers," will be of some use here, my present aim derives equally from an ancient concern of which Fish and Chartier are no doubt aware.[1] Early in Plato's *Symposium,* when Eryximachus proposes the subject of the ensuing conversation, he quotes the tag "mine is not the tale" from Euripides's Melanippe to signal that his subject does not originate with himself but instead with his friend and fellow diner Phaedrus, suggesting that the idea, like the locution, originates with neither of them but nonetheless "belongs" to a far broader group than is, strictly speaking, in attendance at the feast.[2] The allusion to Euripides, by placing the speaker and his meaning at one more textual remove, dramatizes the sharing of texts as a means of encompassing hearers and readers alike in the formation of a community.

The largest question I take up in this essay also begins with Euripides in order to ask: What do Milton's practices as a reader and his conception of the power of books tell us about his idea of education? In seeking answers to this question, I will argue for the importance of thinking about how Milton read specific texts and what material evidence we have of these encounters. The nature of this evidence and the processes it records relate to broader interpretive issues with far-reaching implications for comprehending Milton's thought, such as how he perceived the relative legitimacy of textual interpretations, the utility of such interpretations, and the formative contexts in which interpretations are valorized or debunked. While he holds the validity of an interpretation to be in the first instance absolute, its value ultimately depends upon its particular relation to other interpretations. Moreover, I hope these considerations will shed some new light on Milton's evolving conception of all texts, including his own, as heuristic, not ostensive—that is, leading to the discovery of an interpretation, not providing it.[3] By tracing the hermeneutic concept available and, indeed, advertised in Milton's reading practices, we can further refine our appreciation of fundamental epistemological positions taken and in some respects modified by Milton. I shall discuss how, by first considering Milton's annotating practices, modern readers can deepen their understanding of what Milton says about books in the *Areopagitica* and what such theories might, in practice, look like according to Milton himself.

At some time in 1634, perhaps between the composition of *A Maske* and its performance, Milton bought his copy of Paulus Stephanus's edition of Euripides, as his autograph inscription on the flyleaf indicates.[4] It is clear from the different states of Milton's marginal handwriting that he read both quarto volumes in their entirety at least twice, once before and once after his return from Italy in 1639, before the onset of total blindness in 1652.[5] Even critics such as Samuel Johnson who have examined Milton's annotations have occasionally overlooked the care with which Milton read the books. "The margin," Johnson remarks in the *Life of Milton*, "is sometimes noted; but I have found nothing remarkable."[6] What is most remarkable about the attentiveness of Milton's reading, however, only becomes clear when his annotations are compared with the marginalia of other, later owners of the volumes. Notes in three other hands accompany the two stages of Milton's marginalia. The identity of one of the annotators is certain: Joshua Barnes, editor of Euripides in 1694 and fellow of Emmanuel College, Cambridge, who absorbed some of Milton's conjectures and emendations into his edition (without attributing them) and thereby introduced Milton into the historical collation apparatuses of modern critical editions. About a dozen of his proposed emendations remain accepted readings to this day in modern editions.[7]

The history of Milton's intervention into the mainstream of modern classical editing demonstrates the role of the material book in the transmission of the text and in what William Sherman refers to as "the intertextual and interpersonal quality of Renaissance reading." Although Milton's hand appears to be the earliest to have marked the exemplum, he may not have been its first owner, and, moreover, he likely knew himself not to be its last. Marginal notation ranges, as Anthony Grafton has shown, from the cryptically idiosyncratic to the overtly discursive, a continuum that itself discloses a historical conception of the Renaissance book as material and intellectual property that differs radically from our own. This historical conception of the book in turn relays an idea of authorship quite distinct from modern notions, evincing what Stephen Orgel has called "the legible incorporation of the work of reading into the text of the book." Milton's Euripides marginalia present especially rich evidence of the habits of a seventeenth-century reader because they not only indicate his idea of and interaction with a classical text, but also imply his projection of a future audience for his notes.[8]

The students Milton was tutoring when he reread the Euripides volumes comprise one such audience. Following his return from Italy, most likely "in the autumn of 1639 or early in 1640," Milton began to spend part of each day teaching his young nephews—John and Edward Phillips, then ages eight and nine. From the start, the younger boy probably lived with his uncle, but later in 1640, when Milton found a larger house in Aldersgate, both lived with him, their education becoming a full-time responsibility. In April 1643, when it had become clear that Milton's first wife, Mary Powell, would not be returning any time soon from her "vacation" to her parents' home in Forrest Hill (near Oxford), Milton took in more pupils. In the spring or summer of 1645, Milton began searching for a larger house, and by September or October he had moved into a residence in the Barbican, where, as Edward Phillips recalled, "probably he might have some prospect of putting in Practice his Academical Institution, according to the Model laid down in his Sheet of Education." Among the students Milton probably tutored were Cyriack Skinner, John Overton, Thomas Gardiner, Richard Barry, Richard Heath, Jeremy Picard, William Brownlow, and, later, Thomas Ellwood. In addition, "tho the accession of Scholars was not great," he may have had other students whose names have been lost, since Phillips mentions Milton's "having application made to him by several Gentlemen of his acquaintance for the Education of their Sons, as understanding haply the Progress he had infixed by his first undertakings of that nature." By August 1647, however, Milton had given up the large house in the Barbican and moved to a smaller residence in High Holborn. The death of his own father and of Richard Powell, his father-in-law, had filled the house with relatives and in effect brought to an end what Samuel Hartlib was by then calling "Mr. Milton's Academy."[9]

In the portion of the biography devoted to his years at the Miltons', Edward Phillips memorialized his uncle's "excellent judgment and way of Teaching" and, by extension, the reading practices involved. "By Teaching," Phillips says, "he in some measure increased his own knowledge, having the reading of all these Authors as it were by Proxy."[10] Milton, of course, would have deliberately formulated his curriculum based upon his own vast reading experience, but we can infer from Phillips's description that Milton was rereading "by Proxy" while instructing his pupils. Phillips depicts a pedagogical environment in which students, seated together in Milton's home, take turns reading from his annotated books, sharing their translations aloud, and participating in a conversation with and about the text that involves Milton's written memoranda and, certainly, his oral instruction. Phillips's account, therefore, suggests that Milton's books became communal property while he tutored his pupils and that he might have anticipated this when he wrote in them during this period.

Leaving aside for the moment assessments of the validity of Milton's readings of Euripides, of his metrical and philological proposals for the improvement of his Greek text, I want first to consider the kinds of comments Milton made and, more important, why he made them.[11] Throughout the two volumes, Milton writes out full, discursive comments in Latin where he makes his presence overt and thus the issue of his identity as reader an integral part of the comment. In his pre–1638 hand, he questions his own authority as he alters a word and thereby calls for a plainer sense to line 1145 of *Helena*, "The sense will be plainer, unless I am mistaken" (*ET* 2:584). Similarly, in another pre–1638 annotation, Milton wonders whether proper usage will allow him to change the position of a word in the Latin translation to clarify its syntax: "If linguistic usage permit, I would transfer *pedens*" (*ET* 1:525). These more tentative early comments show the young scholar self-consciously working through the volumes and commenting, most likely to himself, albeit with the knowledge that someone in the future may be reading critically over his shoulder and evaluating his judgments with superior knowledge.

In the earlier marginalia, Milton fashions his voice anxiously in relation to tradition, interjecting *puto ego* ("I think" or "I consider") primarily as a means of differentiating his interpretation from the printed scholia included with his edition. When he corrects the Greek text in his pre–1638 hand, Milton puts on display the same categories of discursive style that he will employ in future evaluations of his reading text, though he makes his own presence a less definite rhetorical feature of his statement: "This way the sense is plainer and more elegant" (*ET* 2:486). After 1638, he introduces one emendation by claiming, "I consider this to be more correct and elegant" (*ET* 1:484). The comment, in Milton's post–1638 hand, interjects the first person singular into the note with *puto* ("I consider"), rather than simply emending the text, as he does in so many other places. He systematically introduces *rectius* and *elegantus*, more correct and elegant, as if they were analytic categories emerging from his own interpretation, bearing witness to his critical judgment.

Positing an authorial identity in judgments announced by the post–1638 hand becomes a repetitive act of self-mythologizing analogous to the formulaic incantation of *cogito*, pronouncing "I think (this)" as a way to proclaim "I was capable of thinking (this)." The implication of authorial possessiveness surrounds the later notes, affecting their mode of address, as when a note marks ownership of an ingenious but suspect onomatopoetic etymology: "I think the word [i.e., διεκαναξε (*diekanaxe*)] comes from the sound of drink-ing wine" (*ET* 2:440). When he thinks a word should be omitted, Milton writes *ejiciendum puto* and explains his rationale instead of simply crossing out the word in his Greek text (*ET* 2:685). When he adds to a text, a rhetorical pause announces the weight of authority he wishes to grant his own margina-lia: "The verse demands it, and I think it should be supplied" (*ET* 2:716).

Marginal annotations are not ordinarily read for their tone, but I would argue that this is because of modern assumptions about the place of margina-lia in a volume that belongs to the private library of an individual collector, assumptions that have little to do with the actual reading practices of the sixteenth and seventeenth centuries. Applying the logic of modern consump-tion to a book owned by Milton implies a misconception about early modern libraries and a commensurate underestimation of marginalia's communal utility. Readers, it is sometimes assumed, tend to address only themselves in the margins of their books—by composing *aides-mémoire* in the form of topic heading and summary—though early modern (like many modern) readers were, of course, often adversarial in their annotating practices, disputing with their texts as if with the authors themselves and registering that active en-gagement in lively marks and comments.[12] While both verbal and nonverbal notation indicate the character of a reader's interaction with a text, the tone of verbal comments, as in Milton's Euripides marginalia, discloses the con-struction of a mode of address and thus an audience, which in turn proposes a conception of the material book as a communicative medium beyond its printed text. Thus, the book becomes the hub of a set of perceived relation-ships among readers extending beyond the horizon of a specific act of textual interpretation.

If these notes convey something of the tone of Milton's address, they nevertheless leave ambiguous the identity of his audience. Milton could, after all, be addressing himself to a time in which he would return to the volumes an older and more experienced reader. Conversely, he may be imag-ining a conversation with a future owner of his books. Again, the rhetoric of a certain kind of inclusion—where the information provided is, strictly speak-ing, unnecessary—hints at Milton's imagination of a broader audience for his conversation with the text. He begins an annotation to the Latin translation of *Suppliants*, line 530, "That verse should rather be rendered thus," instead of simply writing his correction alongside the faulty verse and crossing it out (*ET* 2:30). To whom does he write this?

Other kinds of comments in the post–1638 hand suggest another con-ception of the margins of texts: not merely a space for correction (even of self), they become a space of pedagogy. Milton's marginalia offer exemplary intellectual positions and thus demonstrate the processes at work in reflecting upon a text. Placing readers of his volumes at one remove from the text itself, Milton's comments and corrections attune readers to a debate about the text in order to prompt imitation. If the annotations reconfigure the margin of the book as a pedagogical space, they do so by defamiliarizing the intuitive recognition of meaning and thus making explicit the intellectual processes involved in the act of interpretation. In this way, Milton's marginalia provide a model for what he calls "a well continu'd and judicious conversing among pure Authors," in which "conversing" means not only "discussing," but also (from the Latin *conversari*) "associating" or living among (YP 2:373; cf. 1:883).

The correction to *Hippolytus,* line 998, shows Milton marking up his book with novice readers of the Greek in mind. Here, again in the post–1638 hand, Milton's annotation takes the form of a repeated Latin translation of his Greek correction to the Greek text (see fig. 1). In this passage, Hippolytus— defending himself against his father's charge that he raped his stepmother, Phaedra—invokes his friends as character witnesses. Hippolytus assures his father that his friends are not the kind of people who seek to do wrong, that they are so blameless as to think it shameful merely to "report" shameful things or to perform wicked services in exchange for friendship. Milton changes the word *apaggellein* ("to report" shame) to *epaggellein* ("to order to do" shameful things). Changing the vague hint of evil gossip to a command to do evil, Milton renders the damning behavior in a crisper idiom, one that the editorial tradition has subsequently accepted.[13] By accommodating the sense of the word—adapting the diction to a more decorous relation with the play's overall design—Milton draws a more profound moral distinction in order to deepen the pathos of Hippolytus's response to the accusation.[14] Since Hippolytus is Artemis's "best friend among men" (1332), it is crucial to the tragic structure that Theseus makes the whole question of guilt hinge on the evidence of friendship when he laments, "If there were / some token now, some mark to make the division / clear between friend and friend, the true and the false" (924–26).[15] As it happens, Theseus is as bad at interpreting moral character as he is at interpreting Phaedra's letter, since he has no recourse to the context Hippolytus, using Theseus's own criterion of friendship, tries to supply. Milton's emendation properly focuses the dramatic climax of the play on Hippolytus's severe, moralizing rectitude in contrast with the indecisive evidence of friendship. Thus, Hippolytus tries to contradict "the dead, surest of witnesses [*marturos*]" (972) with a vain wish: "If I had one more witness [*martus*] to my character / if I were tried when *she* still saw the light, / deeds would have helped you as you scanned your friends / to know the true from the false" (1022–25). Unfortunately, as the Nurse says, "words are wounds" (342), precisely because words have the power to indict Hippolytus and therefore to set in motion "deeds," as in his father's curse, which leads to his demise. The indeterminacy of verbal evidence—both the oral testimony of friends and the written accusation of the dead Phaedra—represents the epistemological crisis at issue in the play. The distinction emphasized by Milton's emendation is crucial: by focusing our attention on the force of indeterminate words to cause determinate action, as in a military order or a divine annunciation, Milton elucidates the tragic irony at the heart of Hippolytus's futile response to his father, since it is in fact his austere behavior that has convicted him in the minds of his accusers.[16]

Given that Milton was such a skilled reader of the ancient Greek as to be able to correct diction based on interpretation of context, idiom, and (sometimes) conventions of versification, one wonders why he was rereading the Latin translation at all, much less repeating a correction twice. In his early grappling with the original, he, like any Renaissance student of classical Greek, might well have relied upon the Latin from time to time as an aid to comprehension. Or he may have imagined that some later owner of the book would be helped along in this way. The repetition of his Latin translation *neque inhonesta petere* ("not to solicit shameful deeds") strongly encourages the student-reader to return to the Greek original and serves to illustrate the thrust of the emendation for the novice reading the Latin only as well as for the intermediate reader working primarily through the Greek at the top of the page. (The different functions of printed marginal glosses and paraphrastic footnotes in, say, Norton editions provide a modern analogue.) In all likelihood, as I mentioned earlier, he used these very books when working as a schoolmaster, particularly in the education of his nephews, whom he taught from his home with the volumes in his personal library.

The visual appearance of another set of corrections confirms the intrusive, meticulous, even obsessive nature of Milton's reading practices in a way that cannot be communicated by mere transcription, as the modern edition of Milton's *Works* attempts to do (18:309). When Milton redistributes lines 754–71 of *Suppliants* (see fig. 2), he modifies the text by mechanically crossing out and rewriting the speech prefixes, with the explanation that "these speeches seem rather between Adrastus and the messenger speaking for the chorus, and so should be assigned to Adrastus" (*ET* 2:42). Likewise, when he redistributes lines in *Hippolytus* (353ff.), Milton corrects the speech prefixes in both the Greek and the Latin texts (*ET* 1:527). These corrections, involving the deliberate modification of the reading text rather than simply altering the sense retrospectively by comment, seek to provide a continuity of reading experience while introducing editorial material so that a person reading this book for the first time could incorporate the emendations into the primary experience of the text without pausing to read the editorial rationalization for

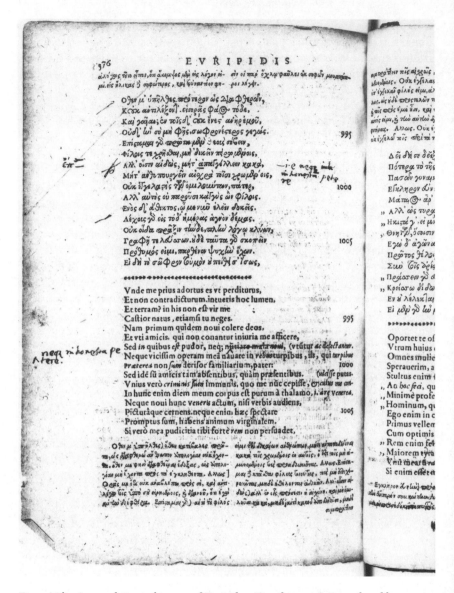

Fig. 1. Milton's emendation to his copy of Euripides, *Hippolytus,* 998. Reproduced by permission of the Bodleian Library, University of Oxford (Don d. 27, p. 576).

them. At the same time, Milton's marginalia produce a de facto edition, illustrating the principles of exegesis by applying them for students.

Furthermore, the inclusion of corrections that do not alter the Greek text—that is, Latin corrections to the Latin translation—appears in this context to have been motivated by practical pedagogy, especially when the corrections carry on at some length. In this vein, Milton's annotations include a new translation of the opening five lines of *Rhesus* (*ET* 2:232). Milton excises the circumlocutions, removes the repetitive and verbose poeticisms, from the printed Latin translation, writing out a sparer literal crib that would act as a help to students interpreting the Greek.

Preparation for teaching was the most likely cause for another variety of marginalia, the cross-referencing note, which proves surprisingly scarce in the extant marginalia, given the extent of Milton's reading. In the Euripides volumes, the only specific edition to which Milton alludes—he mentions Homer, but not an *edition* of Homer—is Scaliger's Manilius, a pioneering work of textual criticism (*ET* 2:29).[17] Another book that survives from Milton's library, the copy of Aratus with his marginal annotation, includes in his post–1638 handwriting the comparison, "Thus Lucretius II, 991, says we are all born of heavenly seed, and all have the same father, etc."[18] The note provides two forms of interesting evidence. First, given that, as Kelley and Atkins suggest, this may have been one of the notes that "were a part of preparation for teaching his nephews," the intertextual reference implies the similarity of Milton's practical curriculum to the theoretical proposal in *Of Education,* where he mentions the importance of "those Poets which are now counted most hard," including among others "*Aratus* . . . and in Latin *Lucretius*" (YP 2:394–95). This account is further corroborated by the testimony of Edward Phillips, who includes both Aratus and Lucretius when he lists some of "the many Authors both of the Latin and Greek" that Milton had his nephews study.[19] Milton's cross-referencing in this instance seems particularly relevant to his teaching, since it links passages from two works he introduces together into the curriculum in *Of Education.* The second point to make about the note is that—like Phillips's description of Milton reading "by Proxy" when his students read or translated aloud—it helps flesh out our picture of the pedagogic environment in Milton's house, especially since Phillips mentions what must have been the edition of Aratus owned and annotated by Milton.[20] In other words, the reference may have been meant to inspire imitation. Milton handwrote the reference to Lucretius but did not mention the place where Saint Paul adopts the thought from Aratus in his address to the Areopagus (Acts 17:28), perhaps thinking this too obvious for mention, perhaps wanting his students to remember the appropriation on their own.[21]

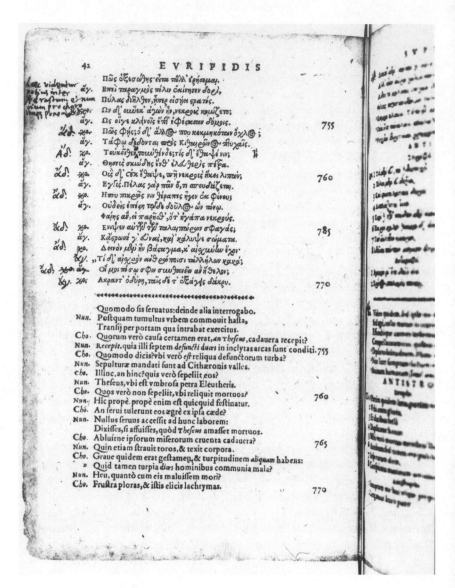

Fig. 2. Milton's emendation to his copy of Euripides, *Suppliants*, 754–71. Reproduced by permission of the Bodleian Library, University of Oxford (Don d. 28, p. 42).

Euripides was one of Milton's most abiding literary interests, next to Homer and Ovid, and remained constantly in his thoughts, as the poet's daughter Deborah reported, even after his blindness prevented him from reading at his leisure.²² As was shown above, Milton reread the volumes in their entirety in exactly the same years during which he acted as a schoolmaster to several young pupils. What effect did reading Euripides at that time have on Milton's writings, and what evidence can his marginalia provide of his conception of the efficacy and potency of books? Milton had rather self-consciously begun to figure his relations with a readership in explicitly pedagogical terms in the antiprelatical tracts published for "the honour and instruction of my country" in the early 1640s (YP 1:810). Milton's idea of the power of a book emerges most fully, however, when he actively and publicly responds to the Licensing Act of 1643. On 14 June 1643, the Long Parliament had issued an Order for Printing that mandated prepublication inspection by Presbyterian censors, an effort to stem the massive influx of dissent (both royalist and sectarian) that was adversely affecting parliamentary control in the capital and drawing momentum away from Parliament's war effort. This largely ineffective order merged with the Stationer's Company bid to secure rights of monopoly over the publishing trade.²³ The *Areopagitica* represents Milton's response to the threat of constricted circulation as a result of the order. How then did Milton conceive of readers responding to a book, whether of poetry or prose, "something so written to aftertimes, as they should not willingly let it die" (YP 1:810)?

We know from *The Reason of Church Government* that Milton thought of his own work and Euripidean drama as analogously "doctrinal and exemplary to a Nation," both as destined for an immediate occasion and as resurrected in posterity (YP 1:815). Since "the Apostle Paul himself thought it not unworthy to insert a verse of Euripides into the text of Holy Scripture, 1 Cor. XV.33," the apostle's citation of the verse affirms the didactic potential of Milton's foray into the dramatic genre of the play from which it was quoted.²⁴ In fact, as Milton says in the *Areopagitica*, Paul "thought it no defilement to insert into holy Scripture the sentences of three Greek Poets, and one of them a Tragedian," whereas "*Julian* the Apostat, and suttlest enemy to our faith, made a decree forbidding Christians the study of heathen learning" (YP 2:508). In *De Doctrina Christiana*, Milton—like Paul in the passage Milton was so fond of—cites Euripides as he discusses the nature of the soul and its fate after the death of the body: "Euripides in the *Suppliants* has given a far better interpretation of this passage than my opponents, without knowing it" (YP 6:407). The identical thought, expressed by the pagan tragedian, can resurrect a vital passage of Scripture through exact interpretation.²⁵

If these allusions to Euripides reveal the way in which the tragedies could become "doctrinal," the quotation from *Suppliants* on the title page of the *Areopagitica* indicates how they could become "exemplary." To put it in the language of the tract, where the allusions in the preface to *Samson Agonistes* and in *De Doctrina Christiana* affirm the activities of the "wayfaring Christian" reader, the epigraph seeks to energize the "warfaring" one. Theseus's retort to the Theban herald—who presumes that Athens, like Thebes, is under the rule of a *tyrannos* (line 399)—was glossed as a "vituperation of tyranny and praise of democracy" in one sixteenth-century edition:[26]

> *This is true Liberty when free born men*
> *Having to advise the public may speak free,*
> *Which he who can, and will, deserv's high praise,*
> *Who neither can, nor will, may hold his peace;*
> *What can be juster in a State then this?*
>
> (*Areopagitica* [1644], title page)

Milton himself marked the speech—though not precisely these lines—in his own copy. In his English version he effects a subtle, but interested, appropriation of Euripides, making the verses more didactic than in the original by changing the mood of the verbs from the Greek's more straightforward, present active indicative to an auxiliary mood of permission, obligation, and condition. In effect, he shifts the mood from "does" to "can, and will." Milton intensifies the sense of civic duty by rendering the "Liberty" expressed by Theseus's hypothetical citizen—who "wishes" (*thelei*) to advise the city—as the native responsibility incurred by "free born men / Having to advise the public."[27]

Voluntary participation, intrinsic to any civic debate, moves to the center of Milton's translation, which accentuates the choice to speak out as a conscious act of reason. In the exordium that follows, proof of character, inhering in the speaker as in the audience, assures "civill liberty" through the practice of civic duty: primarily by means of "the strong assistance of God our deliverer"; secondarily through the exemplary leadership of Parliament and its "indefatigable virtues"; and ultimately in the citizens who, "mov'd inwardly in their mindes," speak "a certain testimony" as a challenge to the "tyranny and superstition grounded in our principles" (YP 2:486–87).[28] Milton allies the ability to speak freely (the "can" of his epigraph), with the conscientious submission of "testimony" that becomes the subject of debate within public assembly (the "will" of his epigraph). When citizens pursue ethical action through political exigency "in Gods esteeme," "when complaints are freely heard, deeply consider'd, and speedily reform'd, then is the utmost bound of civill liberty attain'd" (YP 2:487). The excellence of Parliament, the exordium repeatedly points out, is commensurate with its acknowledgment and obedience of "the voice of reason from what quarter soever it be heard speaking": "there can no greater testimony appear" (YP 2:490). As Melanchthon said in his oration at Luther's funeral, God imparts his blessings upon humankind by calling "forth prophets, the Apostles, teachers and ministers. . . . Nor does He call only those to that warfare who have customary power, but often He wages war against them through teachers chosen from other ranks."[29] The "voice of reason" testifies willingly, is heard freely, and wars against papist "tyranny and superstition."

Milton's argument in the *Areopagitica* centers on his conception of reason, which over the course of the tract undergoes something of a transformation, not unlike Truth, "untill she be adjur'd into her own likenes" at "her Masters second comming" (YP 2:543, 563). Books (such as Milton's own copy of Euripides) are instruments through which reason exercises itself in the educational process, when reason recognizes its likeness in a book: "as good almost kill a Man as kill a good Book; who kills a man kills a reasonable creature, Gods Image; but hee who destroyes a good Booke, kills reason it selfe, kills the Image of God, as it were in the eye" (YP 2:492). Just as the "eye" is the organ that perceives the "Image," the "reasonable creature" comprehends "reason it selfe," the analogy or correspondence between image and likeness; according to Erasmus, "What the eye is to the body, reason is to the soul."[30] As a result of this apparently iconographic exchange, Stanley Fish has attacked the encomiastic portion of the *Areopagitica* as "decidedly *un*Miltonic," arguing that the logic of Milton's praise of books seems grounded in idolatrous practices or worship of the objects themselves.[31] But to characterize Milton's ethical defense of "that season'd life of man preserv'd and stor'd up in Books" as idolatrous is to think too literally about the action "that slaies an immortality rather then a life" (YP 2:493). Where Fish sees the "Image" of the letter that "killeth," Milton comprehends the "Image of God," which is to say the spirit that "giveth life" (2 Cor. 3:6). In this conception of the divine logos as the metaphorical "Image of God," Milton is close to contemporaries such as John Donne, Sir Thomas Browne, and Henry Vaughan, who explicitly deploy the trope during philosophical meditations and inquiries.[32] Futhermore, Milton had only recently revised his conception of the "Image of God" in such a way as to locate the residuum in the human capacity for choice. In *The Reason of Church Government,* as elsewhere in the course of the antiprelatical tracts, Milton had defended the scriptural justification for the Presbyterian "one right *discipline*" against the "English Dragon" of episcopacy on these very grounds: for "the Church hath in her immediate cure those inner parts and affections of the mind where the seat of reason is," the faculty which he refers to later in the pamphlet as "the dignity of Gods image" (YP 1:605, 857, 747, 842). But "the spurre of self-concernment" brought on in the following years by Milton's need to justify the freedom to divorce—ultimately a freedom of choice—refocused Milton's thinking about the place of interpretation (YP 2:226).³³

In the second edition of his *Doctrine and Discipline of Divorce* (February 1643/4), Milton approvingly cites a work that commences with exegesis of Genesis 1:26–27, "And God said, Let us make man in our image, after our likeness. . . . So God created man in his own image, in the image of God created he him" (KJV). In another connection (at YP 2:257), Milton shows that he knew Maimonides's *Guide of the Perplexed* in Johann Buxtorf the Younger's Latin translation, *Doctor perplexum* (Basel, 1629). Maimonides's argument, so influential in both the Jewish and Christian traditions, centers on explaining that the "image" of God is incorporeal, that is, that our "likeness" does not comprise a physical resemblance but rather our "intellectual apprehension," or "the divine intellect conjoined with man."³⁴ Milton, like Maimonides, partitions the "image of God" from idolatry, a division that is absolute. For Maimonides, it is paradoxically by means of this "image" and "likeness" that humanity upholds the Law, which is itself based on the destruction of idolatry and the worship of the one true God. In the exposition on Genesis 1:27 that commences *Tetrachordon,* Milton pursues a similar method to a different end. By "this Image of God," Milton explains, "wherein man was created, is meant Wisdom, Purity, Justice, and rule over all creatures. All which being lost in *Adam,* was recover'd with gain by the merits of Christ" (YP 2:587). Thus Milton explicates the phrase "Image of God" in the light of Pauline theology, favoring a typological interpretation that was common to diverse exponents of reformist doctrine throughout the seventeenth century.³⁵ In *De Doctrina Christiana* (1.18), Milton argues that "the inner man is regenerated by God through the word and the spirit so that his whole mind [*tota mente*] is restored to the image of God" (YP 6:461; CM 15:366). Hence, "the faithful" have "God as their instructor [*edocti a Deo*]," and the regeneration of man's "intellect and will" emerges with "the restoration of the will to its former liberty" (YP 6:478, 462; CM 16:6, 15:370).

This "restoration" then must be logically consistent with the effort to preserve "the pretious life-blood of a master spirit" since the ascent to spiritual regeneration results from the exercise of reason (YP 2:493). Milton makes the case in *Of Education* that all knowledge of God proceeds from observation of the "sensible" to the "intelligible": "[B]ecause our understanding cannot in this body but found it selfe but on sensible things, nor arrive so cleerly to the knowledge of God and things invisible, as by orderly conning over the visible and inferior creature, the same method is necessarily to be follow'd in all discreet teaching" (YP 2:367–69). This passage makes explicit the epistemological assumptions underlying the educational system at work in the *Areopa-*

gitica. The intellect moves from material observation toward theoretical assertion, from inductive perceptions toward deductive demonstrations of truth.[36]
Insofar as the theoretical takes the form of the theological in Milton's formulation, his logic descends ultimately from Aquinas:

All creatures, even those lacking intelligence, are ordered to God as to their ultimate
end, and they achieve this end insofar as they share some similarity with him. Intellectual creatures attain him in a more special manner, namely by understanding him
through their proper activity. To understand God then must be the end of the intellectual creature. . . . A thing is more intimately united with God insofar as it attains to his
substance, which comes about when it knows something of the divine substance,
which requires some likeness of him. Therefore the intellectual substance tends
towards divine knowledge as to its ultimate end.[37]

Aquinas here makes explicit the fundamental rationale for philosophical pur-
suits in the context of Christian piety, a rationale that is not, contrary to the
assertions of Fish and others, considered idolatrous in most seventeenth-
century English Protestant thought. The editors of the Yale prose works, in
their annotations to the methodological passage in *Of Education,* surround
Milton's sentence with echoes from Plato, Dury, Vives, Comenius, and others. Yet the "commonplace" derives the force of its conviction from Aquinas,
who provides the logical connection between the Miltonic defense of "the
Image of God" in books and the intellectual ascent from the inductive contemplation of the sensible to the deductive if limited comprehension of the
intelligible.

Milton's emendations to the Stephanus Euripides demonstrate the principle in action. The "orderly conning" over the "visible and inferior" text
employs the same logical progression as observation of the natural or "sensible" world, the Book of Nature. The hermeneutic circle—building a per-
spicuous context out of the aggregate of analytic details—represents an analogous process, as we have seen in Milton's emendation to *Hippolytus.* A
venerable tradition of Christian hermeneutics has linked the operation of
reason in this way to the speculative approach to truth.[38]

To the extent that readers exercise their reason, they approach the "end
. . . of learning," for by this act only do they regain "to know God aright, and
out of that knowledge to love him, to imitate him, to be like him, as we may
the neerest by possessing our souls of true virtue, which being united to the
heavenly grace of faith makes up the highest perfection" (YP 2:366–67). If in
the imitation of Christ we strive "to repair the ruins of our first parents," then
the specific form of that imitation consists in our exercising the remnant of
divine "likeness," the "Image of God" that is reason. Arguing, as Maimonides
did, against literal interpretation of Scripture, Milton reminds his readers

that many "of most renowned vertu have sometimes by transgressing, most truly kept the law" (YP 2:588). By means of inspired transgression against the material letter of the book, a reader who repairs the ruins of a text by emendation—as Milton did in correcting his copy of Euripides—evinces godly reason. This means that errors (even of typography) relay to readers a didactic message, indirectly reminding them of a fall into print. Thus the duty of an educated reader is "to repair the ruins" of this textual fall. Restoring an Edenic "spirit" of the text, the reader must wrest it away from the "letter" of its manifestation, but always with the knowledge that this "spirit" remains accessible to us only through the material letter modified, emended with spiritual intent. Typography dovetails with typology.

It is as though, for Milton, the truth of a fallen text can only exist in the record of its correction, not in the correction alone. The very transmutability of the material text effects the transformation of its reader because perception of the "spirit" of a text so often registers in perception and modification of an "error" in a book. Milton depicts books as open to inspired modification, while still insisting on an essential conception of their verbal content, "the purest efficacie and extraction of that living intellect that bred them" (YP 2:492). If these two notions of textuality seem mutually exclusive, Milton asks us to remember that the essence of truth, like the intention of an author, can only be achieved provisionally after the fall by a reader who can only partially "repair the ruins" he or she has been bequeathed.

In consequence of the fall, as Sir Thomas Browne remarks in the *Pseudodoxia Epidemica,* there is no longer "a Paradise or unthorny place of knowledge." Our postlapsarian "understandings being eclipsed . . . we must betake our selves to waies of reparation, and depend upon the illumination of our endeavours. For thus we may in some measure repair our primary ruines, and build our selves men again."[39] Browne's epistemological argument bears a structural resemblance to the position Milton articulates with respect to knowledge in *Of Education* and the *Areopagitica.* Just as Browne believes that there exist certain "waies of reparation," so Milton famously encourages the worldly virtue of the *vita activa:* "I cannot praise a fugitive and cloister'd vertue, unexercis'd and unbreath'd, that never sallies out and sees her adversary, but slinks out of the race, where that immortall garland is to be run for, not without dust and heat" (YP 2:515). Far from suggesting an idolatrous insistence upon the letter or indeed the object, Milton's ethical defense of books against prepublication censorship—his likening the intellectual content of books to the "Image of God"—emphasizes the active exercise of reason as a corrective measure against just such literal-mindedness.

To return to the language of *Areopagitica*'s epigraph, the ability to "speak free" stems from the right to interpret or differ in interpretation of

Scripture and, therefore, depends upon the freedom to do so—the "can" of the epigraph. This makes for the apparent paradox expressed in the chapter of *De Doctrina Christiana* devoted to biblical hermeneutics (1.30). Even though "each passage of Scripture has only a single sense"—"the scriptures . . . are plain and sufficient in themselves," and "no inferences should be made from the text, unless they necessarily follow from what is written"— nevertheless "every believer is entitled to interpret the scriptures . . . for himself" (YP 6:580, 581, 583). Each believer "has the spirit, who guides truth, and he has the mind of Christ" (YP 6:583). Hence the centrality of scriptural interpretation: "If studied carefully and regularly, they [Scriptures] are an ideal instrument for educating even unlearned readers in those matters which have most to do with salvation" (YP 6:578–79). The problem of interpretation, however, broadens when considered in the context of the *Areopagitica,* where the consideration of all books, not just sacred Scriptures, is at stake. The category of "things indifferent," as against "those matters which have most to do with salvation," is therefore constitutive of the class of objects open to interpretation as an act of reason.

As soon as interpretation becomes necessary, so does justification. An interpretation, that is, will always be subject to challenge and therefore must rise above other competing interpretations in order to sustain its own claim to validity. Interpretation, of course, first depends on recognizing the proper object of contemplation. The "neighboring differences, or rather indifferences" or "brotherly dissimilitudes" that Milton considers the objects under discussion in the *Areopagitica* seem to have the ability to bring about "things not yet constituted in religion" and, moreover, to assist in the "reforming of Reformation it self" (YP 2:541, 553). The problem, then, is at least in part deciding what belongs in what category. In a tract heartily endorsed by Milton in the *Areopagitica* (at YP 2:560–61), Robert Greville had collapsed the distinction between "things indifferent" and things necessary to salvation. Following the Smectymnuans, Greville writes that it is "Papall, Tyrannical" for the episcopacy to try to differentiate between indifference and necessity: "They will do more than *Adam* did: He gave names to Things according to their Natures; they will give *Natures* according to their owne fancies." Greville asserts that "No Thing, No Act, is *Indifferent* . . . in it selfe, in the thing, but either *necessary* to be done, (if *Best*) or *unlawfull* to be done, if *Bad*." On the other hand, "if Right Reason have not, or cannot determine me; to which side soever I incline, and rest, I sin; because I act *Unreasonably*: being determined by humour, fancy, passion, a wilfull Will." The category of indifference is the province solely of right reason; the Prelates "have no power to determine what is *Indifferent*." Greville goes further than Milton in arguing for what amounts to a libertarian agenda. Unlike the view Milton is developing in the *Areopagitica*, Greville's *Discourse*—following his earlier treatise on *The Nature of Truth, Its Union and Unity with the Soule*—propounds the belief that any man who knows the good will do it, that "recta ratio," as he argues circularly, can itself only be defined by "recta ratio": "But who shall tell us what is *Recta Ratio*? I answer, *Recta Ratio*."[40] Milton's earlier conception of virtue had, like Greville's, derived from the Socratic paradox that doing good is not an act of will, since no one knowingly does evil.[41] As he writes in *An Apology against a Pamphlet*, "the first and chiefest office of love, begins and ends in the soule, producing those happy twins of her divine generation knowledge and vertue" (YP 1:892).[42] The *Areopagitica* of course concentrates on a different but related pair of twins.

In the *Areopagitica*, the whole matter turns on freedom of choice—the "will" of Milton's epigraph. At a critical moment, the speaker argues against those "who imagin to remove sin by removing the matter of sin" (YP 2:527). Milton's philosophical play on the word "matter" induces exactly the kind of consciousness for which he is arguing. The "matter of sin," he implies, is both the incarnation of fallibility that is the flesh and the pattern of thought that engenders such a lapse in spirit. "Matter," then, is both the problem and product of sinfulness in a fallen world, a concept which Milton represents when he collapses form into substance in a moment of ludic concentration, cause becoming interchangeable with effect. Mind, ordinarily held in contradistinction to matter, emerges indistinct from the material world; matter, charged with a vitality ordinarily reserved for descriptions of mind, becomes indistinguishable from the consciousness that saturates it. But the prose describing the desired removal of sin soon takes on language analogous at once to the expulsion of the cosmos from a divine first substance and to the expulsion of Adam and Eve from Paradise: "Suppose we could expell sin by this means; look how much we thus expell of sin, so much we expell of vertue: for the matter of them both is the same; remove that, and ye remove them both alike" (YP 2:527). "Matter" is not merely the location of sin, as it is in more orthodox conceptions, but paradoxically manifests both "sin" and "vertue."[43] And we, in turn, merely discard meaning in the reduction of Milton's telling pun to one or the other possibility.

Reading matter, therefore, cannot be the origin of sin, no more than knowledge itself originates disobedience. If reason is the soul's very "being" (*PL* 5.487), and "reason also is choice" (*PL* 3.108), then in order for "each man to be his own chooser" (YP 2:514), "the Church" cannot have the seat of reason "in her immediate cure" (YP 1:747). On the contrary, the responsibility must fall upon the "umpire conscience" (*PL* 3.195). In the *Christian Morals*, Sir Thomas Browne appositely casts conscience in the role of judge: "Conscience only, that can see without Light, sits in the *Areopagy* and dark

Tribunal of our Hearts, surveying our Thoughts and condemning their obliq-
uities."[44] The only redress for what Milton calls "the fall of learning" is
freedom of conscience: "Give me the liberty to know, to utter, and to argue
freely according to conscience, above all liberties" (YP 2:520, 560). Individual
conscience, guided by reason and the Holy Spirit, awakens the interpretive
faculty to choice, serves as our connection to the divine logos. As he says in
De Doctrina Christiana, "the phenomenon of Conscience, or right reason
[*recta ratio*]" gives evidence of the existence of God (YP 6:132; CM 14:28).
God wills that all may be saved, which is why Milton argues—following
Arminius—that election is simply the salvation available to all believers: "The
condition upon which God's decision depends . . . entails the action of a will
which he himself has freed and a belief which he himself demands from men.
If this condition is left in the power of men who are free to act, it is absolutely
in keeping with justice and does not detract at all from the importance of
divine grace" (YP 6:189). The argument of the *Areopagitica* similarly inheres
in the dilemma posed by freedom of choice. As he says, "many there be that
complain of divin Providence for suffering *Adam* to transgresse, foolish
tongues! when God gave him reason, he gave him freedom to choose, for
reason is but choosing" (YP 2:527). God "trusts him [man] with the gift of
reason to be his own chooser" because obedience to God, unless a conscious
choice, is meaningless (YP 2:514; cf. *PL* 3.103–11).

Therefore, by analogy, human beings must have a certain capacity to will
change if they are to learn. "He who makes you teachable," says Erasmus,
"demands nonetheless your endeavor toward learning." It is "reason," for
Milton as for Erasmus, "from which the will is born," and although "obscured
by sin," it was "not altogether extinguished" by original sin; rather, as Erasmus argues, "If the power to distinguish good and evil and the will of God had
been hidden from men, it could not be imputed to them if they made the
wrong choice. If the will had not been free, sin could not have been imputed,
for sin would cease to be sin if it were not voluntary, save when error or the
restriction of the will is itself the fruit of the sin."[45] Not only sin, but also piety
depends upon the freedom to taste what Erasmus pointedly refers to as "the
fruit of the sin." The matter of them both is the same. For it is not the fruit
but our intention that makes the sin what it is. If an omnipotent, omniscient,
and benevolent God should not have created beings capable of choosing to
transgress his law, then, as Irenaeus argues, "neither would what is good be
grateful to them, nor communion with God be precious, nor would the good
be very much sought after, which . . . would be implanted of its own accord
and without their concern." Irenaeus finds his way out of the supposedly
aporistic "trilemma" (God is benevolent and omnipotent, yet evil exists) by
finding the benevolence of God redolent of his will to educate us: "being

good would be of no consequence" if humankind "were so by nature rather than by will" and thus became "possessors of good spontaneously, not by choice."[46] God formed humankind, as the Father says in *Paradise Lost,* "Sufficient to have stood, though free to fall" (3.99). Our condition in this world necessitates choice, and choice depends on the presence of oppositions (or at least distinct alternatives) from which to choose: "Assuredly we bring not innocence into the world, we bring impurity much rather: that which purifies us is triall, and triall is by what is contrary" (YP 2:515). Milton's recognition of the dilemmas that necessarily face each person in this world fostered one of his most characteristic habits of thought, a pattern in his works memorably described by C. S. Lewis as "the co-existence, in a live and sensitive tension, of apparent opposites."[47] Given "the state of man," Milton asks, "what wisdome can there be to choose, what continence to forbeare without the knowledge of evill" (YP 2:514)? In recognition of this logical dilemma, "the question of censorship," as Edward Tayler puts it, becomes in the *Areopagitica* "ultimately a question of reason in relation to freedom of choice."[48]

Milton therefore depicts the process of learning as a trajectory from choice to recognition, or, as he says in *Of Education,* employing Aristotelian terminology, from "that act of reason which in the *Ethics* is call'd *Proairesis*" (YP 2:396) to *anagnorisis.* Hence the figure of the teacher that ends the brief tractate: teaching is "not a bow for every man to shoot in . . . but will require sinews almost equall to those which Homer gave Ulysses" (YP 2:415). In a counterintuitive move, Milton figures the teacher as Telemachus, not Odysseus. Only Telemachus has "sinews almost equall" to Odysseus's in Book Twenty-One of the *Odyssey,* which is, I think, Milton's way of suggesting that one is both taught and becomes a teacher in the act of recognizing likeness: Telemachus becomes most like himself when he demonstrates that he is most like Odysseus.

Because this comprehension of likeness requires a contrasting perception in order to achieve definition, Milton encourages the recognition of difference, or at least of "brotherly dissimilitudes" that come together to form the Temple of Solomon, the ruins that Reformation seeks to repair. In short, the opportunity to correct error resides in its perception and therefore in the possibility of error's existence. Except in the recognition of difference —the differentiation between "cunning resemblances"—how can we come to see truth in her best likeness?

Good and evill we know in the field of this World grow up together almost inseparably; and the knowledge of good is so involv'd and interwoven with the knowledge of evill, and in so many cunning resemblances hardly to be discerned, that those confused seeds which were impos'd on *Psyche* as an incessant labor to cull out, and sort asunder, were not more intermixt. It was from out the rinde of one apple tasted, that the knowledge of Good and evill as two twins cleaving together leapt forth into the World. (YP 2:514)

Except through the reading of books, how can we find the materials that instigate choice between one portion of truth and another, when the very structure of Truth can only inhere in their composite? Therefore Milton encourages us, "Read any books what ever come to thy hands, for thou art sufficient both to judge aright, and to examine the matter" (YP 2:511). Repairing the ruins of England's "spirituall architecture" entails "an incessant labor" like that which Psyche faced: "to cull out, and sort asunder" (YP 2:555, 514). Thus the effort on behalf of Truth by its very nature entails the considered sorting of opinion, so that what is for royalists the object of withering satire—proliferation of "plainly partiall" expression, even of "unchosen books"—is for Milton a mere statement of our condition in "this World" (YP 2:510, 530). The engraving of Henry Peacham's *The World Is Ruled & Governed by Opinion* (1641) centers on the same metaphor as the *Areopagitica* (see fig. 3), although for Milton it is not the publication of pamphlets but conversely the Licensing Order that "may be held a dangerous and suspicious fruit, as certainly it deserves, for the tree that bore it" (YP 2:507).[49] Books which, like the fruit, tempt with the dangerous knowledge of their arguments, accost both Peacham's "wayfarer" (*Viator*) and Milton's, though a fool waters Peacham's tree. What Milton views as preparatory to virtue, Peacham assumes is destroying it. The fruit, Milton assures us, is not the sin. Booklike "Dragons teeth" may metamorphose into armed men, such as the "warfaring" *Spartoi* that sprang up before Cadmus—seeds, as it were, that sort themselves out.[50] But the chief labor of Reformation activates a "Nation of Prophets, of Sages, of Worthies" working at the "defence of beleaguer'd Truth" in "the mansion house of liberty":

there be pens and heads there, sitting by their studious lamps, musing, searching, revolving new notions and idea's wherewith to present, as with their homage and their fealty the approaching Reformation: others as fast reading, trying all things, assenting to the force of reason and convincement. (YP 2:554)

When Milton translates or emends Euripides, as when he hopes for the "reforming of Reformation" through "books promiscuously read," he advances reasonable choice as the necessary condition for the pursuit of truth (YP 2:553, 517). Freedom of conscience demands freedom of choice, a condition that in turn entails a "perpetuall progression" of alternatives, if reason or virtue is to be exercised (YP 2:543). By a parallel logic, the closing verse of John's gospel resists closure: "And there are also many other things which Jesus did, the which, if they should be written every one, I suppose that even

Fig. 3. Henry Peacham, *The World is Ruled & Governed by Opinion,* engraved by Wenceslas Hollar (1641). Reproduced by permission of the Folger Shakespeare Library.

the world itself could not contain the books that should be written" (21:25, KJV). That Parliament (in the very "mansion house of liberty") would pursue such a policy as represented by the Licensing Order—an even more literal effort at containment—inspired Milton's defense of the integrity of reason as a judge of knowledge's value. Milton's practices as a reader and annotator remain faithful to the paradoxical effort to sustain pure intentions in a fallen world. By scripting their own transmuting exchanges with and within books, readers participate in an ongoing textual conversation. Milton presents an excellent example of how that educational metamorphosis, provisionally re-pairing the ruins of our imperfect and fallen knowledge, arouses the "life beyond life" that is a book's progeny down through history.

Haverford College

NOTES

1. Ben Jonson, *Timber; or, Discoveries,* under the topic *Autodidaktos,* in *Ben Jonson,* 11 vols., ed. C. H. Herford and Percy and Evelyn Simpson (Oxford, 1925–52), 8:563. Stanley Fish, *Is There a Text in This Class? The Authority of Interpretive Communities* (Cambridge, Mass., 1980). Roger Chartier, *The Order of Books,* trans. Lydia G. Cochrane (Stanford, 1994), chap. 1.

2. Plato, *Symposium,* 177a, trans. R. E. Allen (New Haven, Conn., 1991), 116. The irony is even further complicated by the narrative situation: Plato is telling us that Apollodorus reports Aristodamus recalling Eryximachus citing Euripides. Moreover, the remainder of the line, not quoted by Eryximachus, looks forward to Diotima's configuration (208e–209b) of education as reproduction: "Mine is not the tale; my mother taught me" (quoted in Allen's note on 177a). On the relations between education, the transmission of knowledge, and the problematic of textual tradition as intellectual property as seen by Renaissance readers of the *Symposium,* see Kathy Eden, "Friends and Lovers in the *Symposium:* Plato on Tradition," *Friends Hold All Things in Common: Tradition, Intellectual Property, and the "Adages" of Erasmus* (New Haven, Conn., 2001), chap. 2. Since Milton made several specific references to the *Symposium* throughout the divorce controversy, we may be sure he had the text in mind in the period under discussion in this essay. See, for example, *Complete Prose Works of John Milton,* 8 vols., ed. Don M. Wolfe et al. (New Haven, 1953–82), 2:252, 522, 589. Subsequent references to this edition will appear parenthetically as YP.

3. My thinking about this crucial distinction in Milton's thought has profited most imme-diately from related remarks made by William Kerrigan concerning the place of "argument" and "proposition" in Milton's works, particularly the general assessments of "Milton's Place in Intel-lectual History," in *The Cambridge Companion to Milton,* 2d ed., ed. Dennis Danielson (Cam-bridge, 1999), 253–66, and *The Prophetic Milton* (Charlottesville, Va., 1974), 6–7, as well as the more specific treatments of the philosophical use of contradiction in *The Sacred Complex: On the Psychogenesis of "Paradise Lost"* (Cambridge, Mass., 1983), passim. Dayton Haskin, *Milton's Burden of Interpretation* (Philadelphia, 1994), has had a formative influence on my understand-ing of the shift in Milton's conception of biblical hermeneutics in the 1640s.

4. Milton's copy of *Euripidis Tragoediae,* 2 vols., ed. Paulus Stephanus (Geneva, 1602), is now housed in the Bodleian Library, shelfmark don. d. 27, 28. When citing the marginalia, I have

provided where possible the translations found in the Columbia *Works of John Milton*, 18 vols., ed. Frank Allen Patterson et al. (New York, 1931–38), 18:304–25, hereafter cited as CM, though for the sake of future researchers I provide citations to the volume and page number of *ET* in the text, for reasons that should become clear.

5. The Columbia Milton does not differentiate between the states of Milton's hand and offers only a select transcription of the marginalia. Firsthand paleographic analysis makes the distinction between the two states of Milton's handwriting more evident than mere verbal description can. Nevertheless, the most apparent distinguishing features that differentiate earlier from later markings are as follows: the size of the inscription (the later writing being almost invariably larger); the quality of the ink employed and how it has faded over time (the later tends to be lighter in color, more sepia tone showing); the particular features of the lettering, in particular the lowercase letter "e" (Milton prefers the Greek epsilon "È" in the earlier, an Italian "e" in the later) and of the nonverbal supralinear and marginal markings "⁰" (earlier) and "x" (later). The argument from paleographic evidence for dating the two states of Milton's handwriting, based on comparison between Milton's hand in the Trinity Manuscript and the Commonplace Book, was made by Helen Darbishire, "The Chronology of Milton's Handwriting," *Library* 14, 4th ser. (1933): 229–35, a refinement and corroboration of the suggestions made earlier by James Holly Hanford, "The Chronology of Milton's Private Studies," *PMLA* 36 (1921), reprinted in *John Milton, Poet and Humanist* (Cleveland, 1966), 75–125. It is, however, important to keep the limited quantity of evidence in perspective. Peter Beal, *Index of English Literary Manuscripts, Volume II: 1635–1700, Part 2: Lee-Wycherly* (London, 1993), 78–81, argues that the provenance of only seven annotated books from Milton's library can be proven genuine "by virtue of the presence of his authentic signature, inscription or annotations" (79).

6. Samuel Johnson, *Lives of the English Poets*, 3 vols., ed. G. B. Hill (Oxford, 1905), 1:154.

7. *Euripidis Quae Extant Omnia: Tragoediae nempe XX . . .*, ed. Joshua Barnes (Cambridge, 1694). According to the index, Milton is only credited with one emendation, an omission to improve the meter at *Phoenissae* 962 (sig. V2r). Two modern accounts of Milton's *Euripides* marginalia provide critical points of departure for any examination of the books: Maurice Kelley and Samuel D. Atkins, "Milton's Annotations of Euripides," *JEGP* 60 (1961): 680–87; and John K. Hale, "Milton's Euripides Marginalia: Their Significance for Milton Studies," *Milton Studies*, vol. 27, ed. James D. Simmonds (Pittsburgh, 1991), 23–35. Kelley and Atkins helpfully compare Milton's "some 560 annotations" with Bentley's emendations to Horace, remarking that although Bentley "offered over 700 conjectures to the text . . . only one or two have found general acceptance" (686 n. 27, 687). For an evaluation of Barnes's use of Milton's marginalia, see Hale, 25.

8. William H. Sherman, *John Dee: The Politics of Reading and Writing in the English Renaissance* (Amherst, Mass., 1995), 89; Anthony Grafton, *Commerce with the Classics: Ancient Books and Renaissance Readers* (Ann Arbor, 1997), 153; Stephen Orgel, "Margins of Truth," in *The Renaissance Text: Theory, Editing, Textuality*, ed. Andrew Murphy (Manchester, 2000), 107.

9. For biographical material, see William Riley Parker, *Milton: A Biography*, 2 vols., 2d ed., ed. Gordon Campbell (Oxford, 1996), 1:186, 248, 286, 299, 312; 2:836, 882, 837, 922–25; J. Milton French, ed., *The Life Records of John Milton*, 5 vols. (New Brunswick, 1949–58), 2:128; and Edward Phillips, "The Life of Mr. John Milton" (1694), in *The Early Lives of Milton*, ed. Helen Darbishire (London, 1932), 66–68.

For persuasive evidence of a more complex and longstanding relationship between Milton and Hartlib than biographers have often supposed, see Timothy Raylor, "New Light on Milton and Hartlib," *MQ* 27 (1993): 19–31. For more general appraisals of the impact of their intellectual relations, see Barbara K. Lewalski, "Milton and the Hartlib Circle: Educational Projects and Epic *Paideia*," in *Literary Milton: Text, Pretext, Context*, ed. Diana Treviño Benet and Michael

Lieb (Pittsburgh, 1994), 202–19; and Nigel Smith, *"Areopagitica:* Voicing Contexts, 1643–5," in *Politics, Poetics, and Hermeneutics in Milton's Prose,* ed. David Loewenstein and James Grantham Turner (Cambridge, 1990), 105–7.

10. Phillips, "The Life of Mr. John Milton," 60. For a discussion of Milton's Latin curriculum in the context of his teaching environment, see Richard J. DuRocher, *Milton among the Romans: The Pedagogy and Influence of Milton's Latin Curriculum* (Pittsburgh, 2001), esp. 1–18, 171–75.

11. Milton's philological achievement has been the subject of an astute study by John K. Hale, *Milton's Languages* (Cambridge, 1997), esp. 74–80.

12. See Steven Zwicker, "Reading the Margins: Politics and the Habits of Appropriation," in *Refiguring Revolutions: Aesthetics and Politics from the English Revolution to the Romantic Revolution,* ed. Kevin Sharpe and Steven N. Zwicker (Berkeley and Los Angeles, 1998), 101–15.

13. See, for example, *Euripides: Hippolytos,* ed. W. S. Barrett (Oxford, 1964), 134, 349; *Euripidis fabulae,* 2 vols., ed. James Diggle (Oxford, 1981–84), 1:251; and Euripides, [*Works*], 5 vols., ed. and trans. David Kovacs, Loeb Classical Library (Cambridge, Mass., 1994–2002), 2:220–21.

14. On the hermeneutic tradition of accommodation and its origins in ancient rhetorical practice, see Kathy Eden, *Hermeneutics and the Rhetorical Tradition. Chapters in the Ancient Legacy and Its Humanist Reception* (New Haven, Conn., 1997), 1–19.

15. *Hippolytus,* trans. David Grene, in *The Complete Greek Tragedies,* 4 vols , ed. David Grene and Richmond Lattimore (Chicago, 1959), vol. 3.

16. Hence we may observe the continuity between Hippolytus and Pentheus, the self-destructive moralizer of Euripides's later masterpiece, *The Bacchae.* Milton's emendation may have come to mind because of the prominence accorded to *epaggellein* and its cognates in later Greek, especially the New Testament, where *epaggelia* and *epaggellomai* are used to signify announcement or promise. See *A Greek-English Lexicon of the New Testament and Other Early Christian Literature,* 2d ed., ed. Walter Bauer, trans. W. F Arndt et al. (Chicago, 1979), *s.vv.*

17. Milton also cites books referred to in the printed commentaries accompanying his text (cf. Kelley and Atkins, "Milton's Annotations of Euripides," 684). Although (post–1638) Milton refers to Scaliger's Manilius for the work's authority on a particular question of astronomy, the reference nonetheless shows that he had read and considered one of the editions (1579, 1600, and, posthumously, 1655). Scaliger's Manilius would have provided Milton with an exemplary model of textual criticism since "Scaliger began by trying to correct the text" and ended up devising an "exegetical method" that "turned out to be one of his most original creations." See Anthony Grafton, *Joseph Scaliger: A Study in the History of Classical Scholarship,* 2 vols. (Oxford, 1983–93), 1:180–226, esp. 186, 192 (quoted above), 207–8 (on Euripides). For an estimation of the importance of the *Astronomica* to Milton's tutorial and writing, see DuRocher, *Milton among the Romans,* 98–129.

18. Milton's copy of Aratus, *Phainomena kai diosaemia,* ed. Guillaume Morel (Paris, 1559), is held in the British Library Department of Printed Books, shelfmark C.60.L.7. Quotation at 1.

19. Maurice Kelley and Samuel D. Atkins, "Milton's Annotations of Aratus," *PMLA* 70 (1955): 1098–99, 1102; Phillips, "The Life of Mr. John Milton," 60.

20. The relative scarcity of copies makes this almost certain. Aratus was not published in England until the Oxford edition of 1672 (Wing A3596). Consultation of union catalogs has turned up twelve continental editions in Greek, other than that read by Milton, available prior to the Oxford edition.

21. Along with other quotations Paul made before the Areopagus (Acts 17), this verse became one of the most eagerly proffered means of articulating Christianity's relation to pagan classics. See, for example, Saint Augustine, *City of God,* 8.10, trans. Henry Bettenson (Har-

mondsworth, 1972), 312. In the English Renaissance, apologists for poetry such as Thomas Lodge alluded to the passage to counter "that shamelesse GOSSON": "let the Apostle preach at Athens, he disdaineth not of Aratus authoritie" (*Elizabethan Critical Essays*, 2 vols., ed. G. G. Smith [Oxford, 1904], 1:71; compare Sidney, *Apology*, 1:191).

22. The sources for this story are admittedly sketchy. As Dr. Johnson tells it, "The books in which his daughter, who used to read to him, represented him as most delighting, after Homer, which he could almost repeat, were Ovid's *Metamorphoses* and Euripides" (*Lives*, 1:154). A composite of earlier biographies, the story draws upon John Toland, "The Life of John Milton" (1698), in *Early Lives*, 179, for the bit about Homer, though Johnson may have come across relevant details in one of Newton's editions. In addition to recycling the remark about Milton's knowledge of Homer from Toland, Newton says of Deborah Milton, "As she had been often called upon to read Homer and Ovid's Metamorphosis to her father, she could have repeated a considerable number of verses from the beginning of both of these poets, as Mr. Ward, Professor of Rhetoric in Gresham College, relates upon his own knowledge: and another Gentleman has informed me, that he has heard her repeat several verses likewise out of Euripides." See *The Poetical Works of John Milton*, 3 vols., 5th ed., ed. Thomas Newton (London, 1761), 1:lxix, lxxvi.

23. See Stephen B. Dobranski, *Milton, Authorship, and the Book Trade* (Cambridge, 1999), 106–8. The most immediate context for Milton's tract was the response by Presbyterians to the first edition of *The Doctrine and Discipline of Divorce* (1643), which appeared exactly one month after the Westminster Assembly had begun to meet. Milton was condemned by orthodox critics such as Herbert Palmer, William Prynne, and Ephraim Pagitt, among others, including the anonymous author of *An Answer to a Book, Intituled, The Doctrine and Discipline of Divorce*. See Arthur E. Barker, *Milton and the Puritan Dilemma, 1641–1660* (Toronto, 1942), 63–97; and William Riley Parker, *Milton's Contemporary Reputation* (Columbus, Ohio, 1940), 73–75. For an account of the way the tract appropriates the discourses in play in its context as a central technique of its effort to persuade the Erastians in Parliament not to support the order, see Smith, "*Areopagitica:* Voicing Contexts, 1643–5," 103–22.

24. John Milton, *Complete Shorter Poems*, 2d ed., ed. John Carey (London, 1997), 355. Carey notes that, although the maxim is actually from Menander's *Thaïs*, not Euripides, "the fragment in which it survives is found in editions of both Euripides and Menander." All subsequent citations of Milton's poetry will be from this edition and its companion volume, *Paradise Lost*, 2d ed., ed. Alastair Fowler (London, 1998).

25. The scriptural passage in question is Ecclesiastes 12:7 by way of Job 34:14–15 (KJV). The interpretive strategy I attribute here to Milton may be, it is true, a subtle variation on the instruction *spoliabitis Aegyptum*. The Church Fathers referred to God's command that the Israelites plunder the Egyptians (Exod. 3:22, 11:2, 12:35) as a way of justifying the incorporation of the pagan liberal arts into Christian teaching. Pagan "precepts concerning morals" and "even some truths concerning the worship of one God" were, according to Augustine, "their gold and silver, which they did not institute themselves but dug up from certain mines of divine Providence" (*On Christian Doctrine*, trans. D. W. Robertson Jr., Library of Liberal Arts 80 [Indianapolis, 1958], 2.40). By the first half of the twelfth century—according to E. R. Curtius, *European Literature and the Latin Middle Ages*, trans. Willard R. Trask (Princeton, 1953), 466–67—Conrad of Hirsau had broadened interpretation of the passage so that "by the gold and silver of Egypt is meant *litteratura saecularis*." For a history of the *spoliatio Aegyptiorum* from patristic origins to the Renaissance, see Eden, *Friends Hold All Things in Common*, 8–32.

26. Quoted and reproduced in photographic facsimile in David Norbrook, *Writing the English Republic: Poetry, Rhetoric and Politics, 1627–1660* (Cambridge, 1999), 128.

27. See John K. Hale, "*Areopagitica*'s Euripidean Motto," *MQ* 25 (1991): 25–27, responding to David Davies and Paul Dowling, " 'Shrewd books, with dangerous Frontispieces': *Areopa-*

gitica's Motto," *MQ* 20 (1986): 33–37. It is a telling irony that modern critics, fixated on the question of Milton's fidelity to the Greek original, have often missed the tract's other "vigorously productive" appropriations. On Milton's purposeful modifications of source material, see Christopher Grose, "Trying All Things in the *Areopagitica*," *Milton and the Sense of Tradition* (New Haven, Conn., 1988), 85–103.

28. Milton's exordium, like the rest of the speech, employs the conventions of classical oratory, particularly in its emphasis on the ethos of speaker and audience. The conventional *captatio benevolentiae* is described, among other places, in the *Rhetorica Ad Herennium*, 1.4.7–1.5.8, trans. H. Caplan, Loeb Classical Library (Cambridge, Mass., 1954), 12–17. Compare Brian Vickers, *In Defence of Rhetoric* (Oxford, 1988), 69.

29. Philip Melanchthon, "Oration on Occasion of the Funeral of Doctor Martin Luther," *Orations on Philosophy and Education,* ed. Sachiko Kusakawa, trans. Christine F. Salazar (Cambridge, 1999), 257.

30. Erasmus, *De Libero Arbitrio,* in *Luther and Erasmus: Free Will and Salvation,* trans. and ed. E. Gordon Rupp and Philip S. Watson, Library of Christian Classics (Philadelphia, 1969), 49.

31. Stanley Fish, "Driving from the Letter: Truth and Indeterminacy in Milton's *Areopagitica*," in *Re-membering Milton,* ed. Mary Nyquist and Margaret W. Ferguson (New York, 1987), 234–54, esp. 236; and *How Milton Works* (Cambridge, Mass., 2001), 187–214, esp. 190–91.

32. See Donne, *Devotions upon Emergent Occasions,* 9th expostulation, ed. Anthony Raspa (Montreal, 1975), 49; and Browne, *Religio Medici,* 1.16, in *The Major Works,* ed. C. A. Patrides (Harmondsworth, 1977), 78–81. Both Donne and Browne remark upon the expression of the divine image in the Book of Nature as well as the Book of God, which would by Fish's standard equate their thought too with idolatry. Logically, any creation within Nature—anything created as a secondary function of God's creation—may bear the image of an order that is beyond human conception, even when it derives most immediately from a human mind. This is the point of Vaughan's modification of the commonplace in "The Book," where God's "knowing, glorious spirit" is invoked in the final stanza: "Give him amongst thy works a place, / Who in them loved and sought thy face" (*The Complete Poems,* ed. Alan Rudrum [Harmondsworth, 1976], 310).

33. See Haskin, *Milton's Burden of Interpretation,* chap. 3.

34. Maimonides, *The Guide of the Perplexed,* 2 vols., trans. Shlomo Pines (Chicago, 1963), 1:23; compare 2:235 (premises 1–3). See also Milton's refutation by superior knowledge of the context from which Salmasius quotes Maimonides, *First Defense,* YP 4.1:354; CM 7:102. Leo Strauss, *Persecution and the Art of Writing* (Glencoe, Ill., 1952), 23, 192 n., offers a valuable context for juxtaposing the two.

35. John Pearson, *An exposition of the Creed* (1659), 3d ed., Wing P997 (London, 1669), 115–17, interprets Genesis 1:26 in relation to John 1:1–3, bringing Paul's epistles (especially Col. 3:10 and Eph. 4:23) to bear: "The apostle chargeth us to be *renewed in the spirit of our mind,* and *to put on the new man, which after God is created in righteousness and true holiness; and which is renewed in knowledge, after the image of him that created him.*" This "renovation," which as Pearson notes "is called by Paul a 'metamorphosis'" (Rom. 12:2), consists in "a translation from a worse unto a better condition by way of reformation; by which those which have lost the image of God, in which the first man was created, are restored to the image of the same God again, by a real change, though not substantial, wrought within them." In this, Pearson like Milton differs from Calvin, *Institutes of the Christian Religion,* 1.15, trans. Henry Beveridge (1845; reprint, Grand Rapids, 1995), 165: "as the image of God constitutes the entire excellence of human nature, as it shone in Adam before his fall, but was afterward vitiated and almost destroyed, nothing remaining but a ruin, confused, mutilated, and tainted with impurity, so it is now partly seen in the elect, in so far as they are regenerated by the Spirit." Calvin seeks to

debunk Augustine, *City of God,* 11.26, in particular to eradicate the Trinitarian emphasis on the faculties of the intellect.

36. Compare Aristotle, *Prior Analytics,* 68b; *Posterior Analytics,* 71a–72b, 99b–100b; *Nicomachean Ethics,* 1139b.

37. Thomas Aquinas, *Summa contra Gentiles,* 3.25, in *Selected Writings,* trans. Ralph McInerny (Harmondsworth, 1998), 264.

38. For the most notable example, see the magisterial study by Brian Stock, *Augustine the Reader: Meditation, Self-Knowledge, and the Ethics of Interpretation* (Cambridge, Mass., 1996).

39. Browne, *Pseudodoxia Epidemica,* 1.5, in *The Major Works,* ed. Patrides, 185.

40. Robert Greville, Lord Brooke, *A Discourse opening the Nature of that Episcopacy which is Exercised in England,* 2d ed. (1641), Wing B4912 (London, 1642), 13, 26, 25, 31. For Greville's debt to the Smectymnuans, see Barker, *Milton and the Puritan Dilemma,* 54, 56. And see Robert Greville, *The Nature of Truth, Its Union and Unity with the Soule, which is one in its essence, faculties, acts; one with truth,* STC 12363 (London, 1640).

41. Plato, *Republic,* 505d; *Gorgias,* 467a ff., 499e, *Protagoras,* 358b–d. And see Marcus Aurelius, *Meditations,* 4.3. For a trenchant critique of the commonplace expression of the Socratic paradox, see the commentary in *Ion, Hippias Minor, Laches, Protagoras,* trans. R. E. Allen (New Haven, 1996), 159–61.

42. On the interrelation between knowledge and virtue, see Plato, *Meno,* 87c–89a; *Phaedo,* 69a–c; *Protagoras,* 351b–360e. My discussion of Milton's epistemology is greatly indebted to Edward W. Tayler, *Milton's Poetry: Its Development in Time* (Pittsburgh, 1979), esp. 185–213, 261 n.15, 262 n. 26; and "Milton's Grim Laughter and Second Choices," in *Poetry and Epistemology: Turning Points in the History of Poetic Knowledge: Papers from the International Poetry Symposium, Eichstätt, 1983,* ed. Roland Hagenbüchle and Laura Skandera (Regensburg, 1986), 72–93.

43. The concept of substance disclosed in this passage maintains its central structural importance in Milton's thought throughout his writings, at least through the completion of the epic. See John Peter Rumrich, "Milton's Concept of Substance," *ELN* 19 (1982): 218–33.

44. Sir Thomas Browne, *Christian Morals,* 3.15, in *The Major Works,* ed. Patrides, 461.

45. *Luther and Erasmus,* ed. and trans. Rupp and Watson, 73, 48, 50. In the *Areopagitica's* insistence that choice presents a moral dilemma to the reasonable will of a human being, Milton approaches Kant's proposition that "all theodicy should truly be an *interpretation* of nature insofar as God announces his will through it" ("On the Miscarriage of All Philosophical Trials in Theodicy," *Religion within the Boundaries of Mere Reason and Other Writings,* ed. and trans. Allen Wood and George di Giovanni [Cambridge, 1998],17–30, at 24). Although we cannot sincerely claim to comprehend God's will, we must nevertheless be able to aspire to what Kant considers a Jobean "negative wisdom," knowing to know no more (23). This is especially true "if this dismissal . . . is a pronouncement of the same reason through which we form our concept of God—necessarily and prior to all experience—as a moral and wise being. For through our reason God then becomes himself the interpreter of his will as announced through his creation" (24). When, as Abdiel says, "God and Nature bid the same," both freedom and omniscience prevail (*PL* 6.176).

46. Irenaeus, *Against Heresies,* 4.37, in *Ante-Nicene Fathers,* vol. 1, *The Apostolic Fathers, Justin Martyr, Irenaeus,* ed. Alexander Roberts and James Donaldson; rev. ed. A. C. Coxe (1885; reprint, Peabody, Mass., 1994), 520. Free will, as Irenaeus goes on to say, ensures that education ascends to devotion: "having been rationally taught to love God, we may continue in His perfect love: for God has displayed long-suffering in the case of man's apostasy; while man has been instructed by means of it." For a useful survey of thought about the "trilemma," see Mark Larrimore, ed., *The Problem of Evil: A Reader* (Oxford and Malden, Mass., 2001), esp. xviii–xxiv, xxix.

47. C. S. Lewis, *A Preface to "Paradise Lost"* (London, 1942), 7. The sense of good and evil will always be in this world mutually dependent and reciprocally defining, like the two twins conjoined and sundered by the polar meanings embedded in the pun "cleaving." As Victoria Silver, *Imperfect Sense: The Predicament of Milton's Irony* (Princeton, 2001), has persuasively argued, "what Milton suggests is that we apprehend the one in the other, by an interpretive sense of their distinction which requires good and evil to be reciprocally present" (96). Therefore, "In Milton's theodicy, when the true and false, good and evil, are not understood to be practically contingent meanings but instead separate and exclusive, we peremptorily render ourselves incapable of recognizing any of these values" (101).

48. Tayler, *Milton's Poetry*, 194.

49. For a reading of the engraving's politics in the context of royalist use of the Tower of Babel, see Sharon Achinstein, *Milton and the Revolutionary Reader* (Princeton, 1994), 83.

50. While the most commonly cited reference to the Cadmus episode—or to the analogous moment in Jason's story—is Ovid, *Metamorphoses*, 3.103 and 7.102 (*vipereos dentes*), the fullest collection of materials pertaining to Cadmus is to be found in Apollodorus, *The Library*, 2 vols., trans. J. G. Frazer, Loeb Classical Library (Cambridge, Mass., 1921), 3.1.1, 3.4.1–2, 3.5.2, 3.5.4.

THE CONCEPT OF THE "HIRELING" IN MILTON'S THEOLOGY

David Hawkes

"Antichrist is Mammon's son"

I

MILTON'S OBJECTION TO "hireling" priests emerges out of a belief that wage labor in the church led to, and indeed was a form of, idolatry. Milton's attacks on the established church are often launched on financial grounds, and it is possible to distinguish his objections to three kinds of financial abuse. First, he criticizes the prelates for simple avarice, which is displayed in their sins of luxury. Second, he castigates the state church for its monopoly of the trade of preaching, which it protects by intolerance.[1] These two arguments against prelacy are well known, and critics have discussed them at length. I believe, however, that it is possible to discern a third, rather different and relatively neglected, economic charge leveled by Milton against the church. In *The Likeliest Means to Remove Hirelings,* Milton observes that Scripture does not simply attack excessive greed, but focuses on a particular and specific kind of "hire." Its target, he observes, is "not only the excess of hire in wealthiest times, but also the undue and vitious taking or giving it, though but small or mean" (YP 7:280). It is not merely the quantity of "hire" which is criticized, but also its quality. Milton points out that the Bible does not attack luxury only—"not only the excess of hire"—but also the particular *manner* in which priests are rewarded, which is sinful in itself, whether or not luxury is involved.

My purpose here is to determine what Milton understands by this "undue and vitious . . . hire." Among a barrage of biblical texts, Milton begins *The Likeliest Means* with 2 Peter 2:3: "through covetousness shall they with feigned words make merchandise of you" (YP 7:280). Peter objects particularly to that mode of remuneration which makes "merchandise" of people, which treats them as objects to be bought and sold. The specific form of covetousness Peter attacks is one where the spiritual effect is the objectification—or, more precisely, the *commodification*—of human beings. The term "commodity" has become associated with Karl Marx and his followers, but it did not originate with them.[2] The word and concept of "commodity" were widely used and understood in sixteenth- and seventeenth-century England. Famous examples include Shakespeare's *King John* (2.1.573–83), Herbert's "The Pearl" (34), and Bunyan's *Mr. Badman*.[3] Furthermore, discussions of the commodity from this period evince considerable agreement about its psychological effects: it encouraged what was called "idolatry." This connection is stated with great clarity in much of the canonical literature of the age, as for instance in Herbert's "The Church Militant" (111–20), Spenser's *The Faerie Queene* (2.7.39.1–5), or Jonson's *Volpone* (1.1.1–23).[4] In fact, ever since Luther's Ninety-five Theses, Protestant polemicists have drawn causal connections between the ecclesiastical market economy and liturgical idolatry, and Milton enthusiastically endorses this tradition. It is central to his depictions of false religion from *Lycidas* on, and it molds and guides *The Likeliest Means*'s denunciation of ministers whose "sheep oft-times sit the while to as little purpose of benifiting as the sheep in thir pues at Smithfield; and for the most part by som Simonie or other, bought and sold like them" (YP 7:302).[5]

The notion of the "economic" as a hermetic arena that can be thought of in isolation from ethical or spiritual matters was barely emerging in seventeenth-century England, and it was natural to Milton's contemporaries to perceive connections between what we might consider different forms of "economy." The heritage of the Reformation reminded them that the system of monetary exchange that we think of as "the market" had historically been intimately associated with the liturgical practice of the Catholic Church. The great thinkers of the early Reformation did not fully distinguish between religious and lay economies. Martin Luther was convinced that the pope's commodification of salvation was orchestrated by secular capital: "the business is now to be transferred, and sold to Fugger of Augsburg. Henceforward bishoprics and livings for sale or exchange or in demand, and dealings in the spiritualities, have arrived at their true destination, now that the bargaining for spiritual or secular properties has become united into a single business."[6] The trade in and transfer of indulgences were, in fact, the Fuggers's earliest large-scale international transactions and the initial sources of their capital.[7] The implications of such connections for the thinkers of the sixteenth and seventeenth centuries are not easy to discern from a modern perspective. We have been trained to regard ethical critique of the market as eccentric, and today most people who study the exchange economy from an ethical point of view conclude that it is actually a force for moral good. There is even a tendency among some recent commentators to project this attitude back into the seventeenth century. The spiritual implications of Milton's economic rhetoric have recently been the subject of an interesting article in *Milton Studies* by Blair

Hoxby. Hoxby correctly points out that the boundaries of the "economic" realm were far more porous for Milton than they are for modern people. In the course of a detailed analysis of *Areopagitica,* he notes that the tract is "suggestive of how co-involved some contemporaries thought the logic of economic and intellectual exchange really were. Milton and like-minded reformers did not consider the economic analogies in their tracts and sermons mere flowers of rhetoric but vehicles for thinking systematically about the conditions of intellectual exchange that were most likely to generate truth without bound."[8] But Hoxby goes on to claim that Milton attributes beneficent spiritual effects to the secular market economy and that he thought of commodity exchange as a force for redemption and regeneration. Calling attention to Milton's extensive use of commercial imagery in *Areopagitica,* Hoxby suggests that Milton perceived a conceptual as well as an analogical link between the metaphorical "free market-place of ideas" advocated in that tract, and the literal workings of the market economy. Milton, we are told, recognized a causal connection between freedom of speech and freedom of exchange; he "lionizes the psychic mobility and unceasing vigilance that are forced on men by market relations" (191).[9]

   In my view such an interpretation is the product of misguided literalism. Hoxby inflates the commonplace observation that *Areopagitica* uses economic imagery to further its argument into a claim that Milton is literally advocating the virtues of a market economy. He draws from *Areopagitica's* economic tropes the illegitimate inference that Milton "suggests that free markets make free men" (186), and this infatuation with the market involves him in some singular departures from accepted critical opinion. He modifies, for example, the conventional opinion that *Areopagitica* advocates *proairesis.* In Hoxby's reading, this Aristotelian process of deliberate, rational, and conscious choice is elbowed aside in favor of the economic theory of marginal utility:

The notion of a market informs even Milton's famous dictum, "reason is but choosing." . . . [This] is the reason of a consumer society, which can operate effectively only when men may choose freely and openly among ideas. In conditions of unrestricted exchange, men will, on the margin, choose truth over falsehood, and enlightenment will be enlarged. Ideas that ring true will be taken up . . . while those that ring false will lose favor and drop out of the market. (188)

It is fearful to imagine the scorn that Milton would have poured upon this picture of the public perusing ideas as in a shop window and selecting those that "ring true" as one might purchase a favorite brand of cornflakes.[10] The line of reasoning Hoxby attributes to Milton is anachronistically derived from modern apologists for capitalism, who frequently argue that an untrammeled free market in commodities is a prerequisite of free thought and speech.[11]

Hoxby endorses this assumption with polemical fervor, and I assume this is what inspires his literalistic reading of Milton's economic tropes. At times, his enthusiasm for the market goads him into making claims that students of Milton ought to recognize as satanic: "the market is a means by which imperfect men may, in the long term, approximate the wisdom of God" (188). Hoxby thus advances far beyond the reasonable position that Milton's secular economic opinions were basically favorable to commodity exchange. His literalistic interpretation of *Areopagitica*'s imagery drives him to argue that Milton believed the market economy was benign in its *spiritual* impact. We are thus directed away from the traditional critical opinion that *Areopagitica* places its trust in the virtuous and rational capacities of the individual soul: "If Milton begins *Areopagitica* with a rousing apology for the moral import of personal trial, he ends by putting his faith not in men but in a system of commerce and exchange. He puts his faith in the market" (193–94). No one would claim that Milton was opposed to capitalism per se. His father's fortune, on which the poet lived for long periods, was made largely by money-lending. An attempt to collect a debt led to Milton's meeting with Mary Powell, and their marriage may well have been in lieu of a financial settlement. Although he sometimes repeats commonplace criticisms of covetousness, Milton never condemns exchange for profit as such, as many of his contemporaries do. And Hoxby certainly succeeds in establishing that Milton uses the imagery of trade in an apparently nonpejorative fashion in *Areopagitica*. But despite all this, the contention that Milton "puts his faith in the market" is deeply mistaken. Milton did not and could not have regarded the market as a force for spiritual good. As soon as we turn to Milton's substantive discussion of the market, the happy optimism that Hoxby attributes to him rapidly dissipates.

There is one famous passage in *Areopagitica* that would appear definitively to undermine Hoxby's thesis. Milton asks his readers to picture

A wealthy man, addicted to his pleasure and to his profits, [who] finds religion to be a traffic so entangled, and of so many piddling accounts, that of all mysteries he cannot skill to keep a stock going upon that trade. What should he do? fain he would have the name to be religious, fain he would bear up with his neighbours in that. What does he therefore, but resolves to give over toiling, and to find himself out some factor, to whose care and credit he may commit the whole managing of his religious affairs; some divine of note and estimation that must be. To him he adheres, resigns the whole warehouse of his religion, with all the locks and keys, into his custody; and indeed makes the very person of that man his religion; esteems his associating with him a sufficient evidence and commendatory of his own piety. So that a man may say his religion is now no more within himself, but is become a dividuall movable, and goes and comes near him, according as that good man frequents the house. (2.544)

Most critics have taken this passage more or less at face value, as revealing Milton's "contempt of commerce," his "disdain of traders" and his view of "the merchant as a figure of contempt."[12] Hoxby's reading of it is very different: "Milton wants men to be enterprisers in *all* aspects of the public sphere—religious, political, and economic—and he objects to the notion that activity of one sort may substitute for toil of another. . . . A fully autonomous individual takes responsibility for his economic, civil, and spiritual lives: none is a 'dividuall movable' separable from the whole" (192). Perhaps we can concede that Milton's anecdote does not necessarily imply contempt for merchants or the market as such. But Hoxby surely goes too far when he attributes to Milton a quasi-libertarian enthusiasm for "enterprisers" in the spiritual sphere. This passage from *Areopagitica* condemns the alienation of religion—its relegation to a form of property, or "dividuall movable," that can exist in alien form, apart from the person to whom it belongs.[13] The religion of the putative merchant is no longer "within himself"; it has been alienated to another, transferred to "the very person of that man." Milton is appalled by the idea that religion can be conceived of as a thing, an alienable commodity. He is angered by the prospect of a properly subjective experience being given objective form, as when a minister is hired by the merchant to perform his religion for him. While this does not necessarily involve a condemnation of the secular market, it does suggest a finely tuned sensitivity to the spiritual consequences of commodified labor.

The merchant in the above anecdote is presented as selling a part of himself, and such a transaction was offensive to radical Protestant theology. As Laura Brace puts it, "Many of the religious radicals understood their faith, or conscience, as a part of themselves, and so as something which they owned absolutely and individually."[14] The tension in *Areopagitica* is between this notion of an interior, and thus inalienable, core of personal identity, and the merchant's proto-Lockean understanding of subjective activity, or "labor," as an alienable commodity. We can detect in this tension the initial stirrings of a seismic historical rupture. For radical Protestants of the mid-seventeenth century, the fact that one's conscience belonged to oneself meant precisely that it must never be sold—Esau's sale of his birthright provided the biblical referent most often used to establish this point. For political economists of the late seventeenth century, on the other hand, the fact that one's subjective activity was one's own "property" meant that one was entirely free to sell it—in the form of "labor"—to the highest bidder. The difference between these conceptions of the self is twofold. First, at least from our modern perspective, "conscience" is a spiritual matter while "labor" is a matter for the secular world. However, the people of the seventeenth century would not so easily have exonerated "labor" from its spiritual implications. A second kind of difference therefore looms larger than the first in the thought of Milton and his contemporaries—the difference between conceiving of oneself as an integral, unitary, and indivisible being, and the conception that imagines it is possible for one part of the self to alienate, or "sell," another. The latter notion must inevitably imagine the part of the self that is sold as a *thing*, a commodity, and Milton finds this process of alienation and commodification described in Peter's critique of priests who "make merchandize" of salvation.[15]

I hope to show that Milton's use of economic imagery for discursive ends is far from implying the blithe "faith in the market" that Hoxby attributes to him. Hostility to the alienation of spiritual labor lies at the core of Milton's iconoclastic theology and prevents him from regarding the psychological effects of the clerical market with anything but withering scorn and deepest revulsion. Milton is consistent in denouncing wage labor in intellectual affairs. He automatically assumes, for example, that because Salmasius—the "hireling pimp of slavery" (4:461)—or the anonymous "mechanick" of *Colasterion* wrote for wages, they were irresistibly impelled toward idolatrous beliefs and practices.[16] Milton may not have overtly opposed the secular market, but if we can show that Milton unequivocally condemns market practices in the church, we can at least conclude, contra Hoxby, that he would never have suggested that the secular market had laudable *spiritual* effects. I hope to prove, in short, that it would have been inconceivable and impossible for Milton to "put his faith in the market."

II

Milton's "putting his faith . . . in a system of commerce and exchange" would have involved a dramatic departure from the contemporary ethical view of the market. I have discussed in detail elsewhere the ways in which Greek philosophy and Judeo-Christian religion indict large-scale exchange for profit as unethical.[17] For Aristotle and the Scholastics, exchange value was a merely nominal and unnatural imposition on authentic use value, and as such must never be pursued as an end in itself. The biblical tradition, revivified by radical Protestantism, interprets the injunction not to adore "the works of men's hands" as including a prohibition against attaching fetishistic and illusory market value to the products of labor. It is true that by the middle of the seventeenth century the first cracks were beginning to appear in this unvarying façade as the volume of world trade exploded following the European voyages of exploration. So deep was the inherited suspicion of trade, however, that it took more than a century for this "fact on the ground" to achieve theoretical rationalization. The earliest attempts to theorize the operations of the world market in secular terms, such as Edward Misselden's *Free*

Trade and Gerard de Malynes's *The Maintenance of Free Trade* (both published in 1622), are doggedly pragmatic works that make no attempt to defend an exchange economy on ethical grounds. Even Hobbes's *Leviathan*, which provides the most authoritative midcentury rejection of the traditional standard of the "just price" in favor of market value, does so in resigned acknowledgment of ineradicable human selfishness.[18] It is not until Mandeville's *The Fable of the Bees* (1723) that we encounter the argument that the market economy is an ethically benign phenomenon, and even there the author's parodic tone indicates a desire to put a judicious distance between himself and this opinion. So any contention that Milton "puts his faith in the market" seems historically implausible.[19] Nevertheless, Milton was undeniably ahead of his time in many aspects of his thought, and so perhaps we should not hastily dismiss as hopelessly anachronistic the claim that he anticipated the market boosterism of today's libertarians. Instead, let us turn to his actual, substantive reflections on a system of economic exchange and its impact on spiritual affairs.

In Milton's time, the effect of the burgeoning world system of trade was felt most immediately in the growing prominence of money in everyday life.[20] By the middle of the seventeenth century social relations that had traditionally been conducted between individuals in person had, in many spheres of life, been commuted into relations mediated through money.[21] Landlords' rent was now generally paid in cash, as were the wages of most labor, and cash had replaced barter as the medium of exchange in local markets. All money-based economies impose a financial value upon the things of the world, and especially on human activity, or "labor," which functions as the common denominator facilitating the exchange of qualitatively different objects. As people learn to conceive of their surroundings and activities in terms of financial value their habits of thought are correspondingly altered, and this applies particularly to their conception of their own subjective activity. In a word, a market economy demands that people conceive of at least a certain portion of their activity as "labor," a commodity that can be exchanged for a determinate sum of money. The commodification of labor is thus an absolute prerequisite of a market economy, and the forcible transformation of subsistence farmers (who can produce their own livelihood) into landless proletarians (who must sell their labor power as a commodity) is its universal precursor.

Milton's interventions in the tithe controversy analyze this process of "commodification" as it affects the special case of ecclesiastical labor. He leaves no doubt as to the fundamental importance he attaches to the question of priestly "hire." The *Treatise of Civil Power* (1659) opens by declaring: "Two things there be which have bin ever found working much mischief to the church of God, and the advancement of truth; force on the one side restraining, and hire on the other side corrupting the teachers thereof" (YP 7:241). Milton announces that he will devote *Of Civil Power* to the problems created by coercion, while addressing the displacement of "truth" by "hire" in a subsequent tract. This duly appeared a few months later as the polemic against tithes entitled *Considerations of the Likeliest Means to Remove Hirelings.* Here Milton reiterates the political centrality of the matter, repeating for emphasis the *Treatise's* opening identification of "force" and "hire" as the two most pernicious enemies of truth, but this time adding that "hire" is "by much the more dangerous: for under force, though no thanks to the forcers, true religion oft-times best thrives and flourishes: but the corruption of teachers, most commonly the effect of hire, is the very bane of truth in them who are so corrupted" (YP 7:277). Just as *Areopagitica* exempts "popery and open superstition" from toleration, so in *The Likeliest Means* Milton argues that hirelings must always and inevitably be idolaters. Idolatry is grounds for exclusion from the public sphere in *Areopagitica,* and in *The Likeliest Means* Milton presents any involvement in what he elsewhere calls "the ignoble Hucsterage of pidling Tithes"[22] as sufficient cause for exclusion from the church. He had also emphasized this point in *Animadversions,* which explicitly says that it is the status of a "hireling"—as opposed to mere vice or ignorance—that disqualifies a man from the clergy:

And what would it avail us to have hireling Clergy, though never so learned? For such can have neither true wisdom nor grace, and then in vain do men trust in learning, where these be wanting. If in lesse noble and almost mechanik arts . . . he is not esteem'd to deserve the name of a compleat Architect, an excellent Painter, or the like, that beares not a generous mind above the peasantly regard of wages, and hire; much more must we thinke him a most imperfect and incompleate Divine, who is so farre from being a contemner of filthy lucre. (1.720)

By the term "hireling," Milton intends a clergyman who receives compulsory tithes. As several recent commentaries have observed, Milton's objections to tithes differ sharply from those advanced by most other seventeenth-century opponents of clerical "hire." The majority of anti-tithe literature argues that tithes are an inequitable and unscriptural exaction that damages the spiritual and economic welfare of the payers. In contrast, Milton is more interested in the effect of "hire" on the spiritual health of those who receive tithes. As Austin Woolrych puts it, "What distinguishes *The Likeliest Means* from the common run of anti-tithe tracts is that whereas they generally stressed the burden on the consciences and pockets of the payers, Milton cared much more about the corrupting effect on the recipients, and on the whole quality of Christian life" (YP 7:93). Barbara Lewalski notices a similar departure from the usual line of attack: "The rhetoric of Milton's tract is unusual among tithe opponents for focusing less on the wound to conscience than on 'hire-lings' and the evils they import into the church: hire, he claims, is more damaging than persecution because it corrupts the teachers." And Thomas Corns also finds the tract anomalous in this regard: "curiously introverted, focusing not outward on the politics of tolerationism and tithe-abolition, but inward on the promptings of the spirit and on the scriptures."[23] Milton's interest, in fact, is less in the financial hardships caused to the congregation by the exaction of "hire" than in the doctrinal and liturgical price it exacts from the "hireling." *The Likeliest Means* is, in short, a meditation on the psychological and ideological errors that the process of exchanging labor for wages produces in the priesthood.We need to be careful here to specify exactly what Milton objects to. There was, of course, nothing especially new in the general concept of wage labor. The exchange of labor for cash had been the predominant form of employment in the "mechanical" trades for over a century. Indeed, Milton suggests that ministers ought to follow the example of Paul and support themselves by working for wages at manual trades: "But our ministers think scorn to use a trade, and count it the reproach of the age that tradesmen preach the gospel. It were to be wishd they were all trades-men; they would not then so many of them, for want of another trade, make a trade of their preaching: and yet they clamor that tradesmen preach; and yet they preach, while they themselves are the worst tradesmen of all" (YP 7:306).[24] This complex passage contains the key to Milton's argument in *The Likeliest Means*. He urges ministers to become tradesmen so that they may avoid "mak[ing] a trade of their preaching." He is not attacking wage labor in secular life; his objection is to the payment of wages for *spiritual* labor. But before we examine his grounds for this objection, we should establish one more proviso: Milton is by no means opposed to the payment of ministers. He admits that "we cannot justly take away all hire in the church" (YP 7:280), and he draws a careful distinction between "hire" and the "hireling": "Hire of itself is neither a thing unlawful, nor a word of evil note, signifying no more than a due recompense or reward; as when our Saviour saith, 'The laborer is worthy of his hire.' That which makes it so dangerous in the church, and properly makes the *hireling,* a word always of evil signification, is either the excess thereof, or the undue manner of giving and taking it" (YP 7:278–79; emphasis in the original). Milton's target in *The Likeliest Means* is thus much more precise than has usually been realized. He does not object to wage labor in secular life, nor does he object to the financial compensation of ministers. What he argues against, rather, is the financial compensation of *ministers* by *wage labor.* It is acceptable for a "mechanick" to sell his labor, and it is also acceptable for priests to be financially compensated. But Milton finds it morally repugnant and ecclesiastically illegitimate for ministers to sell their labor for wages. Hence, he objects only to compulsory tithes; according to the contemporary terms of debate, voluntary tithes were not legally owed wages but charitable "alms." Clerical wage labor is "the undue manner of giving and taking" payment, the "undue and vitious taking or giving" of money, which Milton distinguishes from his objections to luxury and monopoly.

III

The notion that tithes were wages paid in return for the performance of labor was new and anomalous in seventeenth-century England. Earlier, tithes had been justified, where they needed justification, on the grounds of biblical authority or customary precedent. Here the supporters of tithes were on fairly solid ground. The Bible offers plausible, though not altogether convincing, evidence for a *jure divino* defense of tithes, and the argument from custom had a sound historical basis, as John Selden conclusively established in his voluminous *Historie of Tithes* (1618). The right of ministers to maintenance by tithes had been acknowledged in England for almost a thousand years.[25] Indeed, tithes in Britain predated Christianity, having been established by the fourth century A.D. and confirmed by successive ecclesiastical and lay charters which culminated with the National Synod's imposition of excommunication for nonpayment in 944.

A state church maintained by tithes rests upon a certain set of assumptions about property and labor. Under such a system, the labor of a parish priest is not conceived as a thing which belongs to him and of which he has the right to dispose as he pleases—in other words, priestly labor is not a "dividuall movable" or alienable commodity. A tithe, by extension, is not a wage paid in return for a particular amount of labor. Rather, both labor and its compensation are set in the context of custom and tradition, and the payment of priests by tithes is thought of as external to the market economy. By the 1650s, however, defenses of tithes made on the grounds of custom were more likely to harm than to help their cause in the minds of parliamentarians who were determined to root out all remaining rags of Rome. Furthermore, it had long been obvious to supporters and opponents of tithes alike that the traditional method of tithe assessment was hopelessly anachronistic in a money economy. Tithes were a tax on yield, and customarily payable in kind. The implication was that the ministry formed an organic part of the wider community, and that the minister should therefore share in the fortunes of the community as a whole, prospering in good times and suffering along with the rest in times of dearth.[26] This was a system of taxation designed for and suited to a subsistence, rural economy. And as long as such an economy prevailed, there were few voices raised against the principle of tithing.

The development of the market, and the concomitant commutation of tithes to payment in cash, radically disrupted these assumptions.[27] It became common to substitute the minister's right to a percentage of the livestock with a fixed cash payment. But the hyperinflation of the sixteenth century forced even defenders of tithes to acknowledge the difficulties raised by such methods of collection. In 1607, Cowell's *Interpreter* observed that "those customs of paying a halfpenny for a lamb or a penny for a calf . . . is but very unreasonable in these days, when both lamb and calves are grown four times dearer and more than they were when this price was first accepted."[28] Apart from Selden, the authority most often cited by advocates of tithing was Sir Henry Spelman, whose *Tithes Too Hot to Be Touched* (1640) noted that:

The change and variations of the standard of money is so great and uncertain in all ages . . . that if an hundred pound according to these times, should be allowed for a stipend to a Minister yearly, it may be as much in value as 300 or 400 in the compasses of an hundred years following . . . which hath happened of late times by the discovery of the west-Indies, the trade and commerce thither, and the riches of their monies brought into Europe. (C2)

However, as opponents of tithes quickly pointed out, to link tithes to inflation would be to treat them in the same way as ordinary wages, and thus to imply that ministers were no different from or better than common laborers. If tithes were wages, then ministers were "mechanicks," and the church's protests against "preaching mechanicks" were hypocritical. In 1645, the anonymous author of *Tithe Gatherers No Gospel Officers* suggested that under such a practice, "mercenary praying and preaching will grow contemptible, and our exercising weavers, feltmongers, cobblers etc. be found more to resemble the ministers of the Gospel than your learned doctorships."[29]

Although often aware that they were leaving themselves open to such attacks, the Anglican and Presbyterian clergy were forced by logical necessity into the awkward position that the ecclesiastical tasks they performed were analogous to the secular tasks performed by wage-laborers. Once the justification of tithes by custom came to seem inadequate, it was tempting for radicals and separatists to follow John Wycliffe's opinion that "tithes are pure Alms"[30]—a merely voluntary payment and so unenforceable by law. For obvious reasons the clergy were reluctant to admit this. A possible alternative course was to claim that tithes were comparable to the rent due to landlords. But there were no less immediate and serious dangers involved in making this claim, as is indicated by such conservative tracts as Richard Culmer's *The Minsters Hue and Cry* (1651). This features an outspoken rebel named Robbin Rob-Minister, who declares that "it goes against my will, I mean my conscience, to pay either Tythe-rent or Landlords rent. . . . Thou knowest I was one of those they call Levellers, and if those State-souldiers had not engaged against us, we had put things into better order: Joan my wife should have been as good as my Lady; neither Priest nor landlord, nor any other should have lived upon our labour" (6). So the only safe and credible recourse remaining to the established churches was to argue that tithes were wages paid for labor.[31] This argument was loudly declaimed by William Prynne, the "late hot Quaerist for tithes" (YP 7:294) against whom Milton writes in *The Likeliest Means*. In *A Gospel Plea* (1653), Prynne thundered that tithes were "merited HIRE and WAGES; as much as any deserved hire or wages are due to any other hired servant or labourer whatsoever" (6). Ministers, he declared, have earned "a competent maintenance suitable to their pains and function, as well as any other hired Servants or labourers in the fields" (113), and in fact "of all other labourers they are most worthy of an honourable, comfortable, certain hire, salary, reward" (6). Such arguments could easily backfire. In *Tithes Vindicated from Antichristianism and Oppression* (1659), Giles Firmin intends to bolster tithes when he claims that priests had a right to be paid for their ecclesiastical tasks since they had no other saleable skills: "Paul had his skill of Tent-making before he was called to be an Apostle . . . so were those elders to whom Paul wrote, they had their trades and callings by which they lived in the cities before they heard of a gospel, and could live by their trade, as other citizens did. But tis not so now, unlesse with those Weavers, Taylours, Shoomakers, and other tradesmen, who turn Ministers" (13). But the sectaries volubly responded that it was precisely their ability to support themselves independently of any ecclesiastical hire that qualified such mechanics to preach. The insistence that tithes were wages thus tended to erase the distinction between ordained ministers and lay workers. Prynne's *A Gospel Plea* evinces an obsessive fear of "our new preaching Weavers, Ginger-bread-makers, Smiths, Souldiers, and other Mechanickes . . . who give over their trades and working, to busie themselves only in gathering new Conventicles, new moulding our Church, State, and preaching openly and in corners every where" (44). But his own reduction of ecclesiastical tasks to the status of wage labor suggested that the priestly *opus* was not intrinsically different from secular labor and thus, in defiance of his intentions, helped to advance the doctrine of the priesthood of all believers. In *The Hireling Ministry None of Christ's* (1652), Roger Williams urges ministers to follow his example and to conclude that it is nobler to perform ordinary labor than to commodify the service of God by accepting "hire":

I know what it is to Study, to Preach, to be an Elder, to be applauded; and yet also what it is to tug at the Oar, to dig with the Spade, and Plow, and to labor and travel day and night amongst English, amongst Barbarians. Why should I not be humbly bold to give my witnes faithfully, to give my counsel effectually, and to perswade with some truly pious and conscientious spirits, rather to turn to Law, to Physick, to Souldiery, to Educating of Children, to Digging (and yet not cease from Prophecying) rather than to live under the slavery, yea and the censure (from Christ Jesus and his Saints, and others also) of a mercenary and Hireling ministry?[32]

Even at a purely practical level, the argument that tithes were wages raised far more difficulties than it solved. Unlike secular wage labor, tithing did not involve a contract. The growth of separatist sects created a large and vocal population who had no desire to buy what the priest was selling, and who therefore objected to paying for it. Furthermore, if tithes were remuneration for tasks performed, then failure to perform the tasks ought to free the congregation from the obligation to pay. As Henry Stubbe observed in *A Light Shining Out of Darknes* (1659), "nor indeed could there be any Equity in it, that because 'The labourer was worthy of his Hire,' therefore they who never did hire him, should pay him" (161). Another of Richard Culmer's villains, Tom Tithe-Short, tells the parish minster, Paul Shepherd, "And if you (Goodman Paul) neglect your duty, we need not pay our dues; I made the Pristte where I lived t'other year give me that Sacriment: I sware he should have no Tythes, if we had no Comminion" (16). Answering Culmer, Charles Nichols's *The Hue and Cry after the Priests* (1651) sympathizes with Tom Tithe-Short: "But by what new found Law or Oracle would Mr. Culmer perswade men, that they must pay those who doe no worke for them, he would have men pay those whom they never hired" (9). Thomas Taylor's *A Treatise for the Lord* (1675) also denounces priests for "Suing People at law for Wages, for whom they do no Work" (6).

   To many radicals, including Milton, the view that priestly labor was a commodity not only amounted to idolatry in itself but also produced and confirmed tendencies toward liturgical idolatry among the clergy. As we have seen, the one plausible argument left to the defenders of tithes was that the priest was selling his labor for wages. This suggestion was not necessarily objectionable with regard to the labor of a "mechanick," but the special nature of priestly labor made it appear to be an egregious violation of traditional ethics. The purpose and function of the minister's activities were to save the souls of the congregation. When this activity was equated with a sum of money—when it became commodified—it was hard to avoid the conclusion that salvation was for sale. If it could be shown that the tithe system treated salvation as a commodity, that system would be ipso facto illegitimate. Accordingly, anti-tithe literature examines in forensic detail the argument that tithes were wages. Henry Stubbe, whose *A Light Shining Out of Darknes* has been identified as particularly influential on Milton's tract,[33] used an etymological analysis of the Greek terms for "minister" to demolish the claim that tithes were payable to the office of the priesthood, rather than as compensation for priestly labor. Stubbe asserts that "none of these determinately signifies an Officer, but any one that performs such and such a Work" (1). Even Satan, notes Stubbe, has "ministers," so that the word is "not meant of any particular Function or Office, but a general Performance of any thing accordingly as an Officer, Servant or Minister would" (2). The minister's tithe is thus due to the labor, not the office. It follows that if, as radical Protestants believed, the salvationary functions of the priest could be carried out by any member of the congregation, the rationale for a salaried clergy is immediately undermined. In the greatly expanded second edition, also published in 1659, Stubbe quotes Luther's doctrine of the priesthood of all believers: "These Testimonies do clearly evacuate all visible Priesthood-performances, by making those acts to be Universal, which make up the Essence and Being of a Priesthood, viz. Access to God by Prayer, and the Instructing of others. For what need, what use have we of a Priest, who have no need of any new Mediator or Teacher? Shall we institute an Office or Function without any employment?" (82–83). Their reluctance to admit that tithes were issued by virtue of custom or from charity forced Anglican apologists to claim that they were wages for labor. This acknowledgment benefited their Puritan opponents, such as Stubbe and Milton, who immediately pointed out that such a view of tithes bespoke an idolatrous attitude toward ecclesiastical tasks. A quid pro quo principle of remuneration involved the assumption that priestly labor was efficacious for salvation, and the advocates of this principle thus stood convicted as adherents of Judaic legalism and "works righteousness." Stubbe goes on to cite a speech from Foxe's *Book of Martyrs*, in which William Thorpe informs a prelate:

Since Tithes were the Hire and Wages limited to Levites and to Priests, of the Old Law, for bearing about of the Tabernacle, and for Slaying and Fleying of Beasts, and for burning of Sacrifice, and for keeping of the Temple, and for tromping of Battle before the Host of Israel, and other divers Observances that pertained to their Office: Those Priests that will challenge to take Tithes, deny that Christ is come in the Flesh, and do the Priests office of the Old Law, for whom Tithes were granted. (182)

Tithes, Stubbe argues, were instituted among the Levites as attributable not to the office of a minister, but as compensation for the labor he performed. The assumption was thus that this labor was efficacious in itself. But Protestantism denies that priestly labor is efficacious in itself; therefore, priests who demand compulsory tithes are not Protestants but idolaters (voluntary tithes, in contrast, are alms and not wages, and so they are acceptable). In fact, this logic, by which the sale of priestly labor leads directly to liturgical idolatry, could be described as the cornerstone of Protestantism. It was the original cause of the Reformation: Luther's protests against indulgences, works righteousness, and transubstantiation were all attacks on the fetishization of spiritual labor. The Ninety-five Theses expose indulgences as fetishized certificates representing in abstract form a determinate amount of penitential labor, that is to say, as an ecclesiastical form of paper money. In similar fashion, Luther's objection to the Catholic mass was not to the doctrine of the real presence (in which Luther, of course, believed), but to the notion that the actions of the priest effected a transubstantiation. This notion made the priest's labor into a "finished work," or *opus operatum,* and thus into a thing that could be bought and sold:

there is no belief more widely accepted in the church today, or one of greater force, than that the mass is a good work and a sacrifice. And this abuse has brought in its train innumerable other abuses; and these, when faith in the sacrament has completely died away, turn the holy sacrament into mere merchandise, a market, and a business run for profit. This is the origin of the special feasts, the confraternities, intercessions, merits, anniversaries and memorial days. Things of this kind are bought and sold in the church, dealt in and bargained for, the whole income of priests and monks depending on it. (271)

A century and a half later, Thomas Taylor shows a clear understanding of this connection between economic and liturgical fetishism when he asks the Anglicans, "Do you indeed believe, as in Words you say, That you regenerate the little Infant, by sprinkling a little Water on its Face, and speaking a few Words of your own devising over it, which it knows nothing of. Do you indeed, I say, believe that by this kind of Baptism, they are made the Children of God, the members of Christ, and Inheritors of the Kingdom of God? Or do you not rather do these Things to get Money by?" (7). John Osborne's *Indictment against Tythes* (1659) also points out that priestly labor can only be regarded as valuable—it can only be equated with a sum of financial value—if it is regarded as efficacious for salvation. To regard priestly labor in such a way was, for a Protestant, idolatry. Osborne notes that tithes were originally paid "not to Ministers of Christ to preach the gospel, but to Antichristian idolaters, and to a wicked, idolatrous superstitious end, viz. For satisfaction of the sins of the Donor, to maintain a popish, idle, sottish Clergy . . . And as at the first Tythes were given to Mass-Priests to read and sing the latine-Mass: So they have (for many years) been since continued for reading the English-Mass (the book of Comon-Prayer)" (5). And Anthony Pearson's *The Great Case of Tythes* (1657) makes a similar connection between tithes and the papist belief in justification by good works: "having taught the people that the pardon of sin might be merited by good works, and the torments of Hell avoided by their charitable deeds, it was no hard matter when that was believed, to perswade them not onely to give their tythes, but also their lands" (9).

Milton's *The Likeliest Means* was thus composed in the midst of an intense debate about the spiritual effects of an ecclesiastical market economy. It was regularly being observed that the notion that priestly labor was alienable—that it was a thing that could be separated from the person of the priest—was dangerously close to the Catholic concept of *opus operatum*. This concept reduced the character or faith of the priest to irrelevance: all that mattered was his labor, which was conceived of as a commodity that could be bought and sold. Whereas *Areopagitica* uses commerce as a metaphor for free speech, *The Likeliest Means* engages in a substantive discussion concerning the merits of a market in clerical labor. Modern commentators may find it tempting to accede to the currently prevalent claim that the market and free speech are somehow inseparable or even identical, but such a claim would have seemed deeply idolatrous to Milton. To fully understand the reasons for this, we must now turn to his intervention in the debate whose terms we have just delineated.

IV

For every instance where Milton uses the market as a benign figure or trope, it would be possible to cite several far more derogatory references. Certainly *The Likeliest Means* shows scant respect for market values in its descriptions of tithe-hungry priests exhibiting "a greediness lower than that of tradesmen calling passengers to their shop" (YP 7:298). However, my argument does not depend on Milton's use of trading metaphors but on his rational and discursive opinion regarding the spiritual impact of the ecclesiastical market. It is worth stressing once again that Milton presents this market as the one area where the exchange of labor for wages is unacceptable: "For although hire to the laborer be of moral and perpetual right, yet that special kinde of hire, the tenth, can be not of right or necessity, but to that special labor for which God ordaind it" (YP 7:281). There is no customary "right" to tithes, so tithes can only be wages paid in return for the minister's labor, and it is precisely this that renders them objectionable. Milton admits that in the days of the Old Testament there was a "necessity" for tithes because the priestly caste of Levites were excluded from land ownership. Since then, however, circumstances have changed: "the priest and Levites had not tithes for their labor only in the tabernacle, but in regard they were to have no other part nor inheritance in the land. . . . But our Levites undergoing no such law of deprivement, can have no right to any such compensation" (YP 7:282). Since contemporary priests were not banned from land-ownership, it followed that contemporary tithes can only be wages paid for labor, and because of this Milton pronounces them antichristian.

Throughout *The Likeliest Means,* Milton insists that compulsory tithes are wages, and that wages have no place in the church. The biblical pronouncement that "the laborer is worthy of his hire" is not, according to Milton, a prescription for wage labor. It refers only to "a rule of common equitie which proportions the hire as well to the abilitie of him who gives as to the labor of him who receives, and recommends him only as worthy, not invests him with a legal right" (YP 7:290). The payment referred to in this text is charity, not the "undue and vitious" form of hire, which Milton identifies with wage labor. Furthermore, Milton is convinced that the nature of the priest's labor and payment must inevitably influence his theology. A "hireling," he claims, will automatically be drawn toward idolatry. This is because the conception of labor as a thing for sale involves a process of objectification analogous to that by which divinity is identified with an icon, or by which the civil power asserts control over the spiritual. Milton warns the moderate Independents, who were willing to countenance a tithing state church, that "independence and state-hire in religion, can never consist long or certainly together. For magistrates at one time or other . . . will pay none but such whom by their committees of examination they finde conformable to their interests and opinions: and hirelings will soon frame themselves to that interest and those opinions which they see best pleasing to their paymasters; and to seem right themselves, will force others as to the truth" (YP 7:318). Once again, Milton is careful to specify that his objection is to wage labor only. The term "state-hire" in the above refers to *compulsory* tithes—those enforced by the state. The voluntary payment of ministers by congregations was charity, not wages, and so Milton exempts it from criticism. In his *Letter to a Friend* dated 20 October 1659, Milton expresses the view that the abolition of "forc't" tithes is inseparable from religious toleration. Because of this, he declares that opposition to compulsory tithes is an absolute precondition for participation in government: "If the parlament be thought well dissolv'd, as not complyeing fully to grant liberty of conscience & the necessary consequence thereof, the Removall of a forc't maintenance from Ministers, then must the Army forthwith chuse a councell of State, whereof as many to be of the parlament as are undoubtedly affected to the two condicions proposed" (YP 7:330) Here we see a concise expression of the Miltonic principle that there must be no toleration of idolaters. This principle is one of the few constant factors in Milton's discussions of the forcing of conscience. *Areopagitica* specifically excludes idolaters from the marketplace of ideas, just as *The Likeliest Means* excludes hirelings from religious toleration. The idolater and the hireling, according to Milton, are by definition incapable of exercising freedom in a proper manner. Indeed, the idolater and the hireling often seem coterminus for Milton, as on the several occasions when he cites with approval Paul's reference to "covetousness, which worse than heresie, is idolatry."[34] Defenders of tithes often invoked the rise of "heretical" sects to justify their demands that the church must be bolstered with a regular income, but Milton retorts that it is the inappropriate manner of collecting income that causes such problems: "This is that which makes atheists in the land . . . not the want of maintenance or preachers, as they allege, but the many hirelings and cheaters that have the gospel in their hands" (YP 7:318). Wage labor in the priesthood is an invitation to idolatry, and it is disgraceful that ministers should demand wages "for the verbal labor of a seven day's preachment" (YP 7:285). As Stubbe had emphasized, tithes were instituted among the Israelites as part of the "Judaical ceremonial law" now abrogated by Christ. Milton therefore associates them with the blind adoration of *nomos*, the legalistic fetishization of the sign, which defines idolatry: "He then who by that law brings tithes into the gospel, of necessity brings in withall a sacrifice, and an altar; without which tithes by that law were unsanctifi'd and polluted . . . and therefor never thought on in the first Christian times, till ceremonies, altars, and oblations, by an ancienter corruption, were brought back long before" (YP 7:281–82). Milton's sense of such connections was especially acute, but in the tumultuous 1650s many other opponents of tithes also noticed the homologies among liturgical, legalistic, financial, and political manifestations of idolatry. John Canne's *Query to William Prynne* (1659) commented that "they who cry out loudest for them, are (for the most part) for a Single Person, or for the Interest of Charles Stuart."[35] Like Canne, Stubbe, and other anti-tithe campaigners, Milton perceives how the fetishization of priestly labor leads directly to other forms of idolatry. Following Luther, he notes that the sacrament of penance idolatrously assumes the efficacy of the *opus operatum*. He refers to financial payments "given, as the clergie then perswaded men, for their souls' health, a pious gift; but as the truth was, ofttimes a bribe to God or to Christ for absolution, as they were then taught, from murders, adulteries, and other hainous crimes" (YP 7:307) *The Likeliest Means* objects to compulsory "fees for christenings, marriages, and burials," which are

of such evil note that even the councel of *Trent, l.2 p.* 240, makes them lyable to the laws against Simonie, who take or demand fees for the administering of any sacrament: *Che la sinodo volendo levare gli abusi introdotti &c.* And in the next page, with like severity condemns the giving or taking for a benefice, and the celebrating of marriages, christenings, and burials, for fees exacted or demanded: nor counts it less Simonie to sell the ground or place of burial. (YP 7:297–98)

When the principle of paying wages to priests is admitted, all sorts of idol-atrous absurdities follow. For instance, Milton notes that compulsory tithes and the payment of occasional fees for religious services imply contradictory conceptions of ecclesiastical labor. They cannot both be regarded as wages for a determinate amount of labor: "For if the minister be maintained for his whole ministry, why should he be twice paid for any part thereof? Why should he, like a servant, seek vailes over and above his wages?" (YP 7:298). Of all liturgical matters, the issue of marriage was closest to Milton's heart, and he claims that a sacramental view of the institution is a fetish made plausible by a prior fetishization of the priest's ceremonial labor: "Likeliest it is . . . that in imitation of heathen priests who were wont at nuptials to use many rites and ceremonies, and especially, judging it would be profitable, and the increase of thir autoritie, not to be spectators only in busines of such concernment to the life of man, they insinuated that marriage was not holy without their benediction, and for the better colour, made it a sacrament" (YP 7:299). Fortunately, he notes, marriage has been removed from "the canonical shop" by the Marriage Act of 1653. But Milton views this as only one battle in a comprehensive and continuous war between God and Mammon. Even those critics who wish to portray Milton as a proponent of commerce would presumably try to limit his supposed enthusiasm to the secular, rather than the ecclesiastical, market. But they should bear in mind that in the seventeenth century these spheres were frequently not distinguishable. The declaration Milton makes at the very beginning of his polemical career, that "Antichrist is Mammon's son" (YP 1:590), deserves to be understood as a definitive statement of his iconoclastic theology, and as a manifesto to which he remained faithful throughout his life. As Milton and his contemporaries understood the concept, "Antichrist" was by no means an exclusively ecclesiastical phenomenon.[36] "Antichrist" was not constrained to limit his activities to the church. On the contrary, he was noted for his propensity to range freely up and down the world, entering into every nook and cranny of personal and political life, aiming to dominate all human thoughts and activities while disguising the degree and nature of his dominion through the enticing inducements of idolatrous temptations. As Milton might have put it: like father, like son.

Lehigh University

NOTES

1. On sins of luxury, see, for example, Milton's diatribe against the "unconscionable wealth and revenues" of the prelates, who "snore in their luxurious excesse." From John Milton, *The*

Reason of Church-Government, in *The Complete Prose Works of John Milton,* 8 vols., ed. Don M. Wolfe et al. (New Haven, Conn., 1953–82), 1:856, hereafter designated YP and cited parenthetically by volume and page number in the text. On the monopoly of preaching, see his call for "unmonopolizing the rewards of learning and industry" (YP 1:613).

2. Marx's famous anatomy of the commodity takes up the first chapter of *Capital,* volume 1, trans. Ben Fowkes (London, 1990), 125–77. It is extrapolated into a general theory of false consciousness in Georg Lukacs, "Reification and the Consciousness of the Proletariat," in *History and Class-Consciousness,* trans. Rodney Livingstone (Cambridge, Mass., 1971), 83–222. See also David Hawkes, *Ideology* (New York, 1996), 88–120.

3. John Bunyan, *The Life and Death of Mr. Badman,* ed. James F. Forrest and Roger Sharrock (Oxford, 1988), 108–13. I give many more examples, and provide a far more detailed argument for an awareness of "commodity fetishism" in Renaissance England in *Idols of the Marketplace: Idolatry and Commodity Fetishism, 1580–1680* (New York, 2001).

4. Writers of the English Renaissance did not derive the term "commodification" from their use of "commodity"; instead, they designated this phenomenon by the word "merchandizing," as for instance in Shakespeare's *Sonnet 102:* "That love is merchandiz'd whose rich esteeming / The owner's tongue doth publish every where" (3–4). Quoted from *Shakespeare's Sonnets,* ed. Stephen Booth (New Haven, Conn., 1977).

5. See *Lycidas,* lines 113–32. The main biblical sources for this trope are Ezekiel 34:2–4 and John 10:11–15.

6. Martin Luther, *An Appeal to the Ruling Class of German Nationality,* in *Martin Luther: Selections from His Writings,* ed. John Dillenberger (New York, 1958), 430. Subsequent quotations from Luther are from this edition.

7. See Richard Friedenthal, *Luther: His Life and Times,* trans. John Nowell (London, 1970), 134.

8. Blair Hoxby, "The Trade of Truth Advanced: *Areopagitica,* Economic Discourse, and Libertarian Reform," in *Milton Studies* 36, ed. Albert C. Labriola (Pittsburgh, 1998), 177–202; quotation from 178.

9. For a somewhat more convincing analysis of Charles II's association with trade, see Blair Hoxby, "The Government of Trade: Commerce, Politics and the Courtly Art of the Restoration," *ELH* 66, no. 3 (1999): 591–627.

10. To be fair, Hoxby does not claim any expertise in economics, but his essay nonetheless betrays a disconcerting innocence of the discipline. Discussing Habermas, he asserts: "his treatment of economic questions is undermined by gross misconceptions. In outlining 'pre-suppositions of classical economics' that are 'well-known,' for instance, Habermas says that the value of a commodity is 'gauged' by the 'quantity of labor required for its production.' In other words, he imputes Marx's labor theory of value to classical economics, which utterly rejects the tenet" (ibid., 198 n. 6). The most charitable interpretation of this is that Hoxby has somehow reversed the generally accepted terminology of economics. In reality, the theory that the value of a commodity is gauged by the quantity of labor necessary for its production is indeed, as Habermas says, a fundamental tenet of classical economics, while Marx's refinement of this simplistic thesis is his most basic departure from the classical school.

11. The misconception that *Areopagitica* advocates an economic free market is not exclusive to economic libertarians. Ironically, Hoxby's libertarian reading owes much to Christopher Kendrick's Marxist interpretation in *Milton: A Study in Ideology and Form* (New York, 1986), which claims that in *Areopagitica* "the ways of Truth tend to be one . . . with the ways of the 'free' competitive market" (31). See also Andrew Milner, *John Milton and the English Revolution* (Totowa, N.J., 1981), 54. Dayton Haskin, *Milton's Burden of Interpretation* (Philadelphia, 1994), shows a more nuanced awareness of the seventeenth-century economic context when he resists

the temptation to anachronistically interpret Milton's fascination with the parable of the talents as implying a favorable attitude toward market economics. Haskin shows how Milton read the parable in conjunction with the story of the laborers in the vineyard (Matt. 20:1–16), in which the equation of a sum of money with a quantitative amount of labor time is explicitly rejected (37).

12. On "contempt of commerce," see J. F. Camé, "Images in Milton's *Areopagitica*," *College English* 6 (1974): 23–37, citation from 24; on "disdain of traders," see Alan F. Price, "Incidental Imagery in *Areopagitica*," *MP* 49 (1952): 217–22, citation from 219 n. 9; on a "figure of contempt," see Kevin Dunn, "Milton among the Monopolists: *Areopagitica*, Intellectual Property and the Hartlib Circle," in *Samuel Hartlib and Universal Reformation*, ed. Mark Greengrass, Michael Leslie, and Timothy Raylor (Cambridge, 1994), 177–92, citation from 187.

13. As with the term "commodity," which I discuss above, the word "alienation" boasts a pedigree that may seem surprisingly long. It was regularly used in the seventeenth century to carry the modern sense of an illegitimate or unethical externalization of property. For example, Milton's friend Henry Stubbe, *A Light Shining Out of Darknes* (London, 1659), wrote that "the paying of [tithes] is an Alienation" (171).

14. Laura Brace, *The Idea of Property in Seventeenth-Century England* (Manchester, 1998), 5.

15. There is a vivid example of the psychological impact of alienation in John Bunyan's *Grace Abounding to the Chief of Sinners,* ed. W. R. Owens (New York, 1987), in which the author becomes obsessed by the temptation to "sell" Christ: "I could neither eat my food, stoop for a pin, chop a stick, or cast mine eye to look on this or that, but still the temptation would come, *Sell Christ for this, or sell Christ for that, sell him, sell him.* Sometimes it would run in my thoughts not so little as an hundred times together, sell him, sell him, sell him" (36).

16. I develop this point at greater length in "The Politics of Character in Milton's Divorce Tracts," *Journal of the History of Ideas* 62 (January 2001): 141–60. Milton neglects to mention that he, too, wrote for wages; no doubt he would have considered this irrelevant since they formed no part of his motive for writing.

17. See, for example, Aristotle's *Politics* 1257a1 7–10, 1258b1 49–50, and Psalms 115:4–8, 135:15–18. I cite many other instances and discuss this tradition at length in *Idols of the Marketplace* (27–75), and also in *Ideology* (16–19). On the influence of Aristotle, see especially Odd Langholm, *Wealth and Money in the Aristotelian Tradition* (Bergen, 1984), and Arnaud Berthold, *Aristote et l'argent* (Paris, 1981). On the influence of the Bible, see especially Benjamin Nelson, *The Idea of Usury: From Tribal Brotherhood to Universal Otherhood* (Princeton, 1949), and Norman Jones, *God and the Money-lenders: Usury and Law in Early Modern England* (Oxford, 1989). As J. G. A. Pocock, *Virtue, Commerce, and History: Essays on Political Thought and History* (Cambridge, 1985), notes, "the Western moral tradition displays an astonishing unity and solidarity in the uneasiness and mistrust it evinces towards money as the medium of exchange" (103–4).

18. "The value of all things contracted for, is measured by the Appetites of the Contractors: and therefore the just value, is that which they be contented to give" (Thomas Hobbes, *Leviathan* [London, 1985], 208).

19. On the ways in which early political economy accommodated the moralists' critique, see especially Joyce Oldham Appleby, *Economic Thought and Ideology in Seventeenth-Century England* (Princeton, 1978), 247; Barry Supple, "The Nature of Enterprise," in *The Cambridge Economic History of Europe,* vol. 5, ed. E. E. Rich and C. H. Wilson (Cambridge, 1977), 405.

20. See Immanuel Wallerstein, *The Capitalist World-Economy* (Cambridge, 1979), 5, and Ellen Meiskins Wood, *The Pristine Culture of Capitalism: A Historical Essay on Old Regimes and Modern States* (New York, 1991), 98–99.

21. See Hermann van der Wee, "Monetary, Credit and Banking Systems," in *The Cambridge Economic History of Europe*, 5:290; Glyn Davies, *A History of Money* (Cardiff, 1994), 230; R. H. Tawney, *Religion and the Rise of Capitalism* (Gloucester, Mass., 1962), 137.

22. *Of Reformation* (YP 1:613). See also the references to tithes in *The Tenure of Kings and Magistrates* (YP 3:196, 241), and the *Second Defence* (YP 4:650–51).

23. Barbara K. Lewalski, *The Life of John Milton: A Critical Biography* (Oxford, 2000), 386; Thomas Corns, *John Milton: The Prose Works* (New York, 1998), 113. See also Arthur Barker, *Milton and the Puritan Dilemma, 1641–1660* (Toronto, 1942), 236–59.

24. See Stephen R. Honeygosky, *Milton's House of God: The Invisible and Visible Church* (Columbia, Mo., 1993): "Milton begins by attacking the economics of preachers without another trade, thus, without income; proceeds by endorsing a ministry whose preachers have another trade; and concludes by promoting a spiritual truth—the right and responsibility for any and all (tradesmen) to preach" (189).

25. Favorite texts cited in vindications of tithing include 1 Corinthians 9:9–14 and 1 Timothy 5:18. On right of ministers to tithes, see Christopher Hill, *Economic Problems of the Church* (Oxford, 1956), 77–131.

26. See Sir Henry Spelman, *Tithes Too Hot to Be Touched* (1640): "by payment of tithes in kind out of all profits arising by Gods blessing on our labours, the Clergy doe partake with the people in times of plenty, or suffer with them in extremities, whereas by a certain stipend of money, they would be far less sensible" (C2).

27. On the commutation of tithes to money, see Margaret James, "The Political Importance of the Tithe Controversy in the English Revolution, 1640–60," *History* 26 (June 1941): 1–18, and Eric J. Evans, *The Contentious Tithe: The Tithe Problem and English Agriculture, 1750–1850* (London, 1976), 16–17.

28. Cited in James, "Political Importance of the Tithe Controversy," 2.

29. Cited in ibid., 8. The more acute conservatives foresaw this danger and attempted to forestall it. Spelman, *Tithes Too Hot to Be Touched*, for example, warns that "our Ministers must have no share with us in tilling the land, and matters of husbandry, for they are called from secular cares to spirituall contemplation" (7).

30. Cited in Stubbe, *A Light Shining Out of Darknes*, 163. Arguments for voluntary tithes often cite 2 Corinthians 9:7: "Every man according as he purposeth in his heart, so let him give; not grudgingly, or of necessity: for God loveth a cheerful giver."

31. Laura Brace summarizes the essential paradox: "Anti-tithe writings appreciated the need to defend labour itself, and they portrayed the ministers as parasites attempting to live off the labour of others. Pro-tithers, too, acknowledged the importance of labour as a justification for property, and were concerned to depict the ministers themselves as labourers for the Word who deserved a just reward. . . . The ministers were clearly and categorically claiming a property in tithes derived from their labour, but they did so without reference to the market or to the alienability of labour" (100, 102).

32. Roger Williams, *The Hireling Ministry None of Christ's* (1652), from the epistle dedicatory, n.p.

33. See Austin Woolrych's introduction to YP 7:82–83.

34. See *The Tenure of Kings and Magistrates* (YP 3:196, 241) and *The Second Defence* (YP 4:650–51).

35. From the preface to John Osborne, *An Indictment against Tythes* (1659), n.p.

36. See Christopher Hill, *Antichrist in Seventeenth-Century England* (New York, 1990).

MILTON'S PARABLE OF MISREADING: NAVIGATING THE CONTEXTUAL WATERS OF THE "NIGHT-FOUNDER'D SKIFF" IN *PARADISE LOST,* 1.192–209

Bryan Adams Hampton

Fecisti nos ad Te, et inquietum est cor nostrum, donec requiescat in Te.

Augustine, *Confessions*

WHEN WE FIRST MEET Satan and his cohort of rebel angels in *Paradise Lost,* they are being licked by "livid flames" (1.182) and are ceaselessly tossing upon the furious waves of hell's lake, newly vanquished and desirous of relief.[1] Trying to rouse his fallen troops Satan suggests they raise themselves from the flood and fly toward a "dreary Plain, forlorn and wild" and "there rest, if any rest can harbor there" (180, 185), so that they may hold council about how to proceed. What immediately follows is a lengthy and lavish description of Satan's magnificent body, which is nothing less than a visual feast for the reader's hungry eyes as we find ourselves attracted to this monstrous bulk. In an epic simile, Milton compares him to both the Titans and Leviathan.

Curiously appended to this latter allusion, however, is a short narrative describing an inexperienced sailor who, mistaking the great sea beast for land, moors his small ship upon its back:

> Thus Satan talking to his nearest Mate
> With Head up-lift above the wave, and Eyes
> That sparkling blaz'd, his other Parts besides
> Prone on the Flood, extended long and large
> Lay floating many a rood, in bulk as huge
>
> . . . .
>   [as] that Sea-beast
> *Leviathan,* which God of all his works
> Created hugest that swim th' Ocean stream:
> Him haply slumb'ring on the *Norway* foam
> The Pilot of some small night-founder'd Skiff,

Deeming some Island, oft, as Seamen tell,
With fixed Anchor in his scaly rind
Moors by his side under the Lee, while Night
Invests the Sea, and wished Morn delays:
So stretcht out huge in length the Arch-fiend lay.

                                        (1.192–96, 201–9)

Some readers are tempted perhaps to make little of Milton's "night-founder'd Skiff," relegating it to a mere commonplace. But Milton displays a special fondness for nautical metaphors, scattered throughout his poetry and prose, and such consistent use by a very conscientious man of letters merits that we gauge the image with more import.[2] Alternately, readers may not delve into the implications of the short narrative because the skiff is over-shadowed by Satan's sublime body. But I suggest that this is precisely the point. The idol that Milton carves for our gaze's consumption distracts us from the hermeneutical task at hand: how to read Satan and the physical and spiritual landscape of hell that follows.

In this essay I turn my attention to this short narrative of the "night-founder'd Skiff" in order to invite a novel consideration of Milton's use of the epic simile: as parable.[3] Milton as poet draws upon a theological trope richly explored by Origen, Basil the Great, and Augustine, wherein the individual soul is likened to a ship navigating the perilous waters of spiritual existence.[4] In doing so, Milton as parable maker and preacher accomplishes two things. First, through a negative example the parable teaches his congregation of readers that the individual soul moored upon Leviathan, understood by some expositors to be a figure of Satan in the early modern period, is characterized by spiritual restlessness. Second, Milton's parable of the "night-founder'd Skiff" becomes an object lesson in exegesis whereby virtue (the Latin *virtus* means, among other things, "power" or "skill") becomes the crucial herme-neutical lens for readers of texts.[5] Just as the undisciplined sailor of the skiff incorrectly "reads" the "text" of the physical landscape before him, Milton's undisciplined man who has not properly cultivated virtue will be unable to read correctly the ecclesial and political "texts" before him, as we find that the image of the small skiff becomes conflated with the ships of church and state.

In order to flesh out these spiritual implications for Milton's parable, this essay focuses on three related contexts: the theological, the contemplative, and the homiletic traditions. The first section of this essay traces Milton's rich theological inheritance of the nautical trope with some observations on how Origen, Basil, and Augustine appropriate the image to comment on the necessity of cultivating virtue and spiritual discernment when the believer is confronted with various "texts." Milton co-opts the trope for his parable, and in the second section of the essay I draw out its spiritual implications, arguing that these restless misreaders become indistinguishable from Satan himself as Milton draws upon a notion of virtue that is intimately related to early Christian philosophical contemplation and conversion. Further, I examine Satan's own restless wandering in the poem, for his restlessness and its causes and consequences are the archetypal template for Milton of all restless souls and misreaders: those moored upon Leviathan either by choice or lack of vigilance and virtue. The third section of the essay tries to gather these issues together by exploring more closely Milton's role as preacher/parable maker speaking truth to institutions of power—the ships of church and state—as we find that Milton borrows from the tradition of the medieval exemplum to construct his parable of the "night-founder'd Skiff."

A few words need to be said, however, regarding the parable form.[6] The parable, as Frank Kermode explains in his classic study of the Markan parables, is inextricably bound with the issue of the audience that the parable creates. He argues that the parable is a kind of riddle and that "to divine the true, the latent sense, you need to be of the elect, of the institution. Outsiders must content themselves with the manifest, and pay a supreme penalty for doing so."[7] This is not to say that every parable must be obscure, however, as Madeleine Boucher reminds us, but because the parable form is an "implied comparison" it requires "some insight on the part of the hearer if it is to be apprehended."[8] In his landmark *The Parables of the Kingdom* (1935), C. H. Dodd insightfully comments, "the parable has the character of an argument, in that it entices the hearer to a judgment upon the situation depicted, and then challenges him, directly or by implication, to apply that judgment to the matter in hand."[9] For all of these critics, discernment is required of the parable's audience, and there is no guarantee that the parable will find its audience.

As a discourse of preaching, therefore, the parable form is an exegetical crucible. Given the dynamics that parable imposes upon its audience, we would be remiss if we did not remind ourselves of Milton's own desire, expressed in the invocation to Urania, that his song "fit audience find, though few" (7.31).[10] In using the parable form, Milton implicitly assumes the pulpit and acts as a kind of preacher to his congregation of readers. More will be said of Milton's preaching role a bit later. Presently, however, we need to immerse ourselves with Milton in the perilous waters of the theological tradition in order to see how the nautical trope was variously developed in the patristic tradition. Such a voyage will allow us to see how Milton appropriates the nautical trope, and how the image helps us to flesh out the spiritual and exegetical implications of the parable.

I

As key patristic figures concerned with properly interpreting the Bible, Origen, Basil, and Augustine maintained particular assumptions about texts and readers of texts, whether those texts are pagan epics or entire philosophical systems, and whether those readers are initiates or wizened churchmen. These are assumptions that Milton, as one of the Bible's central interpreters in the seventeenth century, inherited and to which he gave assent. The first section of this essay attempts to delineate one assumption in particular, that virtue is a hermeneutical lens through which readers should read. Why? Because for these churchmen it is the *soul* that reads, a kind of *lectio divina* ("sacred reading"). Without the lens of virtue the soul is in a precarious position, at risk of being deceived or swept away by textual forces more powerful than the reader. Consequently, for Origen, Basil, Augustine, and Milton, there is no better picture of the soul in reading than the ship upon the seas. Potentially, reading is a perilous journey; in this sense, reading is pilgrimage.

The image of the ship navigating the seas belongs to the category of tropes that see the Christian life as pilgrimage. Although she does not mention the nautical metaphor, despite its common use in poems and sermons, Barbara Kiefer Lewalski explains that "such metaphors were understood to be grounded upon true analogies between natural and spiritual things. . . . Also, though they were used in the service of doctrinal exposition, such tropes were not transformed into simple doctrinal statements, but rather provide an imaginative rendering of the experience of living the Christian life."[11] Milton's short narrative of the small skiff moored upon Leviathan is an imaginative picture of the individual "ark of the soul" reading and navigating the waters of spiritual life.

The distinctly scriptural locus for this nautical-metaphysical trope occurs in 1 Peter 3:18–22, in which the apostle allegorizes the Genesis account of Noah's ark. Here Peter indicates that Noah's trial and salvation through water are similar to the ceremony of baptism for believers; by participating in baptism, the believer shares in and identifies with Christ, the new Noah. What seems to be important to Peter, and to many early expositors, is that water is linked to the salvation of God's people through a kind of ceremonial cleansing.

The image of the ark lurching upon the furious waters of salvation/baptism is treated, characteristically, with some measure of hermeneutical "violence" in Origen's *Homily 2 on Genesis*. Origen analyzes the construction of the ark, adopts the language of individual virtue, and assigns spiritual meanings to the mundane. Broadly speaking he likens the ark to the Church and the animals and humans within as its people. The various decks and compartments in the ark represent different levels of spiritual progress within the Church, even though all are saved by one faith through one baptism. Those who progress and live "by rational knowledge and are capable not only of ruling themselves but also of teaching others, since very few are found, represent the few who are saved with Noah himself and are united with him in the closest relationship, just as also our Lord, the true Noah, Christ Jesus, has few intimates." Those believers in the upper decks of the ark who are trained in the practice of virtue, capable of managing and subduing their passions, are to be distinguished from the "multitude" of those of the lower decks "whose fierce raging the charm of faith has not tamed."[12] Implicitly, the virtuous are less affected by the terrors of the storm outside, "anchored" as they are in their relational proximity to the mind of Christ; conversely, the spiritually slothful, whose passions still rule instead of Christ's presence in their hearts, are at the mercy of constant flux and undulation.

In yet another exposition, Origen develops this notion of individual virtue and vice. If a person, seeing that "evils are increasing and vices are overflowing, can turn from the things which are in flux and passing away and fallen, and can hear the word of God and the heavenly precepts, this man is building an ark of salvation within his own heart and is dedicating a library, so to speak, of the divine word within himself." He comments further that the virtuous man's ark (we might substitute "skiff"), his "library," is constructed from planks that are straight and squared, "that is, not from the volumes of secular authors, but from the prophetic and apostolic volumes."[13] The image of the ark upon the waters, then, is an appropriate metaphor for the spiritual life of the believer—the individual soul navigating the spiritual realities of existence where his virtue is tested. Additionally, as Origen makes clear, as much as the nautical metaphor befits an image of the individual soul, it is also a picture of the collective "soul" of the Church, the "one body," though with many members, functioning in union and harmony with Christ. Thus the individual person and/or church that heeds the divine commands and cultivates and exercises virtue will land securely upon Mount Ararat rather than being moored upon a sea beast that will soon be plunging below the waves.

In his treatise To Young Men on Reading Greek Literature, no doubt familiar to Milton, who sought to accommodate pagan literature to Christian understanding, Basil the Great develops Origen's image of the "library" of the soul. He argues that pagan literature may help prepare the young man to receive the mysteries of the church, using the metaphor of a cloth being made ready through various treatments to receive the dye; "so we also in the same manner must first, if the glory of the good is to abide with us indelible for all time, be instructed by these outside means, and then shall understand the sacred and mystical teachings."[14] Here we see that, like Origen, Basil is careful to articulate that the individual exercise of virtue is always with a vision for the ecclesial community; the individual young man learns to practice virtue so that he might be prepared to receive the sacraments of the church, and in this way join its mystical community. In reading the ancient poets and orators, the young man must develop the spiritual virtue of discernment, which is implicitly connected to reading, gleaning that which is helpful in cultivating virtue and jettisoning that which promotes vice.[15]

"[W]henever they [the poets] recount for you the deeds or words of good men," Basil urges, "you ought to cherish and emulate these and try to be as far as possible like them; but when they treat of wicked men, you ought to avoid such imitation, stopping your ears no less than Odysseus did." We can fault Basil for not recollecting the episode of the Sirens correctly in Book Twelve of *The Odyssey*, but his intent seems clear: one is prepared to receive the sacred mysteries of the church through careful and constant spiritual *exercise*, in this case, a kind of virtuous mimesis.[16] Again, we return to the nautical metaphor: the Sirens lured unwary, unprepared, undisciplined sailors to their deaths upon the rocks by the beauty of their tempting song, promising safe refuge. Odysseus is nearly driven mad with desire, and had it not been for his crew stopping their ears, his ship surely would have been lost much earlier than it was.

Virtue can be learned through literary example, argues Basil, but, predictably, so can vice. To Basil, "the soul must be watched over with all vigilance," and pagan poetry has the power to seduce reason, will, and desire. Pagan poetry often depicts men "engaged in amours or drunken [*sic*]" or "define[s] happiness in terms of an over-abundant table or dissolute songs." For Basil such distorted images make a mockery of humanity's telos in conforming to the divine image. Further, they are blasphemous in their depictions of the divine itself when gods are represented in multiplicity, in adulteries, and in brutish actions. So, although Basil sees a value in pagan literature, he sternly admonishes "that you should not surrender to these men once for all *the rudders of your mind*, as if of a ship, and follow them whithersoever they lead."[17] The ship of one's soul will only navigate successfully the raging waters and find its proper moorings in the Church and in divine love with vigilant care. The question for Basil is one of control: Who or what is at the rudder of one's "skiff" as a person navigates the waters of spiritual existence?

It is a question with which Augustine deals in his own spiritual autobiography. Augustine perhaps makes the most extensive use of the nautical metaphor (and pagan poetry) to describe his own spiritual wanderings, his "sacrilegious quest for knowledge." Augustine found himself restless, wandering the churning spiritual waters of Ciceronian rhetoric, Manichaeism,

Skepticism, and Platonic philosophy, until finally finding rest through his conversion to Christianity under the tutelage of Ambrose. Through his conversion he realizes his utter dependence on God and the vanity of trying to define life apart from God: "I sought an object for my love. . . . My hunger was internal, deprived of inward food, that is of you yourself, my God." Augustine's restlessness as he describes it can be attributed to misplaced desire —a "misreading" of his (Christian) telos—and a distorted will. In Book Seven he argues that the wicked mistakenly "feed" their minds and hearts on the things below them in the hierarchy of creation, believing that such things will grant lasting sustenance. His perversity is a twisting away "from the highest substance, you O God, towards inferior things."[18]

Augustine relies heavily on the greatest Latin epic to describe this journey toward conversion, the story of one tossed upon the menacing waves of the Mediterranean, only to arrive finally at his destination in Rome. The influence of *The Aeneid* on Augustine's *Confessions* cannot be overestimated; in many instances, Augustine directly echoes passages from Virgil, only to reinscribe them within the context of his spiritual journey toward God.[19] Throughout the narrative, Augustine sees himself as the spiritual Aeneas, and by implication the epic hero, who cannot rest until he is truly "home." For Aeneas that home is on the seven hills of Palatine along the river Tiber, where Rome will one day flourish. For Augustine that home is in the city of God, a place to which the ravaged soul can always return because it is in eternity.[20] As with Aeneas's journey, Augustine's "skiff of the soul" was not to find the shore for many years, and he would experience much grief and restlessness in the voyage.

Yet for Augustine the Church on earth is the embodiment of this eschatological realization, constituted of individual souls engaged in practicing virtue and navigating their individual way but paradoxically united in their voyage as a collective body under Christ who is at the helm. It is for the edification of the Church, the communion of the saints, that Augustine has written his *Confessions:* "Stir up the heart when people read and hear the confessions of my past wickedness. . . . Prevent their heart from *sinking* into the sleep of despair. . . . I am making this confession not only before you . . . , but also in the ears of believing sons of men, sharers in my joy, conjoined with me in mortality, my fellow citizens and pilgrims."[21] Augustine hopes that the experiences of one man's continued "misreading" of God will teach the community of saints how to properly read his text and respond to its exhortations.

As with Origen and Basil, Augustine collapses the part-whole dynamic, but without diminishing the crucial role of either. The individual soul must be responsible in its own care through personal discipline so that the ecclesial "ship" can properly function; the properly functioning Church continues to offer vision and guidance so that all individuals might be delivered unto a safe harbor. If the "skiffs" of individual souls are "restless" because they are not properly anchored in the discipline and virtue of Christ, then the ecclesial ship will have little hope than to churn restlessly upon the waves as well, or (worse yet) end up "night-founder'd." Clearly then, in the theological tradition the nautical trope is both a figure for the individual soul and the united body of Christ navigating the waters of the world—a kind of sacred hermeneutical circle.

We find this part-whole dynamic at work in Milton's parable as well. If we understand Milton's skiff as a figure of the individual in a hermeneutical relation to a church, then we must pay closer attention to the spiritual aspects of "reading" and the virtue of discernment.[22] For Origen, Basil, and Augustine, individual readers of texts, whether sacred or pagan texts or entire philosophical systems, must exercise care in discerning how these texts impact the (spiritual) course of one's life, for those texts will influence, in turn, the course and direction of the Church. In particular, Milton's parable of the "night-founder'd Skiff" is a picture, then, of both the individual and the corporate soul—Satan and the demonic counterpart of the church—who are engaged in misreading.

II

Milton inherits this rich tradition and works it throughout the fabric of *Paradise Lost*. If we read the passage concerning the "night-founder'd Skiff" as a parable of misreading with this exegetical tradition in mind, what is revealed? In this section I address the spiritual implications of Milton's parable through the early Christian philosophical and contemplative tradition, so influential upon figures such as Basil and Augustine. I want to suggest that we understand early Christian contemplative practice as one species of *lectio divina,* the soul in reading, whereby a person *becomes* that which his mind gazes upon. Within this context the undisciplined pilot in Milton's parable becomes indistinguishable from Leviathan, and the careless soul who has attached himself to Satan will share in his spiritual restlessness and in his destruction. We understand at the outset of the parable that Satan, too, is a reader of texts and is in charge of his own ecclesial vessel, engaged in "talking to his nearest Mate" (1.192). How, then, have the demons fared in their own navigation, in their own sacred reading? What have their minds gazed upon that defines their course and destination? Perhaps more important, what are they becoming in the process?

To address these questions we must begin with the practice of philosophy in the ancient world, for in their desperate attempt to "charm / Pain for a while and anguish" (2.566–67), the fallen angels practice "false Philosophie" (565), a "discourse more sweet" (555) than epic song. In *Philosophy as a Way of Life,* eminent historian of ancient religions Pierre Hadot examines the attitude of many ancients toward the interpretation of philosophical texts. Hadot argues that many Greco-Roman philosophers had a much different conception of the practice of philosophy from moderns. For the ancients, the "philosophical act is not situated merely on the cognitive level, but on that of the self and of being. It is a progress which causes us to *be* more fully, and makes us better." The focus of philosophy in antiquity was not exclusively centered on intellectual argumentation, exegesis of texts, or the learning of abstract theory as seems to be the case with many moderns. Instead, the focus of philosophy among many Stoics, Epicureans, and early Christians was centered on reshaping the self: "It is a conversion which turns our entire life upside down, changing the life of the person who goes through it. It raises the individual from an inauthentic condition of life, darkened by unconsciousness and harassed by worry, to an authentic state of life, in which he attains self-consciousness, an exact vision of the world, inner peace, and freedom." The purpose of philosophy was the shaping and reshaping of the self in all its facets: spiritual, emotional, intellectual. In this sense, the philosophical life was a true exercise in virtue manifested through self-dialogue and meditation in order to understand better one's position in the world, one's experience of it, and the true nature of reality as conceived in each conceptual system. Hadot points out that even though no single treatise exists on the subject of spiritual exercises, a proliferation of fragments and allusions exists in other Greco-Roman writings. Philo of Alexandria, for instance, collected two partial lists of these exercises, which include practices such as research, reading, self-mastery, and meditation. The purpose of these practices is to bring the philosopher into greater self-awareness in order to foster spiritual vigilance; in short, they are meant to gain control over the will.[23]

Meditation, or contemplation, seems especially germane to Milton, who must have spent hours each day in the occupation.[24] Hadot classically defines meditation as "an effort to assimilate an idea, notion, or principle, and make them come alive in the soul."[25] The notion of assimilation has its roots in Neoplatonic contemplation. In both cases, pure contemplation of the Good, the One, the Beautiful results not only in knowing them and their essence, but also in becoming them. In his *Enneads* (6, 9, 10, 14–17), Plotinus describes the moment of transformation through meditation upon an object: "Then the seer no longer sees his object, for in that instant he no longer distinguishes himself from it; he no longer has the impression of two separate things, but *he has, in a sense, become another.*"[26]

The goals of Plotinian philosophy (that is, pure contemplation of the

Good) had a profound impact on many leaders of the early Christian Church, among them Clement of Alexandria, Basil the Great, Gregory of Nyssa, John Chrysostom, and Augustine. Among these figures, Christianity came to be viewed as *the* philosophy, as *the* way of practicing philosophy since it contained the incarnation of the Logos through Jesus Christ. Christianity was concerned with developing an awareness of self as defined in relation to God through Jesus Christ. The Christian philosopher was in constant communion with the active presence of God, and the practice of Christian philosophy was in conforming to the model of Christ, the divine image, through the exercise of reason and will. Hadot quotes Basil: "We must keep watch over our heart with all vigilance . . . to avoid ever losing the thought of God."²⁷ Remembrance of God and meditation upon and obedience to his divine law are central to becoming "fused" with God in will, mind, soul, spirit, action; the object upon which his mind gazes is that which the Christian philosopher becomes. Removing God from one's thoughts was to remove (or, at the very least, limit) God's active presence in one's life. Conversion, for the pre-medieval and medieval Christians, was a daily practice of contemplation, virtue, and obedience rather than a single moment of indoctrination.

This contemplative tradition, therefore, understands that the spiritual life is governed in significant ways by the object of the mind's gaze. When we couple this tradition with the theological tradition, which understands the "skiff" to be a figure of both individual and corporate spiritual life, what is revealed in Milton's parable? We have seen in Origen, Basil, and Augustine that diligence and vigilance must characterize one's treatment of his or her soul, and that this vigilance (or lack thereof) spills over into the community of saints. The question is: to what or to whom does the rudder of one's contemplative soul belong? Upon what is the soul gazing, and in the process *becoming:* the Divine who promises rest, or Leviathan who promises restlessness?

In Milton's parable, the sailor appears to lack the necessary vigilance and discernment required of him to interpret the immediate situation and preserve his small skiff. We gather implicitly that the pilot is inexperienced, perhaps lost, for he is "night-founder'd" and wishes for morning to arrive with greater haste (1.208). By fixing his anchor upon the "slumb'ring" sea beast, the pilot has unwittingly abandoned hope for returning home, finding rest, or simply surviving—a terrifying realization he will have all too soon when he finds himself lurching and plunging at the whims of the great creature. If we push beyond the literal level to the spiritual level of the parable, we find that the sailor of the skiff (the individual soul), in his mooring (in contemplation) on the sea beast, has for all practical purposes given over the control of his craft (mind and will) to Leviathan (Satan) so as to be indistinguishable from the whims (will and desire) of the creature. Such a joining has physical consequences for the sailor (death by drowning) and spiritual consequences for the soul (restlessness and eventual destruction).

Significantly, "Leviathan" derives from the Hebrew *livyâthân* and means "to twine," "to abide with," "to cleave," and "to join." Milton's Leviathan in this passage is an allusion to Isaiah 27:1, in which the Lord "shall punish Leviathan, the piercing serpent, even Leviathan, that crooked serpent; and he shall slay the dragon that is in the sea."[28] The image of the dragon recalls Revelation 12:9 in which John the Divine calls Satan the "great dragon . . . that old serpent . . . which deceiveth the whole world," as well as Revelation, chapter 13, in which the beast "having seven heads and ten horns" (1) rises out of the sea and is given authority by the dragon.[29]

John Calvin offers some relevant insight into "Leviathan," for he, too, explicitly uses the nautical image to describe the perils of the Christian life: "It ought therefore to be observed, that we have continually to do with Satan as with some wild beast, and that the world is the sea in which we sail. We are beset by various wild beasts, which endeavor to upset our ship and sink us to the bottom; and we have no means of defending ourselves and resisting them, if the Lord do not aid us." Calvin emphasizes Satan's "cunning devices" to deceive the elect: "Wonderful are the stratagems with which he comes prepared for doing mischief, and dreadful the cruelty which he exercises against the children of God."[30] The Lord's "aid" is his great sword (Rev. 13:1), but one might also infer that the vigilant soul who cultivates a healthy habit of contemplating the Divine and his workings in the world will be granted a certain kind of illumination to see through the various hermeneutical "stratagems" that Satan sets—the various illusions of stability and safety which threaten the security of the individual and the Church.

Calvin's commentary on Isaiah, chapter 27, also widens the scope of Leviathan's realm to include secular and ecclesial governments. He posits that "leviathan" refers immediately to the king of Egypt, but allegorically extends to Satan and the agents of his kingdom who are constantly at work against the elect. To be sure, the waters of spiritual existence are occupied not only by the solitary figure of Leviathan—he has minions, the "other enemies of the Church,"[31] encompassing the civil and ecclesial powers that may be conspiring against the elect.[32] In Ephesians 6:12 Paul admonishes that the believer wrestles "not against flesh and blood, but against principalities, against powers, against the rulers of the darkness of this world, against spiritual wickedness in high places." Paul indicates that the believer's struggle is ultimately a spiritual one, but some early modern preachers and expositors comment that demonic forces may be at work in current political and ecclesial institutions.[33] This passage, preceded by Paul's exhortation that believers "put on the whole armour of God" (Eph. 6:11), and others focusing on Christian militancy were embraced by the "hotter-sort" of Protestants as legitimate grounds for civil disobedience and even holy warfare.[34]

Clearly for Calvin, "that Sea-beast *Leviathan*" alluded to in Milton's parable is a figure of Satan who will eventually be toppled and brought under judgment. Because the image of Leviathan is associated with biblical prophecy, Milton's allusion to it in the parable becomes apocalyptic.[35] The implicit warning within the parable is that the careless soul and ecclesial community —which lack discernment and discipline, which do not practice virtue, which "gaze" indiscriminately or haphazardly—are in danger of obliteration along with Leviathan, Dragon, and Beast when judgment is rendered.

But while these eschatological consequences are clear, Milton's parable also points to an even more immediate consequence to cleaving to Leviathan: spiritual restlessness, of the sort that occupies the center of Augustine's narrative. In order to draw out this implication we must turn briefly to the figure of the Leviathan of Milton's poem. By examining Satan's own restlessness and peregrinations in *Paradise Lost*, that which occupy the "gaze" of his mind and the minds of his own demonic "ecclesia," we gain greater insight into these spiritual dimensions of the parable as Milton further alerts his congregation of readers to the realities of spiritual life while one is moored upon Leviathan.

One of the recurring motifs in *Paradise Lost* is restlessness and rest: from Satan's trek across the "Illimitable Ocean" of the "wild Abyss" (2.892, 910), through the cosmos to the garden; to the demons' wanderings "O'er many a Frozen, many a Fiery Alp, / Rocks, Caves, Lakes, Fens, Bogs, Dens, and shades of death" (620–21); from the slumber of the angelic throng in heaven "Fann'd with cool Winds" (5.655) and the amorous embraces of the "Blest pair," lulled to sleep by the dulcet songs of nightingales (4.771–75) before the Fall; to the violent surges of biblical history eventuating from the "wand'ring steps and slow" of the solitary pair after their banishment; and finally to the "eternal Paradise of rest" effected by the Son's obedience (12.314). Throughout his epic Milton is preoccupied with divine rest and rebellious restlessness, and he confirms Augustine's assertion, "You have made us for yourself, and our heart is restless, until it rests in you."[36]

We find that what occupies the gaze of Satan's mind and the minds of his demonic ecclesia—that which determines the course and telos of their individual skiffs and collective ship—is nothingness. Recall Augustine's realization that in his spiritual wanderings he became to himself "a region of destitution": "You [my soul] seek the happy life in the region of death; it is not there. How can there be a happy life where there is not even life?"[37] In the poem Satan echoes Augustine's grief when he admits, "which way I fly is Hell; myself am Hell" (4.75). The desolation and pain within, marked by the absence of God's life-giving and life-sustaining Being, are mirrored by the desolation without, in the hellish landscape where the demons "view'd first thir lamentable lot, and found / No rest: through many a dark and dreary Vale / They pass'd, and many a Region dolorous" (2.617–19). Milton goes to great lengths to describe their infernal inheritance, simultaneously a "Dungeon horrible" and a "great Furnace" (1.61–62), whose flames reveal "regions of sorrow" and "doleful shades," and "where peace / And rest can never dwell, hope never comes" (65–66). Much like Milton's Chaos, hell is characterized by its boundlessness and mutability—the only constants are "torture without end," "utter darkness," and "tempestuous fire" (67, 72, 77).

This boundlessness and mutability suggest the demons' inability to contemplate anything of substance for any significant period of time except the pain of their own fallen bodies. But as Peter Fiore explains, within an Augustinian framework even this fixation on their body in pain is *no-thing-ness*. According to Augustine's ontology, wherein "that which exists is good and that which has fallen from existence is evil," the fallen angels now represent "nonentities": non-being.[38] Their fall from God's presence is irreversible. Because Augustinian ontology assumes that every created being has the telos of reaching its particular perfection by participating in God's Being, a "bending back" to God, the fallen angels are no longer able to achieve this perfection and no longer able to participate in Being. Being ("very being itself," as Augustine puts it) contains being, and to change in such a way so as to lose forever one's proper telos is to cease to exist. "I would have no being, I would not have any existence, unless you were in me," Augustine writes. "Or rather, I would have no being if I were not in you, 'of whom are all things, through whom are all things, in whom are all things' (Rom. 11:36)."[39]

No longer participants in the Being that gives being, even the contemplation of their pain—so closely tied to their new identity—is a contemplation of nothingness, and this nothingness gives rise to their restlessness. The demons wander hell's caverns endlessly in search of meaningful occupation and momentary escape from their pain, and the "philosophers" of hell in particular are characterized by their aimlessness, caught "in wand'ring mazes lost" (2.561) as they try to think through the intricacies of a theology with a distorted conception of the *théos*. Like the undisciplined pilot of the skiff they, too, have "cleaved" and "joined" themselves to *livyâthân* in their rebellious misreading, thinking their "dread Emperor" (2.510) to be a secure alternative to the "tyrannous" God, and will hence suffer the same fate. In an odd slippage within the parable, Satan is both reader and text: he is a reader because as a spiritual creature with free will he has been entrusted with navigating spiritual reality; he is a text because he is the Leviathan whose promises for security, presence, and stability are illusory.

If we extend these insights into Milton's parable, we begin to see just how profound its message becomes. To be moored upon Leviathan means for Milton that spiritual life, individual and corporate, is characterized by chronic "misreading," here defined in terms of the shiftlessness of real hunger rather than the anchored discipline of "real presence."[40] One is exiled from the rest afforded by the regenerative and redeeming power of Christ as anchor and ultimate hope—a common meditative emblem in the early modern period.[41] The parable becomes one whose object lesson is centered on a negative exemplum as we conflate the wanderings of Leviathan/Satan and the wanderings of the small skiff anchored upon him.

Nothingness occupies the center of satanic contemplation and theology: the "debt immense of endless gratitude" (4.52) that he cannot pay. His spiritual wanderings stem from his skewed views of grace and obedience, a brand of debtor's theology which Paul addresses on more than one occasion. In Acts, chapter 17, Paul debates the philosophers on Mars Hill who had erected an altar with the inscription "To the unknown God." Concerning this God, Paul declares: "God that made the world and all things therein, seeing that he is Lord of heaven and earth, dwelleth not in temples made with hands; neither is worshipped with men's hands, as though he needed any thing, seeing he giveth to all life, and breath, and all things" (24–25). And in Romans, chapter 4, speaking of Abraham's righteousness, Paul writes: "Now to him that worketh is the reward not reckoned of grace, but of debt. But to him that worketh not, but believeth on him that justifieth the ungodly, his faith is counted for righteousness" (4–5). Paul's sentiment seems to be that God is not and should not be served by human hands as if he needed it, for he is complete in himself and has given everything out of grace as pure gift.[42]

God serves human beings in order to conform them better to his divine image, as we see in Mark 10:45, where Jesus declares that "the Son of man came not to be ministered unto, but to minister, and to give his life a ransom for many." Paul is arguing against the debtor's theology that desires to earn the "wages" of serving God. In Romans 3:23, Paul states that the only "wage" fallen humanity can earn from its "labors" is spiritual death and desolation. The consequence of debtor's theology is that every act of obedience or disobedience then pushes the debtor further into debt, one that cannot be repaid, thereby nullifying the efficacies of grace.

If we return to *Paradise Lost* from our foray into Pauline theology, we find that Satan construes exactly this kind of debtor's theology, and it is this "debt"—this nothingness—which occupies the center of Satan's contemplation. In his soliloquy at the beginning of Book Four, Satan's "bitter memory" (24) of lost Paradise is stirred by his first glimpses of the sun after his fall. He laments not the immediate relationship with the divine that he once had, the proper response to contemplating the visible symbol of God; rather, the beams only remind him of himself in his once glorious state, that "bright eminence" (44) now corrupted, dimming, and ultimately "nonexistent." He meditates on his fall, revealing his fallen theology as well:

> What could be less than to afford him praise,
> The easiest recompense, and pay him thanks,
> How due! yet all his good prov'd ill in me,
> And wrought but malice;
>
> . . . .
>
> The debt immense of endless gratitude,
> So burdensome, still paying, still to owe;
> Forgetful what from him I still receiv'd,
> And understood not that a grateful mind
> By owing owes not, but still pays, at once
> Indebted and discharg'd: what burden then?   (4.46–49, 52–57)

The soul moored upon Leviathan is restless not only because it is has not fastened on an object worthy of contemplation, but also because restlessness is driven by God's constant emanation of grace to complete his work of paradise within. Satan's dilemma stems from a misreading of God's grace. He privileges the contemplation of his *work* of "still paying," that is, continually paying a debt of gratitude over that which he "still receiv'd"; he is "[f]orgetful" (54) of the continual grace and divine love to shape the self in past, present, and future. Satan's theological error is centered on present and future grace, for he cannot envision anything but meaningless repetition that, as he sees it, will never repay the past debt. As Regina Schwartz comments, Satan "depicts an awesome obligation so impossible to fulfill that failure is inevitable: he can only flee such an exacting creditor, declaring moral bankruptcy, as it were."[43] The only wage he can earn for his work is spiritual desolation, a constant emptiness rather than a filling. His debtor's theology assumes the debt *can* be repaid, thus exalting the contemplation of self (not-being) over the divine (very Being itself).

Satan as reader and gazer, as pilot of his own skiff navigating spiritual reality, has substituted a hollow text—himself—for the text that promises a proliferation of meaning and an abundance of rest, the divine name sung in heaven as the "Omnipotent, / Immutable, Immortal, Infinite, / Eternal King; thee Author of all being" (3.372–74). Satan's misreading of the divine text is infectious as he offers his own magnificently carved body, his own "bright eminence," for his cohort of rebellious misreaders to gaze upon rather than upon the Son as messiah (5.756–65). Moored upon this monstrous bulk Leviathan, the demons have little choice but to follow as his ecclesial ship, even as they sluggishly rise from the flames of hell's tumultuous lake.

If we assume Milton's "night-founder'd Skiff" to be a parable of (mis)-reading, Leviathan appears to the undiscerning pilot of the skiff to be a secure text upon which to anchor. But given Augustine's ontology with regard to the fallen angels, Milton's Leviathan as a figure of Satan can finally be no more than a sign without text, unless we understand that text "to be" *no-thing-ness*. In spiritual terms Milton's parable seems to be warning his audience that without conversion, appropriating the Son's obedience in order to cultivate "Virtue, Patience, Temperance, . . . Love" (12.583) so that one might possess the "paradise within thee, happier far" (12.587), human beings are readers without discernment as well as signs without text.

For Milton it appears that proper reading is closely associated with the fruits of divine virtue, carefully tended and maintained through the daily exercise of contemplation and practical obedience. Proper reading for Milton is the discipline of *becoming* that which the soul gazes upon; the ship of one's soul anchoring on the Divine through the reception of a constantly emanating grace and a focused, discerning vision.

III

It is fair to say, however, that Milton is critical of most readers. After all, he is seeking a narrowly construed "fit" audience to receive his poem. So far I have described this fit audience as including those who share Milton's views regarding the role of divine virtue in the act of reading, views that coincide with those of Origen, Basil, and Augustine. It will become clear in this section that Milton's parable of misreaders, those readers who are not anchored in divine virtue, becomes both a lament and an unflinching censure of the powers that be.

Much criticism has focused on Milton's prophetic role as God's sanctified spokesman.[44] Rather than rehearse this line of criticism I want to turn to another context, highly relevant to the parable as a literary form, that is comparatively less discussed but just as compelling: Milton's role as preacher. I hope to make clear that Milton's parable of reading extends to the ships of church and state as a critique of the current historical situation after the Restoration; like the demonic church, they, too, have misread their text(s) for a lack of discernment and have moored upon Leviathan. The same hermeneutical circle between individual skiff and corporate ship is at work in the relation between the individual's exercise of virtue and the properly functioning state. Without Milton's virtuous and disciplined man governing his own skiff, the ships of church and state are in peril of sinking.

Mindele Ann Treip argues that many scholars have neglected the didactic impetus in Milton's epic. She observes that the poem has much in common with homiletics, whose purposes are to "enlighten and instruct fallible man, to comfort and offer hope, and, in the moral sphere, to lead him to the kind of self-understanding and acceptance of individual responsibility which alone can provide a foundation for restoration." Thus the influential Puritan divine John Preston sums up the office of the pulpit when he says that the "end of our preaching is not that you should know, but that you should do and practice. . . . Practice is all in all; so much as you practice, so much you know."[45] Given the didactic purpose of the parable form and the dynamics that it involves with the audience it creates, it is this role that seems most germane to these important passages in *Paradise Lost,* and Milton's own hopes that his poem, composed in his blindness and intended to be read aloud (proclaimed?), find a fit congregation of hearers to interpret and appreciate it. Despite Milton's objection that he decided against a career in the ministry because he was "Church-outed by the Prelats" (*Reason of Church Government,* YP 1:823), he continued to view himself as a preacher and his prose and poetic projects as emanating from his own "Church-outed" pulpit.[46] For Milton, the true minister is one who has the "inward calling of God," whose "own painfull study and diligence . . . manures and improves his ministeriall gifts" (YP 1:715).[47]

Jameela Lares has recently argued that Milton recognized an intimate connection between writing and preaching, and that Christ's College, Cambridge, was the hub of homiletic theory, fostering the work of divines William Perkins, Richard Bernard, William Ames, and William Chappell, Milton's notorious first tutor. Lares insightfully situates Milton within this well-developed homiletic tradition that took its shape from classical rhetoric and was disseminated through the publication of preaching manuals. Milton's decision not to enter the formal ministry was a fairly late one, she argues, and "the idea of the ministry continued to play a role in his imagination and poetics." Additionally, Lares observes that "there is no reason that Milton's desire to be a poet—and especially a godly poet—need displace a ministerial vocation. John Donne continued to write poetry after he took orders, as did George Herbert, Thomas Traherne, and Giles and Phineas Fletcher."[48] In the *Reason of Church Government* (1642) Milton aligns his poetic gifts closely with the office of the pulpit:

These abilities, wheresoever they be found, are the inspired guift of God rarely bestow'd, but yet to some (thought most abuse) in every Nation: and are of power beside the office of a pulpit, to imbreed and cherish in a great people the seeds of vertu, and publick civility, to allay the perturbations of the mind, and set the affections in right tune, to celebrate in glorious and lofty Hymns the throne and equipage of Gods Almightinesse . . . to sing the victorious agonies of Martyrs and Saints . . . to deplore the general relapses of Kingdoms and States from justice and Gods true worship. (YP 1:816–17)

Here Milton collapses the aims of the preacher and the poet: to instill a love of virtue, to address the psychological state of the audience, to foster proper worship, to celebrate the martyrs, and to denounce vice.

One area of homiletic theory and practice that Lares does not consider, however, is the tradition of the medieval exemplum. While the medieval exemplum had largely been eclipsed by Reformation proclamations of the Word and the many sermons aimed at teaching or refuting doctrine, we find Milton creatively reworking that tradition in his parable.[49] In the beast exemplum, popular with lay audiences, snakes, turtles, birds, and whales become the loci for meditations on human nature. One exemplum tells the story of sailors who, mistaking a "sea pig" for an island, disembark onto its back, light a fire, and are subsequently drowned when the creature plunges below the waves.[50] We may imagine that this popular exemplum was used as, among other things, a picture of erroneous discernment and spiritual restlessness. It also appears that Milton participates in the homiletic tradition of the politically charged "public exemplum" with some qualification. Interestingly, Larry Scanlon notes that the public exemplum "had a propensity toward the evil example, toward narratives which demonstrate the efficacy of their *sententiae* by enacting violations of them." Consequently, the negative exemplum insists "on the inherent disorder of the historical world it addresses."[51] Thus it seems likely that exempla are intended to communicate a sense of urgency for political and ecclesial leaders to soberly consider their civic and moral responsibilities.

The negative public exemplum is closely tied to the popular early modern homiletic style of correction and reproof, which "called for the preacher to identify deviations from the standard of virtue and to dissuade his hearers from continuing in such deviations." Jameela Lares quotes William Chappell, Milton's notorious first tutor at Christ's College, who comments on this method: "[The presence of the evil] may be taken chiefly from the proper adjuncts, and opposites without a medium; because that from these we may always argue, both affirmatively and negatively." Thus, she continues, preachers employing this mode are operating on the rhetorical principle, expounded by Aquinas in the *Summa*, that "the straight is the measure both of the straight and of the crooked."[52]

Milton's parable of the skiff centers on just this kind of negative example, and it involves the archetypal figure of moral and spiritual failure. In this context, the long angelic narration of Satan's spiritual rebellion in Books Five and Six can be read as the dramatic subtext and extended negative exemplum story for the compressed parable of the "night-foundered Skiff" whose movements and destiny are soon to be indistinguishable from Leviathan's when the great sea creature awakens.[53] The boundlessness of hell, undisciplined by the divine love of the "Omnific Word" (7.217) that calmed and silenced the churning Abyss at Creation, and the restlessness characteristic of its new inhabitants insist on the inherent disorder of the *spiritual* world that it addresses.

The image of the ship upon the seas can be extended, I would suggest, to include the political and ecclesial worlds as well, such that the image reflects the restlessness and disorder of the historical situation in which Milton finds himself in the tumultuous wake of the Restoration. Consequently, we might consider *Paradise Lost* as its own species of *Fürstenspiegel*, offering incidental lessons of virtue and leadership to church and civil leaders. Governing magistrates, argues Milton, need to develop the virtue of discernment—right reading—as they scan the political and ecclesial situations before them.

But there are important differences between the medieval public exemplum and Milton's exemplum. Where the classical and medieval public exemplum was employed to confer and recenter power on the prince or monarch, Milton the preacher uses it to criticize and to deconstruct the monarch's power by associating the powers-that-be with the undisciplined pilot who lacks the skill, discernment, and necessary virtue to read the text before him and bring his ship into a safe harbor. As Milton argues in the *Tenure of Kings and Magistrates* (1648), titles of authority and kingship are granted "in trust from the People, to the Common good of them all, in whom the power yet remaines fundamentally, and cannot be tak'n from them, without a violation of thir natural birthright" (YP 3:202); the tyrant is "he who regarding neither Law nor the common good, reigns onley for himself and his faction" (YP 3:212).[54] Consequently, while the medieval public exemplum made nobility the exclusive ground for moral law and hence authority, Milton makes the exercise of right reason and virtue under the auspices of obedience to the divine will the bedrock to any governing authority, be it collectively embodied in a representative figure or dispersed in a commonwealth.[55] Milton's tyrant cannot achieve the common good because he lacks personal virtue; the tyrant's version of kingly rule is the exercise of brute power without the virtue of discernment, and the people and nation will suffer because of it.

The basis of freedom, argues Milton (1654), is piety and *self*-government: "to be free is precisely the same as to be pious, wise, just, and temperate. . . . [H]e who cannot control himself . . . should not be his own master, but like a ward be given over to the power of another. Much less should he be put in charge of the affairs of other men, or of the state. . . . If to be a slave is hard, and you do not wish it, learn to obey right reason, to master yourselves" (*Second Defense*, YP 4:684).[56] As Sharon Achinstein comments, "Milton was surprisingly committed to a single goal, that of making his audience fit to achieve self-governance through training in virtue." For Milton virtue and the exercise of self-government, how one navigates his own skiff, are the bases of a just and responsible politics—the governance of the ship of state.[57] Through his parable, Milton the man of virtue and the ideal reader distances himself from the unfortunate sailor of the small skiff, and in the process distances himself from the current civil and ecclesial powers. Milton's pilot has not taken greater care in the learning of his craft, and by his carelessness has anchored himself upon the sea beast.

In *The Reason of Church Government* Milton writes, "there is not that thing in the world of more grave and urgent importance throughout the whole life of man, then is discipline" (YP 1:751). "Discipline" is Milton's mantra throughout the tract. Personal discipline, the government of one's soul, extends for Milton beyond individual responsibility and bleeds into the political and ecclesial realms. For the "disciplined" man, free of spiritual restlessness and anchored in his faith, is he that must be given responsibility for the government of the nation and church. Milton continues:

how much lesse can we believe that God would leave his fraile and feeble, though not lesse beloved Church here below to the perpetuall stumble of conjecture and disturbance in this our darke voyage without the card and compasse of Discipline. . . . [B]ut if it [the happiness of the civil state] be at all the worke of man, it must be of such a one as is a true knower of himselfe, and himselfe in whom contemplation and practice, wit, prudence, fortitude, and eloquence must be rarely met. (YP 1:752–53)

Here we see Milton making full use of the nautical metaphor beyond the auspices of the poem. The "night-foundered Skiff" is no less than the ships of church and state—a common conflation among the early church fathers as well, particularly in regard to the former, as the church negotiated its way upon the dark floodwaters of the world. The ship of state metaphor is an ancient one that appears in Plato's *Republic,* Book Six. In his discussion with Adeimantus about a mutinous crew, Socrates explains that "the true pilot must give his attention to the time of the year, the seasons, the sky, the winds, the stars, and all that pertains to his art if he is to be a true ruler of a ship. . . . With such goings on aboard ship [that is, mutiny] do you not think that the real pilot would in very deed be called a stargazer, an idle babbler, a useless fellow, by the sailors in ships managed after this fashion?" (488d–89).[58] Milton, who surely considered himself one of the "true pilots" of Cromwell's administration, must have been called these names and worse. In *The Readie and Easie Way* (March 1660) he defends his position and the present course: "The ship of the Commonwealth is alwaies under sail; they [the general council] sit at the stern; and if they stear well, what need is ther to change them; it being rather dangerous?" (YP 7:433–34). As is evident, for Milton the rigors of personal discipline can save a sinking church without direction and can guide the citizenry of a nation very nearly into bliss itself.

Milton returns to the nautical exemplum at the end of the poem during Adam's viewing of biblical history as narrated by the archangel Michael. Similarly, the figure of the man in whom are "rarely met" the virtues that Milton esteems appears in Noah, with whom we can now safely intuit Milton identifies. Michael narrates:

> the floating Vessel swum
> Uplifted; and secure with beaked prow
> Rode tilting o'er the Waves, all dwellings else
> Flood overwhelm'd, and them with all thir pomp
> Deep under water roll'd; Sea cover'd Sea,
> Sea without shore; and in thir Palaces
> Where luxury late reign'd, Sea-monsters whelp'd
> And stabl'd.   (11.745–52)

As the saving remnant, itself a trope throughout Scripture, the "true virtue" (790) of those in the ark is contrasted with the "pleasure, ease, and sloth, / Surfeit, and lust . . . wantonness and pride" (794–95) of those without—the same vices Milton often uses to characterize the civil and ecclesial governments.

Thinking themselves safe in their "luxury" and without discernment, the civil and ecclesial governments, too, have moored upon Leviathan. And, as is soon to be the case of our sailor, these institutions have been corrupted and destroyed by their careless attachment, while the sea monsters mock their self-assured resting places, the "palaces" wherein once they "reign'd." Noah is hailed as "the only Son of light / In a dark Age" and the "one just Man alive" (808–9, 818). Despite the horrifying implications for the rest of humanity, Michael's exposition of Noah ends hopefully: "For one Man found so perfet and so just, / That God voutsafes to raise another World / From him, and all his anger to forget" (876–78). In Noah's steadfastness Milton finds comfort that perhaps God will raise another world out of him, a man broken, blind, and dejected in the wake of the Restoration, but a man no less sanctioned as God's own, and God's ideal reader.

Northwestern University

NOTES

I wish to thank Regina Schwartz and Michael Lieb for their seasoned eyes and intellectual generosity, Scott Huelin for the many enlightening conversations on Hadot and spiritual exercises, Jameela Lares for her encouragement and fine research on Milton and preaching, and Albert Labriola for his splendid gift of discernment during this essay's development.

1. All quotations of Milton's poetry are from *John Milton: Complete Poems and Major Prose,* ed. Merritt Y. Hughes (New York, 1957). All quotations of Milton's prose are from *The Complete Prose Works of John Milton,* 8 vols., ed. Don M. Wolfe et al. (New Haven, Conn., 1953–82), cited parenthetically in the text by volume and page number as YP.

2. Compare, for example, *Paradise Lost* 2.285–90, 636–40, 918–20, 1041–44; 4.159–65, 556–60; 5.264–66; 9.513–15; *Paradise Regained* 3.209–10; *Samson Agonistes* 197–200; 1044–45; *Of Reformation,* YP 1:596; *Reason of Church Government,* YP 1:753, 821; *Doctrine and Discipline of Divorce,* YP 2:254; *Tenure of Kings and Magistrates,* YP 3:257; *Eikonoklastes,* YP 3:416, 501; *Readie and Easie Way,* YP 7:433–34, 458.

3. For alternate readings of this epic simile, see Richard J. DuRocher, *Milton and Ovid* (Ithaca, N.Y., 1985), 134–35; Christopher Grose, *Milton's Epic Process* (New Haven, Conn., 1973), 150–52.

4. See Jackson Campbell Boswell, *Milton's Library* (New York, 1975). Milton had an extensive and wide-ranging collection of patristic writings in his library, and the works of Origen, Basil, and Augustine in particular were prominent. While he does not allow his own interpretive authority to be eclipsed by them, Milton does not wholly reject the work of the fathers (compare *Of Reformation,* YP 1:560). For a study of Milton and Origen, see Harry F. Robins, "*If This Be Heresy*": *A Study of Milton and Origen* (Urbana, 1963); for Milton's relation to Augustine, see Peter Fiore, *Milton and Augustine: Patterns of Augustinian Thought in "Paradise Lost"* (University Park, Pa., 1981). Milton's connection to Basil has yet to be fully explored, but he cites Basil in his prose. Compare *Of Reformation* (YP 1:565); *Areopagitica* (YP 2:510); *Tenure of Kings and Magistrates* (YP 3:212); *Eikonoklastes* (YP 3:518).

5. See Henri de Lubac, *Medieval Exegesis: The Four Senses of Scripture,* vol. 1, trans. Mark Sebanc (Grand Rapids, 1998). Significantly, the premedieval and medieval exegetes of Scripture assume the need for personal virtue and discipline *before* one begins the task of interpretation. Without the necessary training, or spiritual exercise, the expositor ran the dangerous risk of running afoul in his interpretation. Thus, interpretation is not so much performed *on* the text as much as it is lived first by the expositor. Provocatively, Milton seems to share this view of the practice of interpretation.

6. See Madelein Boucher, *The Mysterious Parable* (Washington, D.C., 1977). For the purposes of this essay, Boucher's clear and simple definition suffices: "The *parable,* then . . . is a structure consisting of *a tropical narrative, or a narrative having two levels of meaning;* this structure functions as *religious or ethical rhetorical speech*" (23; emphasis in original). Further, "the interpretation of a parable is always ethical or theological discourse" (30). For key contemporary scholarship on the parable, see Frank Kermode, *The Genesis of Secrecy* (Cambridge, Mass., 1979); and *Parable and Story in Judaism and Christianity,* ed. Clemens Thom and Michael Wyschogrod (New York, 1989). For studies of the parable and postmodern theory, see especially the works of John Dominic Crossan: *In Parables: The Challenge of the Historical Jesus* (New York, 1973); *The Dark Interval: Towards a Theology of Story* (Niles, Ill., 1975); *Cliffs of Fall: Paradox and Polyvalence in the Parables of Jesus* (New York, 1980). For a critique of Crossan, see Lynn Poland, *Literary Criticism and Biblical Hermeneutics: A Critique of Formalist Approaches* (Chicago, 1985).

7. Kermode, *The Genesis of Secrecy,* 3. The particular scripture that Kermode has in mind is Mark 4:10–13. See also David Stern, "Jesus' Parables and Rabbinic Literature," in Thom and Wyschogrod, *Parable and Story in Judaism and Christianity,* 42–80. Arguing that the parables of Jesus derive from the rabbinic *mâshal* tradition, Stern observes that the *mâshal* "tends to leave it to the audience to figure out, upon reflection for itself" (58). Boucher, *The Mysterious Parable,*

24–25, maintains that the *mâshal* tradition existed from the time of the composition of 1 and 2 Samuel and 1 and 2 Kings, and that there are at least three examples in the Hebrew Bible when the hearer of a parable utterly fails to comprehend it: 2 Samuel 12:1–14, 14:4–13; 1 Kings 20:39–42.

8. Boucher, *The Mysterious Parable*, 25.

9. C. H. Dodd, *The Parables of the Kingdom* (New York, 1935), 23.

10. For more on how Milton and other revolutionary writers construct a "fit" audience, see Sharon Achinstein, *Milton and the Revolutionary Reader* (Princeton, N.J., 1994). Milton's "aim became not simply to pass on his revolutionary messages in code, but to mold a readership that was increasingly required to know how to decipher conflicting interpretations" (15). See also David Loewenstein, *Representing Revolution in Milton and His Contemporaries: Religion, Politics, and Polemics in Radical Puritanism* (Cambridge, 2001), chap. 7. Loewenstein similarly asserts that *Paradise Lost* "constantly challenges its engaged readers by showing them how to discern the treacherous ambiguities and contradictions of political rhetoric and behavior" (203).

11. Barbara Kiefer Lewalski, *Protestant Poetics and the Seventeenth-Century Religious Lyric* (Princeton, N.J., 1979), 86. The tight and lucid image easily lends itself to early modern emblematic theory. Lewalski quotes Francis Quarles, the collector and author of *Emblemes* (1635), who explicitly links parable and emblem: "An Embleme is but a silent Parable" (sig. A3) (185). In Sir J. A. Astry's *The Royal Politician Represented in One Hundred Emblems* (London, 1700), the trope is extended to the ship of state with the emblem displaying a ship in full sail on turbulent waves, and the prince figured as the ship's pilot. The most extensive use of the nautical metaphor, and most important to Milton, is Dante, *Divine Comedy* (passim) and Spenser, *Fairie Queene*, 2.12.3–29. For examples of sermons in the early modern period that employ the nautical metaphor, see Robert Wilkinson, *The Merchant Royall, being a sermon preached in 1607 in praise of the wife, wherein she is likened to a merchant ship* (London, 1607); Christopher Love, *The naturall Man's Case stated; or, An Exact Map of the little world man . . . in XVII Sermons*, sermon 12 (London, 1652); William Johnson, *A Sermon Preached upon a Great Deliverance at Sea* (London, 1672).

12. Origen, *Homilies on Genesis and Exodus*, trans. Ronald E. Heine, in *Fathers of the Early Church*, vol. 71 (Washington, D.C., 1982), 78–79.

13. Ibid., 86–87.

14. Basil the Great, *Address to Young Men on Reading Greek Literature*, trans. Roy J. Deferrari (Cambridge, Mass., 1934), 385.

15. One might recall that John admonishes: "believe not every spirit, but try the spirits whether they are of God" (1 John 4:1). John's warning is directed to believers to cultivate spiritual discernment in order not to be deceived by false teachers.

16. Basil, *Address to Young Men*, 387–89. See *The Odyssey*, trans. Robert Fitzgerald (New York, 1990). Odysseus did not stop up his ears; warned by Circe of the treacherous song of the Sirens, he was bound to the mast in order to hear the alluring Siren-song (12.190–96). It is provocative to think that Basil's mistake is purposeful, thereby demonstrating to his audience that they were already hyperconscious of such details, and thus prone to the very dangers he is describing.

17. Basil, *Address to Young Men*, 389, 381; emphasis added.

18. Augustine, *Confessions*, trans. Henry Chadwick (Oxford, 1991), 3.3.5, 3.1.1, 7.16.22.

19. See Camille Bennett, "The Conversion of Vergil: The *Aeneid* in Augustine's *Confessions*," *Revue des Études Augustiniennes* 34 (1988): 47–69.

20. Compare Augustine, *Confessions*, 4.16.31.

21. Ibid., 10.3.4–4.6; emphasis added.

22. For more on the spiritual aspects of reading, see Scott G. Huelin, "Spiritual Reading:

Tropology, Discernment and Early Modern European Literature" (Ph.D. diss., University of Chicago, 2002), chap. 1.

23. Pierre Hadot, *Philosophy as a Way of Life*, trans. Michael Chase, ed. Arnold I. Davidson (Cambridge, 1995), 83 (Hadot's emphasis), 84.

24. See Hughes, *Complete Poems and Major Prose*, 1022–23. John Aubrey, an early biographer of Milton, describes a typical day for Milton spent in contemplation. The classic work on Milton (and other poets) with regard to meditation is Louis Martz, *The Poetry of Meditation: A Study in English Religious Literature of the Seventeenth Century*, 2d ed. (New Haven, Conn., 1962).

25. Hadot, *Philosophy as a Way of Life*, 112 n. 38.

26. Quoted in ibid., 101, Hadot's emphasis.

27. Quoted in ibid., 132.

28. Leviathan also appears in Job, chapter 41, during God's rebuke from the whirlwind. Here Leviathan is a fearsome creature, and no one but God can control or tame him. Psalm 104 also mentions leviathan, but in more positive terms as one of God's glorious creations. Milton echoes the Psalmist's version in his retelling of Creation in *Paradise Lost* 7.412.

29. This is the sense that the *OED* captures: "leviathan" is the "great enemy of God, Satan."

30. John Calvin, *Commentary on the Book of the Prophet Isaiah*, 2d vol. (Edinburgh, 1851), 247.

31. Ibid., 246.

32. The *OED* cites Thomas Hobbes's use (1651) of "leviathan": "used by Hobbes for: the organism of political society, the commonwealth."

33. See Bernard Capp, "The Political Dimension of Apocalyptic Thought," in *The Apocalypse in English Renaissance Thought and Literature: Patterns, Antecedents and Repercussions*, ed. C. A. Patrides and Joseph Wittreich (Ithaca, N.Y., 1984): 93–124.

34. See Darren Oldridge, *Religion and Society in Early Stuart England* (Brookfield, Vt., 1998). Oldridge maintains that the discourses of disobedience, persecution, and Christian militancy in Puritan preaching were some of the major factors leading to the English civil war.

35. See C. A. Patrides, " 'Something like Prophetick strain': Apocalyptic Configurations in Milton," in Patrides and Wittreich, *The Apocalypse*, 207–37.

36. Augustine, *Confessions*, 1.1. For an insightful treatment of divine Sabbath rest in the poem, see Michael Lieb, " 'Holy Rest': A Reading of *Paradise Lost*," *ELH* 39 (1972): 238–54.

37. Augustine, *Confessions*, 2.10, 4.12.18.

38. Fiore, *Milton and Augustine*, 16. John Leonard discusses an aspect of this "non-being" in " 'Though of Thir Names': The Devils in *Paradise Lost*," in *Milton Studies* 21, ed. James D. Simmonds (Pittsburgh, 1985): 157–78.

39. Augustine, *Confessions*, 1.2.2.

40. See Regina Schwartz, "Real Hunger: Milton's Version of the Eucharist," in *Religion and Literature* 31 (autumn 1999): 1–18.

41. See Lewalski, *Protestant Poetics*, 200–201. Lewalski observes that John Donne adopted a new personal seal after his ordination, described in Isaak Walton's *Lives* (London, 1670) as depicting the body of Christ "extended upon an Anchor, like those which Painters draw when they would present us with the picture of Christ crucified on the Cross: his [Donne's], varying no otherwise then to affix him to an Anchor (the Emblem of hope)" (56).

42. See Rowan Williams, "On Being Creatures," in *On Christian Theology* (Oxford, 2000). "God creates 'in God's interest' " (74), and God's interest is to act entirely for humanity's sake in "being for" his creation as pure gift.

43. Regina Schwartz, *Remembering and Repeating: On Milton's Theology and Poetics* (Chicago, 1993), 68.

44. See, for example, William Kerrigan, *The Prophetic Milton* (Charlottesville, Va., 1974).

45. Mindele Ann Treip, *Allegorical Poetics and the Epic* (Lexington, Ky., 1994), 222; John Preston, *The Breastplate of Faith and Love* (London, 1634), 2.224–26.

46. Many scholars have recently reassessed the sermon and the role of the preacher in the early modern period. One is *The English Sermon Revised: Religion, Literature and History 1600–1750,* ed. Lori Anne Ferrell and Peter McCullough (Manchester, 2000). Others include Lori Anne Ferrell, *Government by Polemic: James I, the King's Preachers, and the Rhetoric of Conformity, 1603–1625* (Stanford, 1998), and Peter McCullough, *Sermons at Court: Religion and Politics in Elizabethan and Jacobean Preaching* (Cambridge, 1998).

47. See Augustine, *On Christian Doctrine,* trans. D. W. Robertson Jr. (Upper Saddle Hall, N.J., 1958). Augustine's treatise was *the* central patristic text for the development of homiletic theory in the early modern period. Milton shares Augustine's view that the best interpreter of Scripture and the best preacher have a clean mind and heart (1.10). Note in this example Augustine's return to the nautical trope to describe virtue's relation to interpretation.

48. Jameela Lares, *Milton and the Preaching Arts* (Pittsburgh, 2001), 28.

49. See Larry Scanlon, *Narrative, Authority and Power: The Medieval Exemplum and the Chaucerian Tradition* (Cambridge, 1994), esp. chaps. 4 and 5. Scanlon draws a distinction between the sermon exemplum and the public exemplum. The former was increasingly employed by itinerant preachers to teach lay audiences and blended folklore with hagiography. The latter was derived from classical exempla dealing with the *rei publicae* and was used to teach civic leaders about public duty and the centrality of moral order. In this way, notes Scanlon, these public exempla were closely related to the Carolingian *Fürstenspiegel* (mirror of princes) produced by clerics who advised the court on the moral education of princes.

50. G. R. Owst, *Literature and Pulpit in Medieval England* (Cambridge, 1933), 203.

51. Scanlon, *Narrative, Authority and Power,* 81.

52. Lares, *Milton and the Preaching Arts,* 144. By Milton's time the sermon modes had taken solid shape: teaching, rebuttal, training, correcting, and comfort—scripturally derived from 2 Timothy 3:16, and expounded upon in many preaching manuals. William Chappell, *The Preacher* (London, 1656), 155, quoted in ibid., 144. Aquinas quoted in ibid., 145; see 261 n.18.

53. See ibid., 151–58. Lares makes the provocative argument that Raphael's instruction of Adam in these books is an instance of private preaching.

54. Compare John of Salisbury, *Policraticus,* ed. Cary J. Nederman (Cambridge, 1990). Milton shares the bishop's distinction between the prince and tyrant (4.1). Yet Milton would disagree with the bishop's unwavering confidence in nobility and his assertion that the vices of a regent must be tolerated (6.24).

55. On medieval nobility as authority, see Scanlon, *Narrative, Authority and Power,* 111.

56. Compare "On Regeneration" in *The Christian Doctrine* (YP 6:461): "This is how supernatural renovation works. It restores man's natural faculties of faultless understanding and of free will more completely than before." The proper "government" of oneself, it seems, hinges on conversion.

57. Sharon Achinstein, *Milton and the Revolutionary Reader,* 8. See Plato, *Protagoras,* in *The Collected Dialogues of Plato,* ed. Edith Hamilton and Huntington Cairns (Princeton, N.J., 1961), 324d–25b. Milton shares Plato's assumption, made throughout the Socratic dialogues, that the state is only as just as its citizens.

58. Plato, *The Republic,* 488d–89.

"HIS TYRANNY WHO REIGNS": THE BIBLICAL ROOTS OF DIVINE KINGSHIP AND MILTON'S REJECTION OF "HEAV'N'S KING"

Michael Bryson

Kingdom and magistracy, whether supreme or subordinate, is without difference called "a human ordinance."

John Milton, *Tenure of Kings and Magistrates*

I. MILTON AND HIS CRITICS

READING MILTON'S POETRY and prose side by side raises profound questions that tend to recur. Why does John Milton, the antimonarchical rebel who in *Tenure of Kings and Magistrates* defends before all of Europe the beheading of Charles I, subsequently choose to portray God as a king in *Paradise Lost?* Why does the man who declares by way of condemnation in *Eikonoklastes* that monarchy was founded by Nimrod, "the first that hunted after Faction" (YP 3:466), seem to confound his own position by later depicting the Father as an unabashed monarch?[1] One prominent answer to questions of this nature has been that Milton (the political thinker) rejects Charles's earthly kingship while Milton (the orthodox Christian) simultaneously accepts—even embraces—God's heavenly kingship.

Tensions between Milton's representations of heavenly and earthly kingship, however, are not so much purged as *highlighted* by the strenuous and often contorted arguments put forth to reconcile Milton's parallel portrayals of Charles I and the heavenly king. One such argument insists that there is no parallel whatsoever, or, at the very least, that those who find such a parallel are not to be taken seriously; Joan Bennett, in *Reviving Liberty*, insists that finding such a parallel is "Romantic." According to Bennett, "Romantic attempts to link his God with Charles I as monarchs and Satan with Cromwell and Milton as revolutionaries are widely considered to have been mistaken," a statement that seems to imply that the widely held or widely rejected nature of an idea somehow constitutes evidence of the truth or falsity of the idea itself.[2]

Another well-known and influential reaction is that of Stevie Davies, who, in *Images of Kingship in "Paradise Lost,"* offers a curious description of

111

Milton and his project: "England's defender of the regicide, whose epic concerns a rebellion against the monarchy of Heaven together with a defense of that monarchy."[3] To resolve apparent opposition between the political Milton and the theological Milton, and to answer the question of why Milton would impute to his poetic Father the very royal image that he found so repugnant in nonpoetic "real life," Davies elaborates upon a distinction between "oriental" and "feudal" monarchies. The final implication of her arguments is that Satan's monarchy, depicted in terms of "oriental" despotism, is tyrannical, whereas the Father's "western" monarchy is ideal.

Robert Fallon takes a slightly different approach. He suggests that Milton actually has no problem with kingship at all. What Milton does detest, according to Fallon, is the Stuart monarchy. Fallon argues from the fact that Milton had nothing to say about "Philip IV of Spain, Louis XIV of France, John IV of Portugal, Charles X of Sweden, and Frederick III of Denmark," not to mention other absolute rulers with whose regimes Milton would have had at least a passing familiarity in his role as Latin secretary. Somewhat surprisingly, given the evidence of Milton's prose writings, Fallon maintains that "Milton did not reject *all* kings but reserved his condemnation for those who used their power tyrannically." In support of his contention, Fallon declares that the evidence of Milton's prose is "questionable" as a basis for evaluating his attitudes toward monarchy.[4]

In evaluating the evidence of Milton's prose, I believe that it is of the utmost importance to keep in mind that Milton is writing to win. His prose is a competitive instrument, and as such it may seem to present inconsistent views of Milton's theological and political attitudes, especially on the matter of kingship. Reuben Sanchez reminds us that Milton's prose involved shifting self-presentational strategies: "Milton's self-presentation varies from prose tract to prose tract because of the type of argument he makes and the type of persona he creates for the better persuasiveness of that argument. The persona and decorum [and, I would add, the emphasis] of a given tract, therefore, are particular aspects of Milton's response to an immediate occasion."[5] Milton's persona, decorum, and rhetorical emphasis are in some sense the equivalent of battle strategies or game plans; individual elements of Milton's overall belief system are subordinated to the goal of winning whatever argument in which he is involved. The tepid—and somewhat embarrassing—defense of Jeroboam in *A Defence of the People of England* is an excellent example of how Milton, in the pursuit of victory, will make a move that would, in a less immediately agonistic circumstance, be repellent to him. Thus, I think it is problematic at best to focus, as Fallon does, on Milton's flattering of Queen Christina in *A Second Defence,* a strategy Milton pursues in an attempt to advertise and consolidate what he considered to be his triumph over Salmasius.

Quoting from *Tenure of Kings and Magistrates,* Fallon suggests that Milton approves of "just" kings; however, when Milton says, "look how great a good and happiness a just King is, so great a mischeife is a Tyrant" (YP 3:212), this statement is offered in the polemical context of a crisis-ridden nation deposing, and executing, a single unjust king. In and of itself, this passage is not an argument for or against *kingship;* Milton's consistency is not so easily undermined.[6] By the time Milton pens the above-quoted phrase from *Tenure of Kings and Magistrates,* he has already outlined a teleology by which he makes clear his opinion that kingship is a regrettable consequence of the Fall. The rare individual may be a "just" king; but kingship itself is a curse.

In support of his suggestion that Milton rejected only such kings as failed to steer clear of despotism, Fallon, like Davies, suggests that the kingship of heaven is a kind of Platonic archetype, a transcendent reality of monarchy (for which Milton secretly pined) of which earthly kingships are pale and presumptuous imitations:

The Kingdom of Heaven had to be seen as the most splendid imaginable with all the institutions of royal rule carried out to their most dazzling extremes, its subjects more numerous, their praise more exalted, their obedience more unswerving, their knees more willingly bent, and their devotion more profound than any earthly monarch could possibly command. . . . in showing how God rules, [Milton] drew a picture of government truly sublime and warned temporal rulers not to reach for it.[7]

Heaven could not possibly be more oppressive, wearying, and grindingly contemptuous of its vassals than could the Stuart monarchy—except in the formulation that Fallon here suggests is Milton's own.

Painting heaven as an impossibly glorious monarchy is the move of a closet (or open) royalist, a move more befitting Robert Filmer and Thomas Hobbes than Milton. G. Wilson Knight (though he would have argued that Milton's heaven was a model for human monarchy to imitate, rather than a model intended to shame human monarchy out of existence) constructed much this kind of royalist Milton in the service of arguments designed, in part, as a professorial rallying cry in the British war effort against Hitler. Knight argued that Milton was a defender of constitutional monarchy, claimed that Milton's attitude, even during the Republican years, was "sympathetic to the idea of royalty," and resorted to an argument similar to that of Robert Fallon: Milton said nothing derogatory about numerous monarchs and had praise for Queen Christina of Sweden.[8] Though Milton writes to Christina that he has not "uttered a word against kings, but only against tyrants" (YP 4:604), it should not be forgotten that Milton is writing here less out of principle than out of polemical purpose, writing both to consolidate and extend the rhetorical victory over Salmasius achieved with the earlier *Defence of the People of England*.

The odd thing about a monarchical picture of heaven, wedded as it is to a larger claim that Milton opposed only bad or tyrannical monarchies, is that a heaven in which "all the institutions of royal rule [are] carried out to their most dazzling extremes" is a heaven worse than the Stuart monarchy, not better. The fawning and scraping, bowing and continual praise singing of such a heaven is not something "truly sublime," but something oppressive, frightening, and deplorable. In *Paradise Lost,* none of the characters who live (or lived) under heaven's monarchy denies its oppressive nature. When Satan characterizes heaven as a place of cringing and servile adoration, significantly, the unfallen angels *do not disagree.* When Satan accuses Gabriel of having "practis'd distances to cringe" in heaven, Gabriel responds with a taunt of his own: "who more than thou / Once fawn'd and cring'd and servilely adore'd / Heav'n's awful Monarch?" (*Paradise Lost* 4.945, 958–60). Empson has characterized this taunt as evidence of "a very unattractive Heaven," one in which wincing, flinching, and genuflecting have become so ingrained in their angelic (and demonic) practitioners that those who are sycophantic point accusing fingers at the obsequious.[9]

Milton's description in *The Ready and Easy Way* of the fawning and cringing that take place in the court of a human king is of a piece with the angelic and demonic descriptions of heaven in *Paradise Lost:* "a king must be ador'd like a Demigod, with a dissolute and haughtie court about him . . . to pageant himself up and down in progress *among the perpetual bowings and cringings of an abject people*" (YP 7:425–26; emphasis added). How Milton could possibly have imagined that by using "the very practices that he deplored in temporal monarchy" he would be able to "create a King of Heaven so glorious and a court so splendid that it put his idolatrous imitators to shame"[10] is a point none of the aforementioned critics adequately addresses. There is something almost Gnostic about such a view of Milton's purposes, something that goes far beyond Milton's own paradigmatic epistemology of knowing good by knowing evil, and which enters the territory of imagining good by exaggerating the known terms of evil. By this logic, God is simply an impossibly powerful Charles I.

Nevertheless, Fallon has identified something important here: Milton's poetic God is an impossibly powerful tyrannical figure. However, Milton is not creating such an image of God in order to put "idolatrous imitators to shame," but to express his contempt for idolatry itself. Idolatry is worship of an image, the confusion of a representation with that which is represented, and for Milton the image of God as a wildly exaggerated temporal monarch would be one neither to be worshipped, nor to be admired, nor revered. I believe that Milton offers the monarchical image as an object of contempt, not an object of reverence.

I must emphasize, however, that the Father whom Milton presents in *Paradise Lost* should not be perceived as identical to the Father described in *De Doctrina Christiana*.[11] In writing *Paradise Lost*, or any work in which the figure of God appears, Milton works with images and conceptions of God that may not always be used in an attempt to try to define what God is. I contend, in fact, that Milton's image of the Father in *Paradise Lost* is an attempt to portray what God is not. I think we must be extremely cautious about assuming that Milton's poetic representations of the Father are intended to be synonymous with whatever concept or concepts Milton identifies elsewhere with the word "God." The God of Milton's theology is not identical to the Father in Milton's poetry. Each is merely an image, a way of imagining God.

Imagining God has been one of the central difficulties of Christianity since the Gnostics. When they posited the creator of the physical world as evil, the Gnostics were arguing that this god was, for all intents and purposes, actually the devil.[12] However, despite the assiduous labors of such church fathers as Hyppolytus, Tertullian, and Augustine, Gnostic doubts about the Christian God have resolutely refused to be dispelled throughout the ages. The Gnostic image of an evil god has not died; as late as the nineteenth century, Gnostic images continued to appear. William Blake's demiurgic creations Urizen and Nobodaddy manifest the continuing poetic energy and the historical staying power of the idea of divine evil. But the Gnostics accused the creator of the physical world, not to defame, but to defend another image of God. When they argued that the creator is a dark and evil demiurge, the Gnostics were trying to account for the existence of evil in the world while simultaneously placing the blame for that evil on something or someone other than the supreme divinity. The Gnostic move is familiar enough: credit for all good is given to the supreme God, and blame for all evil is placed on a "devil."

The real question, then, that separates the "Orthodox" from the "Gnostic" is not, "Is God good?" but "How is God to be imagined so that his goodness is made obvious?" For both Gnostic and Orthodox early Christians, the goodness of the supreme God was simply assumed. What was at issue was not God's goodness, but the way in which that supreme God was to be imagined. The Orthodox, who clung to the idea that physical creation was good, imagined God as the creator of the physical universe. The Gnostic, who regarded flesh and the physical creation as evil, imagined God as a being higher than the demiurge who created the imperfect earth and the sinful human condition. Each group imagined the other's god as evil; each group believed the other's god to be, in actuality, a devil. But each group also imagined its own god in terms it perceived as good. In essence, each group invented its own arguments to prove that "God" is not the devil.

John Milton was not a Gnostic. For him, certainly, physical creation was not evil. But like the Gnostics, Milton rejected the god imagined by many of his contemporaries. In a discussion of predestination, Milton rejects the way that some imagine the deity: "There are some people, however, who . . . assert that God is, in himself, the cause and author of sin. . . . If I should attempt to refute them, it would be like inventing a long argument to prove that God is not the Devil" (YP 6:166). In *Paradise Lost* and *Paradise Regained,* Milton invents a long argument to prove that God is not the devil. Milton creates a separate god—the moral equivalent of the Gnostics' creator god—in order to reject not physical creation, but monarchy. Kings and kingship; a "heathenish government" given to the people of God as a punishment and, according to Milton, absolutely forbidden to Christians by Christ himself, the institution of monarchy came to be for Milton what the physical was to the Gnostics—a result of evil and the invention of the devil. To imagine God as a king was, for Milton, to imagine God as if he *were* the devil.

Milton's greater and lesser epics are an indictment and rejection of a God imagined in terms of military and monarchical power. For Milton, God is not the devil, but in being conceived in terms of human kingship and the all-too-human desires for power and glory, God has been scandalously and blasphemously imagined in such a way as to be nearly indistinguishable from the devil. Milton pounds this point home by making the Father in *Paradise Lost* his sublime artistic rendering of the execrable tendency to conceive of God in satanic terms. The Father is not Milton's illustration of how God is, but Milton's scathing critique of how, all too often, God is imagined. Similarly, Milton's "long argument to prove that God is not the Devil" does not address what God is, but how God is imagined. Milton writes to reimagine God.

In his prose, Milton departs from ancient—and not-so-ancient—authorities in outlining a teleology by which it becomes clear that monarchy is inherently corrupt.[13] For Milton, the superiority of monarchy to other forms of government is not self-evident (as it was for the classical and medieval writers), and monarchy is the result of the degradation and deterioration of mankind set in motion by the Fall. Milton increasingly comes to emphasize, both in his prose and his poetry, that the real perversion is not the existence of kings (good or bad), but of kingship itself. The fact that Milton has no particular criticism of monarchs from Spain, France, Portugal, Sweden, Denmark, or other countries outside of England is irrelevant. For Milton, England is the country that really and truly matters in a way that none of these other nations can possibly matter.[14]

Quite simply, for Milton, England is—or has the opportunity to be—the new chosen nation of God, the new Israel.[15] In *Areopagitica,* Milton makes his notion of England's special status abundantly clear: God reveals truth "first to his English-men" (YP 2:553), and England is "a City of refuge" (YP 2:553), a "mansion house of liberty" (YP 2:554), and "a Nation of Prophets, of Sages, and of Worthies" (YP 2:554). England, for Milton, had been chosen by God as a special possession, a light to the rest of the world.[16] Abject cringing and fawning servility in the face of the challenges of freedom rendered Milton's countrymen incapable of living up to the rigors of such an ideal, and the dying cries of liberty in Milton's *Ready and Easy Way* attest to this miserable failure of God's "English-men." But during the time in which Milton is writing such antimonarchical tracts as *Tenure of Kings and Magistrates, Eikonoklastes,* and *A Defence of the People of England,* the failure of England has not yet become evident, and Milton has, as yet, no reason to abandon his optimistic view of the English as the newly chosen people of God.

Milton is neither isolated nor particularly radical in adopting the view that England is the modern version of Israel, a new special possession of God. Millenarianism, a movement that had been gaining strength in England since the fifteenth century, had reached a fevered pitch by the 1640s, and Milton is merely the best-remembered and most eloquent spokesman for a spiritual mood that had swept through the time and place in which he lived. Writing in *Areopagitica* that the nation of England was "chos'n before any other, that out of her as out of *Sion* should be proclam'd and sounded forth the first tidings and trumpet of Reformation" (YP 2:552), Milton identifies England with Israel in a manner similar to contemporaries such as Arise Evans, John Reeve, and Lodowick Muggleton (men to the right and to the left of Milton both politically and theologically). In Milton's day, such hopes fed into phenomena as various as the Leveller fight against enclosures of land (echoing the Israelite provision of the Jubilee year, in which lands and properties were returned to their original owners), the Fifth Monarchists' belief that a thousand-year earthly reign of Christ was imminent, and the Diggers' claim that the poor should be able to cultivate common land (based, in part, on the Israelite provision of gleaning—picking up grain fallen on the ground in the normal course of the harvest).

Regardless, however, of the extent to which Milton's millenarianism is a shared phenomenon among his contemporaries, by the time Milton likens England to Israel, it seems no longer possible to fathom either how Milton could regard heavenly kingship as "a picture of government truly sublime,"[17] or how Milton could himself go on to pen anything other than a wholesale rejection of kingship as a foreign imposition. Christopher Hill has argued that the popular myth of the Norman Yoke posited an originally democratic and nonmonarchical constitution as the native English model of society and government. According to this line of reasoning, monarchy was imposed by the invading Normans in 1066, and thus monarchy is an alien institution, and overturning the Stuart monarchy throws off the chains of a foreign tyranny.[18] I do not believe that Milton would refuse such a notion—especially since it appears in his antimonarchical tracts and his *History of Britain*—nor do I believe that Milton could have failed to see the analogy between the myth of the Norman Yoke, with its narrative of kingship as a foreign innovation and imposition, and the biblical narratives of the eventual fall of the Israelites from a commonwealth into kingship "in the manner of all the nations." Davies's suggestion that feudal kingship would have been not only accept-able, but also beautiful, in the eyes of the Milton who writes *Paradise Lost* cannot be reconciled with a view of England as the new Israel. Fallon's contention that because Milton did not specifically reject foreign kings, therefore Milton did not reject kingship also cannot stand up to the test administered by Milton's equation of England with Israel. England should not have kings because Israel was not to have kings.

Kings were given to Israel as a punishment, not as a blessing. Further-more, the fact that the nations surrounding Israel had kings was a sign of their alienation and estrangement from God; the fact that Moab had a king was— or should have been—irrelevant to Israel. God's rejection of kingship in Israel was a rejection of *kingship*. Similarly, Milton's condemnation of kings and kingship in England is tantamount to a censure of kingship everywhere. Like Moab, such European nations as Spain, France, and Portugal are alienated and estranged from God. There would be no point in condemning the sins of nations already rejected by God.

I suggest, by way of contrast to the readings of Davies, Fallon, and Bennett, that the pervasive and historically problematic images of divine kingship in *Paradise Lost* may be reconciled with Milton's increasingly em-phatic opposition to the institution of monarchy by viewing kingship itself through a historical lens different from the perspectives offered by the above-mentioned critics—one demonstrably near and dear to Milton him-self. The earliest portions of the Hebrew Bible (those portions least "cor-rupted" in Milton's eyes[19]) reveal that the roots of heavenly kingship are no less "oriental"—and therefore, in the terms of Davies's analysis, no more "despotic"—than are the roots of the satanic monarchy so vividly realized in *Paradise Lost*. Early biblical narratives, in fact, offer ample evidence that conceiving of God in monarchical terms is a human custom, one that accord-ing to the Bible originated not with the people of the "true" God, but with those peoples who worshipped the "false" gods of the nations. Specifically because Milton makes a point of using biblical precedents (validated by his "internal scripture of the Holy Spirit" [YP 6:587]) to overthrow human "custom" in practically every argument he ever makes, it seems not only possible, but obvious, that he could and would employ the same tactic in the service of a complete poetic rejection of kingship.

II. THE SCRIPTURAL DEVELOPMENT OF GOD AS KING

In writing about both heavenly and earthly realms, I believe that Milton's encyclopedic biblical knowledge leads him ultimately to a position more consistent—and more radical, both theologically and politically—than the partial or tepid condemnations of monarchy commonly ascribed to him by modern interpreters. Milton's passions and positions are never halfhearted; what Milton looses on earth, he looses in heaven. Ultimately, drawing from a rich and complex palette of biblical history and political radicalism, Milton in *Paradise Lost* paints God as a king, not in order to provide a perfect model of the monarchy he abhors, but instead to subject the human custom of commingling the sacred and the profane—divinity and monarchy—to a devastating critique.

Milton is, of course, at least as aware as any of his Bible-reading contemporaries that kingship began in rebellion. In fact, his proficiency in the original languages of the Bible likely makes him more acutely aware of the original biblical nature of kingship than his more limited, theologically and politically jingoistic contemporaries. Milton maintains that for the public interpretation of Scripture, "[t]he requisites are linguistic ability, knowledge of the original sources, consideration of the overall intent" (YP 6:582); as a result of his own ability, knowledge, and consideration, Milton could have been only too aware that the first appearance of the word *mamlakah* (or "kingdom") in the Hebrew scriptures is not in reference to Yahweh, but to Nimrod, "a mighty hunter before the Lord" (Genesis 10:9), whose "kingdom was Babel" (Gen. 10:10).[20] In *Eikonoklastes*, Milton notes this verse explicitly, calling Nimrod "the first that founded Monarchy" (YP 3:466) and later referring to him as "the first King," while noting that "*the beginning of his Kingdom was Babel*" (YP 3:598). Let us be clear about what Milton does *not* say here; he does not say that Nimrod is the first pale imitator of "a King of Heaven so glorious and a court so splendid that it put his idolatrous imitators to shame."[21] Milton does not say that Nimrod is the first that founded human monarchy as an imitation of divine monarchy. Milton does not say that Nimrod got out of bed one morning to declare that "to him shall bow / All knees" (*PL* 5.607–8) on earth because God had long ago made a similar demand in heaven, and Nimrod thought he himself might like to be the object of that knee-crooking servitude. Milton does not qualify the simple statement that Nimrod was "the first that founded monarchy" except by preceding it with the phrase, "reputed by ancient Tradition" (YP 3:466). However, in this instance the firm biblical support for the characterization of Nimrod as a monarch puts Milton's often uncertain relationship to tradition and authority to rest. He does not contest tradition's opinion of Nimrod, which agrees with the Bible's opinion, and with his own opinion. Milton's thorough awareness of the biblical background leads inexorably to a series of realizations: first, that kingship is a foreign ("heathenish") invention that walks hand-in-hand with tyranny;[22] second, that the title *melekh* or "king" is not applied to Yahweh in the Hebrew scriptures until after the kingship of Nimrod; third, that the concept of God as a king comes from human customs of kingship; and fourth, that the model of kingship therefore flows from Man to God, not from God to Man.

The essentially foreign nature of kingship (considered from the points of view outlined in the earliest biblical narratives) is illustrated by a consideration of other Near Middle East deities. The Ammonite deity Molech is a king. El Elyon—the deity of city dwellers like Melchizedek, the king of Salem who invokes him—is conceived of in Syro-Palestinian mythology as a king. The roots of kingship are, in fact, bound up with the roots of cities themselves; Nimrod, the tyrant who as the first biblical king is described by Milton as "first that hunted after faction," was also a builder of multiple cities: Babel, Erech, Accad, Calneh, Ninevah, Rehoboth, Calah, and Resen.

In direct contrast to the city-dwelling worshipers of monarchical gods, the patriarchs Abraham, Isaac, and Jacob dwell in tents, each living as "a stranger and a sojourner" (Gen. 23:4) in the land of Canaan, each worshiping a god specifically not conceived in terms of kingship. Significantly, though Adam names everything with which God presents him (Gen. 1:19, 2:20), he does not use the title *melekh* or "king" in reference to God himself. God is not yet conceived in terms of kingship at this early stage of biblical narrative; throughout Genesis, it is only humans, and specifically humans not in the service of Yahweh, who make use of the term *melekh*. It is not until after the years of Egyptian captivity that Yahweh comes to be referred to as a king. Exodus 15:18 declares that Yahweh "shall reign [*malak*] forever." In the years between Joseph and Moses, something fundamental has changed in the way Yahweh is imagined.

Baruch Halpern explains how this imaginative change may likely have come about. Halpern maintains that Yahweh becomes "king" by delivering the Israelites from Egypt: "In return for a promise of fealty, he [Yahweh] vows to liberate the Israelites from Egypt *and* to settle them in a fruitful land."[23] Halpern suggests a parallel between Yahweh and Marduk in the way each deity achieves the rank of king: though the stories take place on different levels—Marduk's in the assembly of the Annunaki (the collected gods), and Yahweh's in the human realm of Egypt and Canaan—the parallels are striking: "the suzerain contracts to rescue the assembly; he . . . demonstrates his capacity by some sign or test; and he is enthroned on a permanent basis."[24] Both Marduk and Yahweh win their respective kingships by successfully playing the role of Divine Warrior: Marduk's victory is over Tiamat, while Yahweh's is over the pharaoh of Egypt.

It is through this role as Divine Warrior that Yahweh's kingship is established and eventually made "universal." According to Halpern, "such poems as Judges 5:9–13, Deuteronomy 33:2–5, Exodus 15, and Psalm 44:1–5 . . . make use of the myth of the Divine Warrior in their imagery," and such use follows a typical pattern: Yahweh "rescued Israel from its foes, as the Divine Warrior rescued the world from Chaos; therefore [Yahweh] has gained kingship over Israel, as the Divine Warrior earned dominion over the cosmos."[25]

Yahweh's "kingship" emerges during the critical interval between Joseph and Moses; because the God of Israel is a successful Divine Warrior, rescuing Israel from its enemies, he is acclaimed as king, not only of Israel, but also of all the earth. Psalm 47 is a striking example of this pattern of divine acclamation: "O clap your hands, all ye people; shout unto God with the voice of triumph. For the LORD most high is terrible; he is a great King over all the earth. He shall subdue the people under us, and the nations under our feet" (1–3).

The Divine Warrior pattern, however, is (like kingship itself) a foreign import. Marduk is the god of Nimrod, not the god of Abraham, Isaac, and Jacob. Though the biblical account of the "spirit of God" moving across the surface of the waters, the *Tehom* of Genesis 1, retains mythic echoes of the epic struggle between Marduk and Tiamat (a goddess whose name is associated in the *Enuma Elish* with the saltwaters of the ocean), it has been almost completely "nativized" in a way that the elevation of the one-time Bedouin deity to universal kingship cannot be.[26]

Kingship, then, begins as an adoption of the ways of foreign nations, nations not in the service of Yahweh. Yahweh's promises to Abraham at Genesis 17:1–6 that "kings [*melekh*] shall come out of thee," along with his later promises to Jacob that kings shall descend from him (at Genesis 35:11, 12, and 36:9, 15–43), acknowledge that many of the descendants of these men (Ishmael, for example) will not be among the chosen people. Yahweh's promises are also a reflection of the thoroughly "Canaanized" monarchical regimes of David and the later kings of the northern and southern kingdoms under whom the Hebrew scriptures were written and compiled. Kingship remains a sign of the corrupting influence of living among nations not in the service of Yahweh. The provision of kingship at Deuteronomy 17:14–20 is not a recommendation from God that the Israelites adopt a king; rather, it is an after-the-fact justification for kingship during the reign of Josiah (c. 640–609 B.C.E.).

Violence, decay, and the corrupting influence on God's people of living among the nations are nowhere more outstandingly illustrated in the Bible than in the Book of Judges, the last three chapters of which are almost a straight "propaganda piece" for kingship. Possibly written sometime during the reign of the Judean king Josiah, Judges ends with the simple statement, "In those days, there was no king in Israel." This nearly constant refrain in the latter half of Judges lays all corruption and disorder at the feet of the failure of the Judges-period Israelites to adopt the monarchical hierarchies of the surrounding nations.

The urge to centralize is already present in the narrative, however, before this refrain appears. In Judges 8:22–23, Gideon refuses the offer of kingship over Israel, both for himself and for his sons. In refusing kingship for himself, Gideon says to the people, "I will not rule [*mashal*] over you, the Lord will rule [*mashal*] over you." Gideon's son, Abimelech—whose name means "my father is king"—did briefly attempt to reign as a king (and his name suggests that perhaps Gideon had second thoughts about the people's offer). In this early portion of the Judges narrative, a refusal of kingship is considered virtuous, a sign of a healthy and ongoing relationship with Yahweh, the true God. Even here, however, the influence of the surrounding nations with their human and divine kings can be seen taking root in Israelite soil. The primary "king" is now Yahweh. The image of God has already become corrupted, becoming like the images of deity held by the surrounding nations, and this is the first step toward the eventual adoption of human monarchy "like all the nations."

Despite Gideon's refusal of a crown, the Israelites will not be put off permanently in their quest for a centralized, king-based system of governance. 1 Samuel 8 recounts the demand of the elders of Israel that a king rule over them after the manner of the surrounding nations. Samuel tries to tell them that this is not such a good idea, listing a virtual catalog of monarchical abuses that will inevitably follow: the king will take the sons of the people to serve as charioteers and warriors; he will take the daughters of the people to serve as bakers and housekeepers; the king will take the best lands for himself and will tax the produce of all remaining lands. Still, the people insist on having a human king. After telling Samuel that the Israelites have not rejected Samuel but the Lord God himself, Yahweh tells Samuel to grant the request of the people. Thus Saul is anointed as the first king of Israel. Saul is set on his throne by a wrathful God who uses this first Israelite monarch to punish a people who had demanded a king.

With Israel's shift from a commonwealth (what Milton refers to in *Ten-*

ure of Kings and Magistrates as God's "own ancient government" [YP 3:236]) to human kingship, the practice of imagining Yahweh as a king becomes permanently entrenched. The prominence of this image of Yahweh as a king is, in fact, one of the most notable features of the Psalms. The Psalmist prays to "my King, and my God" at 5:2. Yahweh is the "Lord of hosts . . . the King of glory" at 24:10, and "sitteth King for ever" at 29:10. He is "Lord of Hosts, my King, and my God" at 84:3. His "kingdom is an everlasting kingdom" at 145:13.

Nor is God dethroned by the rise of early Christianity. In fact, the image of God as king in the Greek scriptures deepens and extends the pattern seen in the preceding Hebrew examples. 1 Timothy 1:17 proclaims God *basilei ton aionon,* or "king eternal." Conceiving of the Christian God as *forever* a king places him squarely alongside such king-gods as Marduk (declared king of the gods in the *Enuma Elish* prior to his defeat of Tiamat and his creation of Man), and Molech (the king-god of the Ammonites). Matthew 5:35, which describes heaven as the throne of God, refers to Jerusalem as the city of the great king (*basileus*). The adoption of the early Canaanite imagery (specifically the imagery of Molech and Nimrod as kings) and the association with Nimrod as a founder and ruler of cities are now complete. Yahweh (as well as the Christian "Father" based thereon) as king is in fact a portrait drawn from the "oriental" models of Molech, Marduk, and Nimrod.

Arguments from recent scholarship, however, are vulnerable to the charge that Milton's contemporaries—and perhaps Milton himself—read the Bible as a unified text presenting a coherent and reliable chronology of sacred history. Such readers would naturally be unaware of modern theories that assert the influence of Near Middle East cultures on the text of the Bible, regarding Deuteronomy's provision of kingship as an expression of Yahweh's will. Two points can be raised in response to this charge. First, such a reading puts Yahweh at cross-purposes with himself—apparently establishing kingship under Moses, quietly eliminating it at some unspecified later point, then reestablishing it as a punishment during the latter days of Samuel —a situation that in and of itself seems to undermine any assertion of unity or coherence in the text. Second, and more important, the argument that Milton and his contemporaries read the Bible as a unified or coherent text is, at best, problematic. As Regina Schwartz writes, "[Milton] makes distinctions between the authority of an external and internal scripture. Furthermore . . . he takes authority away from the external scripture altogether to confer it on the internal scripture." Schwartz makes this observation in the midst of a complex argument that has Milton using the Bible to authorize his own positions while at the same time using his positions to authorize the Bible. In essence, Milton is involved in a continual exchange of authority with the text he at once rejects and refines. As Schwartz argues, "Because Milton authorizes the Bible, the Bible in turn authorizes Milton."[27]

Christopher Hill has done valuable work in demonstrating that a view of the Bible as a unified and coherent text was far from universally held among Milton's contemporaries. Gerrard Winstanley, for example, "'accepted that the text of the Bible was uncertain'" and "'rejected much Biblical history in favor of allegorical interpretations.'" Winstanley also traced kingship and monarchical power to Cain's killing of Abel and characterized "'Kingly government'" as "'the government of highwaymen.'"[28] Moreover, in Milton's day, antimonarchical sentiment held that kingship was a corrupt innovation introduced by those who had rejected the standards of the true God. Hill gives as an example of this attitude a "near-Digger pamphlet"[29] of 1649, which argues that "'the rise of dukes was from wicked Esau,'"[30] the brother who rejected his birthright and became the founder of the Edomite people.

III. HEAVENLY AND EARTHLY KINGSHIP IN MILTON'S PROSE

For Milton, who writes in *De Doctrina Christiana* that "God is always described or outlined not as he really is but in such a way as will make him conceivable to us" (YP 6:133), the changing portrait of God throughout the Scriptures would not represent a change in God as he is, but rather a change —and a change decidedly for the worse—in the character of God's people, who clamor for a human king "like all the nations" (1 Sam. 8:5). In *Tenure of Kings and Magistrates,* Milton specifically argues that the Israelites' demand for a king reflects a generalized "oriental" tendency toward slavery: "the people of Asia, and with them the Jews also, especially since the time they chose a King against the advice and counsel of God, are noted by wise Authors much inclinable to slavery" (YP 3:202–3). After lumping in Israel with the other "people of Asia," Milton goes on to characterize the giving of a king to Israel as a punishment out of God's wrath: "God was heretofore angry with the Jews who rejected him and his forme of Goverment to choose a king" (YP 3:236). Milton makes his contempt for the Israelites' choice clear in *Eikonoklastes* when he refers to "those foolish *Israelites,* who depos'd God and *Samuel* to set up a King" (YP 3:580). It is unsurprising that this same Milton finds grounds to refer to Englishmen who demand a king as "a race of Idiots" (YP 3:542).

Milton seems to have followed a course of development that starts in the early 1640s with acceptance of kingship as the form of government most likely to be friendly to reformation of the English church, that progresses into the antipathy toward Charles I seen in the antimonarchical tracts of the late 1640s and early 1650s, and that finally develops by 1660 into a full-blown rejection of kingship in *The Ready and Easy Way*. The assumption that Milton was at least nominally royalist in his antiprelatical tracts has long been common in Milton criticism. A World War II–era royalist like G. Wilson Knight is hardly making a dramatic statement when he writes that "Milton's anti-episcopal pamphlets are the work of a fervent royalist." James Holly Hanford describes Milton in his antiprelatical pamphlet period as "with the majority of his countrymen, conservative, assuming the monarchical form of government as that to which the nation is permanently committed." However neatly this line may seem to connect the dots of Milton's published attitudes toward kings and kingship, I believe that this is more a tracing of what he was willing to say publicly than an accurate sketch of changing thoughts Milton may have had. This is also Christopher Hill's contention, as he argues that even before his entry into the church-government controversies of the early 1640s, "Milton [was] at least considering anti-monarchical sentiments which he did not find it expedient to express openly until 1649." Rather than developing an antimonarchical frame of mind through his career of writing prose and poetry, Milton gives clues early on about his negative attitudes toward kings, kingship, and external authority.[31]

Early in his career as a pamphleteer, Milton reveals his predispositions on the subject of the methods of governing. In *The Reason of Church Government* (1641), he writes that "persuasion" is preferable "to keepe men in obedience than feare" (YP 1:746). Nearly thirty years later, the older Milton will put similar sentiments into the mouth of the Son of God, who holds it both humane and heavenly to "Make persuasion do the work of fear" (*PR* 1.223). I believe that this consistency lies at the heart of Milton's attitude toward externally imposed authority of all kinds—church government, secular government, and, ultimately, the human relation to the divine itself. Government must persuade, and it must do so by working with the intellects and consciences of the governed; if government does not function in this manner, then it becomes tyranny, however benevolent it may appear. Government of the "inner man" (*PR* 2.477) is the only true government; external government —kingship both on earth and in heaven—exists only as a result of the deleterious effects of the Fall. Kingship is a daily reminder of the failure of the "inner man."

Milton's belief that this "inner man" is somehow redeemable is made clear in his 1644 treatise *Of Education*, where he outlines the ultimate purpose for human education: "The end then of learning is to repair the ruins of our first parents by regaining to know God aright, and out of that knowledge to love him, to imitate him, to be like him, as we may the neerest by possessing our souls of true vertue" (YP 2:366–67). When Milton suggests that it is possible to "repair the ruins of our first parents" through a vigorous program

of pedagogical self-improvement, he writes in the language of internal relation to the divine. In so doing, Milton is firmly within a Reformation tradition
of imagining salvation as a process of deification, or, less radically, of discover-
ing God within rather than without. Such radical continental Protestants as
Caspar Schwenckfeld, the Silesian nobleman, Teutonic knight, and aristo-
cratic evangelist for reform, regarded God within as the true God: "I cannot
be one in faith with either the Pope or Luther, because they condemn me and
my faith, that is, they hate *my Christ in me*." Schwenckfeld went on to suggest that the purpose of the Incarnation was to make it "possible for man to
become what God is," that is, divine. David Joris, a Dutch Protestant of the
mid-sixteenth century, argued that the purpose of religion was "to achieve
unity with God, a unity which comes only by the inner re-enacting of the
incarnation and Passion of Christ." Quintin of Hainaut, a sixteenth-century
Flemish spiritualist, held that "every Christian becomes, in a pantheistic or
mystical sense, a Christ."[32]

Though English divines in Milton's day stop short of asserting that humans will become divine, they do contend that the divine is to be found by
searching within. The Quaker minister Alexander Parker argues that "Christ
Jesus is the Truth, and he is the Light, and . . . the Light is within . . . all they
who deny to be guided by the light within denies God, Christ, and the
Spirit . . . for God is light, Christ is light, and the Spirit is light."[33] The
equation is clear: the light is to be discovered within, and God is light,
therefore God is to be discovered within. Another famous Quaker, George
Fox, writes his 1654 pamphlet, "To all that would know the way to the
kingdome," as "A Direction to turne your minds within, where the voice of
the true God is to be heard, whom you ignorantly worship as afarre off." Fox
goes on to maintain that, "as the eternal light which Christ has enlightened
you withal is loved, minded, and taken heed unto, this earthly part is wrought
out."[34] When the earthly part is "wrought out," what is left is the divine light,
the inner light provided by God to all those who truly seek. Lydia Fairman
specifically identifies the inner light with an inner Christ when she writes of
"Christ the light in every one of you."[35]

David Loewenstein has argued that "the early Quakers . . . represented
the largest and most dynamic movement of social, political and religious
protest" in the mid-seventeenth century and persuasively demonstrates that
Paradise Regained and "its striking revision of external forms of politics and
kingship; its emphasis on the mighty power of a spiritual kingdom within; and
its depiction of Jesus as a pious and inward saint" adopts many of the same
ideas taken up by the Quakers. "The emphasis in early Quaker writings on
the interiorization of power and kingship" is one shared by *Paradise Regained*, as "this poem does not simply repudiate worldly kingship; it also

makes kingship and power inward . . . redefining them in terms of a spiritual kingdom of the mind."[36]

To argue that education can "repair" the "ruins" produced by the Fall of Adam and Eve is as radical a theological statement as I can find in Milton. This verges on the territory of Pelagius, the fourth- and fifth-century monk who argued that mankind was capable of, and therefore responsible for, its own spiritual regeneration. Milton here reduces everything to one simple principle: love, imitate, and be like God. This cuts to shreds notions of Milton's inconsistency on the issues of kingship and man's proper relation to God, and renders untenable the arguments that would have Milton defending in heaven what he assailed on earth. If Man's greatest achievement, as Milton says in *Of Education* (YP 2:366) and as the Son says in *Paradise Regained* (2.475), is to know God "aright," to imitate and be like God, and if, as Milton argues in *Tenure of Kings and Magistrates,* human monarchy is the end result of a process of falling away from God, then God cannot possibly be a monarch. God is not a king; God cannot be a king because, for humankind to "love him, to imitate him, to be like him," human kingship would have to be approved by God.

Milton's "inner man" will not become like God through unquestioning obedience to any arbitrary authority intent on making equally arbitrary declarations. Authority exercised in this manner can have only negative consequences. A case in point is the proclamation made by the Father in *Paradise Lost* 5.600–15. Here, the Father (presumably without consultation) anoints the Son as a king before whom all must kneel instantly and without question or murmur. Those who fail this test of immediate and *cheerful* obedience are threatened with the direst consequences: they shall be "Cast out from God and blessed vision . . . / Into utter darkness, deep ingulft, his place / Ordain'd without redemption, without end" (613–15). Threats are the currency of the bully; threats are no way to govern the "inner man." Outward complicity is all that such threats will purchase, as evidenced by the consequence of the Father's threats, hypocrisy: "All seem'd well pleas'd, all seem'd, but were not all" (617).

That such governing techniques are doomed to abject failure is a truth all too obvious to the Son after the war in heaven. True government cannot be conducted through fear; rather, it must be undertaken through persuasion. This model of relationship between ruler and ruled, between God and Man, requires subjects capable of being persuaded, subjects educated enough to recognize the good when it is placed before them. Ironically, our ability to recognize the good requires, in the epistemology Milton outlines in *Areopagitica,* a familiarity with evil: "As therefore the state of man now is; what wisdome can there be to choose, what continence to forbeare without knowledge of evil?" (YP 2:514). Milton suggests that the knowledge of evil that is necessary for the ability to recognize and choose the good is the primary benefit of "books promiscuously read" (YP 2:517). Far from the "lowly wise" attitude recommended to Adam (*PL* 8.173), Milton's suggestion reflects an attitude of aggressive knowledge and truth seeking, a model of intellectual and spiritual inquiry similar to that of the Bereans whom Paul referred to as noble because their obedience required persuasion: they "searched the scriptures daily, whether those things were so" (Acts 17:11).

From the antiprelatical tracts to the divorce tracts and through the antimonarchical tracts, Milton continually struggles against human "custom" —an "everyone knows *that*" attitude Milton equates with ignorance—in favor of biblical texts and interpretations that support his arguments. As early as *The Reason of Church Government,* Milton argues for theological and political consistency on at least one level—using the Bible as the source of models for civil and religious authority: "[T]his practice we may learn, from a better & more ancient authority, then any heathen writer hath to give us . . . that book, within whose sacred context all wisdom is infolded" (YP 1:746–747). Milton goes on to insist that just as Moses instructed "the Jewes . . . in a generall reason of that government to which their subjection was requir'd," so "the Gospell" should instruct Christians "in the reason of that government which the Church claimes to have over them" (YP 1:747). In *The Reason of Church Government,* Milton avers that it is "custome" that is "the creator of Prelaty," and that prelaty is "lesse ancient than the government of Presbyters" (YP 1:778). The hierarchy of authority inherent in this statement is a key to understanding Milton's hermeneutical stance toward both theological and political controversies; the ancient models are those that Milton "recovers," excavating them from beneath the dust and rubbish of later "custom." Milton begins his *Tenure of Kings and Magistrates* in precisely the same manner: "If men within themselves would be govern'd by reason, and not generally give up their understanding to a double tyrannie, of Custom from without and blind affections within, they would discerne better what it is to favour and uphold the Tyrant of a Nation" (YP 3:190). Milton continues making his case by returning to original principles, compared to which kingship is "lesse ancient": "I shall here set downe from first beginning, the original of Kings; how and wherfore exalted to that dignitie above thir Brethren; and from thence shall prove, that turning to Tyranny they may bee as lawfully depos'd and punish'd, as they were at first elected" (YP 3:198). Originally, Milton reminds us, "all men naturally were borne free, being the image and resemblance of God himself" (YP 3:198). Kings, then, in Milton's analysis, are the end result of a long chain of events set in motion by the Fall. After "*Adams* transgression, falling among themselves to doe wrong and violence," men "agreed by common league to bind each other from mutual injury, and joyntly to defend themselves against any that gave disturbance or opposition to such agreement" (YP 3:199).

The history and teleology of kingship are sufficient to cast serious doubt on the idea that Milton approved of imagining God as a king. The logical, if absurd, extension of such imagining would posit a heavenly king as one angel elected by the rest to protect the angels from their own descent into "wrong and violence." This is similar to the way Satan imagines the Father in *Paradise Lost*, thinking of the Father as, in Empson's phrase, "a usurping angel."[37] However, Milton elsewhere makes his opposition to heavenly kingship clear enough that we need not rest with logical inference and reasonable doubt.

In the fifth chapter of *The Reason of Church Government*, Milton is already arguing against an identification of divinity with kingship. In refuting Bishop Andrewes's contention that Christ was foreshadowed in Hebrew scripture by both kings and priests, Milton accuses Andrewes of using this (satirically labeled) "[m]arvelous piece of divinity" to "ingage [the king's] power for them [the bishops of the Church of England] as in his own quarrell, that when they fall they may fall in a generall ruine" (YP 1:769–70). Milton's pointed question to Andrewes is an early indication of his rejection of "Heav'n's king": "But where, O Bishop, doth the purpose of the law set forth Christ to us as a King?" (YP 1:770). Milton's answer to his own question makes his rejection clear:

That which never was intended in the Law, can never be abolish't as part thereof. When the Law was made, there was no King: if before the law, or under the law God by a speciall type in any king would foresignifie the future kingdome of Christ, which is not yet visibly come, what was that to the law? The whole ceremoniall law, and types can be in no law else, comprehends *nothing but the propitiatory office of Christs Priesthood*. (YP 1:770–71)

Milton's reference to "the future kingdome of Christ" only makes his discomfort with the idea of divinity conceived in terms of kingship more obvious. "That which never was intended in the Law," the same law that forbids graven images of the deity, was also never intended to become a part of the human imagining of the divine. Some years later, Milton will argue in *Eikonoklastes* that "*Christs Kingdom* [should] be tak'n for the true Discipline of the Church" (YP 3:536). In referring to Christ as "our common King" (YP 7:429), and "our true and rightfull and only to be expected King" (YP 7:445) in *The Ready and Easy Way*, Milton is writing of spiritual kingship, not a "Heavenly" kingship that looks like an impossibly glorious version of the court of Charles I. In other words, "the future kingdome of Christ" is a spiritual arrangement of faith and worship, not a secular arrangement of politics and power (no matter whether such a "secular" arrangement is located on earth or in heaven).

As the Son will later say in *Paradise Regained*, to be truly "kingly" is to exercise spiritual dominion, to govern (in the sense of discipline) the "inner man, the nobler part" (2.477). Each Christian who takes his or her obligations as a Christian in a serious and spiritual sense is thus already "kingly" in this manner and needs no other king on earth or in heaven. Just as Milton relies on a familiar post-Reformation formulation of the "priesthood of all believers" in his antiprelatical tracts (arguing against bishops as an unnecessary and actively deleterious hierarchical layer separating the Christian from God), so he comes to rely on an analogous construction of the "kingship of all believers" (arguing against kings and kingship in the same way) in his later antimonarchical tracts. Much as bishops stood between true Christians (who are "priestly") and a right relationship with God, so also do kings stand between true Christians (who are "kingly") and God. Worse still, the idea of God as a king, an external ruler who demands outward compliance delivered with promptness and ceremony, prevents the Christian from, in the Son's words, "knowing . . . God aright" (*PR* 2.475). In the argument with Bishop Andrewes, Milton has taken his first steps, not only in arguing against the custom of picturing God and/or Christ as a king, but also in redefining what it means to be truly "kingly."

Milton does not stop here, however, but goes on in *Eikonoklastes* to a similar denigration of "custom" in relation to kingship. He refers contemptuously to those "who through custom, simplicitie, or want of better teaching, have not more seriously considerd Kings, than in the gaudy name of Majesty" (YP 3:338). To seriously consider kings, Milton suggests, would be to realize that majesty, in its external and "gaudy" trappings, is not truly kingly. Later, Milton sneers at "the easy literature of custom and opinion," declaring that "few perhaps, but . . . such of value and substantial worth" (YP 3:339–40) will align themselves with Milton's own rejection of such custom. The foreshadowing of the "fit audience . . . though few" of *Paradise Lost* is unmistakable here.

In *A Defence of the People of England,* Milton briefly recalls the account he gave in *Tenure of Kings and Magistrates* of the growth of kingship, but he makes an important addition: the formation of churches. "Men first came together to form a state in order to live in safety and freedom without violence or wrong; they founded a church to live in holiness and piety" (YP 4:320–21). The origin of both kings and churches, then, is the Fall. King and church issue not from blessings but from curses, maledictions cast upon fallen mankind. This insight flowers from the seeds planted in *The Reason of Church Government,* where Milton finds the proper forms of both civil and church governments in the Bible. It is a tantalizing prospect to consider that Milton—who was, according to Thomas Newton, "a dissenter from the Church of England [and] not a professed member of any particular sect of Christians"—may have rejected both king and church, seeing them, finally, as obstacles preventing mankind from knowing God "aright."[38]

Milton goes on in *A Defence of the People of England* specifically and unequivocally to identify the form of civil government recommended in the Bible as a commonwealth, in direct contradistinction to modern interpretations of his writings that would suggest a Miltonic longing for "ideal" or heavenly monarchy: "A republican form of government, moreover, as being better adapted to our human circumstances than monarchy, seemed to God more advantageous for his chosen people; he set up a republic for them and granted their request for a monarchy only after long reluctance" (YP 4:344). Furthermore, Milton argues that God gave the Israelites a king only out of anger: "God was wroth at their desire for a king, not in accordance with divine law but in imitation of the gentiles, and he was wroth furthermore that they desired a king at all" (YP 4:347). In *Ready and Easy Way*, Milton flatly states that God "imputed it a sin to [the Israelites] that they sought [a king]" and further maintains that "*Christ* . . . forbids his disciples to admitt of any such heathenish government" (YP 7:424).

Ample textual evidence demonstrates that Milton considers the "custom" of kingship to be a foreign imposition on God's people; kings are endured as a punishment that, but for the Fall, would never have been necessary. Thus, Milton's portrait of a monarchical Father, a character that has troubled readers and critics alike for centuries, troubles precisely because he is supposed to trouble. The Father's heavenly crown is not an exhibit of heavenly perfection; it is instead a necessary contrast to a perfect form of rule (both heavenly and earthly) that is offered by the Son, who offers the best indication of the system that had the most "obvious beauty" for Milton.

IV. HEAVENLY AND EARTHLY KINGSHIP IN MILTON'S POETRY

Milton's "portrait" of heavenly kingship in *Paradise Lost* is a triptych; the central portion of the piece—with its somber egg tempera image of the Father as a king sitting upon the throne of heaven—cannot be understood properly without reference to the images on its right and left. The panel at the left hand of the Father depicts Satan, while the panel to the right hand of the Father pictures the Son. Each of the peripheral figures represents a balance and contrast to the middle figure; the characters portrayed on the left and right sides of Milton's triptych both offer a challenge to a Father ruling as an "absolute monarch."[39]

The similarity between Satan and the Son as challengers of the Father is a point that cannot be overstressed. Each character rejects the idea of the Father as an unquestioned and unquestionable ruler. For Satan and the Son, the Father will not pass unchallenged as an absolute monarch, certainly not in the terms described by Aristotle (from whom Milton learned much in preparation for his arguments against tyranny): a tyrant is "an individual which is responsible to no one, and governs all alike, whether equals or betters, with a view to its own advantage, not to that of its subjects, and therefore against their will."[40] Critics who engage in what Empson described as "the modern duty of catching Satan out wherever possible" delight in emphasizing Satan's descent into tyranny while trying to avoid—at all costs—coming to grips with the uncomfortable extent to which the Father in *Paradise Lost* fits the definition of a tyrant.[41]

The Father is first referred to as a "supreme King" in *Paradise Lost* at 1.735, after the demonic associations of kingship have been thoroughly rehearsed over the last three hundred lines, and in the midst of a description of the demonic architect whom men, "erring" (1.747), call Mulciber. During the debate in hell, the fallen angels continually refer to the Father as a king: he is twice "the King of Heaven" (2.229, 2.316), and he "first and last will Reign / Sole king" (2.325–25). Satan and his followers take it for granted that the Father is a king, and a tyrannical king at that. They are, in this estimation, correct. A tyrant, according to Milton, is "he who regarding neither Law nor the common good, reigns onely for himself and his faction" (*Tenure of Kings and Magistrates*, YP 3:212). For whom else does the Father rule except for "himself and his faction"? The Father may very well regard "law," but it is difficult to see how he regards "the common good," especially when it is the Son who must vigorously remind him of that good in Book Three of *Paradise Lost*. To argue that the Father gets to define the common good is particularly slippery; this is rather like the argument of Euthyphro in the Platonic dialogue of the same name—piety is piety, not of itself, but because it is dear to the gods, and impiety is impiety, not of itself, but because it is abhorrent to the gods. Variations of this same justification are made in the name of each of history's great tyrannies—the leader knows best, and what the leader defines as the good is the good.

Satan's challenge to the Father is mirrored by the Son's challenge. Left and right are reversed, as in a reflection whose similitude is an illusion, a trick of technique and the manipulation of light and shade. Where Satan is shaded, the Son is light; where Satan's challenge to the Father eventually brings out what is worst in him (his desire to emulate the absolute monarchy he once rejected), the Son's challenge brings out what is best in him.[42] Behind the Son's words in *Paradise Lost* 3.144–66 are the words of Abraham and Moses.

The Son's "that far be from thee" is an almost direct quotation of Abraham's "that be far from thee" during his challenge to Yahweh over the planned destruction of Sodom and Gomorrah at Genesis 18:25.[43]

It should come as no surprise that the often irascible Yahweh looms behind the figure of a poetic character that Milton is careful to identify as Jehovah: "Great are thy works, *Jehovah*, infinite / Thy power" (*PL* 7.602–3). What may surprise is the use to which Milton puts the biblical character in the celestial dialogue of Book Three. Casting the Son in the position of Abraham emphasizes the confrontational nature of the Son's approach to the Father in this scene. Abraham's verbal struggle with Yahweh is no mere polite disagreement. Abraham takes a potentially fantastic risk by challenging the righteousness of his God. Abraham not only asks that Yahweh display mercy to the residents of Sodom and Gomorrah, he asks *repeatedly,* bargaining with Yahweh in an attempt to determine just how far mercy and righteousness may be effective in lessening his wrath. Will fifty "righteous" be enough to avoid wholesale slaughter? How about ten? There are only four, and four turn out to be not quite enough. Yahweh is not testing Abraham; Abraham is testing Yahweh. When Abraham confronts Yahweh in Genesis 18:25 ("Shall not the Judge of all the earth do right?"), he is asking a serious question. Will Yahweh actually kill the innocent with the guilty, making no distinction between righteous and unrighteous? "That be far from thee to do after this manner," declares Abraham. The Son takes a similar position with the Father:

> should Man finally be lost
>
> .   .   .   .
> that be from thee far,
> That far be from thee, Father, who art Judge
> Of all things made, and judgest only right.   (*PL* 3.150, 153–55)

The Father is not testing the Son; the Son is testing the Father.

Another parallel with which Milton works is that between Moses and Yahweh in Exodus, chapter 32. Yahweh tells Moses to leave him alone so that he may destroy the very people whom he has only recently led out of slavery in Egypt: "let me alone, that my wrath may wax hot against them, and that I may consume them" (32:10). Moses, quite understandably, given the effort he has put in over the people Yahweh now threatens to destroy, will have none of this. He tells the deity to stop and think: What will the Egyptians say? "Wherefore should the Egyptians speak, and say, For mischief did he bring them out, to slay them in the mountains, and to consume them from the face of the earth?" (32:12). Such a call to God to consider what the enemy will think and say about the destruction—by God—of God's people is precisely what Milton ascribes to the Son in his dialogue with the Father in Book

Three of *Paradise Lost*. Just as Moses pleads with God to "repent of the evil against thy people" (Exod. 32:12), so also the Son implores the Father not to take an action that will allow Satan to question and blaspheme "without defense."[44] In the context of such challenges, the Son's confrontation of the Father is a demonstration of the passibility, the Yahweh-like emotional volatility and moral ambiguity, of the Father. Michael Lieb has argued that Milton "not only intensifies the idea of passibility, but bestows upon it a new significance" in his portrait of the Father. Lieb concludes, "the figure of God in *Paradise Lost* is portrayed as a fully passible being."[45] Such a being, passible and morally ambiguous, is what the Son confronts in Book Three of *Paradise Lost*.

The Son begins his public career in a manner much less confrontational toward the Father than the stance he adopts in the debate of Book Three. When the Father announces his begetting in Book Five, the Son seems little more than an extension of the Father; the Father's everpresent concern with his "Omnipotence," "Arms," "Deity," and "Empire" (721–24) are echoed by the Son, who describes the controversy in heaven as "Matter to mee of Glory" (737). As the war in heaven is being fought and won, when "War wearied hath perform'd what War can do" (6.695), the Son still speaks of his own glory, but is beginning also to speak in terms of relinquishing the very power he has recently assumed: "Sceptre and Power, thy giving, I assume, / And gladlier shall resign" (6.730–31). After the war and the expulsion of the vanquished, the Son no longer seems so impressed with "Sceptre and Power" as he may have been previously. Mercy is now the Son's focus, not power, not scepter, not even the justice about which the Father rails (at 3.210) in what Empson once described as "the stage villain's hiss of 'Die he or Justice must.' "[46]

The Son's concern with "Glory" and "Sceptre and Power" has completely faded by the time he embarks on the fulfillment of the fatal bargain he made with the Father in Book Three of *Paradise Lost*. In *Paradise Regained,* the Son's expressed contempt for the idea of kingship is devastating in its power. Government, to avoid being tyranny, must be internal, a self-government of each individual guided only by truth, and by "knowing . . . God aright" (2.475). The Son's clear accusation against not only mankind, but against mankind's earthly *and* heavenly rulers is that existing forms of rule have not enabled most to properly know God. Kingship, churches, external rule, threats, and the demand for outward compliance—all of these things have not only *not* enabled mankind to know God "aright," but have actively led mankind astray.

However, this is the kind of external regime that the Son has come to bring to an end, replacing it with a rule of "the inner man" (*PR* 2.477). The

Son has nothing to do with either oriental despotism or feudalism; nor is the Son's rule a "self-renouncing monarchy."[47] The Son promises, and delivers, something entirely different: monarchy-renouncing monarchy. Milton creates a Son for whom to be truly kingly is to "lay down" a kingdom, an action the Son considers "Far more magnanimous than to assume" (2.483). The Son's entire message, if he can be said to have a message in Milton, is that to know God "aright" is to know God as the Son himself knows God, to know that the rule of heaven is not external, but internal. The regime of the Son is not "o'er the body only," but of the "nobler part," a rule where there is no first, but only equality. To know God "aright" is to know that God is not a king.

Like the Son, Satan begins with concern for glory, but his progression is one designed, albeit unsuccessfully, to recover what he feels to be his own lost glory and to accrue more glory through battle and an ascension to a hellish throne. Satan's "ambition" is to "reign" (*PL* 1.262), a concern similar to that the Father expresses in Book Five:

> Nearly it concerns us to be sure
> Of our Omnipotence, and with what Arms
> We mean to hold what anciently we claim
> Of Deity or Empire.   (721–24)

Both the Father and Satan seem primarily concerned with the consolidation, maintenance, or acquisition of power. Satan was, in this sense, right to claim that the Father held "the Tyranny of Heav'n" (1.124). However, Satan's mistake is not his challenge of the Father, but his method. Where Satan chooses military force in an attempt to cause the Father to doubt "his empire" from "terror of this arm" (1.113–14)—a strategy that proves an abject failure—the Son chooses to "make persuasion do the work of fear" (*PR* 1.223), a preference Milton expresses as early as 1642, when in *The Reason of Church Government* he writes that "persuasion is certainly a more winning, and more manlike way to keepe men in obedience than feare" (YP 1:746).

Through the contrasting challenges offered by Satan and the Son, Milton's rejection of the very idea of earthly and heavenly kingship comes sharply into focus. Milton's use of Satan and his rebellion against an absolute monarch in heaven also helps to answer the perennial question of why Satan seems to overwhelm the reader's senses with the scope of his Achillean heroism. Satan is supposed to seem heroic—and not in Fish's sense of misleading the unwary reader line by line. Satan's heroism is real, and therefore his slow degeneration from Book One to Book Ten is not, as C. S. Lewis would have it, farcical, but legitimately tragic. Satan rises against an absolute monarch. So far, so good, Miltonically speaking. The complex of reasons for which he rises comprises both the failure and the wrongheadedness of his rebellion. Satan's sense of "injur'd merit" (1.98), according to his own admission to his closest compatriot, Beelzebub, is what raised him to contend with the Father. As Satan sees it, the issue is simple: Who has the right to reign in heaven? Satan proclaims that in preparation for battle he had "brought along / Innumerable force of Spirits arm'd / That durst dislike his reign, and mee preferring" (1.100–102). Thinking along similar lines, the Father who is concerned with "Deity" and "Empire" (despite the Son's strangely protective and unconvincing gloss of that concern as "derision" [5.736]), seems to indicate that Satan may be more like the Father than many Milton critics would care to admit.

What drives the Son to contend with the Father in Book Three is not a concern with his own merit—injured or rewarded—but mercy for the as yet unfallen human race. Readings of this scene, like Fish's, that insist on the merely rhetorical character of the Father's conversation with the Son in the celestial dialogue deliberately puncture and deflate the swelling drama of what are perhaps the most important passages in all of *Paradise Lost*. If the Father is "determinedly non-affective" and is not talking "to anyone in particular,"[48] then Milton's great poetic triptych has its right hand panel lopped off and is rendered less an artistic marvel of an earlier age than a damaged, but historically significant, curiosity. If denied the emotional weight of speaking back to power in his own voice, the Son is denied the great dignity of Abraham (a frail and mortal man contending with the Almighty over the fate of any righteous men who may live in Sodom and Gomorrah). The Son is also denied the heroism through which, by pleading for mercy to be shown to humanity and offering to die to satisfy the implacable "Justice" of the Father, he displays the greatest bravery imaginable. In a reading that denies him an active and crucial agency in Book Three, the Son is rendered a figure merely ridiculous and sycophantic, the worst—because the most powerful—of the "Minstrelsy of Heav'n" (6.168). Such a Son makes a villain of the Father who creates him. Such a Son hands the moral high ground to Satan.

In contrast to the tripartite structure of Milton's picture of heavenly kingship, earthly kingship in Milton's epics is portrayed rather more simply, nearly always associated either with tyranny or with estrangement from God, or in some combination thereof. Solomon, the "uxorious king" of *Paradise Lost* 1.444, is an example of kings alienated from the true God. A particularly instructive example is Jeroboam, the "rebel king" of 1.472–89, whose Miltonic portrait in *Paradise Lost* is one of apostasy, wickedness, and rebellion against God. However, as Davies has pointed out, Milton, in his polemical argument with Salmasius (in *A Defence of the People of England*), finds himself forced to defend Jeroboam. Milton argues rather weakly: Jeroboam had overthrown his brother Rehoboam (the heir to the throne by birthright), and turned out to be exceedingly pagan and wicked; nevertheless, though Jeroboam and his successors were offenders against the true worship of God, they were not rebels (YP 4:405–6). Davies takes from this seeming inconsistency on Milton's part a most apposite maxim: "This apparent contradiction between prose and poetry may serve as a warning to the reader to modify his expectations of the manner in which the former will elucidate the latter."[49]

Milton's prose and poetry are certainly written in different contexts and for different purposes, and the immediate polemical squeeze into which Salmasius had been able to catch Milton over the rather embarrassing failure of the successors to the Solomonic throne to live up to seventeenth-century English antimonarchical principles was tense and, doubtless, exquisitely uncomfortable. Milton had used Jeroboam as an example of justified rebellion against a wicked king, equating Jeroboam (who deposed Rehoboam) and the English revolutionaries (who deposed Charles I) as "Brethren, not Rebels" in his *Tenure of Kings and Magistrates* (YP 3:209); Salmasius had Milton dead to rights because Jeroboam turned out to be an idolatrous and tyrannical ruler.

Years after his controversy with Salmasius, however, Milton vigorously attacks in poetry what he previously defended in prose because he is no longer faced with a rhetorical situation that demands that he defend an exposed and nearly indefensible flank. I suggest that the characterization of Jeroboam in *Paradise Lost* should be given the most weight because it is more consistent with Milton's view of kingship as a curse, a malediction, a punishment wrought by Sin and the Fall. If readers are to modify any expectations regarding the relationship between the attitudes toward kingship expressed in Milton's poetry and prose, let them look to the teleology of kingship expressed in *Tenure of Kings and Magistrates,* the characterization of kingship in *The Ready and Easy Way* as "heathenish" and forbidden by Christ to those who would follow him, and the impulse of the Son, both in *Paradise Lost* and *Paradise Regained,* to lay down the scepter, step away from the throne, focus on the inner man, and to finish his poetic sojourn "Home to his Mother's house private return'd" (*PR* 4.639).

Readerly expectations should be further instructed by the fact that elsewhere in *Paradise Lost* kings are described as having demonic origins or associations: the "Memphian kings" of 1.694 and the Babylonian kings of 1.721 are entangled in a web of demonic rebellion and rejection of God. Satan's throne in hell is associated with Eastern kings of "Ormus and of Ind" (2.2), while Moloch, the "Sceptr'd king" (2.43), is described in a manner no different from the "Sceptr'd Angels" (1.734) who in heaven rule "Each in his Hierarchy, the Orders bright" (1.737). Thus, Milton tars the hierarchy of heaven with the blackened palette of hell. By first presenting us with kings and kingship in hell (Satan, Moloch, and Death are all described in the language of kingship), and then in the "dark / Illimitable Ocean" (2.891–92) in which Chaos reigns with "the Sceptre of old Night" (2.1002), Milton lays the groundwork for his portrayal of a heaven gone horribly wrong. Milton has not shown us first the kingships of Satan, Death, and Chaos in order to "create a King of Heaven so glorious and a court so splendid that it put his idolatrous imitators to shame";[50] rather, he creates a king of heaven so unworthy of the idea of God to put his fellow post-Restoration Englishmen to shame.

Only in Book Twelve of *Paradise Lost* is there any glimmer of hope. King David of Israel is mentioned with approbation, but he is the all-too-rare exception to the rule of earthly kingship. David, a deeply flawed ruler who used his power to steal another man's wife while simultaneously having the cuckolded victim killed in battle, has much more in common with his earthly and demonic predecessors than he does with the figure who follows him, the Son, "of Kings / The last" (329–30). His reign—the reign of the "inner man"— shall have "no end" (330). Kingship, heavenly and earthly, looks forward to this solitary figure, the Son who in *Paradise Lost* accepts regal power only to lay it down in *Paradise Regained,* who disdains deeds of glory and the pomp and circumstance of the earthly kingships Satan shows him, but who also rejects any form of rule—earthly and heavenly—that does not cause the ruled to know God aright: to know his virtue, patience, and love. Thus, for Milton, the purpose of government, just as the purpose of education, is to repair the ruins of the Fall and to restore the original relationship of humanity and divinity.

If we pull back for a moment from the monumental canvases of Milton's epics and look briefly at an early poem like *Sonnet 19,* it might seem that such opinions on kingship as Milton expresses therein are relatively conventional, but they only seem so until they are placed in relation to the opinions Milton places in the mouth of the Son in *Paradise Regained.* Milton's brief epic is a textbook of antimonarchical attitudes. From Book One's portrait of Satan's continuing obsession with monarchies—earthly and heavenly—to Book Two and Three's depiction of the Son's thoroughgoing rejection of earthly monarchy (including, significantly, Davidic monarchy), and to the Son's radical redefinition of what it means to be truly "kingly" in heavenly and spiritual terms, *Paradise Regained* seems to represent a significant ideological shift from the terms of *Sonnet 19.* Both works, however, focus on what it means to be "kingly," not what it means to be an actual monarch. "Kingly" is a term that need not necessarily be limited to its most literal sense—being, or partaking of, the nature of an actual monarch; it can also refer to traits of character such as nobility, dignity, passion governed by wisdom, justice tempered by mercy, confidence without arrogance, intellectual weight, empathy, and patience.

Sonnet 19 makes reference to a God who has just such traits, a quietist deity who does not need the labors and talents of humans in his service. This

God, whose "State / Is Kingly," imposes only a "mild yoke" (11); and while "Thousands at his bidding speed" (11), those who serve him best are those who bear the mild yoke, including those who "stand and wait" (14) if that is their lot. This is not the military monarch of *Paradise Lost*, a glowering and derisive Father who makes it his business either to create dissent, or to drive it into the open (in Book Five). *Sonnet 19*'s "Kingly" God is a king in the sense of having a "kingly" character. The tolerance and mild yoke of a God who demands nothing more than patience from his blinded and wounded servant Milton are "kingly" in much the same way that the Son's concern with the "inner man, the nobler part" is "kingly" in *Paradise Regained* (2.477). To be "kingly" is not to be either an earthly or a heavenly monarch. To be truly "kingly" is a spiritual, not a political achievement; neither Satan nor the Father, the two characters in Milton's epics most visibly concerned with achieving or maintaining power, gives any evidence of real spirituality of such a "kingly" nature.

I contend that Milton hoped his "fit" audience would recognize that it was the Son, and not the Father, whom he was offering as a lamp to guide their footsteps in the dark world of the restored Stuart monarchy. Challenges to the Father offered by both Satan and the Son show each defying the received opinion of heaven: Satan's challenge is to a position that Abdiel represents in Book Five as a sibling's variation on the classic "I brought you into this world, and I'll take you out" threat of an angry father: "Then who created thee lamenting learn, / When who can uncreate thee thou shalt know" (5.894–95).

Abdiel's behavior in this scene is often portrayed as that of a faithful angel who is bearing solitary witness, under severe duress, to the requirements of true obedience; for example, Stella Revard contends that it is Abdiel, despite his arguments from force, who is being bullied in his argument with Satan.[51] I find it difficult to concur with Revard's assessment of Abdiel's position in this scene, given the fact that he is in no way subjected to reprisal. I am closer to the position of Empson, who sees Satan as displaying a certain nobility in allowing Abdiel to leave unmolested: "we do not find Milton's God being content to differ from someone who contradicts him."[52] Rather than being assaulted, or even seriously threatened, Abdiel is told to leave, told, in fact, to take a message to "the Anointed King" (5.870). The warning that evil might intercept his flight if he does not leave quickly is merely a goad to get him to go and go now. In fact, in this debate, although Satan also argues from force—declaring that "our own right hand / Shall teach us highest deeds, by proof to try / Who is our equal" (5.864–66)—it is Abdiel, rather than Satan, who introduces the theme of uncreation, or death.

Abdiel seems to believe—and significantly, no one contradicts his belief

—that the proper heavenly response to serious dissent is lethal force. Satan is given no immediate verbal response to this dark truism of heaven's monarchical regime, responding instead to this threat as he has responded to the Father's, by demanding proof through the force of deeds. Satan, it would seem, has learned his lessons rather too well; the way to resolve a serious dispute is through violence. Thus, it is entirely predictable that Satan's challenge to the Father is one of military force.

The Son challenges both received opinion and the Father rather differently; in a sense, he challenges the Father's received opinion of himself. Are you, the Son asks, really concerned only with strict, retributive justice? What, then, separates you from your adversary, who is concerned with strict retributive revenge? In another sense, however, the Son is also challenging the Father with the simplistically destructive and bullying terms of Abdiel in mind. Are you really going to uncreate your human creation? "[W]ilt thou thyself / Abolish thy Creation" asks the Son (3.162–63). Are you really the sort of parent who would kill his own children? Are you, in fact, exactly the sort of tyrant that the rebels accuse you of being? If the answer is yes, then "So should thy goodness and thy greatness both / Be question'd and blasphem'd without defense" (3.165–66). Michael Lieb has argued that the Son is not only *challenging* the Father, but also *warning* the Father: "One senses in the challenge that the Son himself would be the foremost among the reprobate in excoriating the Father, should the Father fail to heed the Son's warning."[53] In other words, there will be no defense to be made of a "goodness" and a "greatness" that the Father himself will have proven to be lies. If there is no defense that can be mounted against charges that initially seem to be blasphemous, then there is, strictly speaking, no blasphemy. Truth is not blasphemous, and truth is the basis of the Son's challenge.

Finally, what lies at the heart of the challenges of Satan and the Son is the question of what it means to be truly "kingly"; for Satan, to be "kingly" is to be a monarch, the sense in which most Milton critics today seem to read the term, while for the Son, to be "kingly" is specifically *not* to be a power-wielding monarch, but to be of noble and virtuous character, "to know God aright, and out of that knowledge to love him, to imitate him, to be like him, as we may the neerest by possessing our souls of true vertue" (*Of Education*, YP 2:367). Thus do the kingliness of the Son and Milton's definition of the purpose of education meet: for the Son, to be "kingly" is to have "repair[ed] the ruins of our first parents" (YP 2:366–67). To be "kingly" is to know God and to be like God, a God imagined not as a wielder of power and a giver of orders, but as a soul "of true vertue" (YP 2:367).

Being like God is the promise the serpent makes to Eve in Genesis, and it is the promise Satan makes to Eve in *Paradise Lost*. Raphael's continual suggestions that Adam and Eve may ascend to heaven "under long obedience tri'd" (7.159), and that their "bodies may at last turn all to spirit" (5.497), are variations of the theme of being like God. Ultimately, the question of what it takes to be like God depends upon the answer to a far more fundamental question: *what is God like?* If God cannot be directly apprehended, if the divine is, as Augustine maintained, "unspeakable,"[54] or if, as Milton argued, "God, as he really is, is far beyond man's imagination, let alone his understanding" (YP 6:133), then an even more fundamental question must be asked: *How is God to be imagined?*

Competing definitions offered by Satan and the Son of what it means to be "kingly" are also competing answers to the question of how God is to be imagined. The competition between these definitions and these imaginings, pursued in contrasting challenges to the Father, is the core of Milton's attempt to reject kingship and to reimagine God. Milton wishes to seriously consider kings and kingship and reimagine God in terms other than "the gaudy name of Majesty" (YP 3:338). In so doing, Milton is rejecting the Father and his concern with "Empire" as a proper image of God, and is instead elevating the Son, whose focus is "true vertue."

Satan imagines the Father as a king, while the Son imagines the Father as "kingly." There is all the difference in the world between the two conceptions, and in this last great effort of his life, Milton is England's poetic John the Baptist, a voice crying out in the wilderness of "the easy literature of custom and opinion" to teach his "fit audience . . . though few" to recognize that difference.

DePaul University

NOTES

1. Unless otherwise noted, all quotations of Milton's prose are from *The Complete Prose Works of John Milton,* 8 vols., ed. Don M. Wolfe et al. (New Haven, 1953–82), hereafter cited parenthetically in the text as YP, followed by volume and page number. All quotations of Milton's poetry are from *John Milton: Complete Poems and Major Prose,* ed. Merritt Y. Hughes (New York: Odyssey, 1957), hereafter cited in the text.

2. Joan Bennett. *Reviving Liberty: Radical Christian Humanism in Milton's Great Poems* (Cambridge, Mass.,1989), 33.

3. Stevie Davies, *Images of Kingship in "Paradise Lost": Milton's Politics and Christian Liberty* (Columbia, Mo., 1983), 3.

4. Robert Thomas Fallon, *Divided Empire: Milton's Political Imagery* (University Park, Pa., 1995), 32–33.

5. Reuben Sanchez, "From Polemic to Prophecy," in *Milton Studies* 30, ed. Albert C. Labriola (Pittsburgh, 1993), 27.

6. Michael Fixler, *Milton and the Kingdoms of God* (Evanston, Ill., 1964), has also argued for a consistency in the purpose of Milton's prose writings and has noted that inconsistency may appear as a result of Milton's immediate rhetorical situation: "The unity, particularly of the prose, may be obscured by the apparently different objectives he pursued at different times, but in reality these objectives were only so many means to one end" (76).

7. Fallon, *Divided Empire*, 36.

8. G. Wilson Knight, *Chariot of Wrath* (London, 1942), 44.

9. William Empson, *Milton's God* (London, 1961), 111.

10. Fallon, *Divided Empire*, 42.

11. There are many potential objections to be made to the raising of the controversial theological treatise in an argument about the nature of the Father/Son relationship in *Paradise Lost*. However, despite the eloquent arguments of William B. Hunter and Gordon Campbell et al., I am not yet persuaded that we should abandon the idea of Milton as the author of *De Doctrina Christiana*. See Hunter's argument in *Visitation Unimplor'd: Milton and the Authorship of "De Doctrina Christiana"* (Pittsburgh, 1998), and "Responses," *Milton Quarterly* 33, no. 2 (1999): 31–37; see also the arguments of Gordon Campbell et al. in "The Provenance of *De Doctrina Christiana*," *Milton Quarterly* 31 (October 1997): 67–121.

12. This extreme is not one to which all groups identified as "Gnostic" go, but it is recognizable, for instance, in Marcion. According to Hans Jonas, *The Gnostic Religion*, 2d ed. (Boston, 1991), Marcion's demiurge was primarily conceived in terms of "pettiness" (141) and was merely *just* as opposed to *good*. The Valentinian 'artificer' (demiurge) of the left-hand things" (190) is also recognizable as a devilish kind of anti-God whose main attribute is "ignorance . . . and [the] presumption in which he believes himself to be alone and declares himself to be the unique and highest God" (191).

13. In his *History*, Herodotus, *The History of Herodotus*, trans. George Rawlinson (Chicago, 1955), narrates the argument of Darius for monarchy as the ideal form of government; the Medo-Persian potentate asks, "what government can possibly be better than that of the very best man in the whole state?" (108). Oligarchy and democracy lead inevitably to strife and faction, while Darius insists that monarchs are free to rule with the best interests of their subjects in mind. Plato, *The Republic*, trans. Benjamin Jowett (Chicago, 1955), likewise argues that kingship is the ideal form of rule, calling "the rule of a king the happiest" form of government (419). Aquinas, *Summa Theologica*, vols. 1 and 2, trans. Daniel J. Sullivan (Chicago, 1955), argues that "the best government is government by one" (1:530). He also asserts that "a kingdom is the best form of government of the people, so long as it is not corrupt" (2:309).

14. Christopher Kendrick, *Milton: A Study in Ideology and Form* (New York, 1986), has argued that Milton was a protonationalist: "His whole epic vocation was intertwined with what we might call a form of proto-nationalism. . . . Milton's . . . is a religiously coded patriotism for which the ideal English church . . . is simply one with the nation, and for which the nation represents only a peculiarly chosen member of the collective saintly body" (84).

15. Sharon Achinstein, *Milton and the Revolutionary Reader* (Princeton, N.J., 1994), refers to Milton's equation of England and Israel as a commonplace idea of his time and place: "Israel was not just a model for England, as Rome or Greece might be, but England was a recapitulation of Israel" (17).

16. Barbara Lewalski, *Protestant Poetics and the Seventeenth-Century Religious Lyric* (Princeton, N.J., 1979), has characterized the often-drawn parallels between England with Israel as "genuine recapitulations" in which God "deals with his new Israel as he did with the old" (131).

17. Fallon, *Divided Empire*, 36.

18. Christopher Hill, "The Norman Yoke," *Puritanism and Revolution* (London, 1969), 50–122.

19. In *De Doctrina Christiana,* Milton argues that the text of the Bible as it has been transmitted across the millennia to a seventeenth-century reader is corrupt. The text of the Greek scriptures, in particular, "has often been liable to corruption" (YP 6:587) and should be submitted to the judgment of the individual believer, guided by the Spirit.

20. Scriptural citations are from the Authorized Version of 1611.

21. Fallon, *Divided Empire,* 42.

22. Nimrod is also, for Milton, "the first that hunted after Faction" (*Eikonoklastes,* YP 3.466), and faction is an indispensable ingredient in Milton's recipe for tyranny.

23. Baruch Halpern, *The Constitution of the Monarchy in Israel* (Chico, Calif., 1981), 71. Other works useful for an understanding of the development of the idea of Yahweh as a king include Zafrira Ben-Barak, *The Manner of the King and the Manner of the Kingdom: Basic Factors in the Establishment of the Israelite Monarchy in the Light of Canaanite Kingship* (Jerusalem, 1972); Marc Zvi Brettler, *God Is King: Understanding an Israelite Metaphor* (Sheffield, 1989); and Audrey K Gordon, *Religious Dimensions of Kingship in Canaan and Israel* (M.S., History and Literature of Religions, Northwestern University, 1967).

24. Halpern, *The Constitution of the Monarchy in Israel,* 71.

25. Ibid., 73.

26. For a discussion of the *Enuma Elish,* Genesis, and Milton, see Regina Schwartz, *Remembering and Repeating: On Milton's Theology and Poetics* (Chicago, 1993). Also see J. Martin Evans, *"Paradise Lost" and the Genesis Tradition* (Oxford, 1968).

27. Regina Schwartz, "Citation, Authority, and *De Doctrina Christiana,*" in *Politics, Poetics, and Hermeneutics in Milton's Prose,* ed. David Loewenstein and James Grantham Turner (Cambridge, 1990), 233, 230.

28. Winstanley quoted in Christopher Hill, *The English Bible and the Seventeenth-Century Revolution* (London, 1994), 223, 208, 209.

29. Hill, *The English Bible and the Seventeenth-Century,* 209.

30. Winstanley quoted in ibid., 209.

31. Knight, *Chariot of Wrath,* 27; James Holly Hanford, *A Milton Handbook,* 4th ed. (New York, 1954), 79; Hill, *Milton and the English Revolution,* 91.

32. George Huntston Williams, *The Radical Reformation* (Philadelphia, 1962), 258, 335, 483, 599.

33. Alexander Parker, *A testimony of the Light within . . .* (London, 1657).

34. George Fox, "To all that would know the way to the kingdome" (London, 1654), title page, 2.

35. Lydia Fairman, "A few lines given forth and a true testimony of the way which is Christ . . ." (London, 1659).

36. David Loewenstein, "The Kingdom Within: Radical Religious Culture and the Politics of *Paradise Regained,*" in *Literature and History* 3 (autumn 1994): 64, 63, 74.

37. Empson, *Milton's God,* 103.

38. Thomas Newton, ed., *Paradise Lost* (Birmingham, 1759), lxiii.

39. Bennett, *Reviving Liberty,* 9.

40. Aristotle, *Politics,* trans. Benjamin Jowett (Chicago, 1955), 495.

41. Empson, *Milton's God,* 74.

42. On the Son's challenge to the Father in book 3 of *Paradise Lost,* see Michael Lieb, "Reading God: Milton and the Anthropopathetic Tradition," in *Milton Studies* 25, ed. James D. Simmonds (Pittsburgh, 1989), 213–43, and "Milton's 'Dramatick Constitution': The Celestial Dialogue in *Paradise Lost,* Book III," in *Milton Studies* 23, ed. James D. Simmonds (Pittsburgh, 1987), 215–40.

43. Gordon Campbell, "Popular Traditions of God in the Renaissance," in *Reconsidering*

the Renaissance: Papers from the Twenty-First Annual Conference, ed. Mario A. DiCesare (Binghamton, N.Y., 1992), has pointed out this parallel (501–20).

44. For another expression of this argument, see my "'That far be from thee': Divine Evil and Justification in *Paradise Lost," Milton Quarterly* 36 (May 2002): 87–105.

45. Lieb, "Milton and the Anthropopathetic Tradition," 225, 229.

46. Empson, *Milton's God,* 120.

47. Davies, *Images of Kingship in "Paradise Lost,"* 175.

48. Stanley Fish, *Surprised by Sin: The Reader in "Paradise Lost"* (Cambridge, Mass., 1998), 62.

49. Davies, *Images of Kingship in "Paradise Lost,"* 30–31.

50. Fallon, *Divided Empire,* 42.

51. Stella Revard, *The War in Heaven* (Ithaca, N.Y., 1980), 218.

52. Empson, *Milton's God,* 24

53. Lieb, "Milton's 'Dramatick Constitution,'" 229.

54. Saint Augustine, *On Christian Doctrine,* trans. J. F. Shaw (Chicago, 1955), 626.

MILTON'S "BIRTH ABORTIVE": REMAKING FAMILY AT THE END OF *PARADISE LOST*

Erin Murphy

IN 1652, SIR ROBERT FILMER threw down the patriarchalist gauntlet when he attacked the stories of origin told by contract theorists:

There never was any such thing as an independent multitude who at first had a natural right to a community. This is but a fiction and a fancy of too many in these days, who please themselves in running after the opinions of philosophers and poets, to find out such an original of government as might promise them some title of liberty, to the great scandal of Christianity and bringing in of atheism, since a natural freedom of mankind cannot be supposed without the denial of the creation of Adam. And yet this conceit of original freedom is the only ground upon which not only the heathen philosophers, but also the authors of the principles of the civil law; and Grotius, Selden, Hobbes, Ascham and others raise and build their doctrines of government, and of the several sorts or kinds, as they call them, of commonwealths.[1]

The publication of Milton's *Paradise Lost* faced Filmer's challenge, providing the now defunct commonwealth with a less scandalous origin by telling a story of freedom, complete with Adam and Eve. Though the sadness of the final books of the epic, as well as their much-discussed stylistic frustrations, presents a particularly difficult challenge to the idea that Milton has not given up the fight against the monarchy, reading them with Filmer's challenge in mind allows us to understand their formal qualities as part of a continuing political battle.[2] The poet's move to present the future of Adam's progeny through a genealogical narrative, intriguingly described by Balachandra A. Rajan as stylistically "barren," actually exemplifies his political engagement by plunging us into the conceptual mire of the seventeenth-century family.[3]

In Book Ten, Eve suggests to Adam that they avoid their punishment by refusing to procreate, arguing "So death / Shall be deceiv'd his glut, and with us two / Be forc'd to satisfy his Rav'nous Maw."[4] The tragedy of the Fall she resists is the fall into mortal reproductive time, marked by the proliferation of bodies that die. This fear of reproduction recurs in Milton's writings and mirrors his fear of a royalist government that uses the reproduction of bodies to authorize political power.[5] Though Adam optimistically responds to Eve with the promise of the generation of the Son of God, his hopefulness is undercut by the fact that the reader is left in what has often been described as

145

the bleakest part of the poem. In Books Eleven and Twelve, the archangel Michael chronicles the future of human history for Adam, showing him the sorrows that will befall his progeny. By choosing this genealogical structure to close his epic, Milton places his work at the center of political debates about royal authority. Though Filmer's *Patriarcha* was not published until 1680, his argument deriving the king's legitimacy from the paternal dominion of Adam was already sketched out in his 1652 *Observations Concerning the Originall of Government*, which included an entire section directly critiquing Milton's *A Defence of the People of England*.[6] Representing the Fall not just as a fall into the body, but also as a fall into a strictly reproductive understanding of history, Milton implicitly responds to patriarchalist theories of government. Such theories traced the power of the king back to an original fatherly right, in contrast to contractual theories that located the origins of government in a moment of consent.[7] At a time when patriarchalist imaginings of lineage were a matter of intense political debate, Milton pushes his epic to reinterpret the role of the family in the conception of historical authority. The final books of *Paradise Lost* struggle to detoxify the concept of family by disengaging it from the political realm.

In order to understand the struggle of these books, it is important to begin by unfolding the ways in which Books Eleven and Twelve present family as both an epistemological and a political problem. A close reading of Adam's lament will clarify the epistemological, or narrative, dimension of family, followed by an exploration of the scene of Nimrod's tyranny, which will illuminate the political contours of the problem. With the relationship between these two elements in mind, I will reconsider the question of the form of these final books, analyzing the details of Michael's narrative of lineage as an enactment of the frustrations of family itself. Finally, I will argue that by separating Eve from this scene of historical narration, Milton imagines the domestic as an earthly sanctuary in which the family exists safe from the realm of politics. Thus, Milton transforms family from a crippling symptom of postlapsarian politics into a mode of understanding human existence in the ruptures of fallen time.

The narrative problem of representing history has long been recognized as one of the major issues of the end of *Paradise Lost*. Whether it is Michael's shift from visual to verbal representation, the tension between tragic emplotment and apocalyptic promise, or the style of a flattened poetry, the difficulty of storytelling in Books Eleven and Twelve has been a crucial element in critical discussions of the poem. In these final scenes, the poem shifts to position the reader in a startlingly peculiar moment in time. Like Adam poised on the mountaintop, we are lifted out of the dramatic moment which the previous books have given us into a position of temporal exile. Rather

than enjoying the fiction of having Eden made present, or our typical historical struggle to look backward, we are forced to strain our necks to see our
own past as future. As David Loewenstein has noted, these books look much
like the "dumbshow of history" Milton decries in his *History of Britain*.[8] New
characters are introduced at breakneck speed, but without any of the psychological depth of previous books. Michael's depictions lack the dramatic presence of the fraught soliloquies of Satan, the political intrigue of the devils, the
tender relations of Adam and Eve, or the suspense of the temptation. The
condensation of all of human history into a relatively few short lines puts us
into Adam's position of distance. We can no longer pretend that we are there.

This shift in form can be better understood by considering the problem
Adam bemoans when he learns he will be turned out of Paradise:

> This most afflicts me, that departing hence,
> As from his face I shall be hid, depriv'd
> His blessed count'nance; here I could frequent,
> With worship, place by place where he voutsaf'd
> Presence Divine, and to my Sons relate;
> On this Mount he appear'd, under this Tree
> Stood visible, among these Pines his voice
> I heard, here with him at the fountain talk'd.   (11.315–22)

Though these final books are markedly undramatic, Adam here actually dramatizes a touching scene of narrating the past to his sons, a scene that he
imagines as now impossible due to his exile. Intriguingly, on the list of what
"afflicts him most" is his inability to represent the past to his progeny, the
breaking of the chain of historical memory before it is even formed. Here
Adam begins to understand his relationship to his past as a function of his
relationship to his children, and to understand the intersection of these relationships as a project of storytelling. Like many critics of Milton's work, he
understands history as a narrative problem, but one that becomes a problem
because of a relation to reproduced bodies. C. S. Lewis called the prophecy
of Books Eleven and Twelve the "untransmuted lump of futurity," but Adam
calls his viewing of the future a "Birth / Abortive" (11.768–69).[9] Adam specifically speaks of the impotence of foreknowledge, but the use of this embodied language calls attention to his consciousness that he is entering a biologically reproduced history. Though it enacts a struggle with futurity, this
"lump" actually takes the form of a genealogical narrative.

Like Adam, Michael seems to recognize that one of the issues at stake in
expulsion is the relation between family and historical narrative. Just as Adam
and Eve are separated from God by their exile from Eden, they will eventually be separated from their offspring by death. Both punishments deny the

connection of presence, raising the question of how to bridge the gap between those who are there and those who are no longer. Responding to Adam's inability to "his sons relate," Michael begins by chastising Adam for failing to understand that God is everywhere, but makes sure to acknowledge the particularity of the lament, explaining:

> this had been
> Perhaps thy Capital Seate, from whence had spred
> All generations, and had hither come
> From all the ends of th'Earth, to celebrate
> And reverence thee thir great Progenitor
> But this preeminence thou hast lost, brought down
> To dwell on even ground now with thy Sons.   (11.342–48)

In this moment, the archangel begins to draw out the implications of Adam's narrative problem. In a postlapsarian world, Adam will not be able to gather "All generations" around him. Death denies his ability to sit in this seat of "preeminence" and to tell the past to his progeny. John King points out that in this moment, Adam is "Mourning the loss of his unmediated relationship with the Father,"[10] but he also mourns the loss of another unmediated relationship. Just as expulsion will distance God, the father, from Adam, mortal time will distance Adam, the human father, from his sons. Michael specifically undercuts Adam's historical authority, his ability to make the past present, as he prepares to launch his own story of lineage. In this crucial exchange between God's representative and Adam, the story of family line has been wrested away from the earthly father. The relations between father and sons now operate on one plane, and Adam is denied narrative superiority. When Adam loses his "preeminence," he falls from a vertical position of paternal authority into a horizontal relation in which he must "dwell on even ground" with those to come. The family, like the poetry, has been flattened.

Michael's deauthorization of Adam's familial narrative leads us to a political problem defined by their exchange. The importance of Adam's ability to relate to his sons is not lost on Michael, who mobilizes a narrative of lineage in his most important mission, the expulsion of Adam and Eve. The political charge of his formal choice must be taken seriously. An obsession with family line underlies the imagining of a patriarchalist project and the political controversies of the seventeenth century. In the tracts he published between 1648 and 1652, Filmer argued that the rights of the king could be traced back to Adam's original right as a father: "The first government in the world was monarchical, in the father of all flesh. Adam, being commanded to multiply, and people the earth, and to subdue it, and having dominion given him over all creatures, was thereby the monarch of the whole world. None of his posterity had any right to possess anything but by his grant or permission, or by succession from him."[11] Filmer's justification rests on two claims. The first is one of identity—the right of the king is the same as the right of the father. The second is one of continuity—this right was established with the first man and has existed continuously through to the present. Milton had already challenged the first claim in *A Defence of the English People* when he attacked the royalist work of Claudius Salmasius: "But upon my word, you are still in darkness since you do not distinguish a father's right from a king's. And when you have called kings fathers of their country, you believe that you have persuaded people at once by this metaphor: that whatever I would admit about a father, I would straightaway grant to be true of a king. A father and a king are very different things."[12] Although not the direct target of this critique, Filmer recognized the threat to his theory and responded to Milton directly in his *Observations Concerning the Originall of Government:* "father and King are not so diverse. It is confessed that at first they were all one, for there is confessed *paternum imperium et haereditarium*, page 141, and this fatherly empire, as it was of itself hereditary, so it was alienable by the parent, and seizable by a usurper as other goods are: and thus every King that now is hath a paternal empire, either by inheritance, or by translation or usurpation, so a Father and a King may be all one."[13] When Filmer refers to Milton's confession, he fails to report that Milton goes on to say that royal power originated when "men first came together, not so that one might abuse them all, but so that when one injured another, there should be law and a judge between men" (*A Defence*, 195). By marking a break between a time of paternal rule and the institution of monarchy, Milton denies the transfer of fatherly right to royal right that Salmasius tries to establish through his historical account of several families merging into one government. Strategically omitting Milton's point that families "gave way" to "civil life" (*A Defence*, 195), Filmer tries to force his adversary into admitting the identity of royal and paternal power.

Simultaneously, Filmer mounts the other key plank of his patriarchalism, asserting the continuity of this paternal power across time. Though adding usurpation and translation to inheritance as additional means by which paternal right is transferred from king to king seems to dilute the "fatherly" nature of the "fatherly empire," for Filmer these were just alternative ways to carry on the familial basis of government.[14] After the execution of Charles I, however, some of Filmer's work does reflect discomfort with this easy substitution. His 1652 *Directions for Obedience to Government in Dangerous or Doubtful Times* carefully negotiates the question of usurpation, but ultimately seems to privilege the eventual succession of a lineal heir, arguing that if the right of fatherly government "be usurped, the usurper may be so far obeyed as may tend to the preservation of the subjects, who may thereby be enabled to perform their duty to their true and right sovereign when time shall serve."[15] In 1652, Charles I was dead and England was ruled, in the eyes of royalists, by a usurper. In 1660, seven years after Filmer's death, the time he imagines when the "true and right sovereign" will once again reign returns to England with Charles II. The "fatherly right" could now be properly inherited.

Parliament's proclamation of Charles II's kingship three weeks before his return reveals the relevance of the continuity between fathers and sons to Restoration politics:

Although it can in no way be doubted, but, that his majesty's right and title to his crowns and kingdoms, is, and was every way compleated by the death of his most royal father of glorious memory, without the ceremony or solemnity of a proclamation, yet, since proclamations in such cases have been always used, to the end that all good subjects might, upon this occasion, testify their duty and respect, and since the armed violence, and other calamities of many years last past, have hitherto deprived us of any such opportunity, wherein we might express our loyalty and allegiance to his majesty, we therefore, the lords and commons, now assembled in Parliament, together with the lord mayor, aldermen, and commons of the city of London, and other freemen of this kingdom, now present, do, according to our duty and allegiance, heartily, joyfully and unanimously acknowledge and proclaim, that immediately upon the decease of our late sovereign Lord King Charles, the imperial crown of the realm of England, and of all the kingdoms, dominions and rights, belonging to the same, did by inherent birth-right, and lawful and undoubted succession, descend and come to his most excellent majesty Charles the Second, as being lineally, justly and lawfully, next heir of the blood-royal of this realm; and that by the goodness and providence of Almighty God, he is of England, Scotland, France and Ireland, the most potent, mighty, and undoubted king; and thereunto we most humbly and faithfully do submit and oblige ourselves, our heirs, and posterities, for ever.

God save the King.
Tuesday May 8, 1660[16]

The telling phrase "Although it can in no way be doubted" to introduce the legitimacy of Charles II's succession to the throne belies the fact that the document is designed to quell just such doubt. Despite the claim of a seamless transition between father and son, the proclamation's own language quite self-consciously labors to repress the violence and rupture of the civil wars, referring to Charles I's "death" rather than his "murder" or the "regicide." The "armed violence, and other calamities of past years" did not interrupt the continuity of the royal line; they merely delayed the expression of the subjects' "loyalty and allegiance." Vehemently contradicting the radical claim that in 1649 the rebels had killed the monarchy, Parliament here insists "that immediately upon the decease of our late sovereign Lord King Charles, the imperial crown of the realm of England" descended to Charles II.[17] The emphasis on "inherent birth-right," "next heir," "blood royal," and lineal descent serves to tie the existence and health of the monarchy not to one mortal body, but to a biologically reproduced chain of bodies.[18]

In 1661, Genesis continued to provide a means by which to ground regal authority, as can be seen in Robert Sanderson's preface to James Ussher's *The power communicated by God to the Prince,* a volume dedicated to Charles II:

As soon as Adam was created, God gave to him as an universal Monarch, not onely dominion over all his fellow creatures that were upon the face of the Earth, but the government also of all the inferiour world, and of all the Men that after should be born into the world as long as he lived; so as whatever property any other persons after- wards have or could have in any thing in any part of the world . . . they held it all of him, and had it originally by his gift or assignment.[19]

Like Filmer, Ussher returns to Adam to locate the origin of monarchy, noting the continuity of inheritance through Noah's son as a means of proving that the theory of an original contract is "but a Squib, Powder without shot."[20] In 1663, Charles II reissued Richard Mocket's *God and the King,* a text orig- inally commissioned by James I. Locating the moment of origin at birth rather than in Genesis, the dialogue nonetheless articulates a patriarchalist theory of obedience:

For as we be born Sons, so we are born subjects: his sons, from whose loyns; his subjects in whose Dominions we are born. The same duties of Subjects are also enjoyned by the Moral Law, and particularly (as you shewed in the very entrance unto this our Conference) in the fifth Commandment, Honor thy Father and thy Mother: where, as we are required to honor the Fathers of private families, so much more the Father of our Countrey and the whole Kingdom.[21]

Though Filmer is best known as the spokesperson of patriarchalist theory, the attempt to ground political authority in stories of family continues beyond his death into the Restoration. As Gordon Schochet has shown, "Patriarchal doctrines can be found throughout the Stuart period and in all strata of thought, from well-ordered and self-conscious theories, through the lower level and often implicit rationalization and polemics of tractarians and con- troversialists, to the unstated prejudices of the inarticulate masses."[22] The end of Milton's epic also participates in this genealogical obsession, but it does so in order to reclaim the power of the genealogical form from a pa- triarchalist agenda. Adam knows the importance of narrating the past to his sons, and Michael cannot escape telling the future through stories of prog- eny. It is the inescapability of these reproductive narratives that demands

their reinterpretation in order to loosen them from a patriarchalist framework, purifying them for Milton's antimonarchic purposes.

Milton's antiroyalist sentiment has most often been noted in the scene of
Nimrod at the beginning of Book Twelve, and a closer look at this will help us
to understand how the poet both represents and participates in the political
struggle for conceptual control of the family. Michael shifts his representational mode from vision to verbal description at the same time that he explains that Adam has seen, "Man as from a second stock proceed" (12.7),
allying formal and genetic change. Though God allows Noah to continue the
biological line, Michael's emphasis on the "second stock" marks the flood as a
moment of lineal disjunction. His elimination of Adam's vision places his
entire story at a new level of representational remove, enacting the disconti-
nuity of generations through his shift in form. By reinforcing the loss of
Adam's preeminence, Michael sets the stage for the story of Nimrod. As the
bodies Adam can see disappear, Michael asserts his narrative authority more
strongly with the intriguing phrase, "Henceforth what is to come I will relate"
(12.11). What he proceeds to relate through the figure of Nimrod is a story of
familial and political upheaval. For Milton, the story of Nimrod clearly figures the injustice of divine right, and in Book Twelve Michael describes this
injustice as a family problem:[23]

> till one shall rise
> Of proud ambitious heart, who not content
> With fair equalitie, fraternal state,
> Will arrogate Dominion undeserv'd
> Over his brethren, and quite dispossess
> Concord and law of Nature from the Earth.   (12.24–29)

Nimrod, as the first monarch, misunderstands and manipulates proper familial relations. By describing Nimrod as a bad brother, one who breaks the
fraternal state, Milton emphasizes the conflict between a horizontal and
vertical form of government. Equality and fraternity are contrasted to tyranny and political hierarchy.[24] Adam, described as "fatherly displeas'd,"
speaks out against his progeny, noting that God authorizes no man to exert
authority over another. Annabel Patterson has argued that placing this critique in Adam's mouth is a direct rejection of Filmer's theory of kingship.[25]
But Milton doesn't stop there. Though he uses Filmer's own authorizing
agent to undermine the patriarchalist argument, he then attacks Adam's
ability to authorize. Once again, Michael undermines this father's ability to
place himself above his sons by explaining to Adam that the tragedy of tyranny springs from the "original lapse," just as his children spring from his
loins. Not only is Nimrod on the same level as his brothers, Adam is on the

same level as his sons. Critics have long noted the political nature of this moment as an attack upon monarchy. What I would suggest here is that Milton goes beyond critiquing monarchy as a warped familial system to re-orient the family itself. Royalists in the period will claim that if sin can be inherited, so can monarchic authority.[26] Since his account of the Fall clearly endorses the idea that sin is inherited, Milton must find a way to understand familial connections, or reproductive history, that denies the claims of pa-triarchalism.

Through the story of Nimrod, he clears a space for family outside the realm of politics. Despite Adam's claim, endorsed by Michael, that God "human left from human free" (12.71), the moment of justice before Nim-rod's dominion is still marked by "paternal rule" (12.24). This seemingly contradictory moment makes sense, however, if Milton is trying to make a distinction between the state and the family. In *Defensio Regia*, Salmasius elides this distinction when he describes the coming together of many fam-ilies as "the origin of kingly rule, and the plan and reason for monarchical rule—as the most natural—should be sought in these beginnings. For individ-ual households were held, as if under the kingly rule of one person, of him, of course, who was the first and oldest progenitor of the family" (YP 4:1028). Milton reinterprets Salmasius's account of origins, giving it a particularly contractual spin:

Whence it is quite clear that in the very beginning of nations, paternal and hereditary government very soon gave way to virtue and the people's right. This is the origin of royal power, and the most natural reason and cause. For it was that very reason that men first came together, not so that one might abuse them all, but so that when one injured another, there should be law and a judge between men, whereby the injured might be protected or at least avenged. (*A Defence*, 195).

He goes on to argue that Salmasius's version could only be the story of Nimrod, "the first tyrant." In *Paradise Lost*, he elaborates on Nimrod's tyr-anny, which arises because he, refusing to be "content / With fair equalitie, fraternal state, / Will arrogate Dominion undeserv'd / Over his brethren" (12.25–28). For Milton, familial hierarchy can coexist with the political equality of brotherhood as long as paternal rule does not invade the state. The power of family as a structuring force is too great for Milton to cede to patriarchalism, forcing him to find a place for it safe from politics.

In these final moments of the poem, Milton constantly thematizes the narrative lines of family as a site for political control, as Michael and Adam negotiate who gets to tell the story of the human family. Michael's insistence upon Adam's narrative impotence shows that genealogy must be understood as the domain of the divine. Milton moves the political battle to the level of narrative. Since the familial line must be understood as a story beyond human control, Milton flattens the form of his poem to reflect the incompleteness and contingency of genealogical understanding, emphasizing its illegitimacy as a political authority. By withdrawing the explicit drama of the poetry, these books push the reader to augment his or her reading with a set of biblical allusions and associations, pointing to the realm of Scripture as the proper context for family.

The story of Nimrod provides an important vehicle for the struggle for control of the family because it engages not only the question of the monarchy, but also the problem of language itself. As Sharon Achinstein has shown, royalists used the story of Babel as a means to decry and silence a multiplicity of political voices.[27] Milton participated in the radical reclaiming of this story from the royalists by placing monarchic tyranny at the origin of political confusion. His version ties narrative impotence to the perversion of lineage-based rule. The inauthentic claim of power based on inheritance leads to the disabling of linguistic coherence. By contrast, Filmer interprets the confusion of Babel as consolidating the relationship between family and government, "And for the preservation of this power and the right in the fathers, God was pleased upon several families to bestow a language on each by itself, the better to unite it into a nation or kingdom."[28] Thus, by evoking the story of Nimrod, Milton attacks not only monarchic oppression but also, indirectly, the patriarchalist argument that a story of reproductive lineage can legitimate political authority. Just as Adam must learn that historical authority cannot be derived from a "fatherly" position of preeminence, so also the monarch cannot claim special access to historical truth based on his lineage.

The link between narrative and political incoherence in the story of Nimrod, coupled with the familial questions of epistemology and authority in Adam's lament, suggests that the form of these last two books should be reconsidered as serving Milton's political agenda. Though the defenses of this section of the poem now probably outnumber the negative critiques, many of these recuperative interpretations still try to account for the tragic form by focusing on the presence of absence in this section.[29] The peculiarity of the loss of literariness has been read by Barbara Lewalski and others as representing Milton's desire to move from "shadowy Types to Truth, from flesh to spirit." Other critics have focused on the internalization of the epic, either as a spiritual or psychological event.[30] Still others have turned to the importance of typology to understand how these final books "discourage any attempt to understand human experience in terms of a causally connected linear sequence, and seek an interpretation from above."[31] These strategies acknowledge the importance of what disappears from the end of the poem, but here I would like to concentrate on what remains. Beginning with Adam and Eve's family planning discussion in Book Ten, the epic plunges us into an engage-ment with reproductive time. Although the dramatic unfolding of earlier books is gone and fragmentation pervades Michael's history, the linear cau-sality of reproduction has not disappeared. In fact, Milton's struggle for con-trol of the power of familial narrative requires the presence of this story so that he can reclaim it from royalist propaganda.

Michael's presentation of the future to Adam can be described as a tangle of historical styles, arguably employing a mix of tragic, cyclical, mille-narian, and typological configurations.[32] Indisputably, however, these dispa-rate configurations are brought together in the final books by the structure of a chain of bodies, which continually gain narrative coherence as the arch-angel positions them within a story of reproduction. When Michael first tells Adam to open his eyes, he introduces the scene by explaining how sin will be reproduced in his progeny, "yet from that sin derive" (11.427). Though Adam's children "never touch'd / Th'excepted Tree" (11.425–26), the sin continues on in them. They are corrupted by what is not present. The past is present in them through an inheritance, which is bodily. Though it is divinely ordained, the relationship between Adam and his children does have a con-tinuous logic. At the moment when the first father learns what it means to have children, the messenger of God begins by emphasizing his relation to them as one of inherited sin. Distinguishing the inheritance of sin from the inheritance of political power struck at the heart of Filmerian patriarchalism, as well as Restoration assertions of lineal legitimacy such as those in the 1660 parliamentary proclamation, by defining a connection to past generations that bore no relevance to political power.

Once the primacy of the relation of sin has been established, Michael proceeds to flesh out the family tree. When Adam cries out at the sight of Cain killing Abel, Michael first explains the familial relationships before responding to Adam's question: "These two are brethren, Adam, and to come / Out of thy loins" (11.454–55). This familial frame registers the crime as fratricide, while simultaneously allowing Adam to see these figures as his sons. Of course, Michael is here following the plot of Genesis, but it seems intriguing that an epic dominated by the biblical first father and mother begins its account of postlapsarian history with this originary scene of two brothers. Antimonarchic writers in this period commonly mobilized this story of fratricide to accommodate critiques of oppression, including attacks on the monarchy, naming Cain along with Nimrod as the first earthly king.[33] Milton's telling can be read as part of this movement, but the particular unfolding of the story here requires closer attention. Before Michael provides his explana-tory note, identifying the two men as brothers, the anonymous men have no particular place in history, appearing much like the generic brutes of Thomas

Hobbes's state of nature, subject only to the authority of violence. Though Michael provides an epistemological frame when he informs Adam they are his offspring, infusing the scene with familial relations does nothing to decrease the violence or even to calm Adam's mind. In fact, the first father never acknowledges his paternity. Instead, he focuses on his own individual future, asking, "Is this the way / I must return to native dust?" (11.461–62). As noted above, placing Adam, the authorizing agent of Filmer's theory of the right of kings, as the witness of Nimrod's tyranny pushes the reader to recognize these last two books as an engagement with political theory, particularly patriarchalist thought.[34] By having Adam comment on this scene of human brutality, Milton stages a clash between Filmerian authority and Hobbesian violence.[35] Adam's inability to recognize his own sons, his shock, and then his solipsistic turn back to his own mortality emphasize the instability of a system that puts full faith in the powers of the patriarch. The relation between father and son is one of distance and confusion, prohibiting its use as a political foundation. By representing this break in authority through the figure of the very first earthly father, this moment disrupts the Filmerian argument that the historical presence of Adam provides a sound basis for government.

In the next scene, Michael fills in the picture of the confusion of reproduction by presenting a terrifying picture of bodies in pain:

> Numbers of all diseas'd, all maladies
> Of ghastly Spasm, or racking torture, qualms
> Of heart-sick Agony, all feverous kinds,
> Convulsions, Epilepsies, fierce Catarrhs,
> Intestine Stone and Ulcer, Colic pangs,
> Daemoniac Frenzy, moping Melancholy
> And Moon-struck madness, pining Atrophy,
> Marasmus, and wide-wasting Pestilence,
> Dropsies, and Asthmas, and Joint-racking Rheums. (11.480–88)

The Lazar house tableau again presents anonymous bodies, which Michael positions in relation to their mother as he marks maternal inheritance, citing "th'inabstinence of Eve" (11.476). The connection to Eve here explicitly refers us back to her indulgence, but also shifts the vision from the opening sin of man against man to sins that multiply through the body. The proliferation of suffering flesh fulfills Eve's fear of giving Death "numbers" to feast upon. Adam responds to this sight by echoing her earlier plan, "Better end here unborn" (11.502). Michael provides some comfort, describing a better version of death through the reproductive metaphor of "till like ripe Fruit thou drop / Into thy Mother's lap" (11.535–36), but does not stop there.

Having introduced the horror of maternal legacy, Michael proceeds to present the most explicit scene of inappropriate breeding. The scene of the sons of Seth cavorting with the daughters of Cain, along with the following scene of war, directly connects the act of sexual reproduction with the multi-plication of sin. Though Adam tries to place the blame exclusively on women, Michael merges the paternal and maternal inheritance of the first two scenes to place the origin of man's suffering in the interaction between man and woman. The resulting warring factions bring together the violence of Cain with the propagation of the house of Lazar, as Adam describes how they

> multiply
> Ten thousand fold the sin of him who slew
> His Brother; for of whom such massacre
> Make they but of their Brethern, men of men? (11.677–80)

Michael elaborates the familial relationship by explaining that "These are the product / Of those ill-mated Marriages thou saw'st" (11.683–84). The political terror of war is described as familial, the spread of the problem of brothers.

As we have already seen, this problem arises as a political problem most explicitly with the reign of Nimrod. Despite the flood's potentially purifying project of "depopulation" (11.756), this tyrannical brother refuses his hori-zontal relationship to his siblings and claims dominion. Michael has much to say about this episode, but after silencing Adam's cry by reminding him of his culpability, the archangel falls into a lament of his own, "O that men / (Canst thou believe?) should be so stupid grown, / While yet the Patriarch liv'd, who scap'd the Flood" (12.115–17). Michael bemoans the inability of man to understand his own history, citing the case of Noah's children. Even though Noah still lives, his presence does nothing to remind his offspring of the lessons of the past. A patriarchalist stance requires continuity between gener-ations, as Filmer particularly argues through the case of Noah, "Not only until the Flood, but after it this patriarchal power did continue, as the very name of Patriarch doth in part prove."[36] But if the presence of the "Pa-triarch," his actual living body, cannot establish rightful order, the claim that authentic political authority can be traced back to dead fathers becomes ludicrous. Patriarchal authority suffers yet another blow as Michael shows us that the actual presence of a father makes no difference.

Michael's sadness over the futility of the relationship between father and sons erupts during a moment laden with reproductive promise—the story of Abraham. As Michael explains to Adam that the sinful offspring of Noah cause God to "avert / His holy Eyes" (12.108–9), the angel also reveals that God resolves: "And one peculiar Nation to select / From all the rest, of whom to be invok'd, / A Nation from one faithful man to spring" (12.111–13). In the face of the hope that Abraham's seed will escape the pollution of the other sons, Michael cries out against man's stupidity. The lament interrupts the continuity of this episode, drawing attention to the interruption of the family that follows. Abraham is called "from his Father's house" (12.121), marking a break in lineage. Though God's promise to Abraham is the promise of the reproduction of a nation, it does not follow a clear narrative of lineage. In fact, Michael is so moved by man's inability to establish cognitive continuity across generations that the continuity of narrative line is ruptured by his lament. His cry sits as a warning against patriarchal authority just as we enter into the story of the great patriarch, Abraham.

Like Eve, Abraham becomes the carrier of the promised seed. Michael calls upon Adam to

> This ponder, that all Nations of the Earth
> Shall in his Seed be blessed; by that Seed
> Is meant thy great deliverer, who shall bruise
> The Serpent's head; whereof to thee anon
> Plainlier shall be reveal'd. This Patriarch blest,
> Whom faithful Abraham due time shall call,
> A Son, and of his Son a Grandchild leaves,
> Like him in faith, in wisdom, and renown;
> The Grandchild with twelve Sons increast.   (12.147–55)

The reproductive promise of Abraham's seed runs through the line from father to son to grandson to great-grandsons. The narrative coherence of the genealogical chain of Abraham and his offspring and their favored status in the eyes of God could easily be used to argue for divine right, based on the succession of patriarchs.[37] Milton, however, will allow no such thing. Abraham's seed does lead to a form of government, but the government is not one of patriarchal inheritance, but one of law: "In the wide wilderness, there they shall found / Their government, and their great senate choose / Through the twelve tribes, to rule by laws ordain'd" (12.224–26). As Michael explains to Adam, Abraham's righteous offspring choose to be governed by a senate, not a patriarchal monarch. Milton's description of the senate as chosen by the people departs from the biblical accounts in both Exodus, chapter 24, and Numbers, chapter 11, by emphasizing the people's participation in the formation of their government, introducing the idea that divine authority is granted to the people who then bestow it upon their rulers.[38] Thus, Milton shows how the succession of generations continues without legitimating political authority.

In his tract *The Readie and Easy Way*, Milton argues that this "supreme councel of seaventie" (YP 7:436) was the model republican government, pointing out that one of the benefits of a senate was that it was not subject to the individual mortality of a king, which constantly threatened the stability of the state.[39] Emphasizing the uncertainty of lineage, Milton explains, "the death of a king, causeth oft-times many dangerous alterations," but because a senate exists despite the death of a member, it is "eternal" and "immortal" (YP 7:436). Appearing in April 1660, Milton's tract preceded Parliament's proclamation restoring Charles II by only one month. The political currency of Milton's comments on the destabilizing effect of a king's death appears when Parliament proclaims, "that immediately upon the decease of our late sovereign Lord King Charles, the imperial crown of the realm of England . . . did come to his most excellent majesty Charles the Second."[40] In order to deny the challenge to monarchy posed by the execution of Charles I, the proclamation claims that the death of a king causes no interruption in royal reign because the heir automatically assumes his new role. This reading of history asserts a perfect continuity between fathers and sons, denying the rupture of death. Milton's emphasis on the king's death marks the break between generations, the disjunctive nature of genealogy, and ultimately the failure of a patriarchalist vision of political stability. Like the many interruptions in the familial story of *Paradise Lost,* it denies the ability of "birth-right" and "blood-royal" to authorize political power.

The only individual with a legitimate claim to sovereignty through lineage in the last two books of Milton's poem is the one whose origins are most thoroughly obscured. Michael describes how the Son of God, the "Anointed King Messiah might be born / Barr'd of his right" (12.359–60). In these lines, Michael does not tell of Christ's birth, he only suggests it when he says the Messiah "might be born." William Walker sharply points out that the grammatical uncertainty of these lines emphasizes the impossibility of registering Christ's birth as a temporal event.[41] The problem, however, is not only temporal but also political. The line break marks the division between political right and divine right. Here, the only proper monarch is the divine monarch, and the earthly attempts to understand authority fail to recognize his appearance.[42] If Filmer claims divine right based on the familial connection between Adam and his sons, the displacement of Christ from royal genealogy turns his own argument against him. Michael demonstrates this point formally by introducing the Son of God into his chronology only to withdraw him twice, first for ten lines and then for twenty-eight, before he narrates his birth. The Messiah, who cannot be fully integrated into the linear narrative of generations, is simultaneously the only figure who legitimately "shall ascend / the Throne hereditary" (12.369–70). Through this formal sleight-of-hand, Milton's poetry enacts the theory of divine monarchy he articulates in his prose tract *The Readie and Easy Way,* in which he argues that "the kingdom of Christ our common King and Lord, is hid to this world, and such *gentilish* imitations forbid in express words by himself to all his disciples" (YP 7:429). Though inherited sin binds human generations together and defines Adam's understanding of the future, inherited authority marks only divine relations. The paradox of Michael's description of the Son's inheritance only grows when we consider the circumstances of his birth. Born of a virgin, without a human father, Christ inherits that which is not inheritable.

Yet Michael's lesson is not complete, as he must once more help Adam to truly understand proper familial relations. When Adam finally hears of Christ's birth, he is overcome with tears of joy. His words reveal that part of his joy comes from the relief that he still has a fatherly part to play in this story of redemption, as he exclaims:

> O Prophet of glad tidings, finisher
> Of utmost hope! Now clear I understand
> What oft my steadiest thoughts have searcht in vain,
> Why our great expectation should be call'd
> The seed of Woman: Virgin Mother, Hail,
> High in the love of Heav'n, yet from my Loins
> Thou shalt proceed, and from thy Womb the Son
> Of God most high; So God with man unites.
> Needs must the Serpent now his capital bruise
> Expect with mortal pain: say where and when
> Thir fight, what stroke shall bruise the Victor's heel.   (12.375–85)

Before Adam even asks about the fight between Christ and Satan, he places himself in a genealogical relationship to the savior, emphasizing the importance of "The seed," his "Loins," and Mary's "womb." Michael responds to Adam's joyous inquiry by reminding him not to imagine Christ's victory as a physical battle, telling the story of the Crucifixion and the Resurrection. He ends his intervention in Adam's moment of supposed clarity, however, with a more subtle push away from the body. Through the birth, death, and resurrection of Christ, the reproductive promise made through Adam's seed has been converted. Michael explains to Adam that from the day of Christ's sacrifice,

> Not only to the Sons of Abraham's Loins
> Salvation shall be Preacht, but to the Sons
> Of Abraham's faith wherever through the world;
> So in his seed all nations shall be blest.   (12.447–50)

The promise of the "loins" has been replaced by the promise of "faith." Michael undercuts Adam's emphasis on the human reproduction of Christ by explaining that God's blessing will no longer be derived from biological distinction, but from the mark of faith. Thus, just as Christ cannot be understood within the earthly genealogical narrative, his intervention obliterates the political relevance of genealogical thinking, perhaps posing Michael's greatest challenge to patriarchalist justifications of monarchy. Not only does human genealogy mistake the presence of the true monarch but, through its preoccupation with the "loins" of the father, it also ignores the relevance of Christ's sacrifice.

Christ's elusive nature in Michael's story brings us back to the very beginning of Book Eleven, as well as returns us to the problem I began with— Adam's inability to relate history to his sons. For although Michael continually withdraws the figure of Christ when talking to Adam, Milton directly represents both the Son and his Father before plunging us into the angelic history lesson. In contrast to the conversation with his sons that Adam imagines, Book Eleven begins with an actual father-son chat, but here the discussants are God, the Father, and his Son. Having heard the prayers of Adam and Eve, the Son offers himself up as a link between their language and God's ear, asking, "let me / Interpret for him" (11.32–33). The need for a mediator between God the Father and his offspring on earth confirms Adam's fear that the connection between fathers and sons is now broken. In the relationship of these divine characters, however, Milton imagines a connection of pure presence between generations. Not only is the Son able to fully convey his meaning to his Father, but his meaning also matches the intent of his Father. Though conversation occurs between divine persons, it seems to describe a connection that is already present, rather than attempting to bridge a gap. As the Father explains to the Son, "all thy request was my decree" (11.47). The two are so connected that the Son's request is always already fulfilled by the Father's command. Unlike human fathers and sons, who are separated by time and mortality, this divine pair is indivisible. Unlike the human fathers whom Adam and Michael condemn for their claims of sovereignty, God comfortably sits upon "the Father's Throne" (11.20). Heaven is figured not only as a monarchy but also as a realm of pure presence. In stark contrast, the postlapsarian world Michael conveys to Adam is marked by disjunction at every turn, prohibiting any authenticating claims of merely genealogical connection. The Son addresses the problem of separation directly when he makes his promise for man, pledging that man will be "Made one with me as I with thee am one" (11.44). The promise of a new form of connection to God the Father through the Son encapsulates the mediation and deferment of human generations. The promise of redemption is the promise that the separate links of the genealogical chain will disappear and generations will mark no longer the distance of separation, but the plenty of synchronic existence. At the threshold of the infamous lump of futurity, the poem pushes us to consider the fullness of heavenly discourse, then hurtles us into the brokenness of postlapsarian history.

If the absence of dramatic presence in these final books marks Milton's attempt to show the impotence of familial narratives in authorizing and stabilizing political power, the question of how to read the other major absence still haunts us. What shall we make of the loss of Eve from the familial dispute of these books? As soon as Michael finishes reprimanding Adam for lamenting his inability to "relate" his stories to his sons, he tells him that he has temporarily put Eve to sleep. Oddly, just before the most elaborate reproductive narrative occurs in the poem, the "Mother of all Mankind" drops out of the account. Unlike Adam, Eve differs from the other humans represented in their dialogue since she is present in time, but absent from the conversation. What is the significance of her peculiarly absent presence in these books that are plagued by the postlapsarian problem of distance? Michael's explanation —that this moment is a corollary to Adam's sleeping during Eve's birth— forces us to ask what is being birthed here and why it can only be produced while mother is sleeping.

Feminist thinking requires that we consider that Milton may be co-opting the means of reproduction, letting two male characters (Michael appears in the form of a man in this scene) narrate the relationship among generations while silencing the once vibrant female character. The almost complete absence of women from Michael's story seems to support such a reading. Sarah, Rebekah, and Rachel play major roles in the stories of Genesis, yet only the lascivious daughters of Cain and an unnamed Mary register in this genealogy. Despite his contesting of patriarchalist theory, Milton's divinely narrated genealogy provides no alternative to gendering history male.[43] However, I believe limiting ourselves to this reading would underestimate the political stakes in these final moments. *Paradise Lost* dramatizes one of the most famous male-female domestic relationships of all time. Leland Ryken argues that, like the book of Genesis itself, Milton's poem participates in the genre of "domestic epic."[44] This description, however, fails to acknowledge the shift in these final books. Ryken notes the many scenes of courtship, marriage, and parenting that fill the first book of the Bible, showing how these household moments seem to inform the poem's scenes of domesticity. When Milton moves beyond Adam and Eve to represent the span of Genesis, however, he omits the very scenes Ryken emphasizes, including the complex family stories of Abraham and Sarah, Isaac and Rebekah, and Jacob and Rachel. In these final books, Milton pushes domestic relationships underground. The private family is temporarily put to sleep, but hardly laid to rest. I propose that the sleeping Eve marks a domestic space that must underlie a government that denies family line as its authenticating agent.

The proper place of the domestic became a loaded question during the reign of Charles I. His court reveled in representing itself as the seat of both the family and the government, pushing antimonarchists to attack the appropriateness of love and women in the serious business of government.[45] The royal court was infused with domesticity and the influence of women, while parliamentarian politics "were depersonalized and institutional: alliances in the 1640s and 1650s were not forged so much through personal and familial links as through shared ideological commitment and shared experience in institutions—the army, parliament, and its committees—that were exclusively male."[46] Given this partisan division over the family, the task for republicans was a tricky one. They had to critique Charles I's unmanly conflation of family and state while simultaneously finding a way to define the family for their own agenda.

Citing Milton's *Doctrine and Discipline of Divorce* as his example, James Holstun argues, "The reformed freehold-household of republicans like Milton, Harrington, and Streater sounds remarkably like the gently masculinist 'intimate sphere' of the bourgeois household analyzed by Habermas, which simultaneously nurtures male civic virtue and keeps women out of the public eye."[47] The epic enacts this Habermasian domestic before our eyes as Eve serves Adam and Raphael and then disappears. Unlike Queen Henrietta Maria, Eve's relationship to her mate does not extend to the realm of male discourse. New work on the role of women during the civil wars, particularly those who claimed a public voice through religion as well as those who actively participated in the emergent public sphere as petitioners, complicates prior assumptions that an attack on monarchy necessarily sends women straight to the kitchen.[48] Not all republican women sat quietly at home. Unlike the female petitioners of the civil wars, however, Eve does not take part in the discourse of the end of the poem.[49]

Milton's imagining of a masculine sphere of discourse separate from the realm of the heterosexual couple does not render the family inconsequential, but rather detoxifies it for the republican cause. Though Books Eleven and Twelve are primarily a story of the human family, the domestic realm of the earlier books is palpably missing. Eve's slumber leaves the reader in a history lesson devoid of the dramatic activity of the earlier narrative. Centuries of readers who complain of the dullness of this section of the poem may envy Eve, who leaves a parallel scene of male conversation in favor of a telling that "would intermix / Grateful digressions, and solve high dispute / With conjugal Caresses" (8.54–56).[50] In Book Eight, domestic conversation, inherently linked to the body, is contrasted to the bleakness of homosocial discussion. In Books Eleven and Twelve, the dramatic body of the poem is missing and, not surprisingly, so is Eve. When these final books are described as "dry and undernourished,"[51] the loss of drama is registered through the language of the private realm. Though the poem becomes unrelentingly familial, the Fall has separated us from the nourishing domestic scenes of the earlier books, leaving some critics hungry readers. The lineal family of Michael's genealogical story sits in stark contrast to the fullness of the domestic family, reminding us that the authorizing narrative of Filmerian doctrine can only be understood as a postlapsarian perversion.

By removing the domestic drama from this scene, Milton formally reenacts Adam's reeducation for the reader. Michael constantly denies Adam's attempt to understand the future through the eyes of an authoritative father and forces him to reorient himself. Similarly, Milton denies his readers present tense dramatizations, forcing them to reorient their mode of reading. By keeping Eve away from this scene, however, Milton is able to stage an attack on political patriarchal authority without surrendering the power of the domestic realm. The political necessity of this delicate negotiation is suggested in Maureen Quilligan's contention that "What is left after reformation and regicide is—to put it at its most basic—the political unit of the nuclear family."[52] The force of the domestic at this moment can be seen in the painter Mary Beale's 1667 treatise on friendship, in which she wrote that the curse Eve passed down to her daughters could only be broken when women entered marriages founded on true friendship. Beale's faith in the power of marriage to remake the fallen world, restoring "the marriage bond to its first institution," points us to Milton's deployment of the domestic as a means to replicate Paradise.[53] Beale's language parallels that of Milton's *Doctrine and Discipline of Divorce,* in which he suggests that the performance of "fit and matchable conversation . . . shall restore the much wrong'd and over-sorrow'd state of matrimony, not only to those mercifull and life-giving remedies of Moses, but, as much as may be, to the serene and blissfull condition it was in at the beginning" (YP 2:239–40). The idea that domesticity returns us to an Edenic state much more surely than royalist genealogy suits Milton's political agenda and sits us at the brink of the literary shift to the novel, in which the role of the domestic will increasingly take center stage.[54] By removing Eve from the genealogical narrative, Milton separates the restorative potential of the domestic ideal of family from the corrupt patriarchalist family.

In this way, Milton shares Michael's mission to convey to mankind the promise of the woman's seed by explaining the true promise of reproduction. Many have noted that Milton's portrayal of cyclical decline and continual violence is consistently interrupted by his emphasis on the "one just man" through his representation of Enoch, Noah, Abraham, and, ultimately, Christ.[55] Achsah Guibbory argues that the figure of the one good man who can do right on his own, but cannot necessarily reform his nation, becomes an important theme for the disillusioned revolutionary living in exile. What I suggest, however, is that Milton's emphasis on particular people as markers of these moments of hope continues Adam's exhortation to Eve to reproduce. These are not individual figures portrayed in a vacuum—they appear in a narrative line of generations. As a result, they offer something beyond a model of godly behavior. They offer a sense of futurity that can be fulfilled through the birthing of sons. Their specific promise is reproductive.

When Adam tells Eve they must reproduce in order to enable the eventual birth of the savior, he repeats God's promise and puts faith in the fulfillment of that promise. In this moment, faith in reproduction becomes faith in God. If we turn to Guibbory's definition of typology in these final books, it sounds much like this idea of looking to future generations for salvation: "Typology admits a parallel with a person, action or event in the past, but it stresses the forward movement of history and the superiority of the present to the past, as later antitypes fulfill and surpass the figures that foreshadow them."[56] In a typology like Milton's, where the emphasis is on parallels between people, the relationship between type and antitype is not only one of divine pattern, it is one of genealogical connection. It is crucial to remember that, in light of the conversation between Michael and Adam, this connection must now be understood as incomplete, instrumental, and irrelevant to the political realm. Once Adam and the English people recognize these limitations, however, reproductive promise can resume its rightful place.

Both William Walker and Regina Schwartz complicate Guibbory's definition by discussing Milton's idiosyncratic use of typology in these books as an attempt to register the pessimistic optimism of a moment of historical fulfillment constantly deferred.[57] The idea of fulfillment deferred returns us to Adam's lament about being unable to convey his story to those in the future. Once death becomes a reality, generations will always be separated. In fact, the idea of generations as separate cohorts can only make sense if they cease to exist at the same time. In the face of this dismal inability to connect to the future—the fear of ceasing to be—reproduction becomes a mode of relationship inherently marked by rupture. Though it offers a way to deny the finality of death, it refuses full presence. Progeny will continue the biological line, perhaps even in the spirit of their ancestors, but at some point their ancestors are only spirits. After the Fall, narrative told through family line is always a ghostly form.

These final scenes continually convey the power of narratives structured by reproductive understanding and refuse to abandon them completely. Because of this power, they seem to make two moves to change the role of the familial understanding of time. The first is a move upward—Michael seizes control from the earthly Adam. The second is a move downward—Eve marks the space of an emerging domestic sphere that will ground the development of interiority. As contractualism makes its bid against patriarchalism, the fight over family is fierce. The resonance of family as a structuring principle can not be surrendered to a strict monarchical ideology. In the final books of Milton's epic, the family is relocated. Its power is harnessed and redirected, partially back into a divine scheme and partially into a domestic realm that sleeps while the surgery happens, but awakens to walk out, hand-in-hand.

Boston University

NOTES

For their generous and insightful assistance with this essay, I am indebted to Ann Baynes Coiro, Michael McKeon, Derek Attridge, Albert Labriola, Rachel Hollander, Brian Walsh, and an anonymous reader for *Milton Studies*.

1. Sir Robert Filmer, *Observations upon Aristotles Politiques* (1652), in *Patriarcha and Other Writings*, ed. Johann P. Sommerville (Cambridge, 1991), 236–37.

2. Nigel Smith's important study of the dynamic relationship between literary form and politics, *Literature and Revolution in England, 1640–1660* (New Haven, 1994), suggests the importance of such an approach, arguing that Milton's generic transformations are "the key to our interpretation of Milton's intervention in history" (7).

3. Critical discussions of the end of the poem have generally used the term "narrative" to describe Michael's representation of the future in Book Twelve, marking his shift from visual to verbal representation. Here I am using "narrative" to describe Michael's account of all human history, including both Books Eleven and Twelve. This difference in terminology reflects my belief that even the visions Michael shows to Adam are placed within the linear narrative of an ongoing story—a story of family.

Balachandra A. Rajan's assessment, in *"Paradise Lost" and the Seventeenth Century Reader* (London, 1947), 85, places him in a line of modern scholars who critique the dearth of style in these final books, starting with C. S. Lewis, *A Preface to "Paradise Lost"* (1942; reprint, London, 1961), and including Douglas Bush, *"Paradise Lost" in Our Time: Some Comments* (1945; reprint, Gloucester, 1957); Charles Martindale, *John Milton and the Transformation of Ancient Epic* (Totowa, 1986); and Louis Martz, *The Paradise Within: Studies in Vaughan, Traherne, and Milton* (New Haven, 1964). In a more recent assessment of these books in *The Lofty Rhyme* (London, 1970), Rajan softens his view, claiming, "Severity has its own aesthetic virtues" (98).

4. John Milton, *Paradise Lost* (1667), in *Complete Poems and Major Prose*, ed. Merritt Y. Hughes (New York, 1957), 10.989–91. All subsequent references are to this edition and will appear parenthetically in the text by book and line.

5. In addition to the horrific image of maternity in the allegory of Sin, Louis Schwartz, " 'Conscious Terrors' and the 'Promised Seed': Seventeenth-Century Obstetrics and the Allegory of Sin and Death in *Paradise Lost*," in *Milton Studies* 32, ed. Albert C. Labriola (Pittsburgh, 1995), 63–89, has shown the frightening nature of reproduction in *An Epitaph on the Marchioness of Winchester* and *Sonnet 23*, linking these depictions to Milton's own familial experiences and the high rate of mortality during childbirth in the period.

6. Sir Robert Filmer, *Observations Concerning the Originall of Government* (1652) in Sommerville, *Patriarcha and Other Writings*, 184–234. Filmer also critiques Milton's claim from *The Tenure of Kings and Magistrates* (1649) that the people have a grant from God to choose their government.

7. On patriarchalist theory in the period, see Gordon J. Schochet's pivotal study, *Patriarchalism in Political Thought: The Authoritarian Family and Political Speculation and Attitudes Especially in Seventeenth-Century England* (New York, 1975), 8. In his discussion of patriarchal theories in the seventeenth century, Schochet connects nascent debates about patriarchal authority in the late-sixteenth-century succession debate to the full-scale explosion of such battles during the Exclusion Controversy (47–50).

8. David Loewenstein, *Milton and the Drama of History: Historical Vision, Iconoclasm, and the Literary Imagination* (Cambridge, 1990), 92.

9. Lewis, *A Preface to "Paradise Lost,"* 129.

10. John King, *Milton and Religious Controversy: Satire and Polemic in "Paradise Lost"* (Cambridge, 2000), 170.

11. Sir Robert Filmer, *Observations upon Aristotles Politiques* (1652), in Sommerville, *Patriarcha and Other Writings*, 236.

12. John Milton, *A Defence of the People of England* (1651), in *Political Writings*, ed. Martin Dzelzainis (Cambridge, 1991), 68, hereafter cited in the text by page number.

13. Filmer, *Observations Concerning the Originall of Government*, 203.

14. Salmasius goes a step further on this point, claiming that whether the power of the king is derived from the will of the people or usurpation, it is still " 'paternal' and hereditary, because he who obtains the kingdom in combat or by will of the people, acquires it for himself and his descendants." Unlike Filmer, he makes an argument for paternal legacy, regardless of paternal origin. See *Defensio Regia*, in *Complete Prose Works of John Milton*, 8 vols., ed. Don M. Wolfe et al. (New Haven, 1953–82), 4:1031. All subsequent references to this edition will be cited parenthetically in the text as YP, followed by volume and page number.

15. Sir Robert Filmer, *Directions for Obedience to Government in Dangerous or Doubtful Times* (1652), in Sommerville, *Patriarcha and Other Writings*, 283.

16. *Somers Tracts. A Collection of Scarce and Valuable Tracts . . . Selected from . . . Public as well as Private Libraries, Particularly That of the Late Lord Somers*, 2d ed., 13 vols., ed. Sir Walter Scott (London, 1809–15), 7:430.

17. Paula Backscheider, *Spectacular Politics: Theatrical Power and Mass Culture in Early Modern England* (Baltimore, 1993), notes that the regicide John Cook argued that the king "must die, and monarchy with him" (8).

18. Howard Nenner, *The Right to Be King: The Succession to the Crown of England, 1603–1714* (Chapel Hill, N.C., 1995), argues that upon the Restoration, "These points of indefeasiblity and an unbroken continuity in the succession were being sharply underscored so as not to be lost" (95).

19. Robert Sanderson, preface to James Ussher, *The Power communicated by God to the Prince, and the obedience required of the subject* (London, 1661), sec. 18.

20. Ibid., sec. 18. On the relationship between the thinking of Sanderson and Filmer, see Schochet, *Patriarchalism in Political Thought*, 185–88.

21. Richard Mocket, *God and the King* (London, 1663). See Schochet, *Patriarchalism in Political Thought*, 88–90.

22. Schochet, *Patriarchalism in Political Thought*, 5.

23. On the significance of Nimrod in seventeenth-century political discourse, see Sharon Achinstein, *Milton and the Revolutionary Reader* (Princeton, N.J., 1994), 83–88; Christopher Hill, *The English Bible and the Seventeenth-Century Revolution* (London, 1994), 217–22; David Loewenstein, *Milton and the Drama of History: Historical Vision, Iconoclasm, and the Literary Imagination* (Cambridge, 1990), 109–11; David Norbrook, *Writing the English Republic: Poetry, Rhetoric and Politics, 1627–1660* (Cambridge, 2000), 463–67; Annabel Patterson, *Reading between the Lines* (Madison, 1993), 252–55; Mary Ann Radzinowicz, "The Politics of *Paradise*

Lost," in *John Milton,* ed. Annabel Patterson (London, 1992), 120–41; and Elizabeth Sauer, *Barbarous Dissonance and Images of Voice in Milton's Epics* (Montreal, 1996), 14–34.

24. Radzinowicz, "The Politics of *Paradise Lost,*" interprets Milton's telling of the story of Nimrod as part of his republican politics, noting that Nimrod "ends the pure, brotherly, simple historical commonwealth of Noah's stock" (129).

25. Patterson, *Reading between the Lines,* 253.

26. For a classic literary example of this vein of royalist argument, see lines 769–74 of John Dryden, *Absalom and Achitophel* (1681), in *The Poems of John Dryden,* vol. 1, ed. Paul Hammond (London, 1995), 516.

27. Achinstein, *Milton and the Revolutionary Reader,* 84–85.

28. Sir Robert Filmer, *The Anarchy of a Limited or Mixed Monarchy* (1648) in Sommerville, *Patriarcha and Other Writings,* 145.

29. An important recent exception to this approach is Jameela Lares's argument in *Milton and the Preaching Arts* (Pittsburgh, 2001) that for the contemporary reader these books would resonate with the extremely present form of the sermon (141–68). Though my argument suggests a more explicitly political context, I believe it parallels Lares's contention by attempting to understand the end of the epic as drawing upon a historically specific form.

30. Barbara Kiefer Lewalski, "Structure and the Symbolism of Vision in Michael's Prophecy, *Paradise Lost,* Books XI–XII," *Philological Quarterly* 42 (1963): 25–35. For a discussion of these books as part of a process of spiritual internalization, see Georgia Christopher, *Milton and the Science of the Saints* (Princeton, N.J., 1982), 183–98. See William Kerrigan, *The Sacred Complex: On the Psychogenesis of "Paradise Lost"* (Cambridge, 1983), and Marshall Grossman, *Authors unto Themselves: Milton and the Revelation of History* (Cambridge, 1987), for psychoanalytic analyses of internalization, which subtly complicate the concept of the internal.

31. William Walker, "Typology and *Paradise Lost,* Books XI and XII," in *Milton Studies* 25, ed. James D. Simmonds (Pittsburgh, 1989), 248. See Regina Schwartz, "From Shadowy Types to Shadowy Types: The Unendings of *Paradise Lost,*" in *Milton Studies* 24, ed. James D. Simmonds (Pittsburgh, 1988), 123–41, for a complementary reading of Milton's use of typology to defer meaning in these final books.

32. For a full discussion of the range of configurations Milton employs to imagine history in these final books, see Loewenstein, *Milton and the Drama of History,* 92–125.

33. For a discussion of the range of political meanings assigned to the story of Cain and Abel, see Hill, *The English Bible,* 204–15.

34. Patterson, *Reading between the Lines,* 252.

35. Attacking Hobbes's theory of the state of nature, Filmer, *Observations Concerning the Originall of Government,* specifically disputes claims of originary violence (188). Milton's location of this scene of violence within sacred history provides biblical support for contractual theories of government.

36. Filmer, *Patriarcha* (1680), in Sommerville, *Patriarcha and Other Writings,* 7.

37. Arguing for the godliness of monarchy, Filmer, *Observations upon Aristotle's Politiques,* cites Abraham's reproductive line: "We find it is a punishment to have 'no king', Hosea iii, 4, and promises as a blessing to Abraham, Genesis, xvii, 6, 'that kings shall come out of thee'" (284).

38. In both Exodus 24:1 and Numbers 11:16, God tells Moses to gather seventy of the elders of Israel. Though this "gathering" could have involved a process of election, there is nothing in the biblical accounts to suggest it. Milton's retelling thus provides a distinctively antimonarchical interpretation.

39. Robert Ayers, YP 7:436 n. 129, suggests that Milton here responds to the claims of the patriarchalist Jean Bodin, whose work Filmer drew on extensively.

40. Sir Walter Scott, *Somers Tracts,* 7:430.

41. Walker, "Typology and *Paradise Lost*," 248–49.

42. Since Charles II had chosen to return to London on his birthday, emphasizing the connection between his "birth-right" and his ascension to the throne, Milton's emphasis on the inability of the people to recognize the birth of the one true monarch may also have been an attempt to distinguish between the divine Son and the newly restored son of Charles I. In John Winter's sermon on the day of Charles II's coronation, the connection between the two "sons" is explicitly made: "He enters into his earthly, as Christ entered into his heavenly Kingdome; *through much tribulation*." See John Winter, *A Sermon Preached at East Dearham in Norf. May 29, 1661* (London, 1662).

43. For a radically inclusive representation of the women of Genesis, see Lucy Hutchinson, *Order and Disorder* (1679), ed. David Norbrook (Oxford, 2001).

44. Leland Ryken, "*Paradise Lost* and Its Biblical Epic Models," in *Milton and Scriptural Tradition: The Bible into Poetry,* ed. James Sims and Leland Ryken (Columbia, Mo., 1984), 43–81.

45. See Ann Baynes Coiro, "'A ball of strife': Caroline Poetry and Royal Marriage," in *The Royal Image: Representations of Charles I,* ed. Thomas Corns (Cambridge, 1999), 26–47, and Erica Veevers, *Images of Love and Religion: Queen Henrietta Maria and Court Entertainments* (Cambridge, 1989).

46. Ann Hughes, *Women, Men, and Politics in the English Civil War* (Keele, England, 1997), 18.

47. James Holstun, *Ehud's Dagger: Class Struggle in the English Revolution* (London, 2000), 264. Craig Calhoun, *Habermas and the Public Sphere* (Cambridge, 1992), explains that according to Habermas's analysis, "the family was reconstituted as an intimate sphere that grounded . . . the participation of its patriarchal head in the public sphere" (10). Amid his critique of Salmasius's patriarchalism, Milton consistently mocks his adversary's home life, suggesting that domestic disorder leads to political injustice. See *A Defence,* 153–54.

48. See Lois Schwoerer, "Women's Public Political Voice in England, 1640–1740," in *Women Writers and the Early Modern British Political Tradition,* ed. Hilda Smith (Cambridge, 1998), 56–74; Ann Hughes, "Gender and Politics in Leveller Literature," in *Political Culture and Cultural Politics in Early Modern England,* ed. Susan Amussen and M. Kishlansky (Manchester, 1995), 162–68, and Ann Marie McEntee, "'The [Un]Civill-Sisterhood of Oranges and Lemons': Female Petitioners and Demonstrators, 1642–53," in *Pamphlet Wars: Prose in the English Revolution,* ed. James Holstun (London, 1992), 92–111.

49. On this issue, see Janel Mueller, "Dominion as Domesticity: Milton's Imperial God and the Experience of History," in *Milton and the Imperial Vision,* ed. Balachandra Rajan and Elizabeth Sauer (Pittsburgh, 1999).

50. Starting with Addison's critique in the *Spectator,* the last two books of the poem have often been described as the least pleasing, though during the second half of the twentieth century most critics argue that they are aesthetically purposeful. For a full discussion of this shift, see Stanley Fish, "Transmuting the Lump: *Paradise Lost,* 1942–1979," in *Doing What Comes Naturally: Change, Rhetoric and the Practice of Theory in Literary and Legal Studies* (Durham, N.C., 1989), 247–87. Also see Loewenstein, *Milton and the Drama of History,* 92–93, for a more recent discussion of the debate between the critics and the defenders of these books.

51. Martindale, *Transformation of Ancient Epic,* 148.

52. Maureen Quilligan, *Milton's Spenser: The Politics of Reading* (Ithaca, N.Y., 1983), 13. Arguing from a Marxist history of the division of labor, Quilligan sees Milton as echoing the emerging gendering of production and reproduction.

53. Beale suggests the recuperative power of marriage when she writes, "A Curse, which shee not onely procur'd to Her selfe, but entail'd upon all Her Female Posterity except a small

number, who by Friendship's interposition, have restored the marriage bond to its first institution." See Beale, *Freindship* [*sic*] (1667), quoted in Carol Barash, *English Women's Poetry, 1649–1714: Politics, Community, and Linguistic Authority* (Oxford, 1996), 94.

54. In her analysis of the role of gender in Eve's birth scenes, Mary Nyquist, "The Genesis of Gendered Subjectivity in the Divorce Tracts and in *Paradise Lost*," in *Re-membering Milton: Essays on the Texts and Traditions,* ed. Mary Nyquist and Margaret W. Ferguson (New York, 1987), 99–127, contends, "the domestic sphere with which her [Eve's] subjectivity associates itself will soon be in need of novels" (123).

55. On the importance of the individual believer in these final scenes, see Achsah Guibbory, *The Map of Time: Seventeenth-Century English Literature and Ideas of Pattern in History* (Urbana, 1986), 204–6.

56. Ibid., 188. For a full study of the role of Milton's use of typology, see William G. Madsen, *From Shadowy Types to Truth: Studies in Milton's Symbolism* (New Haven, 1968).

57. The concept of typology as deferred fulfillment is the focus of both Walker, "Typology and *Paradise Lost*," and Schwartz, "From Shadowy Types to Shadowy Types."

PARADISE REGAINED AS RULE OF CHARITY: RELIGIOUS TOLERATION AND THE END OF TYPOLOGY

Phillip J. Donnelly

IN HIS BIOGRAPHY of Milton (1694), Edward Phillips observes that *Paradise Regained* "is generally censur'd to be much inferiour to [*Paradise Lost*], though [Milton] could not hear with patience any such thing when related to him."[1] Why should Milton be so utterly convinced that *Paradise Regained* was at least as good as *Paradise Lost,* if not superior? Historical evidence suggests that he wrote most of the brief epic after writing *Paradise Lost.*[2] In composing the later work between 1665 and 1670, Milton was able to write with some sense of how his earlier poem had been and would be understood, at least by initial contemporary readers. Milton's strong reaction to the comparison of the two epics at the expense of *Paradise Regained* resulted, I contend, from his understanding of the often mistaken basis for such comparison. In his account of the early readers of *Paradise Lost,* Nicholas von Maltzahn shows that the epic's central war in heaven was one of the most important elements of the poem for Restoration readers. Those early readers tended, however, to understand the war not as an imagined prototype of the spiritual battle described in Revelation, chapter 12, but as an endorsement of the traditional epic ethos that valorized warfare and physical coercion.[3] By contrast, the "great duel" central to *Paradise Regained* is explicitly stipulated to be "not of arms" but between "wisdom" and "hellish wiles" (1.174–75).[4] Thus, like Michael's earlier explanation to Adam, that the fight between Christ and Satan does not concern the "local wounds" of physical battle (*PL* 12.386–95), the later epic reminds readers that the most important warfare does not depend on physical coercion.[5] In *Paradise Lost,* the explicit account of Christ's whole life and work on earth is summarized in a few lines (12.359–71, 386–435), whereas *Paradise Regained* presents one segment of that life in a dilated form in order to make a similar point regarding the noncoercive nature of charity. In the later poem we are reminded of Christ's eventual conquest, which will "drive [Satan] back to Hell" with "all his vast force," but the Father observes that first he must "Exercise [the Son] in the Wilderness" (*PR* 1.153, 156):

> There he shall first lay down the rudiments
> Of his great warfare, ere I send him forth
> To conquer Sin and Death the two grand foes,
> By Humiliation and strong Sufferance:
> His weakness shall o'ercome Satanic strength
> And all the world, and mass of sinful flesh.   (1.157–62)

Because of its unmistakable emphasis upon the spiritual nature of the described conflict, *Paradise Regained* could address the apparently common failure to appreciate the earlier epic's war in heaven as a critique of existing assumptions about heroism, ontology, and religious coercion. "A fool will be a fool with the best book, yea or without book."[6] Yet *Paradise Regained* suggests that Milton may not have resigned the earlier poem entirely to such foolish misreading and may have attempted to offer a corrective to such misunderstanding.

Throughout his writing, and long before the composition of *Paradise Regained,* Milton had addressed the question of how humans are to understand divine love or charity, and how such an understanding might guide further biblical interpretation. At one level, the term "charity" is used by Milton as a synonym for sanctification (see, for example, *PL* 12.581–87). "Charity" is also used, however, to indicate the divine "Love without end" that is expressed fully to all creatures by the Son (3.142) and which leads him to redeem mankind (3.213–16). In some respects the former sense of "charity" can be understood as the partial human participation in the latter. The potential for lexical confusion arises, therefore, from the fact that "charity" indicates the divine love that is the source of both redemption and sanctification but refers also specifically to sanctification alone, as the temporal human sharing in divine love as a response to the gift of redemption. Milton's use of the term is further complicated by his appeal to "charity" as a guide to biblical interpretation in his prose works. Protestants commonly cited a "rule of faith" (*analogia fidei*), defined in various ways, as a guide to biblical interpretation.[7] Milton effectively subsumes the "*analogy* of Evangelick doctrine," or "the rule of faith," within his account of charity (YP 2:338–40). In doing so, he argues for the integral role of ethical praxis within intellectual apprehension at the same time that he consistently presumes that the content of charity is to some degree objectively intelligible in the life and work of Christ.[8] Thus Milton's sense of the "rule of charity" as an interpretive guide draws upon his understanding of both charity as temporal sanctification and charity as divine love. Moreover, because he views Christ as the mediator between those two realities, Milton employs a specifically typological poetic in order to articulate the relationship between justification and sanctification. This is why typology, as we shall see, is integral to his poetic attempt to show that authentic Christian faith and practice preclude the use of coercion in support of religious causes.

The argument here unfolds in two stages. Taking as a point of departure Milton's treatment of religious toleration in his prose, the first part explains how the last two books of *Paradise Lost* use biblical typology to present an implacable critique of religious coercion. Central to his poetic strategy is a rearticulation of the relationship between justification and sanctification so that those key Protestant concepts could not be deployed to underwrite religious violence. The second stage of the argument shows how *Paradise Regained* engages the same theological concepts by means of typology, specifically in order to provide an interpretive guide to the Christocentric poetic of the longer epic. In this way, the brief epic can be understood as an interpretive "rule of charity" for *Paradise Lost,* in that *Paradise Regained* offers a more explicit statement of the ethos and ontology that more subtly informs the earlier poem.

I

Although Milton's career-long preoccupation with religious toleration is well known, the way in which his arguments hinge upon the interpretation of key Reformed teachings is less clearly understood. His treatment of the relationship between justification and sanctification is central to his repeated arguments against the use of coercion in religious causes.⁹ Milton follows a similar logic throughout many of his prose tracts, whether arguing for religious liberty, domestic liberty, or the "liberty of unlicensed printing." In each case, he argues that the nature of the unity between Christian faith ("saving knowledge" or justification) and the praxis of charity (sanctification) precludes the use of state coercion regarding either. His specific treatment of the question of religious toleration is most fully elaborated in his *Treatise of Civil Power in Ecclesiastical Causes: Shewing that it is not Lawfull for any Power on Earth to Compell in Matters of Religion* (1659). The tract's first argument (of four) is based on an appeal to the nature of "religion" and begins with a definition of the only two sources of "divine rule or authority" for Protestants. The sole external authority, "without us warrantable to one another as a common ground," is "holy scripture," while the only other is the "illumination of the Holy Spirit" within, "so interpreting that scripture as warrantable to ourselves and to such whose consciences we perswade" (YP 7:242).¹⁰ In elaborating this point, Milton emphasizes that a genuine Protestant is one who "preferrs the scripture before the church, and acknowledges none but the Scripture sole interpreter of itself to the conscience" (243). Thus to force people to "beleeve as the magistrate appoints," much less the church, against their consciences, is antithetical to the nature of Protestant faith, so defined (246). Milton emphasizes that biblical accounts of church discipline are expressly limited to separation from fellowship (245, 269).[11] Thus, Milton does not reject the idea of church discipline per se, nor does his account of conscience entail subjectivism. Rather, he argues that the objective truth of divine love in which both Scripture and conscience participate is inherently noncoercive.

The tract's second main point against the use of force in matters of religion is that even if a magistrate were capable to judge in such matters, "he hath no right" (YP 7:255) because the nature of Christ's authority does not govern by "outward force." In that context, he maintains that the sum of "euangelic religion" "is told in two words, faith and charitie; or beleef and practise" (255). In short, genuine faith is freely accepted, while authentic charity, or sanctification, is necessarily the "fruit of the Spirit" that results from faith (255–56). In this context he cites Galatians 5:22–23 as an elaboration of the meaning of "charity" in order to show the absurdity of trying to coerce people into exhibiting, for example, joy, peace, or patience (YP 7:255–56). Thus the nature of the relationship between justification and sanctification is the crux of his argument against trying to coerce certain actions (good works) that should be the result of saving faith. As a result, his second point also already contains within itself the logic for the other two remaining points of his tract: that coercion in religious causes violates the nature of "Christian libertie"; and that it fails to achieve its own ostensible ends, with respect to God's glory or the benefiting of others. For example, in addressing the claim that coercion is necessary in order to ensure that "prophane and licentious persons" "not neglect the performance of religious and holy duties," Milton points out that such a view falsely assumes that such people are even capable of performing those duties (267). At root is simply a reiteration of the Protestant account of the relation between saving faith and works. In effect, to coerce people to follow certain forms of worship ascribes a saving efficacy to works apart from faith and violates the freedom required to make those actions an authentic expression of charity, or sanctification.

The logic of Milton's argument here is crucial to his larger claim specifically because the Reformed distinction between justification and sanctification had also been deployed to justify religious coercion. The soteriological distinction within the person of each believer, between faith and works, was deployed as a foundation for the ecclesiological distinction between the *forum conscientiae* and *forum externum* in the government of the church.[12] In effect, the use of state coercion in matters of church discipline was justified on the grounds that such matters concerned only temporal or external government and did not pertain to saving faith. The most influential English theorist of such a view was Richard Hooker.[13] Despite his own irenic stance, the logic of his argument ends up legitimating the use of state coercion in matters of church discipline. Hooker did not actually formulate an explicit argument for or against religious toleration per se.[14] Nevertheless, he does indicate that those dissenters who suffer state coercion for their rejection of episcopacy do so as a just consequence of their opposition to civil authority.[15] In effect, Hooker connects the temporal orientation of sanctification with the legitimacy of temporal civil authority. By insisting upon the continuity of all temporal authority, his logic cannot avoid legitimating the use of coercion in support of external religious behavior as distinct from spiritual matters of saving faith. Milton's consistent challenge throughout his poetry and prose is twofold: to preserve the conceptual distinction between justification and sanctification so as not to entail salvation by works, but, at the same time, to articulate the practical unity between them in such a way that shows the incoherence of allowing bodily force any proactive role in promoting the actions of sanctification.

The consistency in Milton's thinking is evident in his use of the same root logic to make similar claims in *Of True Religion* (1673), fourteen years after the publication of *Civil Power*. In the later tract, Milton lists a series of theological issues that are "the hottest disputes among Protestants," but which may nevertheless be "charitably enquir'd into" (YP 8:424). The list includes Lutherans on consubstantiation, Calvinists on predestination, Anabaptists on infant baptism, Arians and Socinians on the Trinity, and Arminians on "free will against free grace" (424–25). Some critics have debated whether Milton does, in this particular tract, identify the Socinian position as his own.[16] Such debate, however, whether arguing for or against Milton's explicit endorsement of Arianism, actually risks obscuring the central point in *Of True Religion*. His primary aim is to persuade a Restoration Parliament that the toleration of dissenters does not entail a susceptibility to the political threat of Catholicism; his rhetorical purpose is not to attack or defend Trinitarianism, but to identify a series of doctrines extrinsic to "saving faith." Before presenting the list of disputed issues, Milton states openly that regarding "all things absolutely necessary to salvation" (that is, justification), these doctrines "will be found less than such" (424). The passage goes on to emphasize that even if such beliefs are disputed among Protestants, such that some might be in error, "it cannot be imagin'd that God would desert [them] ... to damnable Errors & a Reprobate sense" (426). As before, his argument draws on the commonplace Protestant self-identification with *sola scriptura* (against tradition) and *sola fides* (rather than works) (419–24). In short, Milton's reasoning against religious coercion rests on the claim that to make a certain kind of worship (sanctification) a condition of salvation (justification) is to return to salvation by works. In this respect, his argument is also based on an appeal to "charity," or sanctification, understood as the human response to the charity expressed in the divine gift of salvation.

Between the publication of *Civil Power* and *Of True Religion,* Milton published the two epic poems in which he reiterates the claim that Christian charity, or sanctification, necessarily presumes authentic freedom, that is, freedom from bondage to sin, enabling the creaturely response to the always previous action of divine gift, whether the gift of creation or redemption. Milton repeatedly renarrates the embodiment of charity throughout biblical history, citing typological anticipations of Christ. Before presenting *Paradise Regained* as a kind of "micronarrative" version of the rule of charity to guide the reading of *Paradise Lost,* Milton had offered a "metanarrative" version of that rule in the last two books of the longer epic. In the longer epic, typology is more than an ad hoc poetic strategy, but actually becomes the means to situate his story within a renarration of the whole of biblical history and to ensure that charity remains the origin and end of that larger story.[17] In Books Eleven and Twelve of *Paradise Lost,* Milton construes the overarching biblical story as an ethical critique of religious coercion at the same time that he probes the limits of theological formulations with respect to Trinitarian doctrine. In both respects, the implications result from an account of "reason" that is inseparable from Milton's view of creaturely freedom and divine love embodied in the content of the biblical metanarrative.[18]

The revelation of human history that Michael gives to Adam and which takes up most of Books Eleven and Twelve continues, in a most striking way, Milton's conversion of epic modes through biblicist adaptation. In these last two books, however, important changes in the mode of that adaptation require a kind of attention to the poetry that is qualitatively different from the reading of the first ten books. The intertextual situation is largely reversed from the previous books, as the typological elements that had formerly to be explicated are now drawn out clearly on the surface of the text. The switch to the mode of biblical paraphrase can also be potentially misleading, however, with respect to the larger function of that scriptural engagement. For example, what is for the implied epic reader an obvious case of biblical paraphrase of ostensibly past events is for Adam, as an interpreter within the story, an instance of prophetic revelation of future events. We need to keep in view how Milton uses this persistent double focus throughout these books to embody a strategy of indirection that aims to educate the reader's affections as well as Adam's.

With respect to the general use of typology in these books, a slightly different critical mode is required here because the deployment is so much closer to the surface of the text than elsewhere in the epic. First Abel, Enoch, and Noah in Book Eleven, and then Abraham, Moses, Joshua, and David in Book Twelve are each "types" depicting different aspects of the redeeming work accomplished by the coming Messiah to whom they also look forward in hope, just as Adam eventually does. At the same time, the characters within the stories told to Adam, as a result of their own justification through forward-looking faith, also embody different aspects of the sanctified life of charity completed in Christ. But again the difference between Adam and the epic reader is that, because Adam encounters the story as prophecy rather than history, he could understand the typological function of these characters only after the culminating revelation of the Son's life on earth. In this way, Adam's experience emphasizes that typology is simply a Christocentric reading of Scripture in that Christ is the culminating revelation of divine love toward humans.

The obvious extent and density of the deployment of typology in these last two books are, however, worth pointing out, lest Michael's explicit comment regarding the transition from "shadowy types to Truth" (12.303) be misconstrued as a general disparagement of typology. Viewed within its full context, the apparent denigration is striking—immediately surrounded as it is by a particularly dense treatment of the interaction between Moses and Joshua as types of different aspects of Christ's work (12.235–44, 307–14) and more generally embedded within the larger description of typological figures. The "shadowy" quality of the types refers to their unintelligibility apart from their fulfillment in Christ who is "the Truth." But even in that respect, the context of the passage implies also that the types are crucial preparation in order for the truth of the Messiah to be humanly understood at all. The conceptual dynamics of typology are thus not unidirectional; the arrival of the Incarnation of divine love is intelligible only within the context of the history of Israel that the epic summarizes. This is why Michael's prophecy, being addressed to Adam, cannot begin simply with episodes from the gospel narratives. Because the types are fulfilled within time by the one who is the "Truth," they are specifically not "shadowy" in the Platonic sense that they resemble realities belonging to a more real or spiritual world.[19] Thus types persist as the unavoidably particular and embodied instances of divine revelation that are necessary preparation for the fully human temporal apprehension of divine love. At the same time, by including within the epic a condensed summary of the church's history between the Ascension and the return of Christ, Milton emphasizes the continuity between the world of the poem and the world of the implied reader.

Also accessible at the surface level of Books Eleven and Twelve are the central didactic themes that recur throughout. Michael is intent upon the elucidation of three pairs of key concepts and their multiple interactions: the dialectic of freedom versus bondage, the conflict between charity and coercion of conscience, and the relation between internal and external aspects of the human condition. None of the paired terms, as worked through the stories, however, involves a simple correspondence with the other pairs. For example, the bondage discussed within a given story can, in Milton's account, involve internal enslavement to appetites (like those in the Lazar house, or with Noah's peers) or external coercion (whether by Cain or Nimrod). In the case of the Nimrod story, Michael reiterates the point made by Milton in the *Tenure of Kings and Magistrates* that internal enslavement to appetites can lead to external servitude (compare *PL* 12.79–96; YP 3:190–92). Yet elsewhere Milton also develops the theme of internal freedom amid external force (for example, Abel, Enoch, Christ, or the early Church). A favorite topic is the persistence of internal bondage to appetites amid apparent external freedom (for example, 11.791–96; 12.348–59). As these various themes repeatedly recombine within Michael's prophecy, ultimately those who attempt to coerce the consciences of others through a union of civil and religious authority already suffer themselves from internal bondage to base appetites and have thereby lost the *imago dei* capacity for right reason (compare 11.507–25; 12.508–35). Milton implies that all who attempt such coercion suffer from an internal disorder of the affections, though not all kinds of internal enslavement will give rise to such practice. At the same time, the pairing of the terms "internal" versus "external" should not be misconstrued to imply that Milton advocates religious toleration by means of limiting "spiritual truth" to a sphere of "private" religion. Instead, the "internal" order resulting from justification by faith, the restoration of right reason, then results in a virtuous life of visible and temporal sanctification.

At the same time, this recapitulation of the biblical metanarrative is marked at its beginning and end by the invocation of charity. Before Michael presents Adam with the revelation of future events, his explanation of the vision's purpose relates ultimately to Adam's experience of divine love. The intermediate aim of moral education is situated within a still larger intention that Adam should continue to experience God's care. In bemoaning his expulsion from Eden, Adam specifically regrets that he will not be able to set up shrines to memorialize for his children where he met with God (11.317–27). Michael responds:

> Doubt not but in Valley and in Plain
> God is as here, and will be found alike
> Present, and of his presence many a sign
> Still following thee, still compassing thee round
> With goodness and paternal *Love*, his Face

Express, and of his steps the track Divine.
Which that thou may'st believe, and be confirm'd,
Ere thou from hence depart, know I am sent
To show thee what shall come. . . .

. . . .

                                thereby to learn
True patience, and to temper joy with fear
And pious sorrow, equally inur'd
By moderation either state to bear,
Prosperous or adverse: so shalt thou lead
Safest thy life, and best prepar'd endure
Thy mortal passage when it comes.

                          (11.349–57, 360–66; emphasis added)

In short, the ultimate purpose of the revelation is to strengthen Adam's faith (trust) in God's continued love toward him and his progeny. Thus the exhortation to virtue which the narrative embodies for Adam is part of the divine care for creaturely happiness within a world of freedom, action, and consequence.

At the conclusion of Michael's prophecy, the didactic purpose of the revelation is again emphasized, though in slightly different terms. At the culmination of his postlapsarian education, Adam responds to Raphael by summarizing the lessons that he has learned about virtue and declaring his own trust in the coming "Redeemer" (12.561–73). Michael responds by acknowledging that what Adam has learned is "the sum / Of wisdom" (575–76); indeed, he recommends the superiority of such knowledge to Adam over knowledge of "all Nature's works" (578). Michael also indicates, however, that the intellectual apprehension that Adam possesses is not sufficient in itself for him to experience the full restoration of God's image, that "paradise within":

                                Only add
        Deeds to thy knowledge answerable, add Faith,
        Add Virtue, Patience, Temperance, add Love,
        By name to come call'd Charity, the soul
        Of all the rest: then wilt thou not be loath
        To leave this Paradise, but thou shalt possess
        A paradise within thee, happier far.   (12.581–87)

Lest this passage be misconstrued as evidence of a latent rationalist-voluntarist binary, it should be pointed out that the repeated use of the word "add" suggests a similar construction found in 2 Peter 1:5–7, which begins with faith and culminates in charity. The "soul," or living form, as it were, of the "paradise within" is constituted not through private inner knowledge, but through active and often outwardly accessible action. The key point here, however, is that "divine love" progresses through the course of Books Eleven and Twelve from being something external to Adam, something of which he needs assurance, to being something internal to him in the restoration of the divine image. In effect, given that Adam and Eve have already evidenced repentance and the seeds of saving faith (11.1–44) (justification), the goal of Michael's prophecy is to strengthen the human trust in divine love (11.348–58) so that these first parents are able, however partially, to embody that love themselves (the "paradise within" of sanctification) and thereby prefigure its fullest revelation in Christ.

Also coincident, however, with these two moments of emphasis upon charity within the poem are clear references to the cooperation of the Father, Son, and Holy Spirit. Just before Adam's final confession of faith, Michael begins the last segment of his prophetic narration by describing the life of the Church after Christ's Ascension. In a manner strikingly similar to the account of Adam's situation a few lines later, Michael describes the operations of divine love upon the hearts of the first disciples after Pentecost. Moreover, he does so in terms that are at least generally Trinitarian:

> From Heav'n
> [Christ] to his own a Comforter will send,
> The promise of the Father, who shall dwell
> His Spirit within them, and the Law of Faith
> Working through love, upon thir hearts shall write,
> To guide them in all truth, and also arm
> With spiritual armor, able to resist
> Satan's assaults, and quench his fiery darts,
> What man can do against them, not afraid.   (12.485–93)

Intertextually, several important things are happening at the same time within this passage. First, the "fiery darts" allude to the devotional themes earlier engaged in Book Six of the epic, where Ephesians 6:11–17 had shaped the account of spiritual warfare. Second, the last two lines are consistent with Milton's emphasis throughout Books Eleven and Twelve, upon showing how inward or spiritual restoration often results in certain kinds of outward actions or conditions. Third, the inscription of the "Law of Faith" by the Holy Spirit clearly evokes the restoration of the *imago dei* as conscience or "right reason," but it does so in a way that links that restoration to all three members of the Trinity and to the internalization of divine love. Thus, finally, as with Adam, the restoration of the divine image is expressed specifically in terms of "faith" and "love" (justification and sanctification, respectively). The Son sends the Holy Spirit, who is promised by the Father, in order to regenerate within individual believers the image of God in which right reason embodies a unity of faith and love, and, in being true, impinges upon the world with consequence. Thus Milton's brief summary of the Church's history also emphasizes his understanding that people who experience such an inner restoration often experience persecution by civil authorities because their religious practices are not merely private.

The reader has already been prepared for such threefold divine action at the very outset of Book Eleven, where the members of the Trinity each play a role in Adam and Eve's repentance and forgiveness:

> Prevenient Grace descending had remov'd
> The stony from thir hearts, and made new flesh
> Regenerate grow instead, that sighs now breath'd
> Unutterable, which the Spirit of prayer
> Inspir'd, and wing'd for Heav'n with speedier flight
> Than loudest Oratory.
>
> . . . .
>
> Then the glad Son
> Presenting, thus to intercede began.
> See Father, what first fruits are sprung
> From thy implanted Grace in Man, these Sighs
> And Prayers, which in this Golden Censer, mixt
> With Incense, I thy Priest before thee bring.   (11.3–8, 20–25)

In the lines that follow, the Son, as "Advocate," goes on to offer to the Father his "Merit" and "Death" to redeem mankind so that, as he says, "All my redeem'd may dwell in joy and bliss, / Made one with me as I with thee am one" (11.43–44). The Holy Spirit enables prevenient grace to induce repentance. The phrase "Spirit of prayer," with reference to sighs "unutterable," alludes to the description of the Holy Spirit's role in prayer found in Romans 8:26. Taken as a whole, the above passage clearly invokes the different roles of the Father, Son, and Holy Spirit in effecting human salvation from sin, or justification. This kind of threefold action in effecting salvation history is not the whole of orthodoxy; however, it does emphasize that the justifying work of redemption is the full expression of divine love toward specifically fallen humans. The last phrase, however, equating the unity between Father and Son with the unity between Christ and humanity (line 44), is noteworthy. As a paraphrase of John 17:20–21, the line is both perfectly biblical and deeply ambiguous with respect to any clearly Trinitarian or Antitrinitarian interpretation. Yet, however one views the interpretive openness of this particular line, Michael clearly invokes the Father, Son, and Holy Spirit as integral to the human experience and the embodiment of charity at the beginning and end of his summary of biblical history.

The crucial question is how best to understand the meaning of Milton's biblicism. Any answer is, of course, complicated by the longstanding debate over the precise nature and meaning of Milton's Antitrinitarianism. Customary formulation of Trinitarian belief describes the three persons as subsisting in a relation of charity, and what remains undeniable is that *Paradise Lost*, at two key narrative moments, explicitly links the cooperation of the Father, Son, and Holy Spirit with the work of charity. As I have demonstrated elsewhere, the rigor of *Paradise Lost*'s biblicism ensures that the epic cannot be used any more effectively than the Bible itself to show that the poem is "Arian," or "Antitrinitarian."[20] An appeal to biblicism is, however, often intrinsic to Antitrinitarian arguments.[21] It is thus possible to debate whether the biblicism serves a secret Antitrinitarianism, or whether the apparently weak Trinitarian formulation is only an incidental result of the biblicism. But the very attempt to resolve such a question obscures a more important point Milton makes about the connection between true belief and genuine transformation. By Milton's own explicit account in *Of True Religion*, belief or unbelief in "the Trinity" per se is not "necessary to salvation" (YP 8:424–25). What is crucial is that people hold the scriptural view that Christ is "both God and their Saviour" (425). Milton's statements in both *Paradise Lost* and the 1673 tract reveal an express purpose to avoid textual susceptibility to strong interpretations along either Trinitarian or Antitrinitarian lines. But we can now understand also that the biblicism and interpretive openness in Milton's poetry are integral to his elaboration of the claim that charity and religious toleration are inherent to true religion. Milton eschews the doctrinal formulations in such a way that emphasizes the charity that is the essence of the biblical godhead, but he simultaneously offers strong criticism of those who would try to join ostensibly Trinitarian belief with religious coercion. Indeed, one of the central functions of the concluding books, with respect to "reader response," is to provoke a reaction of extreme discomfort among Erastian readers who find repeatedly throughout the summary of biblical history that their deployment of civil authority locates them in opposition to divine love. For those in seventeenth-century England who held heretical views, any argument for religious toleration involves an unavoidable element of self-protection as a matter of course. Yet Milton was sufficiently adept as a rhetorician to understand that such an argument could not be based on an appeal to those same heretical views. His genius is to advance the critique of religious coercion precisely by means of the very biblical texts and terms that the orthodox would use as a basis for their theological views. In effect, by using biblicism to resubmerge, as it were, the doctrine of the Trinity, Milton foregrounds the sad contradiction of demanding ostensible orthodoxy in such a way that violates the same charity the doctrinal formulation attempts to articulate.

Because the story of Books Eleven and Twelve embodies the kind of Christocentric typological reading that informs the rest of the poem, Michael's prophecy, in some sense, functions as an interpretive "rule of charity" for the rest of the poem. Milton achieves this effect by summarizing the biblical metanarrative in such a way that preserves elements of its irreducible particularity. Thus, for the fit readers of the epic, the memory of the explicit typology in Books Eleven and Twelve becomes the guide for discerning the charitable interpretation of the preceding ten books. Milton's strategy presumes a second reading of the poem that keeps in mind the previous reading. The poem thus implies the central importance of memory in the readers' response to its central thematic preoccupations. Moreover, such charitable educative reading aims at more than an apprehension of doctrinal formulations that would risk leaving the reader a "heretick in the truth" (YP 2:543). Instead, the dramatization of biblical events is made inextricable from an account of charity that incarnates the relation between liberty, virtue, and reason—the last term unfolding simultaneously through the discourses of conscience, ontic-logos, and Christology. In his prose, Milton effectively claims that religious coercion is anti-Christian, that it opposes the nature of the Protestant understanding of the gospel. In *Paradise Lost,* he attempts to show through a renarration of the whole of biblical history in its particularity that to admit religious coercion is inherently satanic and necessarily entails an inversion of the Protestant account of the relation between justification and sanctification as found in Scripture. Thus the poet requires readers, amid various hermeneutic operations, to make a choice, not simply between advocating religious toleration or siding with Satan, but between accepting religious toleration or rejecting the Protestant view of salvation, charity, and freedom, a view that Milton holds to be integral to the overarching biblical story.

II

The problem, which Milton seemed to recognize, was that most readers of *Paradise Lost* failed to appreciate sufficiently its critique of epic violence and coercive power. By offering a more explicit statement of the Christocentric poetics and ontology informing the longer epic, and thereby making the connection between charity and religious toleration unavoidable, *Paradise Regained* serves as an interpretive guide to *Paradise Lost*. Because Milton's account of the relationship between justification and sanctification is central to his critique of religious coercion, it is important to understand that *Paradise Regained* is not primarily about Christ's work of atonement, or the forgiveness of sin. The brief epic does ultimately clarify Milton's account of redemption, but it does so indirectly. The concluding angelic chorus of *Para-*

dise Regained states explicitly that when Christ thwarted Satan's temptations in the desert, he "regain'd lost Paradise" (4.608). The tendency to equate the regaining of Paradise with Christ's work of atonement is the main cause for the common puzzlement over Milton's choosing the particular story of Christ's temptation for poetic dilation rather than one of the gospel Passion narratives. For example, Christopher Hill observes that Milton's "failure to mention the crucifixion more than incidentally is . . . a startling departure from orthodoxy in a poem about the recovery of Paradise for all mankind."[22] But such a departure is startling only if one equates the "Eden rais'd in the waste Wilderness" (*PR* 1.7) with the forgiveness of sin resulting from Christ's work of atonement. As we have observed, in *Paradise Lost* Milton had already used the phrase "Paradise within" to indicate specifically the temporal embodiment of virtue, whose "soul" is "Charity" (*PL* 12.581–87). The process of developing such virtue, or sanctification, is clearly distinguished in *Paradise Lost* from the earlier forgiveness of Adam and Eve's sin as a result of the Son's mediation in response to their prayer of repentance (11.1–44). Thus, if the spiritual "Eden" that Christ establishes in *Paradise Regained* is comparable to the "paradise within" of the earlier epic, then the "Paradise" that is restored by Christ in the brief epic is the authentic practice of charity (sanctification) rather than the forgiveness of sins (justification) per se.

With respect to the customary formulations of the relationship between justification and sanctification, however, the situation of the Son in *Paradise Regained* is utterly unique in that not only is he sinless and therefore not in need of forgiveness, but also his very embodiment of charity will eventually culminate in the sacrificial death that will make (and, in a sense, has always already made) the forgiveness of human sin possible. This singular condition involves *Paradise Regained* in a logic that is both analogous to and a reversal of the customary human experience of the relationship between saving faith and virtuous action. Milton emphasizes the practical unity between trust and virtue within the life of Christ—rather than, for example, the conceptual distinction between faith and works in the life of a believer. As a result of the Son's complete trust in the love of the Father, he resists Satan's multiform temptation to establish the Kingdom of God on earth by any means other than charity. The poem thus emphasizes the incoherence of treating Christ's Passion in isolation from his entire virtuous life of charity. This point is important in two respects. First, there is nothing inherently good about suffering or being executed, even unjustly. The work of atonement itself has meaning only if Christ's entire life is virtuous and without sin. Moreover, it is not enough for that charity to remain as potential; it must be embodied. Second, Christ's temporal practice of charity, although it will result in his death, does not depend upon death for its reality or intelligibility. The Son's condition is like a reverse mirror image of the way in which justification in the life of a believer necessarily results in, but does not depend upon, sanctification. Thus Milton's choice to focus on Christ's temptation rather than his Passion is not simply a result of bloodless rationalism, or a reaction against the Counter-Reformation emphasis upon Christ's suffering. The poem implies that, although the response of divine love to the specifically human problem of sin involves sacrifice, death is not ontologically necessary to charity.[23] This ontological claim is, of course, important for Milton's stance on religious toleration in that, as we have observed, he consistently argues for the incoherence of any attempt to coerce the human practice of charity.

This clarification of the theological basis for the poem results in important implications for how we understand its central themes. Because of its emphasis upon Christ's temporal embodiment of charity, the didactic core of the poem is exemplary rather than theologically demonstrative. Such an emphasis does not, however, imply that Milton ascribes saving efficacy to human attempts at following Christ's example.[24] Anne Krook makes a similar observation that "Christ's action in the poem is predominantly exemplary." But because she does not sufficiently allow for the distinction between justification and sanctification in the life of the believer, Krook suggests that Milton advocates salvation by human effort.[25] The difficulty arises, once again, from presuming that the "regaining of Paradise" is synonymous with salvation from sin rather than with Christ's embodiment of charitable virtue that will result in that salvation. To suggest people could be saved from sin by simply following Christ's example of virtue is to ascribe to *Paradise Regained* the very stoicism which the poem openly rejects (*PR* 4.300–308). The individual believer can share in Christ's virtuous establishment of a paradise within, but that sanctification is a result of saving faith, not a basis for salvation.

This understanding clarifies what would otherwise seem a strange shift in tenses at the beginning and at the end of the poem. At both points, Christ's resistance to Satan's temptation is described as that which completes the action of establishing paradise (*PR* 1.1–7; 4.606–14). Yet also at both points the Son's victory is described as a still future event that follows the temptation (1.150–62; 4.615–35). As the closing passage makes clear, Christ has yet to "reinstall" the "chosen Sons" of Adam within the Paradise that he has just established (4.613–17). That event is described in the future tense, not because any amount of human striving will ever result in that reinstalling, but because the atonement is yet to come (compare 1.155–62).[26] Consistent with Milton's lifelong insistence upon the primacy of saving faith, *Paradise Regained* maintains that only the forgiveness of sin made possible by Christ's death and Resurrection could result in the freedom required for anyone besides Christ to share in that Paradise constituted by a life of charity.

In elaborating the gospel accounts of Christ's temptation in *Paradise Regained,* Milton deploys a biblicist strategy similar to the earlier epic's elaboration of the Genesis story. He makes similar use of typology to engage within an immediate narrative framework the whole of biblical history.[27] We can see this in the explicit connections and comparisons made between Adam (*PR* 1.51–52, 115; 2.133–34), Job (*PR* 1.47, 369, 424–26), and Christ, the last being a completion or fulfillment of the truth that was incomplete or only intimated by aspects of the former two. The same typological dynamic is also at work in the several parallels drawn between the temptation story and the heavenly war in Revelation, chapter 12.[28] Although in one sense the repeated mention of "Wilderness" simply follows the gospel narratives, and is part of Christ's identification with Israel's forty years in the desert, the coincident and repeated descriptions of the temptation as a battle also connect that wilderness to the one into which "the Woman" and the "remnant of her seed" are pursued by the dragon that attempts to "make war" against them (Rev. 12:13–17). Structurally, the poem's use of the angelic song as a kind of dramatic chorus is similar to the angelic chorus and/or the "voice in heaven" that speaks throughout the Apocalypse.[29] This alternation between heavenly and earthly perspectives, which is also used in *Paradise Lost,* results in what Joseph Mede calls, in his commentary on Revelation, "the apocalyptick theater," in which the reader is able to glimpse the connections between temporally distant events. But the apocalyptic theater is, in effect, a function of typological interpretation.[30] By connecting distant events through time in order to depict the relation between heavenly and earthly perspectives, *Paradise Regained* emphasizes the unity between divine love and human virtue, between the divine gift of justification and the human embodiment of sanctification.

If we consider some of the key points in *Paradise Regained* at which Milton dilates the biblical narrative, we can understand why the poem does not explicitly invoke "charity," but instead intimates Christ's embodiment of the complete unity between charity as the divine love that he shares with the Father and charity as sanctification. One of the most important changes that Milton makes to the biblical versions of the temptation story is the conclusion of the final temptation, in which Satan falls from the top of the temple. By arranging that the final defeat of Satan's last effort to tempt Christ results in Satan's own fall from the temple pinnacle, rather than in Christ's falling into sin (4.562–81), Milton makes a series of further biblical connections. Most immediately, the fall constitutes a parallel with the heavenly war in Revelation, chapter 12, that results in Satan's "second" fall, as it were (see *PL* 4.3). Thus the closing angelic song relates Satan's immediate fall from the temple both to his past defeat "long of old" (*PR* 4.604) and to his future final defeat

(619–35). Consistent with the typological strategy in *Paradise Lost,* however, *Paradise Regained* does not collapse the various similar events into a single form or identify them entirely with one another. Although the fall of Satan from the top of the temple at the end of *Paradise Regained* is like his earlier fall from heaven and his future fall from earth into hell, the narrative preserves the temporal framework and does not imply that these events are simply reenactments of a single eternal pattern. Rather, the typological similarity between the three events allows the recognition of a resemblance that does not deny their respective singularity. As we shall see, Satan's blindness to charity is precisely what prevents him from understanding the singular meaning of Christ's Incarnation. The prediction of Christ's final judgment, like the earlier war in heaven, and unlike the immediate situation in *Paradise Regained,* is a response to Satan's freely chosen demand that God's power be proven by force to match his own. But the point of invoking the Last Judgment within *Paradise Regained* is that precisely such retribution cannot be exercised by humans who, before the eschaton, can only best follow the example of the incarnate Christ. The invocation of the future judgment thus serves as a reminder of the penultimate character of all temporal regimes and their use of force. Moreover, by alluding to the same biblical locus of Revelation, chapter 12, Milton emphasizes the typological correspondence between the event which occupies the center of *Paradise Lost* and the event at the end of *Paradise Regained,* thus weaving the conclusion of the later poem back into the center of the earlier one.

We encounter a different typological elaboration of the gospel narratives in the most sustained treatment of Job within the poem, in Book Three. There Christ responds to the temptation to pursue imperial power for fame and glory by citing Job as an example of true virtue which remains little known among humans. Job's character occasions sustained comment on his position as someone who is better known in heaven than on earth, whose true glory is, although publicly intelligible, not concerned with political power. He therefore eschews the use of bodily force to acquire fame or glory among men:

> They err who count it glorious to subdue
> By Conquest far and wide, to overrun
> Large Countries, and in the field great Battles win,
> Great Cities by assault: what do these Worthies,
> But rob and spoil, burn, slaughter and enslave
> Peaceable Nations. . . .
>
> . . . .
>
> But if there be in glory aught of good,
> It may by means far different be attain'd
> Without ambition, war, or violence.   (3.71–76, 88–90)

This description of true glory is offered by Christ as part of an explanation of the nature of Job's exceptional life (3.60–70, 92–95), a life that is itself a prefigurement of the life that Christ embodies fully.[31] But Job also, in a sense, becomes here a figure for the hidden character of the true church at the same time that his rejection of worldly power clarifies the distinction between the two views of reality.[32]

But the similar deployment of typology in the two epics should not obscure crucial differences in emphasis between them. *Paradise Regained* invokes the terms of spiritual battle by reference to an apocalyptic framework similar to that deployed in Book Six of *Paradise Lost,* but in a much different immediate setting. The particular choice of Christ's temptation story as a framework also enables Milton to foreground the question of biblical inter-pretation as it relates to the practice of liberty versus license, and to the belief in the primacy of charity versus coercion. At the very end of Book Two, at what is, in effect, the center of *Paradise Regained,* we find the end of Christ's response to Satan's appeal to wealth as a means to achieve "Conquest, and Realms" (2.422). At first Christ observes, in terms generally analogous to a classical account of virtue, that the man who controls his own desires is "More a king" (467) than one who rules other people (450–72). But the culmination of Christ's rejection is that which Satan seems unable to antici-pate and which leaves him "mute confounded" (3.2):

> But to guide Nations in the way of truth
> By *saving Doctrine,* and from error lead
> To know, and knowing *worship* God aright,
> Is yet more Kingly; this attracts the Soul,
> Governs the inner man, the nobler part;
> That other o'er the body only reigns,
> And oft by force, which to a generous mind
> So reigning can be no sincere delight.
> Besides, to give a Kingdom hath been thought
> Greater and nobler done, and to lay down
> Far more magnanimous than to assume.
>
> (*PR* 2.473–83; emphasis added)

The passage begins with an emphasis upon the way in which "truth" involves a practical unity between justification ("saving Doctrine") and sanctification ("worship"), a unity that shows by contrast the weakness of bodily force. But what Satan seems most unable to anticipate is the experience of gift. Satan seems to know that the Messiah will obtain a kingdom. But because he is unable to imagine what it would mean "to give a Kingdom" or to be given one, Satan's strategy for temptation consistently revolves around the question of how to take one. Whether he specifically proposes force or some other means, his logic depends upon taking rather than giving a kingdom.

Satan's incapacity to allow for the nature of divine gift-love relates directly to the central interpretive emphasis within the dramatic action of the poem. That the nature of the "battle" between Christ and Satan turns upon biblical interpretation is generally understood.[33] Similarly, Barbara Lewalski has demonstrated the central thematic importance of the question regarding how to interpret Christ's identity.[34] Yet the precise character of Satan's most important interpretive failure, evidenced dramatically in the final temptation, requires further illumination. In the lines immediately preceding the climactic moment at which he transports Christ to the top of the temple, Satan reveals the full extent of his puzzlement and anxiety over Christ's identity. He is worried about the exact meaning of the words spoken from heaven after Christ's baptism in the Jordan—an event that is recounted here for the fourth time within the poem and for the second time by Satan himself:

> by voice from Heav'n [I]
> Heard thee pronounc'd the Son of God belov'd.
> Thenceforth I thought thee worth my nearer view
> And narrower Scrutiny, that I might learn
> In what degree or meaning thou art call'd
> The Son of God, which bears no single sense;
> The Son of God I also am, or was,
> And if I was, I am; relation stands;
> All men are Sons of God; yet thee I thought
> In some respect far higher so declar'd.   (*PR* 4.512–21)

Satan claims that his final "method" (4.540) of testing Christ is compelled by his determination to know if Jesus is "more . . . than man, / Worth naming Son of God by voice from Heav'n" (4.538–39). At that moment when Satan "with amazement" falls from the temple (4.562), he seems to recognize that Jesus is indeed the same "first-begot" "Son of God" who had driven him from heaven (compare 1.86–93; 4.560–62, 596–635). But until then, his persistent reduction of the meaning of Jesus' sonship to a function of power reveals Satan's incapacity to understand the full meaning of the epithet "belov'd." In his earlier recounting of the same event to the demonic council, he characterizes the "first-begot" Son as the "Monarch of Heaven" who, if he and Jesus are one and the same, is sure to benefit from the favoritism of his almighty Father (1.86–93). Satan puzzles over the meaning of the sonship and openly admits his incomprehension of the descending "perfect Dove" (1.83), but that he simply presumes he knows the meaning of "belov'd" is reducible to a kind of favoritism that enables political and coercive power. This leads him to mistake his present situation as being similar to his earlier defeat in heaven. The previous "fierce thunder," which drove Satan and his peers to the deep (1.90), was a just response to those who, having denied dependence on any creator, demanded that God's power be proven in answer to their own force (*PL* 5.859–69). By contrast, the Son's incarnation and eventual humiliation are in response to the specific needs of the human problem of evil that resulted, in part, from deception (3.130–32, 227–97). In effect, even as *Paradise Regained* implies comparison among the past, present, and future spiritual battles between Christ and Satan, Satan as a character within the story fails to understand the crucial differences between those battles. This point shows the typological insistence upon the particularity of the events being compared, but it also demonstrates the central place of divine gift-love to a correct deployment of such comparison.

The repeatedly stated but ignored epithet "belov'd" indicates the basis for the Son's response to Satan's temptations: his trust in the Father's love. That the brief epic manages structurally to state four times the emphasis upon the Father's love for the Son shows that Milton is making a point beyond the usually single reference to the Father's announcement in the gospel narratives.[35] The same divine love which, in *Paradise Lost,* is the source of all reality is emphasized in *Paradise Regained* as the basis for Christ's virtue. In this way, the later epic presents a direct reversal of the connections between ontology, identity, and coercive action that Satan exhibits in *Paradise Lost*. It may seem that the sense of "charity" as virtue, or sanctification, in the story of Christ's temptation is muted by his isolation. But it must be remembered that, although Christ is alone in this story, he is neither independent nor self-concerned. The love he shares with the Father is the basis and origin of his action, while the explicitly stated goal of his resistance to Satan's temptation is ultimately the redemption of humanity (*PR* 1.259–67)—hardly a case of spiritual solipsism. In effect, *Paradise Regained* offers in the temptation story, and through its use of typology, an embodiment of charity in the life of Christ. The poem openly invokes both the divine love of the transcendent godhead and the "paradise within" which is Christ's enacting of perfect human virtue; however, the poem does not explicitly use the term "charity" because Christ himself embodies the mediation between the two realities of divine love and human sanctification. Moreover, Milton's rhetorical aim is not simply to induce a comfortably vague verbal affirmation regarding the importance of charity, as an explicit invocation of the term might do. Instead, he provokes a choice between accepting Christ's virtuous action as the substantive content of charity, or endorsing religious coercion. And in this way, *Paradise Regained* makes more explicit the connections between typology, the rule of charity, and the Christocentric poetics that remain implicit in most of *Paradise Lost* (Books One through Ten). The surface narrative of the brief epic thus presents more openly the account of peaceful ontic charity that underlies Milton's poetics.[36] The later poem's shift in emphasis is unmistakable, and that difference explains the aversion to *Paradise Regained* on the part of those who, by Milton's own account, enjoyed the earlier epic for the wrong reasons.

In both of Milton's epics we find then that the intertextual dynamics of biblical typology are, in effect, a Christocentric interpretation of the overarching biblical story intended to ensure that charity rather than coercion is understood as the basis for reality and for authentic human freedom. In both poems, Milton develops from within his biblicism an account of sanctification that guards against the kinds of Protestant ecclesiology that permitted coercion in such "external" or temporal matters as church discipline. In *Paradise Lost*, Books Eleven and Twelve function as a version of the rule of charity writ large, as it were, through the whole of biblical history. In *Paradise Regained*, the direction of the scale for the Christocentric poetics is reversed so that the whole of Christ's work is engaged from within the narration of one part of his life. By making more explicit the nature of charity (in both senses) that inheres to Milton's poetics, the brief epic identifies in more direct terms the kind of choices involved in the spiritual battle depicted at the center of *Paradise Lost*. Thus, if Books Eleven and Twelve function as a metanarrative version of the rule of charity for the preceding books of the longer epic, *Paradise Regained* offers a micronarrative version of the rule of charity that specifically eschews the risk of being misunderstood as an epic celebration of violent warfare. In this way, the brief epic could offer a corrective to those early readers who mistook the nature of the epic battle at the center of *Paradise Lost*.

Thus, like the earlier epic, *Paradise Regained* offers an intertextual dilation of biblical narrative that becomes inextricable from the accounts of liberty and charity that underwrite Milton's stance on religious toleration. The brief epic's intertextual dynamics also similarly weave together elements from the whole range of biblical narration, from Genesis to Revelation. *Paradise Regained* presents that interweaving, however, from the location of the incarnational midpoint of the overarching biblical story. At the same time, the later poem more explicitly rejects, at its beginning, middle, and end, any enthusiasm for carnal warfare that would miscelebrate the central battle of *Paradise Lost*. Those who tended to view the war in heaven as a literal "glorification" of violence, and who possibly ignored the critique of such attitudes presented in, for example, the Nimrod story (*PL* 12.24–37), would have been utterly disappointed by *Paradise Regained*. The potential for such a mistaken understanding of *Paradise Lost,* as a basis for comparing it with *Paradise Regained,* would explain to a great extent the vehemence of Milton's response to those who viewed the later poem as inferior to the longer epic. Thus, *Paradise Regained* offers, through its portrayal of Satan's interpretive practice and its defeat, a quasiprophetic account of how *Paradise Lost* could be misunderstood. At the same time it embodies an antidote to such a misreading that would mistake the ontology of the earlier poem for one of coercion rather than charity.

Baylor University

NOTES

I am grateful to the Social Sciences and Humanities Research Council of Canada and the Ontario Graduate Scholarship program for their financial support in the early stages of the research for this essay. For their helpful responses to an earlier version of this essay, I am thankful to Albert Labriola and David Loewenstein. I am especially grateful to Nicholas von Maltzahn for his help with the research that provided the basis for this analysis of *Paradise Regained.*

1. Edward Phillips, *The Life of Mr. John Milton* (1694), in *The Early Lives of John Milton,* ed. Helen Darbishire (London, 1932), 75–76.

2. Ibid., 75. Even if one remains skeptical regarding Thomas Ellwood's claim that he, in effect, prompted Milton to write *Paradise Regained* by his reaction to *Paradise Lost,* the basic chronology of Ellwood's account fits with that given by Phillips. See Thomas Ellwood, *The History of the Life of Thomas Ellwood* (London, 1714), 233–34, 314, 450–51. For a fuller account of the circumstances under which Milton likely composed *Paradise Regained,* see Barbara K. Lewalski, *The Life of John Milton: A Critical Biography* (Oxford, 2000), 443–60, 489–94.

3. Nicholas von Maltzahn, "The War in Heaven and the Miltonic Sublime," in *A Nation Transformed: England after the Restoration,* ed. Alan Houston and Steve Pincus (Cambridge, 2001), 155–72.

4. Quotations of Milton's poetry are from *John Milton: Complete Poems and Major Prose,* ed. Merritt Y. Hughes (New York, 1957), hereafter cited parenthetically in the text.

5. This is not to imply that such spiritual battle has no bodily dimension. As the poem clearly states, the "Humiliation and strong Sufferance" (*PR* 1.160) involved in that battle include the body. Rather, the point is that the nature of the power deployed by the Son is not coercive. Compare Fish, *How Milton Works* (Cambridge, Mass., 2001), 349–52.

6. *Complete Prose Works of John Milton,* 8 vols., ed. Don M. Wolfe et al. (New Haven, 1953–82), 2:521. Citations of Milton's prose are from this volume, hereafter designated YP, and cited in the text parenthetically by volume and page number.

7. For a general account of how English Protestants variously deployed appeals to "the rule of faith" as a guide to biblical interpretation, and Milton's relation to such appeals, see Dayton Haskin, *Milton's Burden of Interpretation* (Philadelphia, 1994), 54–83.

8. My account of Milton's position here contrasts with that of Stanley Fish in *How Milton Works,* 216–48. In discussing "the question of interpretation in Milton's early prose" (215), Fish contends that the need for charity itself to be continually reinterpreted renders it inadequate as a

constraint or guide for interpretation (245–48). Such a view, however, depends upon a presumed reduction of all ethical praxis to subjective egoism (e.g., 252–54). For a fuller response, see Phillip J. Donnelly, *Rhetorical Faith: The Literary Hermeneutics of Stanley Fish* (Victoria, 2000), 57–74, 93–102. The present account of Milton's position involves a substantial revision of my previous argument, which dealt almost exclusively with the treatment of charity in *De Doctrina Christiana*. The treatise simply follows the general Protestant practice of identifying charity with works, or sanctification (YP 6:637–38).

9. Although Milton draws distinctive implications from these categories, his deployment of them is generally consistent with commonplace Reformation usage. In conjunction with their emphasis upon salvation by faith alone, reformers like Calvin and Luther distinguished between the saving faith that allows the believer to experience forgiveness of sin (justification), and the practical outworking of that faith in a righteous life (sanctification). See John Calvin, *Institutes of the Christian Religion*, 2 vols., trans. Henry Beveridge (Grand Rapids, Mich., 1983), 3.3.9–13, esp. 3.11.1–4. Compare Martin Luther, *Two Kinds of Righteousness*, trans. Lowell J. Satre, in *Luther's Works*, vol. 31, ed. Harold J. Grimm, Helmut Lehmann, and Jaroslav Pelikan (Philadelphia, 1957), 293–306. The emphasis upon both the distinction and the unity between the two aspects of God's work is crucial in any reformed account of salvation. The conceptual distinction is necessary in order to avoid implying salvation by works—in effect, justification does not depend upon sanctification. But the practical unity between them is no less important in order to avoid letting the doctrine of salvation by grace become an excuse for license or antinomianism (Calvin, *Institutes*, 3.3.14). In effect, "justification" pertains to the eternal destiny of a person, whereas "sanctification" concerns the necessary temporal embodiment that results from saving faith. According to such a formulation, good works do not cause saving faith or result in justification, but they are a necessary consequence of faith. Thus the conceptual distinction is crucial in order to avoid ascribing salvific efficacy to human works, while the simultaneous insistence upon their practical unity is necessary to ensure that the doctrine of justification does not legitimate vice or the violation of charity.

10. Against the widespread tendency to ascribe to Milton a kind of ecclesiastical solipsism, it is worth noting two important implications of the last phrase regarding those "whose consciences we perswade." First, it demonstrates that Milton does not view the conscience as some incommunicable source of divine knowledge that is isolated within the subject, but as something that clearly has an intersubjective dimension and is therefore susceptible to persuasion and involves other humans. Second, the emphasis upon persuasion, without recourse to coercion, indicates precisely the limit of such interpersonal discursive practice. Because of the widespread influence of the biographical tradition descending from John Toland and Samuel Johnson, the central difficulty for critics today is to join Milton in imagining that truth could be objective but not coercive. Such imagining requires resisting the attempt to make truth (including the truth of Milton's biography) serve the ends of either an antireligious political program (as in Toland's case) or a national church (as with Johnson). See John Toland, *The Life of John Milton* (1698), in *The Early Lives of Milton*, ed. Helen Darbishire (London, 1932), 83–197, esp. 195. Samuel Johnson, "John Milton," *Lives of English Poets: A Selection* (London, 1975), 47–106, esp. 84. Both Toland and Johnson contend that Milton was ecclesiastically isolated at the end of his life. For Toland, the story offers a perfect model for the public atheism that is the aim of his own political program (which is the driving motivation for his republication of Milton's prose works in 1698, the occasion of the biography). For Johnson, simply following Toland's lead on this point, the story serves as a perfect illustration of how Dissenting religion necessarily ends in anarchy and atheism. The generally uncritical acceptance of this biographical tradition has tended to render Milton's ecclesiology incoherent, by preemptively denying any alternative to a dichotomy between secular and confessional versions of civic religion.

11. Conversely, Catholicism is construed as a "Roman principality" rather than a genuine religion at all, and is dubbed a "heresie against the scripture" and necessarily excepted from toleration "for just reason of state more then [*sic*] of religion" (YP 7:254). Milton's view on this point is not unusual and has precedents from well into the previous century. In "Persecution and Toleration in the English Reformation," *Studies in Church History* 21 (1984): 163–87, G. R. Elton contends that at no time in the sixteenth century, according to either English civil law or official church doctrine, was Catholicism condemned as a heresy in Britain (173–74, 180–82). Notwithstanding the repeated Catholic charge of religious persecution, the legal statutes required that Catholics were always prosecuted for treason (181–82). For those who would fault Milton for not extending toleration to Catholics, it should be clarified that for Milton the issue was simply a matter of logical consistency. Given his definition of "popery" as religious coercion, the toleration of such an institution would involve him in the obvious contradiction of tolerating religious coercion.

12. W. J. Torrence Kirby, *Richard Hooker's Doctrine of Royal Supremacy* (New York, 1990), 44.

13. For instances of the same basic distinction that runs throughout Hooker's writing, see his *Laws of Ecclesiastical Polity*, vols. 1–4, in *The Folger Library Edition of the Works of Richard Hooker*, 6 vols., ed. W. Speed Hill et al. (Cambridge, Mass., 1977–82; Binghampton, N.Y., 1993), 2.8.5–6; 3.3.2–3.

14. John W. Allen, *A History of Political Thought in the Sixteenth Century*, rev. ed. (London, 1957), 239–41.

15. Hooker, preface to *Laws of Ecclesiastical Polity*, 3.15.

16. Here is the passage which has occasioned some of the competing interpretations:

> The Arian and Socinian are charg'd to dispute against the Trinity: they affirm to believe the Father, Son, and Holy Ghost, according to Scripture and the Apostolic Creed; as for the terms of Trinity, Triunity, Coessentiality, Tripersonality, and the like, they reject them as Scholastic Notions, not to be found in Scripture, which by a general Protestant Maxim is plain and perspicuous abundantly to explain its own meaning in the properest words, belonging to so high a Matter and so necessary to be known; a mystery indeed in their Sophistic Subtilties, but in Scripture a plain Doctrin. (YP 8:424–25)

For contrasting views, see William B. Hunter, *Visitation Unimplor'd: Milton and the Authorship of "De Doctrina Christiana"* (Pittsburgh, 1998), 100–104, and John P. Rumrich, "Milton's Arianism: Why It Matters," in *Milton and Heresy*, ed. Stephen B. Dobranski and John P. Rumrich (Cambridge, 1998), 75–92, esp. 78. The key point here is that, even if Milton were rehearsing customary Arian misgivings, such a reiteration would not imply his adopting them as his own, unless we deliberately disregard the obvious context of the tract and its presumed readers. As Stavely points out, the overall concern of the tract is to address the issues raised by a pending bill in Parliament, by taking advantage of the recent "No Popery" agitation in such a way as to argue for the toleration of dissenting Protestants (YP 8:413). Thus, for example, Milton's repeated invocations of the Thirty-Nine Articles in this particular piece of writing are part of his larger attempt to appeal to the Anglican orientation of the Restoration Parliament. To maintain that the above passage indicates Milton's own adherence to Arianism would ascribe to him an exceptional rhetorical ineptitude. Why should Milton alienate his most important intended readers? Even if Rumrich is correct in insisting that Milton's views on the Trinity are represented in some form within *De Doctrina*, that belief could have no relation to the ostensible meaning of the text in *Of True Religion*, given the latter's rhetorical purpose.

17. Despite some recent attempts to qualify or otherwise play down Milton's use of biblical

typology, the central place of that kind of interpretive strategy within his poetry remains unde-niable. For an account of how Milton's use of typology enables his biblicist poetic strategy as it relates to issues of both Christology and theodicy, see the final sections of my essay, "The *Teloi* of Genres: *Paradise Lost* and *De Doctrina Christiana*," in *Milton Studies* 39, ed. Albert C. Labriola (Pittsburgh, 2000), 85–97. See also Dennis R. Danielson, "Through the Telescope of Typology: What Adam Should Have Done," *Milton Quarterly* 23 (1989): 121–27. The general account of typology presumed by the present analysis is drawn from Erich Auerbach, *Mimesis: The Repre-sentation of Reality in Western Literature,* trans. Willard R. Trask (Princeton, N.J., 1953), 48–49, 63–67, 73–76. One of the seminal monographic studies of typology in Milton's poetry is William G. Madsen, *From Shadowy Types to Truth: Studies in Milton's Symbolism* (New Haven, 1968). For an account of how typological interpretation specifically changed the critical reception of Books Eleven and Twelve of *Paradise Lost,* and eventually the whole poem, see Stanley Fish, "Transmuting the Lump: *Paradise Lost* 1942–1979," *Doing What Comes Naturally: Change, Rhetoric, and the Practice of Theory in Literary and Legal Studies* (Oxford, 1989), 247–93. Fish recounts how the critical tradition of giving strong attention to the use of typology, especially in the last two books of the poem, extends from the work of William Madsen and F. T. Prince in the late 1950s, through H. R. MacCallum and B. A. Rajan in the 1960s, to Edward Tayler at the end of 1970s (276–87). The influence of that tradition, which often contrasted typology with allegory, resulted in a tendency to emphasize Milton's avoidance of allegory. It is, therefore, against the weight of such a tradition that Kenneth Borris and Catherine Martin offer their accounts of allegory in *Paradise Lost.* See Kenneth Borris, " 'Union of Mind, or Both in One Soul': Allegories of Adam and Eve in *Paradise Lost*," in *Milton Studies* 31, ed. Albert C. Labriola (Pittsburgh, 1995), 45–72, and Catherine G. Martin, *The Ruins of Allegory: "Paradise Lost" and the Meta-morphosis of Epic Convention* (Durham, N.C., 1998). Although the present analysis is con-cerned with typology, I suggest that Milton does at certain points invoke allegory as a mode of biblical interpretation and as a more explicit strategy for poetic representation, though not for the reasons cited by Borris or Martin. In *Milton and the Preaching Arts* (Pittsburgh, 2001), Jameela Lares contends that "the last two books of *Paradise Lost* are better understood in terms of Homiletics than in terms of pedagogy or even typology" (168). Without denying the impor-tance of preaching as a genre within the epic, the fact remains that Milton consistently favored typology as the exegetical means to reach the suasive ends of his poetry. Indeed, typology is the predominant exegetical form that enables Milton to unite conceptually the full range of rhetori-cal arts and his own sense of prophetic vocation within his biblicism.

18. Throughout this analysis, my use of the phrase "biblical metanarrative" (or overarching biblical story) is influenced by John Milbank's account of "metanarrative realism" in *Theology and Social Theory* (Oxford, 1995), 385–88. The term "metanarrative" is thus deployed here to indicate something distinct from the customary use of the word, as for example in Jean-François Lyotard, *The Postmodern Condition: A Report on Knowledge,* trans. Geoff Bennington and Brian Massumi (Minneapolis, 1984). In Lyotard's account, the "metanarratives," about which there is so much skepticism, are specifically Enlightenment metanarratives (xxiv). As such, those overarching accounts of the trajectory of human social life depend specifically on Enlightenment versions of "the unfolding of foundational reason" (Milbank, *Theology,* 386)—whether referring to Kantian, Marxian, or Freudian accounts of history. By contrast, the "biblical metanarrative" stands in opposition to Enlightenment attempts to narrate the world by means of a constitu-tionally contentless, or purely instrumental, rationality. Thus it is that Milton participates in a pre-Enlightenment Christian tradition of "faith seeking understanding," which eschews claims to anything "total," in the modern sense. On the basis of that kind of inquiry (*quaerens*), he maintains that the life of charity and fidelity, the right exercise of reason, and the content of biblical narration are ultimately inseparable.

19. For a comparable account of how Milton's use of typology entails a contrast with the "two worlds" doctrine of Platonism, see Madsen, *From Shadowy Types to Truth,* 85–113. The key point here is that all the events and characters described in the "heaven" of *Paradise Lost* are no less creaturely than those on earth. The account of heaven, both in Books Three, Five, and Six, makes it clear that Milton does not construe "heaven" along the lines of a Platonist analogy that would make it simply the location of static forms within the mind of the Creator.

20. Donnelly, *"Teloi* of Genres," 88–93. That part of the essay also demonstrates how the debate over Milton's view of the Trinity is inseparable from the debate over his authorship of *De Doctrina Christiana.* My own fuller account of what *De Doctrina* does with the Trinity can be found in *Rhetorical Faith,* 49–56, 97–102.

21. Maurice Wiles, *Archetypal Heresy: Arianism through the Centuries* (Oxford, 1996), 141–47. Compare John Carey, introduction, YP 6:55, 62–63.

22. Christopher Hill, *Milton and the English Revolution* (London, 1977), 419.

23. My account of how Milton's view of charity avoids a supplementary relation to death or sacrifice has been influenced by John Milbank, "Can Morality Be Christian?" *The Word Made Strange: Theology, Language, Culture* (Oxford, 1997), 219–32. Milbank contends that, in order for a Christian account of the good to avoid inscribing the Gnostic logic whereby virtue is dependent upon evil for its goodness, divine love must be understood as the "gift and counter-gift" that ontologically precedes all else (228–29). In this respect, Milbank's account, like Milton's, risks being misunderstood as antinomian in that its emphasis upon the Resurrection "ruins the possibility" of "any reactive moral order, which presupposes the absoluteness of death" (229).

24. Throughout his writing career, Milton consistently repudiates salvation by works or by anything other than explicit faith. See, for example, *Of Reformation* (YP 1:519–21), *Of Civil Power* (YP 7:242–46, 255–56), and *Of True Religion* (YP 8.419–20).

25. Anne K. Krook, "The Hermeneutics of Opposition in *Paradise Regained* and *Samson Agonistes," SEL* 36 (1996): 134–35.

26. The poem actually implies two future victories for Christ. The first is the victory over "Sin and Death" "By Humiliation and strong Sufferance" (*PR* 1.159–60), in effect, the work of atonement which then allows forgiven humans to be "reinstall[ed]" in the virtuous Paradise that Christ has established by overcoming temptation. The other "future" victory in relation to the poem's temporal framework concerns the ultimate driving of Satan and his companions from earth altogether and back to hell (4.618–35; compare 1.153). Including the main action of the poem, *Paradise Regained* thus implies three occasions of Christ's victory on earth, each with distinct theological importance: the temptation, the Passion and Resurrection, and the eschaton.

27. For what remains the definitive study of typology and biblical precedent in *Paradise Regained,* see Barbara K. Lewalski, *Milton's Brief Epic: The Genre, Meaning and Art of "Paradise Regained"* (London, 1966). Compare Northrop Frye, "The Typology of *Paradise Regained," Modern Philology* 53 (1955): 227–38.

28. In "Milton's Biblical Style in *Paradise Regained,"* in *Milton Studies* 6, ed. James D. Simmonds (Pittsburgh, 1974), Emory Elliott lists twenty-four allusions to the Book of Revelation in *Paradise Regained,* ten of those occurring in the final fifty lines (231). As with *Paradise Lost,* whether or not one argues that the Book of Revelation governs the structure of the whole poem, the simple parallel between Satan's "fall" in both poems and the heavenly war in Revelation, chapter 12, is readily apparent.

29. Compare *Paradise Regained,* 1.168–81; 4.593–635; Revelation 5:6–14; 12:10–12.

30. Joseph Mede, *The Key of the Revelation, Searched and Demonstrated out of the Natural and Proper Characters of the Visions,* trans. Richard More (London, 1650), part 1:30. Mede derives the very idea of an "apocalyptick theater" specifically from his delineation of typological

correspondences between the heavenly throne in Revelation 4:2–11 and the "ancient encamping of God with Israel in the wilderness" in Numbers 1:52–2:34 (1:30–37).

31. Lewalski, *Milton's Brief Epic*, 178–82.

32. Compare ibid.,180–81.

33. See, for example, Krook, "Hermeneutics of Opposition," 132–36; Elliot, "Milton's Biblical Style," 227–39; and Mary Ann Radzinowicz, *"Paradise Regained* as Hermeneutic Combat," *University of Hartford Studies in Literature* 15–16 (1984): 99–107.

34. Lewalski, *Milton's Brief Epic*, 133–63.

35. The basic story, which involves Jesus' baptism, the descent of the Holy Spirit in the form of a dove, and the voice of the Father from heaven calling Jesus his "belov'd Son," is offered first by the narrative voice (*PR* 1.25–32), then by Satan during the demonic council (1.75–85), by Christ himself (1.270–286), and finally by Satan again, just before the final temptation (4.510–13).

36. For a brief account of how the ontology of *Paradise Lost* is rooted in peaceful charity rather than, for example, the indeterminacy of chaos, see Donnelly, *"Teloi* of Genres," 82–84, esp. 98–99 n. 5.

"ILL FARE THE HANDS THAT HEAVED THE STONES"[1]: JOHN MILTON, A PRELIMINARY THANATOGRAPHY

Carol Barton

APPARENTLY RELYING ON the testimony of Milton's servant, Elizabeth Fisher, and her sister Mary, Charles Symmons, David Masson, William Howitt, Sir John James Baddeley, and William Riley Parker all report that, late after he retired for the evening on Sunday, 8 November 1674, John Milton, gentleman, died in his sleep, a month short of his sixty-sixth birthday, and a few blocks from the Bread Street address where he was born.[2] As far as we can determine (primarily from the report of Mistress Fisher, who discovered the body that Monday morning),[3] the poet and statesman passed away as peacefully as he had lived those last few years, in the "somewhat commodious" four-hearth dwelling that stood then across the road from the "bone hill" fields to which the doleful overflow of Saint Paul's churchyard had been carted in the mid-sixteenth century (fig. 1), just a few hundred yards from the military training installation known as Artillery Ground—all of those locations within what is now the Corporation of London's "Square Mile."[4] Cyriack Skinner reports that Milton "dy'd in a fitt of the Gout, but with so little pain or Emotion, that the time of his expiring was not perceiv'd by those in the room."[5] On 12 November 1674, they buried him, another few blocks away, in what was then the chancel of the ancient church of St. Giles, Cripplegate, in the Barbican (fig. 2), in a crypt beneath the stone floor of an edifice that has in one form or another stood in its present location since the eleventh century.

Masson reports that his funeral service was conducted "according to the rites of the Church of England"; his older nephew, Edward Phillips, says he "had a very decent interment according to his Quality" (Darbishire); and as it was described by Toland, the final tribute to John Milton occurred in the company of "all his learned and great Friends in *London,* not without a friendly concourse of the Vulgar," at "the Church of *S. Giles* near *Cripplegate* . . . where the Piety of his Admirers [would] shortly [Toland believed] erect a Monument becoming his worth."[6] Thereafter, his coffin (probably made of wood, and encased in a leaden outer shell, as befitted someone of his social

Fig. 1. Bunhill Fields Cemetery, Bunhill Row, Islington, London. Photograph courtesy of the author.

status)[7] was interred next to, or on top of, that of his father, John Milton Sr., who had died more than twenty-seven years before.

If it were really that simple, the formal story of John Milton's life and times would end where most of his biographies do, here at the north end of the church at what is now the foot of the altar steps (see fig. 3)—save for the postmortem details of the filing of the poet's nuncupative will by his brother Christopher in November 1674, accounts of what became of his family and descendants (the last of whom, his granddaughter Elizabeth Foster, died in 1754, and was buried in Bunhill Fields),[8] and chronicles of posthumous events like the discovery of the manuscript of *De Doctrina Christiana*. But like most of his life, the death of England's greatest epic poet is the subject of considerable controversy: Did he die at Artillery Walk (or Artillery Wall, or Artillery Way, or Artillery Garden Walk, or Bunhill Row)?[9] Did that unhappy event occur during the night of the eighth of November (Fisher, Symmons, Masson, Howitt, Baddeley, Parker), or was it the morning of the ninth—or even the tenth (Aubrey, citing Milton's Apothecaryes Booke, and A. C. How-

Fig. 2. St. Giles, Cripplegate, in the modern Barbican, City of London (EC2). By permission of photographer Geoffrey Rivett, M.D.

ell and French, citing Aubrey)?[10] Did the poet die in penury (George Steevens,[11] and the anonymous poem Jonathan Richardson says his "Son found written in the Spare Leaf before the Answer to *Eicon Basilike*"),[12] or in relative comfort (Phillips, also cited by Richardson)? Was Milton's third wife and widow "rapacious" (Steevens),[13] a "Termagant" (Richardson),[14] and "a woman of most violent spirit, . . . a hard mother in law to [Milton's] children" (Newton),[15] or "kind and careful of him" (his brother Christopher)[16] and "a gent. (genteel?) person, (of) a peaceful and agreeable humour" (Aubrey, parentheses in original)?[17] Did Cripplegate's "most famous parishioner"[18] ever actually attend the church in which he was interred? Of what sectarian persuasion was the church at that time, and what sermon was preached, by whom, at his funeral?[19] Finally, just whose bones did a company of "merry-meeting" revelers "tremble not to grasp"—and make away with—116 years later? This preliminary thanatography collates and supplements the existing body of available data relevant to Milton's death and burial and the macabre unearthing of "dem bones," while exorcising some vintage misperceptions about the participants in the intrigue and their motives. In the process of accomplishing that objective, it will unveil a mystery, expose a possible cover-up, and reveal some new discoveries about the people who were involved in this centuries-old intrigue.

The trail of misinformation and uncertainty surrounding the death and remains of England's foremost poet begins (as I have already demonstrated) with confusion about the location of the house in which he died, the hour of his passing, the value of his estate, the devotedness of his widow, and even the age and religious persuasion of the church that was entrusted in perpetuity with the custody of his casket. Much of this material is covered reliably by other sources; where that is the case, I will merely cite the pertinent reference, giving detailed acquisition information in the endnotes for primary texts that are not readily accessible to the general public; where it is not, I will do my best to provide substantiated corrections of the inaccuracies and misperceptions of the past, to avoid their replication in the future.

Beginning at the end, then, St. Giles Without Cripplegate is an old and respected monument to church antiquity, dating from the year 1030, or 1090, or 1099, according to the various accounts. Despite the local disagreement, the consensus seems to be that its first incarnation took place at some point during the reign of William the Conqueror.[20] Even in 1674, what is now known as St. Giles' Church Cripplegate could already boast of having hosted a procession of British luminaries: William Shakespeare attended his nephew's christening there in 1603; Ben Jonson had been a parishioner; Lancelot Andrewes was vicar from 1588 to 1605; John Foxe and John Speed and Martin Frobisher were buried in its hallowed grounds; and twenty-one-year-

Fig. 3. Milton's gravestone beneath the altar steps at St. Giles, Cripplegate, lower center (directly below the two knee cushions at right). It reads: "JOHN MILTON, author of Paradise Lost, Born 1608—Died 1674." Photograph courtesy of the author.

old Oliver Cromwell had exchanged wedding vows with Elizabeth Bouchard at its altar in 1620. But the old stone church that would later withstand even the Luftwaffe's carnage does not seem to have been honored *in vita* by the attendance of its most distinguished son.[21] Very few twentieth-century writers even mention the purported desecration of the poet's grave by a trio of (probably inebriated) lay church officials and their equally "merry" friends 116 years after his body's interment, and those who do (James Holly Hanford, Sister M[ary] Christopher Pecheux, John T. Shawcross, Michael Lieb, and William Parker among them) do so only in passing, in most cases with a healthy dose of skepticism. Allen Walker Read notes that in the nineteenth century David "Masson does not so much as allude to the affair . . . even in his inviting section 'Posthumous Miltoniana,' "[22] and observes that "in [John] Mitford's [1834] *Life*, the most important before Masson . . . only the [following] sentences [occur]: 'On the disinterment of the *supposed* coffin and corpse of Milton in August, 1790, see the *Pamphlet of P. Neve, Esq.* and

Todd's Life. p. 139. The exact place in the church where Milton and his father lie, is not ascertained.' "[23]

Perhaps the most concise and least biased contemporary synopsis of what Mitford calls Neve's *"Pamphlet"* and the aftermath of its publication is the review that appeared in *The Gentleman's Magazine* regarding "A Narrative of the Disinterment of Milton's Coffin, in the Parish Church of St. Giles, Cripplegate, on August 4, 1790, and of the Treatment of the Corpse, during that and the following Day." Despite its several errors—the date of violation of the coffin, the minor inaccuracy as to Mrs. Hoppey's name, the mischaracterization of her role and the roles of several of the others in the initial disinterment, the number and members of the Smyth family who are buried nearby,[24] and the date of John Milton Sr.'s death—it is an unusually fair representation of an incident that occasioned a good deal of controversy at the time. It reads as follows:

Curiosity having been awakened to avail itself of the present repairs of Cripplegate Church, whose roof and upper windows are going to be made new, in search for Milton's body, whose father was buried here, according to the parish-register, March 15, 1656-7 [actually, 1646/7], and his son, according to tradition, under the clerk's desk in the chancel, i.e., where that desk once stood, for it is now opposite to the former, Messieurs Strong, F.A.S., vestry-clerk, Cole, church-warden, Laming and Fountane, overseers, Taylor, surgeon, from Derbyshire, on a visit to Mr. Laming, Ascough, hereditary parish-clerk, Mrs. Hoppers, sexton, and two others, opened the grave, August 3, and found a leaden coffin, old, and much corroded, without inscription or plate, 5 feet 10 inches long, and 1 foot 4 inches broad over the shoulders, lying on a wooden one, supposed his father's. The ground was immediately closed, but opened next morning by the church-wardens, &c., in consequence of a *merry-meeting* at Fountane's house.[25] They cut open the leaden coffin, from the head to the breast, and found the corpse done up in its shroud; on disturbing which, the ribs fell. They knocked out the teeth, cut off the hair, *six inches long,* which had been *combed and tied together,* and after pulling the bones about, left the whole a prey to the grave-digger,[26] who made money by shewing it till Thursday four o'clock, when the ground was closed.—Mr. Philip Neve . . . of Furnival's Inn, the writer of this pamphlet, has not a doubt of the authenticity of the body, from the site and hair, notwithstanding over the spot is a monument to a father, mother, and two sons of the family of *Smith,* buried *near that place,* 1653, 1655, 1664, 1674, to a *daughter* of which, a writer in *The St. James's Chronicle,* Sept. 4–7, inclines to give it; and it must be confessed, the length of the hair, and the state in which it was found, rather favours the opinion. Be this as it may, the dead have been shamefully violated, and most probably a fiction imposed on the publick for truth; which we sincerely wish may have been the case, and that our honoured Bard still rests in peace.[27]

Thompson agrees that "this occurrence involved a shocking violation of the dead, which is equally reprehensible whether the body be that of a poet or a pauper" (363); however, most of the biographical references to the disinterment made prior to the twentieth century are based on Henry John Todd's *Some Account of the Life and Writing of John Milton*,[28] which treats the issue somewhat less dramatically, and they do likewise. "In August, 1790," says Todd,

the spot where [Milton's] body had been deposited, was opened; and a corpse, hastily supposed to be his, was exposed to publick view. A Narrative of the disinterment of the coffin, and of the treatment of the corpse, was published by Philip Neve, Esq. The Narrative was immediately and ably answered in the St. James's Chronicle, in Nine Reasons why it is improbable that the coffin, lately dug up in the Parish Church of St. Giles, Cripplegate, should contain the reliques of Milton. Mr. Neve added a Postscript to his Narrative. But all of his labour appears to have been employed in an imaginary cause . . . [and] whether the remains of that body which once was Milton's, or those of any other person were thus exposed and set to sale, death and dissolution have had their empire over these. [All that truly matters is that] the spirit of [Milton's] immortal works survives invulnerable. (139)

Todd's conviction that the body in question was not Milton's relies on his recollection that "the late Mr. [George] Steevens, who particularly lamented the indignity which the nominal ashes of the poet sustained, ha[d] intimated in his manuscript remarks on this Narrative and Postscript, that the disinterred corpse was supposed to be that of a *female*, and that the minutest examination of the fragments could not disprove, if it did not confirm the supposition" (139). Steevens's "remarks" were delineated in his "MILTON. Reasons why it is improbable that the Coffin lately dug up in the Parish Church of St. Giles, Cripplegate, should contain the Reliques of Milton," which first appeared anonymously in the *St. James's Chronicle, Or British Evening Post* on 4 September 1790 (no. 4583). Originally, Steevens's disquisition contained eight "reasons"; by the time it resurfaced in the September issue of the *European Magazine and London Review*, the arguments had been expanded to nine.[29] In his attribution of the "Reasons" to Steevens, Howell observes,

that Steevens had first-hand evidence on which to base his nine reasons[, which] is proven by an entry in *Isaac Reed's Diaries, 1762–1804* (Berkeley, Calif.: U. of Cal. Press, 1946, p.180), where under the date of Tuesday, August 17, 1790, Reed notes, "Went with Mr. Steevens to St. Giles Cripplegate to search for the body of Milton. Found what was supposed to be him." August 17 was the date of the second disinterment [and the date Neve gives for the exhumation at which the surgeon Dyson, was present[30]]. Evidence for Steevens' authorship of the *St. James* [sic] *Chronicle* article occurs in James Boaden's *Memoirs of the Life of John Philip Kemble* (London: 1825), in which the author, after summarizing Neve's pamphlet, quotes liberally from the Chronicle article, attributing the arguments to Steevens. He gives practically the entire last page verbatim, indicating that Steevens wrote it. (21)[31]

In fact, the "Postscript" to Neve's *Narrative. . . . The second edition, with additions* (London, 1790, with a postscript, dated 8 September 1790), which was published less than a month after the original release of the pamphlet, was an able rebuttal of Steevens's "[Eight] Reasons," cogently argued and carefully documented as to names, dates, and events.[32] In spite of the meticulousness of Neve's investigation, though, it seems that, for a good number of contemporary correspondents, the challenger prevailed. Charles Symmons, for example, remarks somewhat melodramatically in 1806 that

in august [*sic*] of 1790, the grave, as it was imagined, of the great poet, was opened; and his remains exposed for some time to the public view. . . . The people pressed from all quarters for a sight of the bones: and happy was the man, who, availing himself of the mercenary spirit of the parish-officers, could become the possessor of any portion of the sacred reliques.[33] This profanation of the ashes of the illustrious dead was warmly resented by some of the writers of the day; but, much curiosity having been excited on the subject, the skeleton was subjected to a very accurate inspection, and proved to be that of a female; a fact, which, showing that the coffin of Milton was yet unviolated, relieved the uneasiness of his admirers. (503)[34]

Despite his respectability among Shakespearean critics, however, George Steevens's credibility in other matters was, to put it mildly, dubious, and later commentators, such as Ashton (1887) and Howell (1963) are not so impressed. The *DNB* confirms that Steevens "at one time owned a share in the 'St. James's Chronicle' "—a fact that would put him in some control over what was or was not published in that newspaper—and says that " 'Reasons why it is probable that the coffin [usually alleged to] contain the body of Milton should really contain that of Mrs. Smith' (*St. James's Chronicle*, 7 Sept. 1790; reprinted in the *European Magazine*, Sept. 1790, p.206), was 'a skit on a dry antiquarian pamphlet on the subject of Milton's burial by Philip Le Neve [q.v.].' "[35] Steevens was notorious for such "skits": his "pretended description of the upas tree of Java in the 'London Magazine' on the authority of a fictitious Dutch traveler, was conceived in a like vein," the *DNB* continues, enumerating some of Steevens's other literary "pranks"—of which "less can be urged in defence." For example, Steevens "contributed to the 'Theatrical Review' (1763, i. 61–66) a forged letter purporting to be a description by George Peele of a meeting at the Globe with Shakespeare and others," and engaged in "a practical joke of a more laboured kind . . . [when he] devised to pay off a trivial score against Richard Gough, director of the Society of Antiquaries." This involved embarrassing that organization with an elaborately faked "discovery" of the tombstone of Hardecanute—not to mention half a dozen other escapades of an equally unscholarly nature. Introducing the reader to "this impish gentleman, called 'the Puck of Shakespeare commentators,' " Howell is somewhat less than amused. He dismisses Steevens as "a notorious hoaxer of antiquaries in his day, though he did make some good emendations of Shakespeare's text."[36] Read concurs, noting that Samuel "Johnson defended [Steevens], it is true: upon Lord Mansfield's assertion that one could believe only half of what Steevens said, Johnson retorted that one could never be sure which half deserved credence" (1061). Even the *St. James's Chronicle* links the two events, lamenting that "—The present year has proved most inauspicious to Antiquarian researches. A false Hardickanutian Marble and the body of a spurious Milton, are objects that will not speedily be forgotten" (4–7 September 1790, no. 4584).

Be that as it may, Steevens's rebuttal is still the only substantive challenge to Neve's *Narrative* of all of the documents currently extant. The eight-reason version was answered both by Neve's second edition on 8 September 1790 and by a letter to the editor published in *The Gazetteer and New Daily Advertiser* (14 September 1790, no. 19,274) under the pseudonym "Benevolus," which argued that "the reasons given by Mr. Anonymous [i.e., Steevens], about the body which has been taken up in Cripplegate church, do not seem to be confirmed by scarce any one reason that it is not Milton's." Indeed, the most compelling reason of the eight (or nine) given is the sixth, "—Because Milton was not in affluence—expired in an emaciated state,—in a cold month, and was interred by direction of his widow. An expensive outward coffin of lead, therefore, was needless, and not likely to be provided by a rapacious woman, who oppressed her husband's children while he was living, and cheated them after he was dead—" but there is certainly no historical reason to believe Steevens's characterization of Elizabeth Minshull Milton as "rapacious." As previously indicated, Christopher Milton had testified under oath as to his brother's appreciation of his sister-in-law's devoted care. Mark Pattison affirmed that, "during the remaining eleven years of his life [after his marriage to Elizabeth in February 1663], the poet was surrounded by the thoughtful attentions of an active and capable woman," and repeated Aubrey's characterization of her "peaceful and agreeable humour," himself remarking that "it is certain that she regarded her husband with great veneration, and studied his comfort."[37] Furthermore, in the collection of Cripplegate memorabilia compiled by Anne S., identified by the British Library as "Topographical and Historical Collection Relating to the Parish of St. Giles, Cripplegate,"[38] the account of an auction held at Sotheby's entitled "Memoranda of Milton, the Poet, and James Boswell, Esq." notes that

On the 30th of June, 1825, Mr. Sotheby, of Waterloo-bridge, Strand, sold by public auction the library of James Boswell, Esq., . . . when among the rest were sold the office copy of the will of Elizabeth Milton, the poet's widow, and other papers related to her death, for 20*l*.9*s*.6*d*. by Thorp, bookseller. Three receipts, with the signatures of the poet's daughters, Anne Milton, Mary Milton, and Deborah Clarke and her husband, on receiving [£]100 each from their stepmother, as their portion of the estate of their father, for the sum of 18*l*. 7*s*. 6*d*., [were also sold] by Thorp.[39]

Certainly, then, their stepmother does not seem to have "cheated them after [their father] was dead," as Steevens alleged, especially in consideration of their uncle's affirmation in his deposition of 5 December 1674 at the Prerogative Court of Canterbury[40] that John Milton intended "to leave to the unkind children [he] had by [Mary Powell Milton]" only presumably equal interests in their mother's uncollected dowry, and otherwise "noe part . . . noe other benefit of [his] estate."[41]

Indeed, whether the last Mrs. Milton was "rapacious" or not, "contemporary accounts of the funeral"—most notably, Phillips's, and later, Todd's—"seem to indicate that [Milton's] was not a poor man's affair." "Surely," Howell remarks, "Sir Christopher Milton and John Philips [*sic*] would have provided a leaden coffin in honor of their distinguished relative if the widow had not."[42] It is indeed possible that John Phillips would have made such a contribution; it is more likely, though, that it would have come from his brother Edward, since it was the latter who maintained conspicuous contact with the poet during his declining years. Even in the absence of such family generosity, Milton's close friends—Andrew Marvell (d. 1678), Thomas Ellwood (d. 1713), Cyriack Skinner (d. 1700), Dr. Nathan Paget (d. 1700), and perhaps even Marchamont Needham (d. 1678) and John Dryden (d. 1700)—would presumably have acted on the deceased's behalf, seconded by his casual admirers and acquaintances.[43] But such charity does not appear to have been necessary: Phillips tells us that Milton "is said to have dyed worth 1500 *l*. in Money (a considerable Estate, all things considered) besides Household Goods"[44]—hardly the kind of penury that Steevens would hold accountable for Elizabeth's depriving him, either of a decent funeral, or of the leaden coffin befitting a man of his means.[45]

In an edition of *Paradise Lost* issued within two years of the disinterment, Capel Lofft seems unconvinced by either argument about the identity of the body, though in the preface to Book One, he is vocal in his indignation about the acts of vandalism wreaked upon the exhumed corpse, "whether the remains of that body which once was Milton's, or those of any other person [had been] . . . thus exposed and set to sale" by the vandals entrusted with their preservation.[46] "Mr. Lofft," Todd writes, "noticing the burial of the poet in St. Giles's church, has eloquently censured 'the sordid mischief' committed in it" by those who attended what churchwarden John Cole (silversmith, Barbican) called a "merry-meeting" at the home of Jonathan Fountain—a "victualler" or publican of Beech-Lane, and one of the parish overseers—the night before the sacrilege was perpetrated.[47] Lofft is clearly disgusted by "the market made of the eagerness with which curiosity or admiration prompted persons to possess themselves of [Milton's] supposed remains" (140). However, convinced that there is "reason to believe [that], far from being Milton's, [these] were the bones of a person *not of the same age or sex,*" *Scots Magazine* (no. 52, London, 1790), likewise reassures its readership that "notwithstanding the circumstances here [in Neve's *Narrative*] described, we have the satisfaction to think that the ashes of Milton have not been disturbed. The unhallowed visitors of the silent grave have, it seems, been upon a wrong scent; and (according to some,) have actually sold, as precious relics, the teeth, and other bones, of a female corpse, for those of the ever venerable author of paradise lost."[48] That pronouncement is repeated verbatim in the *Monthly Review* (November 1790), to the great relief (one imagines) of the parish sexton, who was "from home the whole day" while her enterprising colleagues were engaged in their ghoulish mischief.[49] In a letter to the editor recorded in *The English Chronicle and Universal Evening Post* (August 1790, no. 1705, pp. 24–26) and paraphrased in both *The London Times* (23 August 1790, no. 1658) and the *Gazetteer and New Daily Advertiser* (26 August 1790, no. 19,258), THE SEXTON (Mrs. Hoppey) reports that:

On Tuesday last some Antiquarians hearing that the vault of Milton, in Cripplegate Church, has been lately opened, went to the spot in order to obtain some further degree of information relative to that Poet.

When they arrived they found that the coffin, supposed to be Milton's, had already been opened, and that the hair was all taken off, and several teeth carried away as reliques. The skull otherwise remained perfect, and from its *smallness,* as well as the *openness of the forehead,* carried the marks of originality. To ascertain this further, they sent for a Surgeon, who on opening the skull, declared it to be that of a *male.* So far so good; all then that remained was to obtain some of the hair that was taken off, to see whether it corresponded with that colour which is given him by all his biographers.

The hair was recovered when lo! instead of a *light brown,* the well-known colour of Milton's hair, it was a *raven black.*[50]

This closed the inquiry in that instance, and after depositing the skull in its former place, the Antiquarians took leave, "tired but not satisfied," though we should not be surprised shortly to hear "a full and true account (from the *first inquirers*) of some late and *important* discoveries relative to that immortal bard."

The official inquiry may have been concluded to Ann Hoppey's satisfaction[51] (and indeed, neither Denton nor Baddeley makes mention of it),[52] but the public was not yet quite tired of the story. A month after the first disinterment, *The English Chronicle and Universal Evening Post* noted that there was a "Curious advertisement in Bowling-lane, near Duke's-place. 'To be fou–d within, *a hundred and four* real *teeth* of the famous Milton, vich the [s]eller will make oath dat he took out of dat great poet's *mout* himself at Cripple-gate'" (4–7 September 1790, no. 1800)—the *Chronicle's* editor grumbling that "there is scarce a *Jew pedlar* that has not some of poor Milton's hair for sale." Indeed, says he, "the head of the poet must have vegetated a great variety of hair, and of *various colours,* as the Public are alternately presented in the street with *grey, black, red* and *auburn* hair, each of which they are *solemnly* assured is *real* and *genuine*" (7–9 September 1790, no. 1801).⁵³ The *Gazetteer and New Daily Advertiser* agrees: on 3 September 1790 (no. 19,265) its editor reports that "several dozens of *teeth* have lately been very profitably disposed of as the genuine *grinders* of Milton, and six or seven *jaw-bones* are now on sale from the same undoubted authority." The next day, the same paper (no. 19,266) remarks that "more teeth and hair of Milton have been disposed of than could possibly belong to one individual, and yet there still remains on the market a sufficient quantity to supply the demand." Mrs. Hoppey's cause is again taken up by *The English Chronicle and Universal Evening Post* in the issue of 18–21 September (no. 1806), its editor observing that "a morning paper says, the body of Milton proved at last to be that of a lady; but luckily the mistake was not discovered, till the numerous tribes of writers, both in prose and verse, had exerted their genius on the occasion."⁵⁴

But though several contemporary poets (Cowper, Hunt, Keats, and "Albertus" among them) did indeed wax rhapsodic on the rape of the Miltonic locks, journalistic prose is the genre of primary interest here, for in that mode (as we have seen) there is a good deal of sardonic fun. Many late 1790 newspaper accounts lampoon the St. Giles parish and its officials with such high mock gravity that later readers have been gulled into confusing these "reports" with fact. Charles Gould, for example, remarks that,

two opposing parties now sued the luckless overseers. . . . The rector of St. Giles firmly believed that it was Milton who had been exhumed, and not having received any tithe of the hair and bones, he began a suit against his parish "for the recovery of dues so unjustly withheld from him.". . . Meanwhile, the descendants of the Smiths were bringing an action for the violent treatment to which the remains of their presumed ancestor or ancestress had been subjected.⁵⁵

This is no doubt derived from the report in the *St. James's Chronicle* of 7 September 1790 (no. 4584) that "we hear, that the Rector of St. Giles's, Cripplegate, having received no *tithe* of the hair and bones of *Milton,* has commenced a suit against his parish, for the recovery of dues so unjustly withheld from him."⁵⁶ "-It is likewise whispered," the column continues, "that the descendants of the *Smith* family are seeking redress from the same parish, it being now satisfactorily proved that the corpse which underwent such extraordinary treatment, was that of a Miss *Smith,* one of the daughters of *Richard Smith,* Esq., who died in 1675." The latter is reiterated two days later (7–9 September 1790, no. 4585) in the editorial comment that "in this Paper of Tuesday last, it was observed, that the *Smith* family were preparing a prosecution on account of the late unworthy treatment of one of their deceased relations in Cripplegate church," but in fact—as Read discerns—none of that is actually the case (1061). Though Howell also seems to accept these statements as fact, Neve points out that the Smyth family monument could not "have been erected until many years after the death of the last person mentioned in the inscription; and it was then placed there, as it expresses, not by any of the family, but at the expence of friends" (Neve 26–27), for no member of the immediate family was likely then alive.[57] Such spurious allegations sometimes provoked serious responses, even among the contemporary audience: the *St. James's Chronicle* for Saturday, 11 September 1790 (no.4586), reports that "A law correspondent in this paper of Thursday last, very truly observes, that any indifferent person may proceed in the case of a misdemeanour: of all offences which fall under this description, brutal and wanton insults on deceased persons are least to be forgiven.—But *Milton,* and others who are numbered with the dead, may safely entrust their rights to the protection of an English jury." Invariably, such statements were the product of contemporary wit and not empirical fact, a contention that can only be demonstrated by multiple recitation. For example, with a heavy dose of mischief, the *St. James's Chronicle* of 31 August 1790 (no. 4581) intimates that "one of the Parish Officers of Cripplegate, who violated the bones of Milton, has since been deranged in his intellects, and supposes himself to have been grasped by a cold hand, which has occasioned torpidity in his animal system. His wife, on this occasion, is inconsolable, and heartily wishes he had never meddled with what she calls a poetical Cramp-fish."

Taking the same rascally tack, *The Public Advertiser* (3 September 1790, no.17,522) reveals that

The researches into Milton's grave having occasioned much conversation, the author of a pamphlet, just published [i.e., Neve], gives us his opinion on the subject in the following words:

. . . A correspondent, passing along Barbican about a week ago, picked up the following curious bit of parcels, which we publish for the information of our readers, who may expect, after their graves are paid for, to lie quiet in them.

Ebenezer Ashmole, Esq.; F[ellow of the] S[ociety of] A[ntiquarians]

Bought of Timothy Strip-dead, Grave-digger to the parish of St. Giles, Cripplegate.

Aug. 3, 1790	*l.*	*s.*	*d.*
To two eye-teeth of one Mr. Milton	0	4	0
To a grinder of ditto	0	3	0
To a bit of winding sheet of ditto	0	2	6
To ditto of shrowd of ditto	0	2	6
To lock of light hair of ditto	0	4	0
To ditto black of ditto	0	2	6
To bit of wooden coffin of ditto	0	2	6
To ditto of leaden of ditto	0	3	0
To finger bone of ditto	0	5	0
To jaw-bone of ditto, with one broken tooth in it	0	7	0

As I sell these articles on account of one of the Parish Officers, I hope your honour will consider me a trifle.

N.B. All the above goods are warranted; there being counterfeits abroad.

No doubt, this piece is based on another wry comment made under "Literature" in the *Gazetteer and New Daily Advertiser* of the day before (no. 19,264) regarding "The Disinterment of Milton's Coffin" that "Mr. NEVE, after relating with great particularity the circumstances that accompanied the discovery of the pretended Coffin of Milton, and stating the precise sums which he paid for the recovery of locks of hair, teeth, and bones ravished from the sacred, though doubtful skeleton, sums up his narrative in a strain of holy indignation, with which some of our readers will sympathize, and at which some of them will smile." On 15 September 1790, *The Gazetteer and New Daily Advertiser* (no. 19,275) reports that "the wise men of Cripplegate parish have never been deficient in strength of digestion—but the *bones* they have lately encountered are likely to *stick in their throats!*"

Likewise, on 25 September 1790, upon the death of the duke of Cumberland (who per no. 17,543 was to be buried on the 28th), *The Public Advertiser* (no. 17,541) puckishly imparts the news that "strict orders have been given that none of the Parish Officers of Cripplegate shall be permitted to enter the Royal Vault in King Henry VII's Chapel. The same notice, in very polite terms, has been sent to the Antiquarians—as the determination is to keep out *all* the light-fingered gentry."

These are but a few examples of the satiric flavor of London journalism in the 1790s, which as a consequence must sometimes be taken with a rather large grain of salt. In periodical after periodical, such entries pervade all but the most somber segments of the news and are virtually indistinguishable from factual accounts. Unfortunately, because that is the case, and because each successive chronicler has tended to rely on the ones who preceded him or her for information, it is also true that, as demonstrated in this article, not all of the accounts of the desecration and its aftermath are as accurate as one might wish. Reliance on them—particularly the older ones—must therefore be tempered by a good deal of caution.

A case in point is Howell's confusion over Steevens's reference, in the first of the latter's "Reasons," to the Smyth family monument, which Steevens invokes as proof that the Smyths in general were buried in that section of the chancel from which the disputed remains were unearthed: "First,—Because Milton was buried in 1674, and this coffin was found in a situation previously allotted to a wealthy family, unconnected with his own. See the mural monument of the Smiths, dated 1653, &c. immediately over the place of the supposed Milton's interment." Conflating this remark with Steevens's later assertion (in the fifth reason) that "there is reason to believe that the aforesaid remains are those of a young female (one of the three Miss Smiths) for the bones are delicate, the teeth small, slightly inserted in the jaw, and perfectly white, even, and sound," Howell concludes (erroneously) that "the *Chronicle* writer [that is, Steevens] believed that the corpse was that of a female named Elizabeth Smith, buried near the column, according to an inscription on the adjacent wall, in 1665."[58]

The "inscription on the adjacent wall" to which Howell refers is actually the inscription on the Smyth family cenotaph, which was at that time mounted on a center aisle *column* (not a wall), near the present altar steps—and not far from Milton's gravestone; Baddeley provides a photograph of it.[59] The only female memorialized on the plaque is Elizabeth Smyth, the *mother* of the "three Miss Smiths"—and it is she who died on 25 May 1664, at sixty-four years of age, per the burial register, of jaundice—as corroborated by the cenotaph itself and her husband's entry in the *Obituary*, indicating that his "dear wife (*hei mihi*) M[is]. Elizabeth Smith died this dismall night; buried y[e] 28 of May" (60).[60] The dates on which the younger Smyth females expired are unknown; only the deaths of two of their brothers, Richard—aged seventeen, 1653, and John—aged thirty-two, 1655—are recorded on the monument, which also indicates that "their tender loving mother" "had 5 sons and 3 daughters" by "M[r]. Richard Smyth; sometymes Secondary of the Poultry Compter . . . whereof 2 only survived her," all of them unnamed.[61] But in the *Obituary*, Smyth laments that on 6 May 1655, "My only and eldest son, John Smith, beloved of all men (proh dolor), died at Micham in Surry, and buried in Lond. May 9, at St. Giles, Cripplegate"[62]—which means that the two surviving children had to be female, since by the death of their mother in 1664 all of the Smyth boys had passed away, too. Mrs. Smyth "willed this monument to be erected" in memory of her sons, the cenotaph inscription continues, "w[ch] after her death was (by her appointment) at her owne private cost (by her friends) performed" (parentheses in original). Since their father did not pass away until 26 March 1675, at the age of eighty-five, it was probably one or both of the two remaining Smyth girls (Martha Smyth Hacker and/or Anne Smyth Fleetwood) who had his name inscribed on the monument, but the identity of the third sister (who predeceased their mother) has thus far been impossible to determine. She may or may not have been an Elizabeth, and may or may not have been buried in the church. With respect to her identity, Lieb, following Howell, replicates the error of his source, just as that source perpetuates the errors of his source, and of all prior sources, going back to the original.[63]

It is Philip Neve himself who initiates the confusion in the first place. Aware in the first edition of the *Narrative* that the "Elizabeth Smyth" whose name is engraved on the "monument to the family of *Smith*" is "the mother, aged 64" (26), he concludes his second edition *Postscript* to Vestry Clerk Thomas Strong "with this declaration, that I should be very glad if any person would, from facts, give me reason to believe, that the corpse in question is rather that of *Elizabeth Smith,* whose name I know only from her monument, than that of *John Milton*" (50). He may have said so somewhat ironically, conscious that Elizabeth Dean Smyth's coffin contained the remains of the only identifiable female in the vicinity—and a female of virtually the same age at her death as Milton was at his—or he may have misassociated the mother's epitaph with her daughter's body. One way or the other, the two became synonymous forevermore in the ensuing scholarship.[64]

There can be no doubt, however, that whomever the body unearthed at Cripplegate church belonged to, it had been brutally vandalized, its rib cage disintegrated, the hair torn from its skull, the teeth smashed out of its jaw with a stone, and many of its bones removed. No one was quite certain then (or can say with confidence now) whether or not the coffin whence these curiosities came contained the remains of England's greatest poet, but as we have seen, the typical contemporary response to news of the desecration is to hope "that the poet's remains still rest undisturbed since their interment in 1674"—and that, "later inquiries . . . [having] produced some doubts of the identity of the corpse . . . his ashes have been violated only by proxy." Some comments are more indignant, and more pointedly political. Thompson makes reference to the "sarcastic correspondent" quoted in the *St. James's Chronicle* of 7 September 1790 (no. 4584), who notes,

—What different reflections will the same occurrence excite in people of opposite ways of thinking! The Tory *Dr. Johnson,* had he been alive, would have considered the disturbance of *Milton's* ashes as a late though certain judgment from Heaven, on the reviler of King Charles the First. On the contrary, Mr. *Hollis,* of Whiggish memory would have styled our poet's disinterment as an act of sacrilege committed on the bones of a patriot, a desecration which nothing less than the blood of the whole offending parish could expiate.[65]

In 1825, James Boaden, Esq.—who is Howell's authority for the provenance of the "[Nine] Reasons"—is convinced that "the only reason for supposing the body to be the poet's is, that it was found exactly in the situation which tradition had assigned to it; I mean, under the clerk's desk, as it stood in Milton's time; everything else is against it." Boaden even goes as far as to suggest that "the elders of Cripplegate" might deliberately have moved Milton's body in response to Charles II's treatment of the remains of Crowmell, Ireton, and Bradshaw, fearing that "what they had already seen in the case of the regicides, they might behold in the case of him, who certainly did not aid, but as certainly did *justify* all that [the regicides] had done." Perhaps following Boaden, Clement Ingleby suggested rather darkly in 1838 that it may have been the Tories themselves who were the perpetrators of the desecration—thus anticipating the sort of conspiracy theory with which modern history is so rife:

Mr. George Steevens, the great editor of Shakespeare, who justly denounced the indignity *intended,* not offered, to the great Puritan poet's remains by Royalist land-sharks, satisfied himself that the corpse was that of a woman of fewer years than Milton. Thus did good Providence, or good fortune, defeat the better half of their nefarious project: and I doubt not their gains were spent as money is which has been "gotten over the devil's back." Steevens' assurance gives us good reason for believing that Mr. Philip Neve's indignant protest is only good in the general, and that Milton's "hallowed reliques" still "rest undisturb'd within their peaceful shrine." (19–20).

McMains's summary is more noncommittal: his thumbnail sketch of the desecration says little more than that "public controversy flared as to whether the corpse was Milton's."[66]

Mark Pattison, on the other hand, shares Neve's conviction that the body belonged incontrovertibly to the poet. In 1880, he writes that "the disgusting profanation of the leaden coffin, and dispersion of the poet's bones by the parochial authorities, during the repair of the church in August, 1790, has been denied, but it is to be feared that the fact is all too true" (160).[67] A note published in *The Quiver,* vol. 1, no. 50 (785–87) by "W.D." on Saturday, 1 September 1866, reflects the indignation of those who concur:

Is a church always the trustworthy guardian of the dead buried within its walls? "Undoubtedly," many will say; "once let the gravestone be placed, and the long repose shall not be broken, until the mysterious trumpet of judgment shall call forth the sleeping ones to the light of endless day." Such may be the true answer in many cases, but what do men say about the grave of MILTON? . . . Those who believe that the body thus shamefully disturbed was [his] . . . might be reasonably indignant; but scepticism utters the consoling whisper, that the wrong grave had been opened, and that the poet still rests in an undisturbed grave. It is, however, to be feared that no mistake was made; and some private collection may at this moment boast of its stolen Miltonian relics.

Charles Gould agrees, remarking in 1930 that "it is strange that no final disproof has ever appeared, and still more curious that the incident seems to have been forgotten since that time."[68] His contemporary, Read, is equally vehement in his denunciation of the claims that the vandalized bones belonged to one of the daughters of antiquarian Richard Smyth (1590–1675): "The refutation of [the *Narrative*] has consisted almost entirely of pious hopes," he declares, "and the constant repetition of them has, in general, induced belief." To reinforce his point, he cites Howitt's 1847 assertion that "there is every reason to believe that [Milton's] remains were, on this occasion of raising the chancel and removing the stone, disturbed. The coffin was disinterred and opened. . . . The matter at the time occasioned a sharp controversy, and the public were at length persuaded to believe that they were not the remains of Milton, but of a female, that by mistake had thus been treated." "None have ever questioned the authenticity of Neve's material," Read reminds us. Rather, "they have tried merely to escape his conclusions . . . [that] the body disinterred in 1790 at St. Giles, Cripplegate, was that of the poet Milton." Howell would seem to concur: upon observing that J. Milton French has called Read's "the most comprehensive treatment of the event" to date, Howell affirms that he "arrived independently at almost the same conclusions, after examining much the same material."[69]

As Michael Lieb's very cautious affirmation suggests, Read's verdict may not be as "inescapable" as he would like us to perceive it to be,[70] but I too am certain that the bones hawked as relics of John Milton were not the remains of one of the daughters of Richard Smyth. The tale that leads me to that conclusion is a fascinating one, full of twists and turns and missing links and unexpected outcomes—and like all good tales, it is part fact, part myth, and part fantasy. To what has been said before, I can add several significant pieces of illumination either unknown to or ignored by those who have blazed this trail before me.

The first is that Philip Neve, Esq., of Furnival's Inn, Holborn (whose writing, as Read says, "is dispassionate and reserved, and appears quite like a lawyer's brief") was in fact a barrister of the Inner Temple (and later a magistrate of London's Marlborough Street Police Station), and therefore had the municipal power and wherewithal to see the offenders punished.[71] Certainly, Neve would have known how to go about such a prosecution, and we have already seen that he had the inclination. All the more curious, then, that John Laming and Jonathan Fountain were still performing their regular duties as Overseers of the Poor of the Parish through May 1791, and that no record of their indictment, or of any charges against them (or the mysterious grave digger, Elizabeth Grant) is extant at the Metropolitan Archives, Guildhall, or the Corporation of London Record Office.[72]

The second is that the "Dr. *Hunter*" under whom Neve's forensics specialist "Mr. *Dyson*" "received his professional education" (46) was the celebrated Scots physiologist John Hunter, "the leading anatomist of his day, being appointed Surgeon Extraordinary to King George III (1776)," according to the *DNB*.[73] The latter is important to our understanding of the events of the desecration because Dyson, the forensics expert whose Christian name is not given in the *Narrative*, was the "experienced surgeon of the neighborhood" who at the church's request performed the second medical examination of the desecrated body—by then missing almost all of its ribs, its lower jaw, and one hand (Neve 44–45)—and pronounced it to be that of a male of Milton's approximate age.[74]

The third is that "Mr. Dyson" was in fact Theophilus Dyson (1760–1809/10), author of such articles as "A Description and Dissection of a diseased Spermitic vein" and "A Case of inverted Uterus after parturition."[75] Beginning 1 June 1775, he served a seven-year apprenticeship to Samuel Dyson, a surgeon and apothecary of Leeds (though no apparent relation), and became qualified in those disciplines himself in 1782. Dyson first appears in the Society of Apothecaries' membership rolls in 1794, when he is listed as a yeoman residing in Fore Street (his address still in 1790, when he is called in to examine Milton's bones). By the third mention of Dyson's name in *Eighteenth Century Medics,* the surgeon resides (or practices, or both) in New Basinghall Street,[76] has become a Member of the Royal College of Surgeons, and is no longer referred to as an apothecary.[77]

On that basis, it is significant to this study that, upon evaluation of the pelvis and skull in question, Dyson concurred with the findings of Gabriel Taylor (who Neve says hails from Staunton, Derbyshire, and is also "a surgeon of considerable practice and eminence in his county"[78]) that the bones belonged to a man (and not a woman); and that he moreover pronounced them the bones of a man who was younger than Richard Smyth, aged eighty-five at the time of his demise. Luckily for posterity, a parish grave digger was on hand as well to lend some credibility to these forensic speculations; he, too, was certain that the body was that of a man (Neve 40, 46–48). It seems significant in light of this that the construction workers who located what they supposed was Milton's corpse had not found the bodies of Smyth's sons, Richard and John (mentioned earlier) in the vicinity of the older man's grave. Were the desecrated corpse Elizabeth Dean Smyth's (or even that of her husband), one would expect it to have been buried in closer proximity to the bodies of the other members of the Smyth family, assuming that the children of Richard and Elizabeth Smyth had in fact been buried with their parents in the first place, which does not seem likely at all.[79]

To better understand the evolution of this macabre series of events, one must travel a little over eleven decades backward in time to 1679, when, as Aubrey says, "the steppes to the communion table were raysed," and Milton's "stone was removed."[80] Probably relying on this information, most commentators report that the grave remained unmarked for 116 years. In 1963, however, Howell points out that "some manuscript jottings" made by engraver George Vertue which "are now . . . in the British Museum and quoted in *Notes and Queries* for July 6, 1861 (p. 2)" indicate that "there was . . . a grave stone for Milton in [Saint Giles's] Cripplegate, where he was buried; but in repairing the church lately [the note was written about 1721] they have taken it away and it is lost, though there are people who know perfectly [well] the spot of ground where it stood, which was shown to me. Upon that grave stone was [only cut] J.M."[81] For some reason unpreserved for posterity, that modest monument was neither reinstated nor replaced: "It is curious," wrote Thompson in 1890,

that from four years after Milton's death until 1793 no monument existed to mark the place where his remains had been deposited. . . . and if its removal were necessary in connexion with repairs or alterations in the church it is strange that it was not replaced or—if that were not practicable—that no other monument was erected to point out where the poet's remains rested, an oversight which gave rise to a most melancholy occurrence a hundred and sixteen years after his death.[82]

Indeed, as we have seen, the lack of a proper monument gave rise to a *singularly* "melancholy occurrence." It is curious, too, that that poor, mangled corpse in its hopelessly ransacked coffin was not apparently accorded the respect of a dignified reburial; rather, it seems to have been unceremoniously plopped back into the crypt "as is," without so much as a memorial service to make amends for the indignities it had suffered. Whomever it belonged to, his or her closest relatives were long dead, too, and Philip Neve was (apparently) the only living soul motivated to insist on its proper reinterment.[83]

Given the very public hue and cry that raged for several months over this affair, one would think the St. Giles "spin doctors" would have seized on the opportunity to make formal—and lavish—amends. They do not seem to have done so, though; nor does an extensive search of the appropriate records and documentation at the British Library, the Guildhall, the Metropolitan Archives, the Public Record Office, and the U.S. Library of Congress indicate that the "merry meeting" attendees were ever fined or punished, though a similar incident in a nearby parish was more swiftly and decisively dealt with.[84] As indicated previously, Fountain, Laming, and Taylor were still serving the parish in their official capacities some nine months later. Other than drink and the devil, and an opportunistic disregard for the sanctity of the grave, it is difficult to imagine what could have provoked the members of an otherwise apparently law-abiding parish that had been home to so many of England's illustrious dead to disturb—and brutally desecrate—the final resting place of the author of *Paradise Lost* almost twelve decades after his bones were duly committed to the church's protection. "Suspicious. Reasonless," as Milton's Satan might say. Except, of course, that they did it because Samuel Whitbread asked them to.[85]

The motive behind the famous brewer's request was hardly as sinister as its outcome. Aside from the fact that his "intire" or "entire butt" beer may well have been the libation served to the revelers at that notorious merry-meeting, Samuel Whitbread, M.P. for Bedford, was a prominent philanthropist who (like so many of his contemporaries) considered it disgraceful that the body of John Milton had lain for so long with nothing to mark the place.[86] Todd remarks that, Milton's original gravestone having been "removed not many years after his interment," his remains were not "honoured by any other memorial in Cripplegate church, till the year 1793; when by the munificence of the late Mr. Whitbread, an animated marble bust, the sculpture of Bacon, under which is a plain tablet, recording the dates of the poet's birth and death, and of his father's decease, was erected in the middle aisle.[87] *To the Author of Paradise Lost"*—and *not,* we might note, to the author of *The Tenure of Kings and Magistrates,* or the author of *Eikonoklastes*—Todd continues, "a similar tribute of respect had been paid, in 1737, by Mr. [William] Benson;[88] who procured [Milton's] bust to be admitted, where once his name had been deemed a profanation, into Westminster Abbey" (140–41).[89] These were the only monuments to Milton in all of London at the time, so that Whitbread's commissioning of the sculpture finished in 1793 was a significant event: "this unintended injury has in our days been amply compensated by the erection, in the same church, of a marble bust of the great poet, by the hand of Bacon and the liberality of [the late] Mr. Whitbread," says Symmons, extolling the latter as a man "whose virtues reflected honor on his species . . . the charities, which this excellent man has distributed with silent and sagacious beneficence, amounted annually to no less a sum than [£]10,000."[90] W. D. in the *Quiver* is more succinct in his praise: "Here is a fact for the cynic," he writes: "the greatest epic poet of England was buried in Cripplegate Church in 1674; and, one hundred and [nineteen] years after, MILTON's countrymen erect a monument near his grave!"[91]

Given that the elder Mr. Whitbread was so prominent and influential a member of St. Giles, Cripplegate parish,[92] it is not difficult to imagine that any "request" he might make ex officio to the lay officials of the church would reverberate with political overtones: they were all local businessmen themselves, and Whitbread's power and influence in the community would doubtless have had an almost coercive impact on the parish's willingness to be accommodating. As a result, we should not be put off by Neve's nondescript plurals in the second paragraph of the *Narrative*—where he says that,

it being in the contemplation of some persons to bestow a considerable sum of money, in erecting a monument, in the parish church of *St. Giles* Church, to the memory of *Milton,* and the particular spot of his interment, in that church, having for many years past, been ascertained only by tradition, several of the principal parishioners have, at their meetings, frequently expressed a wish that his coffin should be dug-for, that incontestable evidence of its exact situation might be established, before the said monument should be erected. (7)

Use of such devices ("some persons," "several of the principal parishioners") to protect the identities of individuals is common practice even today, and the plural terminology could just as easily refer to Whitbread alone. Such a theory is supported by the fact that, on 31 August 1790, in the fourth column on the front page, the *St. James's Chronicle* (no. 4581) announces that "Mr. Whitbread, the opulent Brewer, is prepared to raise a magnificent Monument to the memory of Milton, in the Parish Church of St. Giles, Cripplegate, the place of our poet's recent and ever-memorable disinterment." No other monument to the poet seems to have been planned for the parish at that time, unless those who were originally interested in doing so receded into the shadows when the more prominent Mr. Whitbread emerged. It seems likely therefore that it was his request to churchwarden Cole that induced the latter to direct the construction men—who were then already engaged in performing a £1,350 renovation contract in the church's behalf, per the *Narrative* (9)—to look for Milton's coffin. Of course, neither Whitbread nor Cole could have anticipated the mayhem that ensued, and disappointingly, if any correspondence ever existed between them or between Messrs. Whitbread and Bacon on the subject of the statue, it does not exist in the archives of the Whitbreads, or of the Royal Academy.[93] Absent any such evidence to the contrary, then, it would appear that Whitbread was the "principal parishioner" of whom Neve spoke.

The story of what happened to the Whitbread/Bacon bust after its creation in 1793 is almost as bizarre as the story of the posthumous "adventures" of Milton's bones. It, too, has been shrouded in the mists of misinformation and error, though it has been less susceptible of mayhem than the poet's remains. The bust was the work of John Bacon, the elder, a neoclassical sculptor born in London on 24 November 1740. According to the *Encyclopedia Britannica* (Macropedia, vol. 1, 1998 ed.), in 1754, Bacon was apprenticed in a porcelain works at Lambeth, painting small ornamental pieces of china. By 1769, he had won the first gold medal for sculpture given by the newly instituted Royal Academy for a bas-relief representing the escape of Aeneas from Troy, and in 1770 he earned a second gold medal from the Society for the Encouragement of the Arts for his Mars and Venus, and was made an associate of the Royal Academy. Some of his best works are still on display in Westminster Abbey.[94]

"An Account of John Bacon, Esq., F.R.A." affirms and amplifies the above, noting that "when he was already famous for his Mars and Venus, the Archbishop of York commissioned Bacon to do a sculpture of the king for the hall of Christ-Church College at Oxford, after which he received a royal patronage, and began sculpting a series of commissioned pieces, two more for the king, then several for the dean and Fellows of Christ-Church."[95] At the time of the publication of this article, which predates the Whitbread bust, Bacon was known to be working on a likeness of Dr. Johnson as well.

Evidently modeled on the Faithorne portrait of Milton, the Whitbread bust consists of a white marble likeness of the poet's head and upper torso, mounted on a small pedestal over a large engraved plaque, just as it was described by Todd above. Originally secured to the third column from the altar in 1793, it had been moved to a more prominent location by the time Thompson saw it in 1890, since he reports that it

now stands in a memorial shrine of Caen stone, designed by the late Mr. Edmund Woodthorpe, and erected in 1862. The base bears the following inscription:—

> John Milton
> Author of Paradise Lost
> Born December, 1608. Died November, 1674.
> His Father, John Milton, Died March, 1646.
> They were both interred in this Church.
> [Samuel Whitbread posuit, 1793][96]

Beneath this are the serpent and the flaming sword, symbolical of the fall and expulsion from Paradise.[97]

According to Baddeley, Woodthorpe's "canopied shrine of Caen stone, elaborately carved and supported by columns, composed of different coloured marbles, granite, and alabaster," was "12 feet in height, and nearly 8 feet wide at the base"—a rather gaudy affair, by modern standards. It is pictured with the bust at its center on page 96 of Baddeley's *Account,* apparently still housed in the interior of the church (fig. 4). The bust itself, which appears in *SGC,* page 41, can be seen more clearly in figure 5.[98]

The memorial shrine of Milton is placed in the south aisle, directly facing the north door of the church.   Beneath its canopy, is a bust giving a striking likeness of the poet, the work of John Bacon, a noted sculptor,

who executed about the same time (1793) the monuments of William Pitt, Earl of Chatham, in Westminster Abbey, and in the Guildhall, City of London.   The bust was the gift of Samuel Whitbread, Esq., head of the great brewing firm in Cripplegate, and a respected member

Fig. 4. The Caen stone shrine designed by Edmund Woodthorpe (1862), which formerly housed the Whitbread/Bacon bust of the poet seen at its center. The shrine was apparently destroyed by the Luftwaffe, but the bust was undamaged and survives intact today. By permission of the British Library (shelfmark 4705.e.27).

Fig. 5. The Whitbread bust, sculpted by John Bacon (the elder), F.R.A. (1793). Its commissioning was the indirect cause of the discovery and desecration of the poet's grave. By permission of photographer Ruth I. LuSan.

It is still there, in the Woodthorpe shrine, but moved "outside the western door," when A. C. Howell sees it in 1931. He reports that by 1960, "only a small stone marked [Milton's] grave [see fig. 3] . . . both the bust and its shrine, and the statue outside the western door [(the bronze Horace Montford likeness commissioned by Baddeley, 1904) having been] destroyed by the bombings which all but obliterated this section of London" in World War II. "It seems only fair to observe that the poet chose an unquiet grave," says Howell, "a grave which through the vicissitudes of time has been more than once disturbed"—lamenting that Milton "got but half the wish he expressed in *Mansus*, for though his face was carved in marble, he did not rest in peace."[99]

That part of the story, at least, has a happy ending. Neither the Whitbread bust nor the Montford statue, nor even the now-decaying pedestal designed by E. A. Richards on which the Montford statue once stood, were obliterated by Hitler's incendiary bombs as Howell (and French before him) supposed. Pecheux explains that, having been blown off its base twice by the Luftwaffe when it stood in the St. Giles courtyard during the most devastating attacks on the Barbican area (August 1940), the Montford statue was moved for safety to its present position inside the church, where it is very much intact even today (see fig. 6).[100] The pedestal, now missing almost all of its artwork but for the moss-covered and barely distinguishable "BADDELEY" engraved at its base, remains outside in the church courtyard (fig. 7), a monument to the ravages of war. As for the Whitbread bust, that is in fine shape, too: Pecheux saw and described it in 1981[101]; Ruth Lu San saw and photographed it in October 1993 (see fig. 5); and in a less prominent position (though probably in the same place), I, too, saw and photographed it in December 1999 (fig. 8). It was still there, mostly hidden by the cloth-wall screens that conceal the makeshift storage area over which it currently presides, at Easter 2001, but I have the assurance of the Reverend Katharine Rumens, the new vicar of St. Giles, Cripplegate Church, that it will once again be displayed where parishioners and visitors can see it clearly, perhaps in the alcove next to the place where the Milton Quadricentenary Window will be installed in 2008, in direct line of sight of Milton's fading gravestone, and the bones it was meant to honor.

"Ill fare the hands that heaved the stones," indeed! Early in this investigation, I was convinced that the body in question was John Milton's, that the officials of St. Giles, Cripplegate, knew that it was, and that, as Neve darkly suspects, they conspired to silence him when he tried to obtain redress on behalf of a victim for whom there was no one else to speak (Neve, 38–39). I still think so—and the more data I have uncovered about this bizarre set of events, the more certain I have become; only now I think that for practical reasons, Philip Neve himself became party to the cover-up.

Fig. 6. The bronze Horace Montford statue commissioned by Lord Mayor Baddeley, 1904, atop the E. A. Richards pedestal. By permission of the British Library (shelfmark 10349.gg.47).

Fig. 7. The E. A. Richards pedestal outside the church today. The no longer legible inscription on the base quotes *Paradise Lost* 1.17–26 ("spirit . . . what in me is dark / Illumine . . ."). Photograph courtesy of the author.

Fig. 8. "Milton, god of AV": The Whitbread bust as I first saw it, hidden behind shelving and audiovisual equipment in a storage area at St. Giles, Cripplegate. It has since been relocated to a more prominent location on the same wall. Photograph courtesy of the author.

As a summation of the evidence that leads me to draw that conclusion, I would like to counter George Steevens's "MILTON. Reasons why it is improbable that the Coffin lately dug up in the Parish Church of St. Giles, Cripplegate, should contain the Reliques of Milton" with a set of "reasons" of my own. I think it is not only probable, but almost certain, "that the Coffin . . . dug up in the Parish Church of St. Giles, Cripplegate [in 1790] . . . contained the Reliques of Milton," based upon the following considerations:

First, that the only candidate corpses, given their position relative both to the original chancel of the church, and to the markers that by historical consensus indicated the proximate location of their bodies, were those of John Milton Sr. (d. 1647, aged almost eighty-five); the poet (d. 1674, aged not quite sixty-six); Richard Smyth (d. 1675, aged eighty-five); and his wife, Elizabeth Dean Smyth (d. 1664, aged sixty-four). Neve's argument that the four Smyth bodies mentioned on the family cenotaph (that is, the parents and their sons Richard and John) should have been found together notwithstanding, the sons (who died long before their parents did) seem to have been buried in the churchyard, while Richard Smyth and his wife were demonstrably buried in the church, according to the official register. That would account for the two bodies being found, off by themselves, in that vicinity of the crypt, and reinforce the idea that they did not belong to the Miltons. It would also invite the speculation that, rather than that of a "young female" (one of Elizabeth Smyth's daughters), the body unearthed may indeed have been that of the mother herself.

However: since Richard Smyth lived some eleven years beyond the demise of his spouse, it would have been *his* coffin, and *not* Elizabeth's, that would have been the uppermost.

Second, that the surgeon who at parish request examined the remains of the remains at the second exhumation on 17 August 1790 determined that the body was not Richard Smyth's (based on the octogenarian's age), that the corpse was determined to be the body of a man significantly younger, and that there were no other bodies buried in the near vicinity. This would tend to increase rather than reduce the likelihood that the desecrated bones were John Milton's.

Third, that that same surgeon, Theophilus Dyson, was a trained forensics expert who had studied under John Hunter, the father of forensic medicine, and was a member of both the Society of Apothecaries and the Royal College of Surgeons. The credibility of his findings would therefore be much greater than that of the average physician or barber-surgeon of the period.

Fourth, that Dyson's opinion was seconded by Gabriel Taylor/Tayler, apothecary and surgeon to the St. Giles, Cripplegate, workhouse (and by the unnamed male grave digger as well).

Fifth, that the author of the *Narrative of the Disinterment* (which re-counts the events surrounding the desecration in meticulous detail) was not only a Milton aficionado and an antiquary, but a barrister of the Inner Temple, and later a magistrate of the Marlborough Street Police Station as well. As such, he was very familiar with the rules of evidence and was careful to record the names, addresses, and occupations of all involved, in addition to the extent of their participation in the desecration and its aftermath.

Sixth, that despite the fact that Philip Neve expressed the desire and had the means to see that the perpetrators were punished, Fountain and Laming were still serving as overseers of the poor, and Taylor as apothecary and surgeon of the workhouse, the following spring.

Seventh, that other individuals in nearby parishes (including the apoc-ryphal female grave digger?) were prosecuted and punished for committing crimes of the same type against less prominent "victims" as soon as they were apprehended.

Eighth, the unlikelihood that Neve would have been indignant enough about the desecration to write and publish the *Narrative* and an almost immediate second edition (appending his letter of complaint to Strong)—and so devoted to Milton's memory that he would take the time and trouble to locate and buy back the purloined "reliques" at his own expense so that they could be restored to the poet's coffin—but could at some point thereafter be seized (as Boaden would have us believe he was) by the conviction that Steevens's "Reasons" "were absolutely unanswerable," so that he simply abandoned his cause, forgot his quest to have the remains reburied in a new casket, and went on to other matters.

Ninth, the fact that, ridiculed publicly and relentlessly for the malfea-sance of its "merry" lay officials, the church was so anxious to divert public attention from the parish that it (allegedly) barred Neve from continuing his investigation (see Neve, *Narrative,* 2d ed. letter to Strong, 38–39). Had the parish officials truly believed that the defiled remains belonged to someone other than the poet, they would perhaps have been more inclined to pomp and circumstance, and made use of the ostensible opportunity for the "dam-age control" that a formal, dignified public reburial of the vandalized bones would have accomplished. But the truth was scandalous, and to admit con-clusively that the body was Milton's would be to invite even more censure than the Cripplegate congregation had already endured. Vicar George Wat-son Hand and senior churchwarden John Benjamin Cole and the others seem to have been unwilling to risk it.

Tenth, that somehow, once the sexton had published her announcement that the body was a female's, the Cripplegate officials managed to silence their opposition and the media so effectively that the general public took

Mrs. Hoppey at her word and turned its attention elsewhere. Bribery alone would not likely account for that, especially in Neve's case (given his personal character and zeal), and there were simply too many people and too much notoriety involved for payoffs to have been a practical solution in the other instances. Nonetheless, the silence is pervasive, in November 1790 and beyond.

Eleventh, that, despite their continuous (and almost vicious) attention to the story of the desecration and its aftermath from August through October 1790, the major London newspapers suddenly and without explanation elected to drop commentary on the subject from their pages that November, never to be mentioned by contemporary journalists again.

Twelfth, that the report that the female gravedigger (Elizabeth Grant) was remanded to Newgate for her part in the desecration is an apocryphal one, evolving out of the casual speculation of a journalistic feature writer.[102]

Thirteenth, that (though the entries for this period are extant), there is no indication in the *Vestry Minutes* for August 1790 that the desecration (of Milton's grave or anyone else's) ever occurred—and one would think such a scandal worthy of at least "honorable mention," especially among innocent bystanders.[103]

Fourteenth, that there is similarly no indication in the *Vestry Minutes* that Fountain, Laming, Taylor, Grant, Ellis, or any of the subsequent malefactors in this incident ever received as much as a reprimand for violating the sanctuary of the dead, and that in fact they all retained their parish positions, and most received raises, during the six months subsequent. (Unfortunately, the *Churchwarden's Registers* for 1790 and 1791, where such records might also appear, have been lost or destroyed.)

As I noted earlier, there were two things that bothered me throughout this investigation: first, the lack of any suggestion in any of the records I examined that (regardless of whose corpse it was) those poor mangled bones were interred in a new coffin and received a dignified reburial; and second, the idea that anyone would have been able to stop Philip Neve dead in his tracks and silence the newspapers and broadsheets as simultaneously and as effectively as the church seems to have done. The possibility that the Cripplegate officials just tossed the body back into the ground, broken casket and all, when they were finished with it was so repugnant that it led me to check the parish burial registers for August through October 1790 in search of some indication that John Milton or the young woman I then believed was "Elizabeth Smyth" had been officially reinterred.[104]

I found no entries for "Smyth" or "Smith" or "Smythe." I did, however, find a curious entry for "Milton," corroborated by the ledger of burial fees.[105] It concerned the demise of one James Milton, a child of the poor of indeterminate age, who died of "convulsions" in White Hart Yard (which, per Henry A. Harden, F.S.A., *A Dictionary of London*, 1918, was "north out of Fore Street in Cripplegate Ward Without," on the west side of Coleman Street, north of the White Horse Inn—that is, just a few hundred yards from Cripplegate church). Aside from the resonance of his name, the interesting thing about this item is that neither the child's age nor his parentage is given (though either or both appear in the entries for other parish children who expired under similar circumstances), and that, because he was poor, James Milton would have been buried at parish expense.[106] By the time Fountain, Laming, Taylor, Ellis, and Hawkesworth were done with it, what was left of Milton's body would have been small enough to fit into a child's coffin (much less costly than an adult's). There would have been no one left of his immediate descendants to attend a funeral (Elizabeth Foster having died in 1754), so there would be no need for ostentation; and they would have had to put something in the registers to justify the expense, since the church's books and records of account were subject to audit by the faculty of St. Paul's.

The mischievous speculation that occurred to me as a result—that is, could "James Milton" and John Milton have been one and the same?—led me to a theory that resolves the second of my major concerns: suppose that, in exchange for a promise not to continue his journalistic war of words with George Steevens, and to refrain from prosecuting any of the people who were involved in the desecration, Hand, Strong, and Cole had given Neve what he wanted most: a dignified reburial of Milton's remains, including what he had recovered from the grave robbers? They might then have appealed to the newspapers in unison to let the matter drop. That would explain both Neve's sudden abandonment of his mission and the deafening journalistic silence after October 1790. Furthermore, since both the bishop of London and the dean of St. Paul's had jurisdiction over the Cripplegate parish, one might expect to find internal correspondence between those ecclesiastical agencies and George Hand among their documents; but there is nothing relating to this matter in the records of Bishop Porteus at Lambeth Palace, nor in the visitation records or in the Faculty Register of the Dean of St. Paul's at Guildhall[107] that would support or refute the supposition that the "gag order" was a joint venture between Neve and the parish officials. This then seems the most plausible answer, though of course it also reflects some wishful thinking on my part, based on the conviction that Neve would not willingly have let the matter die in any other case.

Taking a cue from *Areopagitica* (YP 2:549), Michael Lieb in *Milton and the Culture of Violence* draws an elegant analogy between the author of the *Narrative,* "sad friend of Milton's body," going "up and down gathering up [the pieces of Milton] limb by limb still as [he] could find them," and "the carefull search that Isis made for the mangl'd body of Osiris."[108] As the first female investigator to follow (conceptually) in Neve's footsteps, I would like to invoke both Lieb's analogy and Milton's original appropriation of the Isis/Osiris myth in *Areopagitica* in my own behalf to emphasize that the purpose of this study has been to gather, consolidate, and rectify as much as it is possible to do so the corpus of Truth that is left to us on "the treatment of [Milton's] corpse" 213 years after the fact, and 329 years after his death and burial. The trail one must follow to restore to him what was so rudely taken away is a complicated one, its navigation rendered even more difficult by the blind alleys of documents lost, discarded, or destroyed in at least one major fire, and the errors, misperceptions, and misinterpretations of those who did their best to piece this story together in the past. I respect and am grateful to the scholars who preceded me, and acknowledge the obstacles they overcame with less advanced technology (and worldwide collegial support) than I was fortunate to have at my disposal.

His face was carved in marble. May his spirit rest in peace.

In quintum Novembris 2001

Danville, Virginia

NOTES

I am deeply grateful to John T. Shawcross for his tireless guidance, encouragement, and support throughout my work on this complicated project, and for the many references that are cited here from his forthcoming *Milton: A Bibliography for the Years 1624–1700: Revised, and for the Years 1701–1799* (published electronically in *Iter*, and in hard copy by Medieval and Renaissance Essays and Studies). Many thanks also to Michael Lieb and William B. Hunter, who read (and re-read) this article in manuscript and contributed many valuable comments and suggestions; and to Geoffrey Rivett, M.D., for the chance remark about the disinterment made during our "cook's tour" of St. Giles, Cripplegate, in December 1999 that would lead me all over London before I understood the significance of "Milton, god of AV," and learned the real history behind the local legends surrounding the grave it was intended to adorn. The cooperation of the other archivists and scholars whose names appear below has likewise been invaluable, since without their aid and participation, this project would have been infinitely more difficult to accomplish.

Unless otherwise specified, all eighteenth-century periodicals referenced were published in London. Additionally, because some of the texts would otherwise be difficult to locate, wherever possible I have indicated their Library of Congress (LOC) and Folger Shakespeare Library (FSL) call numbers, and/or their British Library (BL) and Guildhall (G) shelfmarks.

1. The title tag is from the fifth stanza of William Cowper's "On the Disinterment and Multiplied Sale of Milton's Bones," first published in *The Gazetteer and New Daily Advertiser*, 11 September 1790, no. 19,272, and later retitled "Stanzas on the late Indecent Liberties taken

with the Remains of the Great Milton.—Anno. 1790." See A. C. Howell, "Milton's Mortal Remains and Their Literary Echoes," in *Ball State Forum* 4 (1963): 23; Corrie Leonard Thompson, "John Milton's Bones," in *Notes & Queries,* 1890, 361–64, 395; and Sister M[ary] Christopher Pecheux, *Milton: A Topographical Guide* (London, 1981), 91.The stanza reads:

> Ill fare the hands that heaved the stones
> Where Milton's ashes lay,
> That trembled not to grasp his bones,
> And steal his dust away!

Thompson reprints the poem in its entirety, along with a transcript of Leigh Hunt's "To [Robert Batty,] M.D., On his giving me a lock of Milton's Hair"; see also John Ashton, *Eighteenth Century Waifs: Essays on the Social Life and Biography of the Eighteenth Century* (1887; reprint, Detroit, 1968), 55–57.

2. These are by no means the only commentators; see, for example, John T. Shawcross, *John Milton: The Self and the World* (Lexington, Ky., 1993), 280.

3. David Masson, *The Life of John Milton: Narrated in Connexion with the Political, Ecclesiastical, and Literary History of His Time, 1859–80,* 6 vols. (London, 1894), 6:731. Per 731 n. 1, the testimony was recorded in the "Evidence of Elizabeth Fisher and Mary Fisher in the case of Milton's Nuncupative Will."

4. The phrase "somewhat commodious" is John T. Shawcross's (*Self,* 272). See Pecheux, *Milton,* 65–66.

5. Cyriack Skinner, "The Life of Mr. John Milton," in Helen Darbishire, *Some Early Lives of Milton* (London: Constable & Co., 1932), 33. Based on Peter Beal's recent discovery of two authentic examples of Skinner's hand (and confirming William Riley Parker's earlier inference), Gordon Campbell, introduction to *A Milton Chronology* (New York, 1997), x, now affirms that the identity of the heretofore "anonymous" biographer has been established conclusively. I am grateful for Professor Campbell's 6 August 2000 e-mail elaboration on his source for n. 7. It is worth noting that in "Milton's Gout," *Bulletin of the History of Medicine* 28 (1954): 301–11, Edward A. Block discusses the "gout struck in" from which Milton died and suggests that a modern diagnosis would be heart failure.

6. John Toland, "The Life of Milton," *A Complete Collection of the Historical, Political, and Miscellaneous Works of John Milton* (London, 1698), 46. Masson, *The Life of John Milton,* 6:731; Darbishire, *Some Early Lives,* 76.

7. See Philip Neve, *A narrative of the disinterment of Milton's coffin, in the Parish-Church of St. Giles's, Cripplegate, on Wednesday, the 4th of August, 1790; and of the treatment of the corpse during that, and the following day* (London, 1790), 13–14, 27. Signed on page 34, "Philip Neve. Furnival's Inn, 14th of August, 1790"; hereafter cited in the text.

8. J[oseph] Milton French, *The Life Records of John Milton,* 5 vols. (New York, 1966), LOC call no. PR3581.F72, 352: "With Mrs. Foster's death, the direct line of descendents of Milton came to an end, though the families of his sister Anne [Milton Phillips] and his brother Christopher have continued into the twentieth century."

9. The name is given variously by different authors, but the general consensus is that, as Pecheux, *Milton,* indicates, "Milton's last home was located in BUNHILL ROW, also known as Artillery Walk or Artillery Row" (63). (See my *"Dem Bones": Milton beyond the Grave,* forthcoming, for additional details.)

10. Aubrey comments that "he died in Bunhill opposite to the Artillery garden-wall . . . of ye gowt struck in the 9th or 10th of Novemb. 1674 as appeares by his Apothecaryes Booke" (Aubrey f.68, in Darbishire, *Some Early Lives,* 4–5, and French, *Life Records,* 96–97), the latter remarking that "anywhere from the 8th to the 10th would be appropriate" (97). Howell, "Milton's Mortal

Remains," gives Aubrey without dispute (17). In *The Life of John Milton* (1822; reprint, New York, 1970), LOC/PR3581.S8.1970, p. 425, Charles Symmons asserts that it was the eighth, as does Masson, *The Life of John Milton*, 6:731; William Howitt, *Homes and Haunts of the Most Eminent British Poets. In Two Volumes*, vol. 1 (New York, 1847), LOC/PR109.H6, p. 115; Sir John Baddeley, *An Account of the Church and Parish of St. Giles Without Cripplegate, in the City of London/compiled from various old authorities, including the churchwarden's accounts, and the vestry minute books of the parish* (London, 1888), 94–95, hereafter *SGC*; and William Riley Parker, *Milton: A Biography*, 2d ed., ed. Gordon Campbell (Oxford, 1996), 1:640, agree, all of them apparently relying on the depositions of Elizabeth and Mary Fisher, as to the day of the week of Milton's demise, as indicated above. However, French notes that "both Elizabeth and Mary Fisher testified that Milton died on Sunday, November 15" (98), which was also the date that Cripplegate parishioner and antiquarian Richard Smyth recorded in "A Catalogue of all such Persons deceased whome I knew in their Life time . . . from the year of our Lord M.DC.XXVIII" (BM Sloane MS. 886, f. 73v, *The Obituary of Richard Smyth*, 1849, Publications of the Camden Society, no. 44, p. 104; as edited by Sir Henry Ellis, K.H., who says (preface, i) that the whereabouts of the original cannot be determined. The work is also known as the *Obituary of Richard Smyth, Secondary of the Poultry Computer, London: Being a Catalogue of All Such Persons as he knew in Their Life: Extending from A.D. 1627 to A.D. 1674* [London, 1849]); cited hereafter as "the *Obituary*." See also Baddeley, *SGC*, 99: "1674 . . . Novem 15 Iohn Milton. Died at Bunhill near morefields in Criplegate Parish. blind some time before he Died." That of course conflicts with the clear entry in the parish burial register (Guildhall microfilm MS L92.6419, vol. 9, 1674), showing that "<u>John: Milton, Gentleman</u>" was buried on "<u>Nov. 12</u>. 1674," the 'L' that precedes his name signifying that he resided at the time of his death on land originally leased to the Lord Mayor and commonality of the City of London by Robert Baldock in 1315, in behalf of the Lords of the Manor of Finsbury, generally referred to as "the Lordship." Control of this suburb of London proper was held by the Lord Mayor until it passed to the Ecclesiastical Commissioners in 1867, per Ernest Ryan, KW, in *Cripplegate, Finsbury, & Moorfields*. London: Adams Brothers & Shardlow, 1917. (I am indebted to Ms. Claire Frankland, Islington Local History Centre, Finsbury Library, for this information.)

11. The comment is made in the anonymously published "MILTON. Reasons why it is improbable that the Coffin lately dug up in the Parish Church of St. Giles, Cripplegate, should contain the Reliques of Milton," *St. James's Chronicle, Or British Evening Post*, 4 September 1790, no. 4583, later identified as the work of George Steevens (see appendix B.)

12. Darbishire, *Some Early Lives*, 276, citing Samuel Richardson (1734), xcv, who remarks, even as he is about to transcribe the poem that appears below, that he has "heard it Intimated, [Milton] Left at his death 1500 *l.* besides his Goods" (Darbishire, *Some Early Lives*, 279):

> Upon *John Milton's* not Suffering for His
> Traiterous Book when the Tryers were Executed 1660.
> That thou Escapd'st that Vengeance which o'ertook,
> *Milton*, thy Regicides, and thy Own Book,
> Was Clemency in *Charles* [II] beyond compare,
> And yet thy Doom doth prove more Grevious farr.
> Old, Sickly, Poor, Stark Blind, thou Writ'st for Bread,
> So for to Live thou'dst call *Salmasius* from the Dead.

13. See the *St. James Chronicle*, 4 September 1790, no. 4583.

14. Darbishire, *Some Early Lives*, 280.

15. Mark Pattison, *Milton* (New York, 1880),145, citing the remark made by Thomas "Newton, Bishop of Bristol . . . in 1749."

16. *Ad Interrogatoria,* cited in Henry John Todd, *The Poetical Works of John Milton, with Notes of Various Authors. To Which are Added Illustrations, and Some Account of the Life and Writings of John Milton. The Second Edition, with Additions, and with a Verbal Index to the Whole of Milton's Poetry,* 7 vols. [London, 1809], 5:172, reissued with a new title page, unless otherwise noted; LOC/PR3581.T6.1809; FSL/PR3551.M622.1809, 175.

17. Pattison, *Milton,* 145.

18. Frank Major, text, and Geoffrey Rivett, modern photography, *St. Giles' Church, Cripplegate* (London: St. Giles' Church, Cripplegate, 2000), 5.

19. The vicar of the church at the time of Milton's death was John Pritchett (1664–1681), whom Baddeley, *SGC,* characterizes as a notorious pluralist, reporting that, at the time of his death, Pritchett held, "in addition to the vicarage of Saint Giles, the Bishopric of Gloucester, the living of Harlingdon, and a stall in St. Paul's Cathedral" (65). The sermon "Queries to be put to the ministers" (1679), wing P3528A, may be his, but it clearly was not preached at Milton's funeral. Per the web page of the Diocese of Ely at http://www.ely.anglican.org./history/talk-19990209/andrewes.html, "the diarist John Evelyn notes on 4th April 1679 that the Bishop of Gloucester, John Pritchett, preached Andrewes-style with many sub-divisions, and 'with much quickness,' in a manner by then out of date" (15 June 2001).

For an account of the fluctuating religious politics of St. Giles, Cripplegate, Church during this period of its history, see Sharon Achinstein's forthcoming *Zion's Ashes: The Poetics of Dissent in Restoration England.*

20. 1090 is the date given on the official web page of St. Giles, Cripplegate, Church, per Eatick and Thornton. However, under the heading "St. Giles Without, Cripplegare [*sic*], Ancient Church," a curious undated article from *City Notes and Queries* signed "Humphry Clinker" (and compiled by Anne S.) indicates that "Neve, Seymour, and Newton agree to the statement [made by "Mr. Miller, in a foot note to his *Milton Memorial,* 16"] that the church was built in 1030," and observes that Stow's *Survey* would seem to concur (since it says that the church was built "[in] the reign of William the Conqueror, who died in 1087")—though the *Survey* itself gives the date as 1099. Other sources—equally conflicting—are cited in my *"Dem Bones."*

21. One assumes that he attended the funerals of John Milton Sr. and his father-in-law, Richard Powell, both of which he would have arranged and paid for, but no record of those events (or the sermons preached at them) appears to be extant. Per Baddeley, *SGC,* St. Giles was without a rector from the time of the ouster and imprisonment of William Fuller, D.D., by Oliver Cromwell in 1642 to the installment of Samuel Annesley by Richard Cromwell in 1658, and that fact may have a good deal to do with the absence of such records. The books of account—cited by Baddeley in *SGC* in 1888 but no longer extant—showed that itinerant preachers such as Kelly in 1646 and Samuel Torshell in 1648—the latter of whom died, according to Smyth's *Obituary* on 22 March 1649/50—were sometimes hired in the interim. I have been able to locate only one sermon attributed to any of them, in this case preached to Parliament by Torshell, "A Design About Disposing the Bible into an Harmony; or, An Essay, Concerning the transposing the order of Books and Chapters of the holy Scriptures" (London, 1647); Folger shelfmark 137752/wing T1936, but it is clearly not a funeral piece.

22. See James Holly Hanford, *John Milton, Englishman* (New York, 1949), 249. Pecheux's remarks are representative. Affirming that "the facts surrounding the notorious incident of the alleged disinterment of Milton's body have been disputed from the beginning," she notes that, though "the truth of [Neve's] account was denied almost immediately . . . the most recent investigator (Read, in *PMLA* 45) believes that the [*Narrative*] was substantially true" (*Milton,* 90). The "notoriety" of the incident might well be disputed, except as to the first three months immediately after its occurrence, since more than half a century passed between the publication of Read's article (1930) and Pecheux's citation of it (1981); and Read's remains the last extensive

commentary on the subject even now, twenty years after Pecheux's acknowledgment of his work. See Allen Walker Read, "The Disinterment of Milton's Remains," *PMLA* 45 (1930): 1050–68.

23. The reference is to *The Poetical Works of John Milton, printed from the original editions, with a life of the author by the Rev. John Mitford* (London 1851). FSL/PR3551.1851.v1. Read, ibid., cites vol. 1, p. 125 n. 8 (1066).

24. It should be noted that Smyth consistently spells his own name "Smyth," but most often uses the modern spelling ("Smith") when referring to family members. I have standardized the spelling to "Smyth" except in direct quotation from a primary source.

25. As Neve confirms, only overseers John Laming, [Jonathan] Fountain, and [parish apothecary and surgeon Gabriel?] Taylor (with the assistance of Samuel A[y]scough's apprentice, Benjamin Holmes) were responsible for the initial desecration, which took place early on the morning of 4 August 1790 (C^v/16). [Thomas?] Ellis, Thomas Hawkesworth, and Elizabeth Grant were later participants in the ghoulery (22), and senior churchwarden John Benjamin Cole; vestry clerk and solicitor Thomas Strong; and sexton [Ann—widow of former Sexton James] Hoppey were not present at the desecration (or the paid exhibition) at all. The "two others" who opened the grave (but not the coffin) on the *third* of August were Cole and Strong, who respectfully declined even to move the upper casket aside so that they could positively identify it as Milton's from the inscription they thought would still be legible on the lower one, presumably containing the remains of his father. All of the bracketed Christian names are added for the first time at this writing; except as noted, Neve's *Narrative* gives only their surnames. Using a combination of the *St. Giles, Cripplegate Vestry Minute Book, 1793 [sic]–1818* (Guildhall MS 6048–3, the first entry of which actually occurs on Easter Monday, 12 April 1784; hereafter *Vestry Book*) and the *Poor Tax Assessments* for the parish from July 1790 through March 1791 (Guildhall MS 6104/205–208, hereafter *Assessments*) in conjunction with other documents and information identified elsewhere herein, I was able to determine that the people named were in fact the individuals involved. For the purposes of confirming his identity, it is worth noting that, according to Hughson's *London,* 361 (excerpted by Anne S., n.p.), Thomas Strong, Esq., F.A.S., died on 19 November 1794, aged fifty-eight; Bernard Nurse, librarian of the Society of Antiquaries of London, confirms that Strong was elected a fellow of the society on 19 December 1776, and indicates that notice of his death was printed in the *Gentleman's Magazine,* vol. 64., pt. 2 (November 1794, p. 1063), with a longer obituary in the section for December 1794 (1107). Please see my *"Dem Bones"* for additional details.

26. Elizabeth Grant, who worked for Ann Hoppey, and about whom there appear to be no extant records, other than Neve's mention of her in the *Narrative.* The *Churchwarden's Registers* for 1790 and 1791 (where payments for Grant's services would most likely have been recorded, and where any remarks Cole might have wanted to make about the desecration would have been entered) are not available, either. The Guildhall archives contain only MS 6049/1 (for 1724–1779), and MS 6049/2 (for 1792–1810).

27. *The Gentleman's Magazine and Historical Chronicle for the Year MDCCXC,* vol. 60, pt. 2, "Review of New Publications" (London, 1790), 837. The article uses Neve's spelling of "Ascough," which is given as "Ayscough" in the *Vestry Notes* and *Assessments.* The *Narrative* is provided in full text at appendix A.

28. Henry John Todd, *Some Account of the Life and Writing of John Milton* (London, 1801). Michael Lieb, introduction to *Milton and the Culture of Violence* (Ithaca, N.Y., 1994), 3 n. 3, remarks that "in the twentieth century, the disinterment receives little or no notice at all," and directs the reader to "the brief descriptions" in Hanford, *John Milton, Englishman,* 249; A. N. Wilson, *The Life of John Milton* (Oxford, 1983), 259; and French, *Life Records,* 5:136. I would add Charles Gould, "Milton and the Ghouls," *The Saturday Review of Politics, Literature, Science, and Art* 150 (1930): 662–63; Read, "The Disinterment of Milton's Remains"; Howell,

"Milton's Mortal Remains," 17–30; Pecheux, *Milton*, 88–91; and John Walter Good, *Studies in the Milton Tradition* (New York, 1971), 275–76, which erroneously refers to Neve as "Le Neve"—they were two different people—and expresses doubt that "some teeth and bones [were] actually sold as precious relics"; Clement Mansfield Ingleby's *Shakespeare's Bones: The proposal to disinter them, considered in relation to their possible bearing on his portraiture. Illustrated by instances of visits of the living to the dead* (London, 1838), reprinted 1974, 18–20; Gordon Campbell's recent edition of Parker, *Milton: A Biography* (2:1158 n. 11); John T. Shawcross's entries in *A Milton Encyclopedia*, 9 vols., ed. William B. Hunter (Lewisburg, 1978–83), including "William Cowper," 2:93, and "Philip Neve," 5:199–200; and his *Self*, 280; as well as H. F. McMains, *The Death of Oliver Cromwell* (Lexington, 2000), 2:169–70—some of whom Lieb mentions elsewhere in *Culture of Violence*.

29. The eight-reason version also appears in *The Gazetteer and New Daily Advertiser* for Monday, 6 September 1790, no. 19,267. It is expanded to nine reasons under the same title (hereafter referred to as "[Nine] Reasons") in *The European Magazine and London Review*, 18 (September 1790): 206–7 (archived by Anne S., n.p., as *The London Review*), and resurfaces in *Walker's Hibernian* (or simply *Hibernian*) *Magazine, or Compendium of Entertaining Knowledge, for the YEAR 1790, From July to December, Inclusive* (October 1790), 367–68. It is also included in Ashton, *Eighteenth Century Waifs*, 70–75.

30. Thompson, "John Milton's Bones," says that, in addition to Dyson, "several other surgeons" agreed that the desecrated body was male; in fact, only Taylor is credited with concurrence in Neve's account (363).

31. But for its repetition of Todd's 1809 assertion in *Some Account* that "the late Mr. Steevens" was its author (139), Boaden's attribution of the "[Nine] Reasons" to "the commentator on Shakespeare" (20) is unsubstantiated. See James Boaden, *Memoirs of the Life of John Philip Kemble* (London: 1825). He gives only six of Steevens's reasons (with some paraphrase), and his account of a supposed meeting between John Philip Kemble, Esq., and "Ellis the player [who] showed him the spoils he had brought away from the grave" is undocumented, as is his assertion—allegedly on the authority of Ellis—that Neve, "on being shown the objections of Mr. Steevens, . . . said they were absolutely unanswerable; and . . . added, 'Ill as the commentator [Steevens] has always behaved to me, I always admired the force of his mind, and am happy that he has exerted it, as I think, triumphantly, on the present occasion' "(24). It is self-evident from the argument of the second edition of the *Narrative* that Neve thought no such thing—and though Boaden invokes Ellis's name as if it were eponymous, except for Neve's reference to him by surname and occupation, the identity of the actor(?)/comedian(?)/dresser(?) is in fact so obscure that at this point we can only guess at whom he may have been. A more cogent basis for the attribution of the "Reasons" to Steevens is contained in a letter dated 4 September 1790 from Michael Lort, a well-known antiquary, to Bishop Thomas Percy. It is cited in part by Read: "Notwithstanding Mr. Neve's positive assertion in the inclosed pamphlet, that he has relics of Milton's corpse, our friend Steevens insists that it is all a flam, for that is the body of a Miss Smith, not of Milton and he will prove it ("The Disinterment of Milton's Remains," 1060). In any case, *caveat lector:* Howell's blithe reliance on Boaden is highly questionable, as is much of the data he provides (see appendix C).

32. Both the first and second editions of Neve's *Narrative* are available on microfilm, from Eighteenth Century Research Publications (BL1417.e.22, Reel 3287[6], and BL79.e.30, Reel 2460[7]. See G/PAM 879, LOC/PR3585.M5. Neve's information is accurate and verifiable (directly from church records, or by affirmation via the independent testimony of others) on all points but two, and the seeming inconsistencies here may be the result of misinformation or simple error in transcription, as follows:

1. Though it is certainly possible that she was too poor to have owned or leased property in her own name (or that she may have roomed with others, which would make her exempt from taxation), Neve may have erred about the grave digger's surname: there is no "Elizabeth Grant" in the Poor Tax Assessment records, though there is an "Elizabeth Hunt," in Butlers Alley near Flying Horse Court, whose dwelling is assessed at a modest £16 (146). Since the statements he recorded were all obtained verbally, Neve may have misheard "Grant" for "Hunt."

2. Ellis may have been both a "victualler"/publican (the *Vestry Book*) and an aspiring actor/comedian (Neve). Though volume 5 of *A Biographical Dictionary of Actors, Actresses, Musicians, Dancers, and Other Stage Personnel in London 1660–1800*, ed. Philip A. Highfill Jr., Kalman A. Burnim, and Edward Langhans (Edwardsville, Ill., 1978), does indicate that "the Drury Lane accounts show occasional payments of 9s a week to Mr. Ellis, one of the men's dressers, from 1789–90 through 1813–14" (55), given Ellis's intimate engagement in the desecration, and the fact that no one outside the circle of lay church officials and construction workers seems to have been directly involved, it is probable that he was the Thomas Ellis who was appointed sidesman on 5 April 1790 (*Vestry Book*, 38) and admitted to fine (that is, excused from serving, for a fee) on the twentieth of the same month (41). In that case, he lived on Flying Horse Court, his dwelling rated at £30 (*Assessment*, 146)—not "No. 9, Lamb's Chapel" (a court off Monkwell Street), as Neve reports—the latter address dubious on its face since as the *Assessments* of the period demonstrate, the numbering of houses was not common practice in Cripplegate Ward at that time. On the other hand, Denton notes in 1883 that "the Flying Horse Tavern, Little Moorfields, which had an entrance in what is now New Union Street, was long renowned as a suburban place of entertainment. The yard of this inn had apparently been arranged for the theatrical entertainments before theatres were built for this purpose" (108).

33. This seems unlikely, given that Ms. Grant at first charged "6d. and afterwards . . . 3d. and 2d. each person" (Neve, *Narrative*, 21). Had people "pressed from all quarters" as Symmons, *The Life of John Milton*, imagines they did, the grave digger would not have had to lower her price twice within a few hours of admitting her first customer.

34. The quotation may be found in note o [*sic*] on page 503 of the first volume of his initial biography, the "Life of Milton," in *The Prose Works of John Milton; with a Life of the Author, Interspersed with Translations and Critical Remarks*, 7 vols. (London, 1806), FSL/PR3569.1806, and 427 n. 53 in his 1822 *Life*.

35. Sir Leslie Stephen and Sir Sidney Lee, eds., *The Dictionary of National Biography: From the Earliest Times to 1900* (London, 1921–22). As indicated above, the reference to "Le Neve" is incorrect; the antiquary John Le Neve (1679–1741), author of *Fasti Ecclesiæ Anglicanæ*, to whom Sir Sidney Lee is presumably referring, and the antiquary Philip Neve (15 March 1749–? July 1824), who is referenced but does not actually appear in the *DNB* are two different persons. Citations to the *DNB* are hereafter credited in the text.

36. But, says Howell, "Milton's Mortal Remains," he is "not without interest to Milton scholars, for he was probably the author of the romantic story of the Italian girl, who, 'seeing Milton asleep left a verse quotation beside him' (CM, XVIII, 535)" (21). The Columbia Milton, *The Works of John Milton*, 18 vols. in 21, ed. Frank Allen Patterson et al. (New York, 1931–38) (hereafter cited as CM), cites Todd's 1801 edition (1:21–22), and says that the story "is probably a romantic invention of the eighteenth century or even earlier"; but see the Salisbury *County Magazine* 2, no. 36 (1788): 182, available at the British Library, for further elaboration.

37. Pattison, *Milton*, 145.

38. Anne S., "Topographical and Historical Collection Relating to the Parish of St. Giles, Cripplegate," unpublished ms., London, 1889, listed as "A Collection of Extracts from Books, Cuttings from Newspapers, Engravings, Lithographics, [etc.] relating to the Parish of St. Giles' Cripplegate." British Library shelfmark b. 14, 1–2.

39. The releases signed by Anne, Mary, and Deborah are among the current holdings of the New York Public Library.

40. *Deposition Book, 1674*, f.238v.

41. French, *Life Records*, 91.

42. Howell, "Milton's Mortal Remains," 22.

43. Interestingly, in this context, Masson remarks in "Posthumous Miltoniana" (*The Life of John Milton*, 6:778) that "the gossip Aubrey" informed Anthony Wood on 18 May 1675 that "Mr. Marvell has promised me to write minutes [i.e., a biography] for you of Mr. Jo. Milton"—but that the notes were never written, and "Marvell, who might have been the first biographer of Milton, was dead in August 1678."

44. Darbishire, *Some Early Lives*, 78.

45. Parker, *Milton: A Biography* (with no apparent conviction), reduces this sum to "a pitiful £900" (648), based on Masson, *The Life of John Milton*, 6:743–44, though he also acknowledges that Masson's figure is based solely on conjecture.

46. *Paradise lost. A poem in twelve books. The author John Milton. Printed from the first and second editions collated. The original system of orthography restored; the punctuation corrected and extended. With various readings: and notes; chiefly rhythmical.* By Capel Lofft (London, 1792).

47. Neve gives his name only as "Fountain," but using a combination of the Cripplegate *Vestry Book* and the *Assessments* for the parish, I have been able to establish that he was the same Jonathan Fountain, "victualler" (*Vestry Book*) or "publican" (Neve) of Beech Lane who was elected sidesman on 24 March 1788 (*Vestry Book*, 26), and an overseer of the poor of the parish on 24 April 1790 (*Vestry Book*, 37). Like Cole's and Laming's, his home's assessed value was £22, suggesting a comfortable degree of affluence. The relative assessment values levied on the homes of the key figures in the *Narrative* are consistent with their social standing: the home of Theophilus Dyson, MRCS, surgeon, New Basinghall Street, is assessed at £36; the home of Thomas Strong, solicitor and vestry clerk, Frying Pan Alley, is assessed at £30; the home of Gabriel Taylor, apothecary and surgeon to the parish workhouse, Little Moorfields, is assessed at £26; the homes of Andrew Wright, baker and senior churchwarden, Cock Alley, and of John Price (presumably Dyson's partner), Bull Head Court, are assessed at £23; the home of William Ayscough, coffin maker and vestryman, Fore Street, is assessed at £16; and the home of James Hoppey (given as Hopper in the *Assessments,* and Hoppey in the *Vestry Book*), sexton—and his wife, widow, and successor in that position, Ann (secular occupations unknown)—Hanover Court, is assessed at £8.

48. "A Catalogue of New Books," *Scots Magazine*, no. 52 (London, 1790), 552.

49. *Monthly Review*, no. 3 (London, November 1790); parish sexton's whereabouts from Neve, *Narrative*, 20.

50. According to Dr. William Masselas, medical examiner of the City of Roanoke, Virginia, in a telephone conversation dated 11 September 2001, in fact the hair on the heads of deceased humans can change to almost any color ("including blue"), depending on the moisture, temperature, and chemical content of the soil, as well as the age of the remains.

51. On Ann Hoppey's involvement in the desecration, see above. Neve gives the sexton's name only as "Mrs. Hoppey," and James Hoppey appears as sexton in the *Vestry Book* until his death is reported on 27 May 1785; three days later, Strong notes that "at a Vestry held at the Questhouse on Monday May 30th 1785 . . . Mrs. Ann Hoppey Widow of Mr. James Hoppey the

late Sexton Deceased—was Unanimously Elected and chosen Sextoness of this Parish in the Room of—her said late Husband" (13).

52. Rev. W. Denton, Records of St. Giles, Cripplegate (1883). In Baddeley's case, the omission seems to be a pointed one since, rather incredibly, his chronology for the 1700s ends in the year 1760, with the affirmation that "Nothing further of particular interest occurred in Cripplegate during the remainder of the century." See Sir John James Baddeley, *An Account of the Church and Parish of St. Giles Without Cripplegate, in the City of London/compiled from various old authorities, including the churchwarden's accounts, and the vestry minute books of the parish* (London, 1888), 98; hereafter cited as *SGC*.

53. One such relic may be seen at the Cottage at Chalfont St. Giles, the country house Thomas Ellwood procured so that Milton and his family might escape the London plague, and the only one of his homes still standing. Unremittingly gray, this lock, too, has a rather questionable pedigree. Relying on French (*Life Records*, 5:135), Howell, "Milton's Mortal Remains," says that "it belonged originally to a lecturer at St. Giles Cripplegate, who got it from the head of the poet when the grave was opened in 1790. His great-granddaughter, a Mrs. Bouchard of Lee, presented it to the Milton Cottage at Chalfont St. Giles" (28)—but French (whom Howell misquotes) does not cite a source, and the assertion is not corroborated by any records of the Milton Cottage Trust (see appendix C). Until I conducted my investigation (and the acquisition records were examined in detail in preparation for public release of that information for the first time), it had been traditionally assumed that the lock now on display at the cottage was purchased outright in 1927 by the Milton Cottage Trust as one of a number of items of supposed Miltoniana (including a purported lock of Betty Minshull Milton's hair) offered for sale by Hunter Charles Rogers, who was later exposed as a forger of documents allegedly signed by William Shakespeare and Isaac Pennington. The circumstances surrounding that transaction were bizarrely consistent with the rest of this story, so it also seems fitting that, at this point, neither the curator of the cottage, Edward Dawson, nor the chairman of the Milton Cottage Trust, Philip Birger (who has served in that capacity for over twenty years), can say with any certainty exactly where and how the lock now in their possession was acquired (though the cottage has kept an acquisitions log since its inception, including detailed records for every other holding, and itemized negative inventory entries for the items returned to Mr. Rogers). Nothing about this dubious piece of Miltoniana appears there, or in the cottage's minute books, either.

54. For examples of the resulting poetry, see Cowper, "On the Disinterment," and Albertus, "The Ghost of Milton," in *The Gazetteer and New Daily Advertiser*, 15 September 1790, no. 19,275, also published in *The Public Advertiser*, 16 September 1790, no. 17533, and published as "Milton's Ghost. An Elegy. Written in the year 1790, when a report prevailed that the grave of Milton had been discovered in Cripplegate Church-yard, on which Occasion the supposed Remains of this famous Poet were dug up, and suffered for some days to remain exposed to public view," in *An Asylum for Fugitive Pieces in Prose and Verse* (London, 1793), vol. 4, 123–25.

55. Gould, "Milton and the Ghouls," 663. This is also reported as "fact" by Thompson, "John Milton's Bones," 312, and Howell, "Milton's Mortal Remains," 20.

56. The remark is paraphrased in the *General Evening Post*, 7–9 September 1790, no. 8882.

57. Howell, "Milton's Mortal Remains," 20. Per Sir John James Baddeley, in *Cripplegate: One of the Twenty-Six Wards of the City of London* (printed for private circulation, London, 1921), 98:

> The entries in the Registers are as follows:—
> Rich : sonne of Rich: Smith Gent. 12 Aug. 1653
> John Smith Gent.—Consumption 9th May 1655

Elizabeth wife of Richard Smith, Gentleman, Jaundice, Church, 28th May 1664
Richard Smith, Gentleman, Aged, Church, 1st April 1675

The notation "church" after the names of the antiquarian and his wife would seem to indicate that they were buried in the crypt beneath the church floor, while their sons were buried in the churchyard that then existed outside (see the Anne S. manuscript for several good sketches of St. Giles at this stage of its evolution). This would be consistent with the ages and social standing of the sons, and makes it even less likely that the desecrated body belonged to one of the Smyth boys. We have Dyson's assurance that it did not belong to their eighty-five-year-old father, and it is unlikely (because her husband's body would have been the uppermost, Elizabeth having predeceased him) that it belonged to their sixty-four-year-old mother. I have been unable to ascertain the date of Martha Smyth Hacker's or Anne Smyth Fleetwood's deaths, or their places of burial; but since they were likely born before 1640 (when their mother was of childbearing age), there would have been no one left who cared very much by the time the bones in that ancient coffin were disturbed 150 years (or so) later.

58. Howell, "Milton's Mortal Remains," 20.

59. Baddeley, *SGC*, 98.

60. See also ibid., 99.

61. Per entries in the *Obituary*, the sons include: Richard #1 ("a twinn"), d. 11 August 1628 (5); William ("a twyn"), d. 9 November 1632 (7); Thomas, d. 8 August 1640 (17); Richard #2, d. 10 August 1653 (35); and John, d. 6 May 1655 (40). The daughters are Martha Smyth Hacker, the eldest, and her father's favorite, as well as his executrix (preface, xi), and Anne Smyth Fleetwood; the third sister, who predeceased her parents, is unnamed. See the partial genealogy given on page iii of the Ellis edition, and Smyth's report that, on 20 September 1669, he and "my daughter [Martha Smyth] Hacker, daug. Smyth [apparently, his daughter-in-law, the widow of his son, John Smith]; and daugh. Edney [were] invited to [an acquaintance's] funerall" (83). The latter entry (identifying Ms. Edney as his "daughter") is probably an oversight: since all of Smyth's sons were dead by 1664, and only two of the Smyth children survived their mother per the cenotaph—Anne Smyth Fleetwood and Martha Smyth Hacker, judging from the *Obituary*—it is likely that Smyth's previous (34, 70) and subsequent (104, 105) references to his "sister [or sister-in-law?] Edney" correctly reflect the relationship between them. Both of the biological daughters Smyth mentions in the *Obituary* (Martha and Anne) were widows at this point, William Hacker having been "murthered near Franckfort in Germany" on 26 March 1651 (30), and Jeffry Fleetwood having "died in ye Tower, leaving . . . Anne, his wife, and 6 small children behind him" on 18 April 1665 (63). Though the phrases "daug. Smith" in the entry for 20 September 1669 (83) and "my daugtr Smith" in the entry for 1 October 1669 (84) could therefore mean either of them, or the (unmarried?) third sister, the fact that Smyth refers to Martha as "my daughter Hacker" in the former case suggests that "daughter Smith" means his eldest son's widow— and not his own third female child.

62. *Obituary*, 40. This is repeated in Francis Peck's *Desiderata Curiosa* (1732), 536, and in Ashton, *Eighteenth Century Waifs*, 72. Peck's entry reads: "MDCLV. May vi, died my (now) only and eldest son, John Smith (*Proh Dolor*, beloved of all men!) at Mitcham in Surrey. Buried May ix in St. Giles, Cripplegate."

63. Lieb, *Milton and the Culture of Violence*, 7.

64. Ironically indeed, because it is likely that their sons were buried in the churchyard rather than in the subfloor vault with their parents (see note 50, above), the bodies of Richard and Elizabeth Dean Smith/Smyth may also have been interred one atop the other, isolated from their near neighbors as the remains thought to be those of John Milton Sr. and his son would have been. In that case, though, Richard's would have been the uppermost, since Elizabeth predeceased him by a decade.

65. "The poet's remains still rest undisturbed" and extract is from Thompson, "John Milton's Bones," 363; "later inquiries . . ." is from *European Magazine* 18 (September 1790): 205–7.

66. Boaden, *Memoirs*, 23, 24, 19–20; McMains, *The Death of Oliver Cromwell*, 169.

67. Pattison, *Milton*, 160.

68. Gould, "Milton and the Ghouls," 663.

69. Howitt, *Homes and Haunts*, 115; Read, "The Disinterment of Milton's Remains," 1066–68; Howell, "Milton's Mortal Remains," 19 n. 2.

70. Lieb, *Milton and the Culture of Violence*, tempers his pronouncement with a qualifier, then adopts the passive voice to reinforce the tentativeness of his assent: "*Assuming* Neve's account is accurate," he tells us, "*we are made to conclude* that the body in question is none other than Milton's" (5; emphasis mine). It is difficult not to be somewhat skeptical under the circumstances. For example, though Read is the most thorough and persuasive of the commentators on the disinterment up to the present time, even he neglects to mention when invoking Howitt that the latter proves a most unreliable witness in at least two instances in the passage cited. "Dr. Johnson," he reports, "supposed that [Milton] had no inscription, but Aubrey distinctly states that 'when the two steppes to the communion table were raysed in 1690, his stone was removed.'" What Aubrey actually says is that Milton "lies buried in Sᵗ Giles Cripplegate upper end of chancell at the right hand . . . his stone is now removed; about two yeares since [now 1681] the steppes to the communion table were raysed" (Darbishire, *Some Early Lives*, 5; brackets in original). The error in the year would be significant, even if the quotation were otherwise accurate: it was 1679, not 1690. Similarly, the sentence that follows the last one Read quotes from *Homes and Haunts* ("The matter at the time occasioned a sharp controversy . . .") indicates that since "the workmen [Cole commissioned] had the inscribed stone before them, and dug down directly below it, what doubt can there be that the remains were those of the poet?" (Howitt, 115). This, of course, is historically untrue: the whole reason for Cole's instigation of the search (at Whitbread's or some other benefactor's request) was that the grave had been unmarked, except perhaps briefly during the period to which Vertue, *Notes and Queries* (6 July 1861), referred, for 116 years.

71. Read, "The Disinterment of Milton's Remains," 1050. The *DNB* has no entry for Philip Neve. However, the *British Biographical Index*, ed. Laureen Baillie and Paul Sieveking, fiche 1, reel 811, 1998, 108–9, LOC/86/901(c) and CT773.B75 1998, contains the following entries:

(1) Neve, Phillip, Esq. One of the Magistrates of the Marlborough Street Police Office. A Letter to the Rev. William Corkburne, occasioned by his account of Lord Camelford's Death, 1804. [From Watkins, *A Biographical Dictionary of the Living Authors of Great Britain and Ireland, comprising literary memoirs and anecdotes of their lives, and a chronological register of their publications, with the number of editions; including some notices of foreign writers whose works have been occasionally published in England* (London, 1816), 108, LOC/Z2010.B61 (also attributed to William Upcott).]

(2) Neve, Philip, Esq. "Cursory Remarks on some of the Ancient English Poets, particularly Milton." London, 1789. Narrative of the Disinterment of Milton's Coffin. London, 1790. A Letter to the Rev. William Corkburne . . . [From Robert Watt, *Bibliotheca Britannica: or, a general index to British and Foreign Literature* (1824; reprint, New York, 1965), 698–99. LOC/Z2001.W34 1965.]

I am indebted to James Travers and Dr. Amanda Bevan of the Public Record Office (PRO) for their identification, respectively, of a letter dated 20 June 1794 from Philip Neve to an unknown recipient (shelfmark FO 95/3/3), and a record of the magistrate's "Oath of S. H. Rankin sworn before P. Neve," 19 July 1810 (shelfmark FO 95/8/6); and of Neve's will (dated 17 June 1814 and redeclared on 28 February 1821, PRO shelfmark PROB 11/1688, folio 241–

241v), which identifies him as a barrister of the Inner Temple. He is sworn in as a justice of the peace in 1792 (PRO shelfmark C202/180/5), and by 1799, Philip Neve of 17 Furnival's Inn appears in the annual Law List as a Commissioner of Bankrupts and a Magistrate of the Great Marlborough Street Police Office. Dr. Clare Rider, archivist of the Inner Temple, affirms that "Philip Neeve son and heir apparent of Gabriel Neve of the Inner Temple London gent." (ADM/4/6)—who was himself "son and heir apparent of Gabriel Neve of the parish of St. Michael Cornhill, London, gentleman" (ADM/4/5)—was admitted to the Inner Temple on 2 February 1760, and called to the bar on 8 February 1793 (BAR/4/1) thirty-three years later. Further details, along with additional biographical data pertaining to Philip Neve's activities post 1790, will be included in my "Dem Bones." I should note that neither the Society of Antiquaries of London, nor the Westminster Library, nor the Magistrates' Association held records pertaining to the author of the Narrative.

72. Frank Major, the parish historian, informed me on 18 December 1999 of the local mythology that holds that an (unnamed) female grave digger was solely responsible for the desecration, and was carted off to Newgate for her crime. The source of the story may be an article entitled "St. Giles, Cripplegate" and signed only "RGI" in Pen and Ink Sketches of London. By J.B. (preserved by Anne S., n.p., n.d.). As RGI records it,

> [Milton] died in the year 1674, in Artillery-walk, now called Bunhill-row, and was buried in the vaults of St. Giles's Without Cripplegate, where a monument was erected to his memory by Samuel Whitbread, Esq. and another in Westminster Abbey, erected by William Benson, Esq. These monuments are still to be seen at Westminster Abbey and in the choir of St. Giles's Without Cripplegate Church; but his remains, it is reported, have been most sacrilegiously removed away from their wonted resting-place *by some villainous gravedigger. It may be supposed, and justly so, to have been the one who was tried and convicted at Newgate some few years since, for stealing the brass inscription plates and lead coffins from the vaults of another church.* (Emphasis mine)

It is possible, of course (but not likely), that Grant lived outside the parish. Probably, she lived in Cripplegate Ward but was too impoverished to appear in parish poor tax assessment records (where the rate basis was the valuation of one's owned or rented real property). Some female taxpayers are recorded, and valuations of dwellings from as little as £6 (Jane Milton, Castle Court, Assessments, 91) appear. Only the name of the actual lessor of the property would appear on the tax rolls, however, so if Grant shared lodgings with other tenants, her name would not be recorded. Whatever the reason, and as previously indicated, with the possible exception of the Cripplegate birth and death registers, which were not examined for this purpose in the current investigation—Grant is not mentioned anywhere in any of the extant records of the parish at that time.

73. The entry for Hunter, John (1728–93), in the DNB reads "Anatomist, Physiologist, and Surgeon," though he apparently started life as an apprentice cabinet maker. Upon joining his brother William in London, it continues, "he made rapid progress in the study of anatomy and surgery and became the leading anatomist of his day, being appointed Surgeon Extraordinary to King George III (1776). He laid the foundation of comparative anatomy; pioneered the art of tissue grafting and dissection; established a museum which was subsequently presented to the Royal College of Surgeons of England; was elected to several leading Royal Academies; and was Deputy Surgeon General to the Army from 1786."

74. Though Neve refers to him as "Dr." Hunter, in fact it was only his older brother William who had obtained an M.D.; like many surgeons of the period (Gabriel Taylor among them), John Hunter was technically not entitled to be called " doctor"—but by the time of Neve's Narrative, Dr. William Hunter was already dead, so "Dr. Hunter" is unquestionably John.

75. Theophilus Dyson, "A Description and Dissection of a diseased Spermitic vein," in *Memoirs of the Medical Society of London*, I.ii, p. 556 (1792), and "A Case of inverted Uterus after parturition" (Ub. Vi.118, 1805), cited in Watt, *Bibliotheca Britannica*, 326(s).

76. On Rocque's map of London (1747), only Basinghall Street exists, running north-south from London Wall, which is parallel to and very close by Fore Street (fig. 6). But in Bacon's plan of London (1888), New Basinghall Street is an extension of Basinghall Street, running north from London Wall to join Fore Street, which runs east-west from St. Giles to Bethlem Hospital (fig.7).

77. P. J. and R. V. Wallis et al., eds., *Eighteenth Century Medics: Subscriptions, Licenses, Apprenticeships*, 2d ed. (Newcastle upon Tyne, 1988), 179. Many thanks to Dr. Steven Greenberg, MSLS, reference collection access librarian for the History of Medicine Division of the National Library of Medicine in Bethesda, Maryland (e-mail of 6 March 2000); and especially to Dr. Lesley A. Hall, senior assistant archivist (Outreach), Archives and Manuscripts, Wellcome Library for the History and Understanding of Medicine (e-mails of 25 January 2001, and prior); and Ms. Dee Cook, MA, DARM, RMSA, archivist to the Society of Apothecaries (e-mail of 7 March 2001), for their assistance in establishing a positive identification for Dyson. I also acknowledge and appreciate the assistance of Ms. Tina Craig, deputy librarian, Royal College of Surgeons of England, for her confirmation that Dyson became a member (MRCS) upon completion of examinations given at the Surgical Theatre, Surgeon's Hall, on 3 July 1788 (fax and e-mail, 23 March 2001).

78. Neve gives only his surname, and may have been confused about his residence: more than likely, he refers to the same Gabriel Taylor who is already serving as apothecary to the workhouse of the parish on 12 April 1784. That man receives the following additional responsibilities from Cripplegate Ward on 28 March 1785; and becomes Apothecary and Surgeon to the Workhouse on 24 March 1788, when

> he is to provide the medicines for all the Poor in the said Workhouse and Bleed them when necessary, and to attend the Master and Mistress of the Workhouse and provide them with Medicines, To do all the Surgery Business wanting in the Workhouse, including the foul Patients, and man midwifery in all desperate Cases, and to—attend the Sick Poor in the different Wards of the Workhouse three times every Week at the least, and oftner when required by the Officers, for all which he is to receive a salary of Fifty Guineas ayear [*sic*]. (*St. Giles, Cripplegate, Vestry Minute Book*, 1793 [*sic*]–1818, 10)

Taylor is not listed in Wallis, but per Dee Cook, archivist of the Society of Apothecaries (e-mail, 17 April 2001), an apothecary named Gabriel Tayler was apprenticed to John Griffin of Kington, Hereford, on 27 April 1752 for seven years (for a fee of £30). Strong reports Taylor's death to the *Vestry* on 30 October 1793, at which point St. Giles is forced to perform a search for his replacement; the dates seem consistent with one another. There is no evidence that Taylor/Tayler ever became a Member of the Royal College of Surgeons (MRCS), but as Ms. Cook also points out (18 April 2001), the titles "apothecary," "surgeon-apothecary," and "surgeon, apothecary, and man-midwife" were all common terms for nonspecialist medical men before the Victorian era, so Taylor's was likely a parish-bestowed honorific. On the other hand, his status in Cripplegate Ward is suggested by the fact that only Strong (£30) and Dyson (£36) own houses valued at more than his in Little Moorfields (assessed at £26).

79. Ironically, the patriarch of the Smyth family is the antiquarian Richard Smyth, who entered the following in the St. Giles register, according to Baddeley (*Ward*, 100): "Nov. 15 [*sic*], 1674—John Milton died at Bunhill near Morefields in Criplegate parish, blind some time before he died." Entry 1717 of the secondary bibliography of Shawcross, *Milton: A Bibliography for the Years 1624–1700*, elaborates:

London, British Library. Sloane MS886.

Richard Smyth, "A Catalogue of All Such Persons deceased Whome I knew in their Life time [etc.] from M.DC.XXVIII," entry, f.73v. Smyth died in 1675 (391).

The notice also appeared in *Desiderata Curiosa,* item XIV, pages 48–49, and in the expanded (1779) edition of the same book, Vol. II, page 552.

Though Neve in part bases his conviction that the desecrated coffin was Milton's on the assumption that the members of the Smyth family named on the cenotaph were buried together somewhere near their memorial, in fact there may have been only two of them there (see note 64 above).

80. Darbishire, *Some Early Lives,* 5.

81. Howell, "Milton's Mortal Remains," 18; the bracketed statement dating Vertue's note is Howell's. The quotation occurs at the end of the *Notes & Queries* entry entitled "MILTON.—August 10, 1721," in which Vertue describes his meeting with seventy-year-old "Mrs. Clarke," that is, Deborah Milton, the poet's youngest daughter. It ends with the passage Howell slightly misrecords (corrected in brackets). Actually, says John T. Shawcross, *Notes & Queries,* 2d ser., 12 (1861): 1–2,

> the reference is to a letter written by George Vertue to Charles Christian, dated 12 August 1721. He reports visiting Deborah; her reaction to a "'portrait'" and her comments on the two younger pictures of Milton (the Janssen and the Onslow) and his hair are mentioned. [The letter] is quoted in part in Masson's biography, Vol. I, p. 277 note; see also Masson, VI, 751–58. *N&Q* makes the relation with St. Giles, Cripplegate. The letter was published in *Monthly Magazine* 37 (May 1814): 330, [and can be found] in the British Library in MS Harleian 7003, ff. 175v–176. A copy was transcribed by Thomas Birch in MS Additional 5016°, f. 11–11v (formerly f. 71–71v and misdated). All [known] references to the letter have been to Birch's transcription rather than to the original. (E-mail dated 16 August 2000)

82. Thompson, "John Milton's Bones," 361. Henry Gerald Hope's objection to Thompson's article on page 396 of *Notes & Queries,* 1890—citing Howitt's remark (*Homes and Haunts,* 115) that since "the workmen had the inscribed [grave]stone before them, and dug down directly below it," there could be no doubt "that the remains were those of the poet"—is thus unfounded.

83. In the postscript to the second edition of the *Narrative,* Neve records his suspicion, confirmed by "a principal person of the parish . . . that the parish-officers had agreed among themselves, that from [his] frequent visits and enquiries [he] must have an intention of delivering some account of the transaction to the world," and had expressed an interest in "stop[ping] the narrative from going forth" (38–39). Also contained in the postscript is Neve's letter of 25 August 1790 to the solicitor, Mr. Strong, vestry clerk and a Fellow of the Antiquarian Society (F.A.S.), which reports that the Cripplegate church officials

> are all, as I find, very fond of deriving honor to themselves from Milton, as their parishioner; perhaps the mode, which I have hinted, is the only one, which they have now left themselves, of proving an equal desire to do honor to him. If I had thought that in personally proposing to the parish-officers a general search for and collection of all the spoils, and to put them, together with the mangled corpse and old coffin, into a new leaden one, I should have been attended to, I would have taken that method; but when I found such impertinent inventions, as setting-up a fabulous surgeon to creep-in at a window, practised, I felt that so low an attempt at derision would ensure that whatever I should afterwards propose would be equally derided, and I had then left no other means than to call in the public opinion in aid of my own, and to hope that we should at length

see the bones of an honest man, and the first scholar and poet our country can boast, restored to their sepulchre. (42–43)

It should be noted that Read reports similar sentiments expressed by a contemporary royalist: in a "plea" published in *The Town and Country Magazine, or Universal Repository of Knowledge, Instruction, and Entertainment*, 22 (October 1790): 465, 468; entitled "Milton and His Remains" and signed only "A Whit." The writer calls for "the 'discovered dust' . . . [to] be transferred to Westminster Abbey," declaring, "In this age of taste, genius, and freedom, the literati should immediately assemble, and see that the remains of *Milton* be honorably interred, and a monument, by subscription, erected to his memory" (1063). Even George Steevens was moved to demand justice, though he—apparently—took no action to ensure it. "*—Cape saxa manu, cape robora Pastor!*," he cries at the end of his "Reason"; "—But an Ecclesiastical Court may yet have cognizance of this more than savage transaction. It will then be determined whether our tombs are our own, or may be robbed with impunity by the little tyrants of a workhouse."

Be that as it may, an e-mail I received from Stephen Freeth, keeper of manuscripts, Guildhall (8 February 2000) responds with "regret that a search of the baptisms and burials for the month of August 1790 [made at my request] has failed to reveal any reference to the re-burial of either John Milton or Elizabeth Smith." I subsequently made the search of the Cripple-gate records myself, through October 1790, once I discovered Neve's error about "Elizabeth" Smyth's name, and could find no suitable alternative entry.

84. On page 28 of the *St. James's Chronicle* of Saturday, 25 September 1790, no.4592 (Thursday, September 23 to Saturday, September 25), there is a report on the desecration of a number of graves at St. Peter Le Bailey, in which the editor congratulates the rector for his swift reprisal: "But it is with pleasure we hear the Parish have laudably undertaken a legal investigation of this matter, and have already buried the bones. We shall not therefore at present particularize the Culprits, nor endeavor to pre-judge them; or prejudice the minds of those who may be their judges, before they are legally called on to do justice to the publick." A similar account appears in the *General Evening Post* of 28 September 1790 (25–28 September 1790, no. 8891; see "Extract of a Letter from Oxford, Sept. 24") and in *The Gazetteer and New Daily Advertiser* (1 September 1790, no. 19,263; see "Public Office, Bow-Street"). It is very curious, then, that a sacrilege of national significance committed at St. Giles in which the perpetrators were known and the prosecution (as evidenced by Neve's *Narrative*) was diligent should have gone (apparently) unpunished—particularly when one considers that Philip Neve was himself an officer of the peace.

85. It seems significant that on 14 August 1790, when Neve published the first edition of the *Narrative*, he already knew that a "sumptuous monument to the memory of *Milton*" had been commissioned for the church—so that "several of the principal parishioners have . . . frequently expressed a wish . . . that incontestable evidence of [his coffin's] exact situation might be established, *before the said monument should be erected*" (7; emphasis mine). Now calling for a dignified reburial of the recovered remains, Neve opines at the end of the same publication that "unless that be done, in vain will the parish hereafter boast a sumptuous monument to the memory of *Milton*: it will but display their shame in proportion to its magnificence" (33)—suggesting that he already knows the "sumptuous" and "magnificent" details of the proposal. While it is possible that Samuel Whitbread (the elder) was able to contact, commission, receive, and approve a design from John Bacon (the elder), and thence negotiate the terms of a three-year contract for what would become the Whitbread bust in the ten days intervening between the date of the desecration (August 4) and the date of the first publication of the *Narrative* (August 14)—it is unlikely that he did so.

86. On 6 August 2000, the "People and Events" section of the Whitbread Corporation's website (at www.corporate.whitbread.co.uk/html) confirmed that Samuel Whitbread Sr. elected M.P. for Bedford Town in 1768, was a vocal supporter of prison reform and the abolition of slavery, and gave generously to the founding of hospitals and charity schools; he also donated a ward for incurable cancer patients that still exists at Middlesex Hospital today.

87. This is reported in *The St. James's Chronicle,* 5–7 September 1793, no. 5071, as follows:

A small neat marble monument has been just set up in the middle of the aisle of Cripplegate Church, to the memory of the great Poet Milton. It consists of a bust, as "animated" as the chisel of the artist can make it, the sculpture of Bacon. There is no "storied urn," but underneath is a plain tablet, with the following inscription: "John Milton, Author of Paradise Lost, born Dec. 1608, died Nov. 1674. His father, John Milton, died March 1646. They are both interred in this church."

88. One of the Auditors of the Imprest, "better known as Auditor Benson," whose contribution Good describes as follows:

Under Whig influences, a Monument was erected to Milton in Westminster Abbey, in the year 1737; though sixteen years earlier the name of Milton had not been permitted to appear in that sacred place upon the inscription to the memory of another poet. The donor was William Benson . . . a public spirited man, with sufficient means at command to carry out at least some of his plans. He had a Milton Medal made; had Rysbeck [Michael Rysbrack] to make two busts of Milton; and later gave William Dobson £1,000 for a *Translation of Paradise Lost into Latin Verse,* which appeared in 1750–53. (Appendix J, Milton's Monument, Grave, and Family, 274)

The Benson bust remains on display in Poet's Corner at Westminster.

89. Symmons, *The Life of John Milton,* commends "Mr. Benson, . . . who in 1737 introduced a . . . memorial of Milton into Westminster Abbey, to the walls of which venerable building his very name had been considered, only a few years before, a species of pollution." Samuel Johnson, "in his biographical libel on Milton," had said that when "the monument of Philips [the poet, not Milton's nephew John Phillips], in which he was said to be soli Miltono secundus [second only to Milton], was exhibited to Dr. Sprat then Dean of Westminster, he refused to admit it; the name of Milton was in his opinion too detestable to be read on the wall of a building dedicated to devotion." Mitford, who describes the interment and the Whitbread bust (*Poetical Works of John Milton,* lxxxix–xc), but ignores the disinterment except as noted above, confirms that, remarking that "this anecdote was related to Johnson by Dr. Gregory. 'Such has been the change of opinion,' he added, 'that I have seen erected in the church the statue of that man, whose name I once knew considered as a pollution of its walls.' " The bust is still in Poet's Corner, also.

90. Symmons, *The Life of John Milton,* 1806 ed., 501–2.

91. W. D., *Quiver,* vol.1, no. 50 (1 September 1866): 785–87. Notice of the Whitbread/Bacon bust also appeared in *St. James's Chronicle,* 5–7 September 1793, no. 5071; *The Universal Magazine of Knowledge and Pleasure* 93 (7 September 1793): 235; *The European Magazine* 24 (1793): 236; and *The Annual Register; or, A View of the History, Politics, and Literature for the Year 1793,* vol. 35, 41. Though the *New England Courant,* no. 22 (1 January 1721/22), remarks that a monument to Milton is to be erected in Westminster Abbey, in 1734, people are still complaining that no such tribute exists. See *The Weekly News and Daily Register,* no. 203 (26 January 1734), which discusses the political and religious reasons why this is the case, and *The Weekly Miscellany by Richard Hooker,* no.73 (4 May 1734), which again makes mention of the proposed monument, as well as note 72 above.

92. According to Denton, *Records of St. Giles, Cripplegate,* "the present firm of Whitbread's Brewery was founded by Mr. Samuel Whitbread, of Southill, Bedfordshire, who in the year 1750 removed the business he had carried on from 1742 at the Brewhouse, Old Street, St. Luke's, now occupied by Messrs. More and co. to the existing premises in Chiswell Street [in St. Giles parish], which appears to have been used for the same purpose, previously." Samuel Whitbread Sr. was "succeeded by his son, Samuel, and from 1799, the business was conducted under the style of 'Whitbread & Co.'" (137).

93. This was confirmed by Linda Sofianos of the Whitbread Brewery (e-mails dated 9–29 September 2000) and Andrew Potter, research assistant, Royal Academy Library (e-mail dated 3 October 2000), who assured me that no correspondence is held by Whitbread Museum or the Royal Academy that would establish the date of or precise reason for the commission.

94. *Encyclopedia Britannica,* Macropedia, vol. 1 (1998), 777.

95. "An Account of John Bacon, Esq., F.R.A.," *The European Magazine and London Review* (August 1790) (J. Sewell, Cornhill, 1 September 1790), which also appeared in *Hibernian Magazine,* pt. 2 (1790): 243–44.

96. This part of the inscription, which Howell, "Milton's Mortal Remains," Thompson, "John Milton's Bones," and Baddeley, *SGC,* all omit—though Howitt, *Homes and Haunts,* includes it (116), and so does Pecheux, *Milton,* 92—is partially visible in figures 4 and 5, and is accurately described in Walter Thornbury et al., *Old and New London: A Narrative of Its History, Its People, and Its Places,* 6 vols. (London, 1879–85), 2:231. The donor's line is likewise omitted in accounts given in *The London Chronicle; or, Universal Evening Post* report of 7–10 September 1793 (no. 5784), and the "Historical Chronicle," 7 September 1793, in the *Universal Magazine of Knowledge and Pleasure* 93 (1793): 235.

97. Thompson, "John Milton's Bones," 363.

98. Baddeley, *SGC,* 97. Photograph courtesy of Ruth I. LuSan, with special thanks for her kind permission to use it here. Her e-mail of 6 August 2000 says that when this shot (in which the name "WHITBREAD" at the base of Bacon's sculpture is partially visible) was taken, in October 1993, the bust was mounted on a column on the north side of the church ("as I faced Milton, the altar was to my right"). "Unlike the nearby monument to John Speed," she continues, "it bore no plaque indicating that it had been repaired after bomb damage." Though I could not get as close to it as she did in December 1999 (because it was two or three feet above my head, behind some equipment and shelving, as shown in fig. 5), the bust I affectionately dubbed "Milton, god of AV" because of its location looked perfectly intact to me as well.

A pen-and-ink sketch of the Whitbread/Bacon bust done circa 1795 by an anonymous artist may be viewed at http://collage.nhil.com/cgi-bin/collage/browsing/collage.pl; search for "Milton," or go to directly to Record 2668.

99. Howell, "Milton's Mortal Remains," 24–25. French, *Life Records,* also reports that "before the last war busts or statues of him stood both outside and inside the church, but both were broken by the war bombings" (99). Like the Whitbread bust, however, the statue commissioned by Sir John James Baddeley and created in autumn 1904 by Horace Montford (Baddeley, *Ward,* 102–3) still stands in the church today, though its badly deteriorated and barely recognizable base (designed by E. A. Richards) now stands alone in the northeastern church courtyard. See figure 7; originally, says Baddeley, "a bas-relief on the eastern side of the pedestal represent[ed] the Expulsion from the 'Garden of Eden,' and one on the western side a scene from 'Comus'" (105). See also the letter to the editor of the *London Times* written by Lionel Cust of the National Portrait Gallery on 3 November 1904 (4 November 1904, no. 37,543), p. 7[f]), and the bulletin *St. Giles' Church, Cripplegate* (2001).

100. Pecheux, *Milton,* 94. A photograph of it as it looked when it was unveiled by Lady Egerton on 2 November 1904 can be found in Baddeley (*Ward,* 105).

101. Pecheux, *Milton,* 92.

102. See note 72 above.

103. *Vestry Minutes,* August 1790, Guildhall MS 6048/3.

104. *Baptisms and Burials, St. Giles Cripplegate,* vol. 2 (August–October 1790), Guildhall MS L92 6420/2.

105. *Miscellaneous Records Relating to Burials,* 1774–1793, "Burial Fees," MS L2 6095/1.

106. The entry for 10 August 1790 in the burial register (*Baptisms and Burials, St. Giles Cripplegate,* vol. 2 (1777–1792) (Guildhall MS L92 6420/2), reads: "James Milton, a child, convulsions"; the ledger entry under "Buryings in August 1790" in the "Miscellaneous Records Relating to Burials, 1774–1793," Guildhall MS L2 6095/1, reads: "[August] 10. James Milton, a child, White hart y^d.—conv." (with a caret over the "v"), and in the column where the fee received would customarily appear, says merely "Poor."

107. GL MS 25664/5.

108. *Areopagitica,* 2:549; Lieb, *Milton and the Culture of Violence,* 5.

A

NARRATIVE

OF THE

DISINTERMENT

OF

MILTON's COFFIN,

IN THE

PARISH-CHURCH OF ST. GILES, CRIPPLEGATE

ON WEDNESDAY, 4TH OF AUGUST, 1790;

AND OF

THE TREATMENT OF THE CORPSE,

DURING THAT, AND THE FOLLOWING DAY

The second edition, with additions

*—nec mortuis parcunt, quin illos de requie
sepulturae, de asylo quodam mortis, jam alios,
jam nec totos, avellant, diffcent, distrabant.*

TERTULL. Apologet. Cap.37

LONDON

Printed for T. and J. EGERTON, *Whitehall*

MDCCXC

A NARRATIVE, &C.

HAVING read in the Public Advertiser on Saturday, the 7th of August, 1790, that *Milton's* coffin had been dug up, in the parish church of *St. Giles,* Cripplegate, and was there to be seen, I went immediately to the church, and found the latter part of the information untrue; but, from conversations on that day, on Monday the 9th, and on Tuesday, the 10th of August, with Mr. Thomas *Strong,* Solicitor and F.A.S.[1] Red-cross Street, *Vestry-Clerk;* Mr. John *Cole,* Barbican, Silversmith, *Churchwarden;* Mr. John *Laming,* Barbican, Pawnbroker, and Mr. *Fountain,* Beech-lane, Publican, *Overseers;* Mr. *Taylor,* of Stanton, Derbyshire, Surgeon; a friend of Mr. *Laming,* and a visitor in his house; Mr. William *Ascough,* Coffin-maker, Fore-street, *Parish-clerk;* Benjamin *Holmes* and Thomas *Hawkesworth,* journeymen to Mr. *Ascough;* Mrs. *Hoppey,* Fore-street, *Sexton;* Mr. Ellis, No. 9, Lamb's-chapel, comedian of the royalty-theatre; and John Poole (son of Rowland Poole), watch-spring-maker, Jacob's-passage, Barbican; the following facts are established.

It being in the contemplation of some persons to bestow a considerable sum of money, in erecting a monument, in the parish church of *St. Giles,* Cripplegate, to the memory of *Milton,* and the particular spot of his interment, in that church, having for many years past, been ascertained only by tradition, several of the principal parishioners have, at their meetings, frequently expressed a wish, that his coffin should be dug-for, that incontestable evidence of its exact situation might be established, before the said monument should be erected. The entry, among the burials, in the register[7]-book, 12th of November, 1674, is *"John Milton,* Gentleman, consumpcon, *chancell."* The church of *St. Giles,* Cripplegate *St. Giles,* Cripplegate was built in 1030; was burnt down (except the steeple) and rebuilt in 1545; was repaired in 1682; and again in 1710. In the repair of 1682, an alteration took place in the disposition of the inside of the church; the pulpit was removed from the second pillar, against which it stood, north of the chancel, to the south side of the present chancel, which was then formed, and pews were built over the old chancel. The tradition has always been, that *Milton* was buried in the chancel, under the clerk's desk; but, the circumstance of the alteration in the church not having of late years [B^v/8] been attended to, the clerk, sexton, and other officers of the parish have misguided enquirers, by shewing the spot under the clerk's desk, in the present chancel, as the place of *Milton's* interment. I have twice, at different periods, been shewn that spot, as the place where *Milton* lay. Even Mr. *Baskerville,* who died a few years ago, and who had requested in his will to be buried by *Milton,* was deposited in the above-mentioned spot of the present chancel, in pious intention of compliance with his request. The church is now, in August of 1790, under a general repair, by contract, for 1350*l.* and Mr. *Strong,* Mr. *Cole,* and other parishioners, having very prudently judged that the search would be made with much [B/9] less inconvenience to the parish at this time, when the church is under repair, than at any period after the said repair should be completed, Mr. *Cole,* in the last days of July, ordered the workmen to dig in search of the coffin. Mr. *Ascough,* his father, and grand-father, having been parish clerks of *St. Giles* for upwards of 90 years past. His grandfather, who died in February, 1759–60, aged 84, used frequently to say, that *Milton* had been buried under the clerk's desk in the chancel. John *Poole,* aged 70, used often to hear his father talk of *Milton's* person, from those who had seen him; and also, that he lay under the common-council-men's pew. The common-council-men's pew is built over that very [B2^r/10] part of the old chancel, where the former clerk's-desk stood. These traditions in the parish, reported to Mr. *Strong,* and Mr. *Cole,* readily directed them to dig from the present chancel, northwards, towards the pillar, against which the former pulpit and desk had stood. On Tuesday

Neve, *A Narrative* (London, 1790, with a postscript, dated 8 September 1790), personal transcription from the actual manuscript at Guildhall, shelf-mark PAM 879.

afternoon, August 3d, notice was brought to Messrs. *Strong* and *Cole*, that the coffin was discovered. They went immediately to the church; and, by help of a candle, proceeded under the common-council-men's pew, to the place where the coffin lay. It was in a chalky soil, and directly over a wooden coffin, supposed to be that of *Milton's* father; tradition having always reported, that *Milton* was buried [B²/11] next to his father. The registry of the father of *Milton,* among the burials, in the parish-book, is *"John Melton,* "Gentleman, 15th of March, 1646–7." In digging through the whole space, from the present chancel, where the ground was opened, to the situation of the former clerk's-desk, there was not found any other coffin, which could raise the smallest doubt of this being *Milton's.* The two oldest, found in the ground, had inscriptions, which Mr. *Strong* copied.; they were of as late dates as 1727 and 1739. When he and Mr. *Cole* had examined the coffin, they ordered water and a brush to be brought, that they might wash it, in search of an inscription, or initials, or date; but, upon its being [12] carefully cleansed, none was found. The following particulars were given to me in writing, by Mr. *Strong,* and they contain the admeasurement of the coffin, as taken by him, with a rule. [Each line of the following offset is preceded by quotation marks in the original. Line breaks are indicated by forward slashes (/).]

A / leaden coffin, found under the com- / mon-council-men's pew, on the north / side of the chancel, nearly under the / place, where the old pulpit and / clerk's-desk stood. The coffin ap- / peared to be old, much corroded, / and without any inscription, or plate upon / it, [*sic*] It was in length five feet ten in- / ches, and in width, at the broadest / part, over the shoulders, one foot four / inches.

Conjecture naturally pointed out, both to Mr. *Strong* and Mr. *Cole,* that by moving the leaden coffin, there would [13] be a great chance of finding some inscription on the wooden one underneath; but, with a just and laudable piety, they disdained to disturb the sacred ashes, after a requiem of 116 years; and having, as far as might be, satisfied their curiosity, and ascertained the fact, which was the subject of it, Mr. *Cole* ordered the ground to be closed. This was on the afternoon of Tuesday, August the 3d; and when I waited on Mr. *Strong,* on Saturday morning, the 7th, he informed me, that the coffin has been found on the Tuesday, had been examined, washed, and measured by him and Mr. *Cole;* but that the ground had been immediately closed, when they left the church:—not doubting that Mr. *Cole's* [14] order had been punctually obeyed. But the direct contrary appears to have been the fact.

On Tuesday evening, the 3d, Mr. *Cole,* Messrs. *Laming* and *Taylor, Holmes,* &c. had a *merry-meeting,* as Mr. *Cole* expresses himself, at *Fountain's* house: the conversation there turned upon *Milton's* coffin having been discovered; and, in the course of the evening, several of those present expressing a desire to see it, Mr. *Cole* assented, that if the ground was not already closed, the closing of it should be deferred, until they should have satisfied their curiosity. Between 8 and 9 o'clock, on Wednesday morning, the 4th, the two overseers (*Laming* and *Fountain*) [15] and Mr. *Taylor* went to the house of *Ascough,* the clerk, which leads into the church-yard,² and asked for *Holmes;* they then went with *Holmes* into the church, and pulled the coffin, which lay deep in the ground, from its original station, to the edge of the excavation, into day-light. Mr. *Laming* told me, that, to assist in thus removing it, he put his hand into a corroded hole, which he saw in the lead, at the coffin foot. When they had thus removed it, the overseers asked *Holmes* if he could open it, that they might see the body. *Holmes* immediately fetched a mallet and chisel, and cut open the top of the coffin, slantwise from the head, as low as the breast; so that, the top being doubled backward, they could see the corpse: [Cᵛ/16] he cut it open also at the foot. Upon first view of the body, it appeared perfect, and completely enveloped in the shroud, which was of many folds; the ribs standing-up regularly. When they disturbed the shroud, the ribs fell. Mr. *Fountain* told me, that he pulled hard at the teeth, which resisted, until some one hit them a knock with a stone, when they easily came out. There were but five in the upper-jaw, which were all perfectly sound and white, and all taken by Mr. *Fountain:* he gave one of them to Mr. *Laming;* Mr. *Laming* also took one from the lower-jaw; and Mr. *Taylor* took two from it. Mr. *Laming* told me, that he had at one time a mind to bring away the whole under-jaw with the teeth [C/17] in it; he had it in his hand, but tossed it back again. Also, that he lifted up the head, and saw a great quantity of hair, which lay straight and even, behind the head, and in the state of hair, which had been combed and tied together before interment: but it was wet; the coffin having considerable corroded holes, both at the head and foot, and a great part of the water, with which it had been washed, on the Tuesday afternoon, having run into it. The Overseers and Mr. *Taylor* went away soon afterwards; and Messrs. *Laming* and *Taylor* went home to get scissors to cut-off some of the hair: they returned about ten; when Mr. *Laming* poked his stick against the head, and brought [C2ᵛ/18] some of the hair over the fore-head; but, as they saw the scissors were not necessary, Mr. *Taylor* took up the hair, as it laid on the forehead, and carried it home. The water, which had gotten into the coffin, on the Tuesday afternoon, had made a sludge at the bottom of it, emitting a nauseous smell, and which occasioned Mr. *Laming* to use his stick to procure the hair, and not to lift up the head a second time. Mr. *Laming* also took out one of the leg bones, but threw it in again. *Holmes* went out of the church, whilst Messrs. *Laming, Taylor,* and *Fountain* were there the first time, and he returned when the two former were come the second time. When Messrs. *Laming* and *Taylor* had finally [C2/19] quitted the church, the coffin was removed, from the edge of the excavation, back to its original station: but was no otherwise closed, than by the lid, where it had been cut and reversed, being bent down again. Mr. *Ascough,* the clerk, was from home the greater part of that day; and Mrs. *Hoppey,* the sexton, was from home the whole day. Elizabeth *Grant,* the grave-digger, and who is servant to Mrs. *Hoppey,* therefore now took possession of the coffin; and, as its situation, under the common-council-men's pew, [20] would not admit of its being seen without the help of a candle, she kept a tinder-box in the excavation, and, when any persons came, struck a light, and conducted them under the pew; where, by reversing the part of the lid which had been cut, she exhibited the body, at first for 6d. and afterwards for 3d. and 2d. each person. The workmen in the church kept the doors locked to all those who would not pay the price of a pot of beer for entrance, and many, to avoid that payment, got in at a window at the west end of the church, near to Mr. *Ascough's* counting-house.

I went on Saturday, the 7th, to Mr. Laming's house, to request a lock of the hair; but, not meeting with Mr. *Taylor* at home, went again Monday the 9th, when Mr. *Taylor* gave me part of what hair he had reserved for himself. *Hawkesworth* [21] having informed me, on the Saturday, that Mr. *Ellis,* the player, had taken some hair, and that he had seen him take a rib-bone, and carry it away in paper under his coat, I went from Mr. *Laming's,* on Monday, to Mr. *Ellis,* who told me, that he had paid 6d. to Elizabeth *Grant* for seeing the body; and that he had lifted up the head, and taken, from among the sludge under it, a small quantity of hair, with which was a piece of the shroud, and, adhering to the hair, a bit of the skin of the skull, about the size of a shilling. He put them all into my hands, with the rib-bone, which appeared to be one of the upper ribs. The piece of the shroud was of coarse linen. The hair, which [22] he had taken, was short: a small part of it he had washed, and the remainder was in the clotted state, in which he had taken it. He told me, that he had tried to reach down as low as the hands of the corpse, but had not been able to effect it. The washed hair corresponded exactly with that in my possession, and which I had just received from Mr. *Taylor. Ellis* is a very ingenious worker-in-hair, and he said, that thinking it would be of great advantage to him to possess a quantity of *Milton's* hair, he had returned to the church on Thursday, and made his endeavors to get access a second time to the body: but had been refused admittance. *Hawkesworth* took a tooth, and broke off a bit [23] of the coffin; of which I was informed by Mr. *Ascough.* I purchased them both of *Hawkesworth,* on Saturday the

7th, for 2s; and he told me, that when he took the tooth out, there were but two more remaining; one of which was afterwards taken by another of Mr. *Ascough's* men; and Ellis informed me, that, at the time when he was there, on Wednesday, the teeth were all gone; but the Overseers say, they think that all the teeth were not taken out of the coffin, though displaced from the jaws, but that some of them must have fallen among the other bones, as they very readily came out, after the first were drawn.—Haslib, son of William Haslib, of Jewin-street, undertaker, took [Dᵛ/24] one of the small bones, which I purchased of him, on Monday, the 9th, for 2s.

With respect to the identity of the person; any one must be a skeptic against violent presumptions, to entertain a doubt of its being that of *Milton*. The parish-traditions of the spot; the age of the coffin; none other found in the ground, which can at all contest with it, or render it suspicious; *Poole's* tradition, that those, who had conversed with his father about *Milton's* person, always described him to have been thin, with long hair; the entry in the register-book, that *Milton* died of a consumption, are all strong confirmations, with the size of the coffin, [D/25] of the identity of the person. If it be objected, that against the pillar, where the pulpit formerly stood, and immediately over the common-council-men's pew, is a monument to the family of *Smith*, which shews that "*near that place*" were buried, in 1653, *Richard* Smith, aged 17; in 1655, *John* Smith, aged 32; in 1664, *Elizabeth* Smith, the mother, aged 64; and, in 1675, *Richard* Smith, the father, aged 85; it may be answered, that if the coffin in question be one of these, the others should be there also. The corpse is certainly not that of a man of 85, and, if it be supposed one of the first-named males of the *Smith* family, certainly the two later coffins should appear; but none such are found; nor could [D2ᵛ/26] that monument have been erected until many years after the death of the last person mentioned in the inscription; and it was then placed there, as it expresses, not by any of the family, but at the expence of friends. The flatness of the pillar, after the pulpit had been removed, offered an advantageous situation for it; and "*near this place*," upon a mural monument, will always admit of literal construction. As *Holmes*, who is much respected in that parish, and very ingenious and intelligent in his business, says, that a leaden coffin, when the inner wooden case is perished, must, from pressure and its own weight, shrink in breadth, and that, therefore, more than the present admeasurement of this coffin, across [D2/27] the shoulders, much have been its original breadth. There is evidence, also, that it was incurvated, both on the top and at the sides, at the time when it was discovered. But the strongest of all confirmations is the hair, both in its length and color. Behold Faithorne's quarto-print of *Milton*, taken ad vivum,[3] in 1670, four years before *Milton's* death. Observe the short locks growing towards the forehead, and the long ones flowing from the same place down the sides of the face. The whole quantity of hair, which Mr. Taylor took, was from the forehead, and all taken out at one grasp. I measured, on Monday morning, the 9th, that lock of it, which he had given to Mr. *Laming*, six inches and a half by a rule; [28] and the lock of it, which he gave to me, taken at the same time and from the same place, measures only two inches and an half. In the reign of *Charles* II. how few, besides *Milton*, wore their [own] hair! *Wood*[4] says *Milton* had light brown hair; the very description of that which we possess: and what may seem extraordinary, it is yet so strong, that Mr. *Laming*, to cleanse it from its clotted state, let the cistern-cock run on it, for near a minute, and then rubbed it between his fingers, without injury.

Milton's coffin lay open from Wednesday morning, the 4th, at 9 o'clock, until 4 o'clock in the afternoon of the following day, when the ground was closed.

With [29] respect to there being no inscription on the coffin; *Holmes* says, that inscription-plates were not used, nor invented, at the time when *Milton* was buried; that the practice then was to paint the inscription on the outside wooden coffin; which, in this case, was entirely perished.

It has never been pretended that any hair was taken, except by Mr. *Taylor*, and by *Ellis* the player; and all which the latter took would, when cleansed, easily lie in a small locket. Mr. *Taylor* has divided his share into many small parcels; and the lock which I saw in Mr. *Laming's* hands, on Saturday morning, the 7th, and which then measured 6 inches [30] and an half, had been so cut and reduced by divisions among Mr. *Laming's* friends, at noon, on Monday, the 9th, that he then possessed only a small bit, from two to three inches in length.

All the teeth are remarkably short below the gum. The five, which were in the upper jaw, and the middle teeth of the lower, are perfect and white. Mr. *Fountain* took the five upper-jaw teeth; Mr. *Laming* one from the lower jaw; Mr. *Taylor* two from it; *Hawkesworth* one; and another of Mr. *Ascough's* men one; besides these, I have not been able to trace any; not have I heard that any more were taken. It is not probably that more than ten should have been brought [31] away, if the conjecture of the Overseers, that some dropped among the other bones, be founded.

〰

In recording a transaction, which will strike every liberal mind with horror and disgust, I cannot omit to declare, that I have procured those relics, which I possess, only in the hope of bearing part in a pious and honorable restitution of all that has been taken:—the sole atonement, which can now be made, to the violated [E^v/32]rights of the dead; to the insulted parishioners at large; and to the feelings of all good men. During the present repair of the church, the mode is obvious and easy. Unless that be done, in vain will the parish hereafter boast a sumptuous monument to the memory of *Milton:* it will but display their shame in proportion to its magnificence.

I collected this account from the mouths of those, who were immediate actors in this most sacrilegious scene; and before the voice of charity had reproached them with their impiety. By it, those are exculpated, whose just and liberal sentiments restrained their hands from an act of violation; and the blood of [E/33] the lamb is dashed against the door-posts of the perpetrators, not to save, but to mark them to posterity.

PHILIP NEVE.

Furnival's Inn
14th of August 1790.

FINIS [F^v/34]

〰

POSTSCRIPT

As some reports have been circulated, and some anonymous papers have appeared,[5] since the publication of this pamphlet, with intent to induce a belief that the corpse mentioned in it is that of a woman, and as the curiosity of the public now calls for a second impression of it, an opportunity is offered of relating a few circumstances, which have happened since the 14th of August, and which, [F] in some degree, may confirm the opinion that the corpse is that of *Milton*.

On Monday the 16th I called upon the Overseer, Mr. *Fountain,* when he told me, that the parish-officers had seen a Surgeon, who on Wednesday the 4th had got through a window into the church, and who had upon inspection pronounced the corpse to be that of a woman. I thought it very improbable, that a Surgeon should creep through a window, who could go through a door for a few halfpence; but I no otherwise expressed my doubts of the truth of the information, than by asking for the Surgeon's address. I was answered, [F^{v}2/36] "that the gentlemen begged not to have it known, that he might not be interrupted by enquiries." A trifling relic was, nevertheless, at the same time withholden, which I had expected to receive through Mr.

Fountain's hands; by which it appeared, that those in possession of them were still tenacious of the spoils of the coffin, although they affected to be convinced that they were not those of *Milton*. Their contradictions, however, I reserved for the test of an inquiry elsewhere.

In the course of that week I was informed that some gentlemen had, on Tuesday the 17th, prevailed on the Churchwardens to suffer a second disinterment of the coffin, which had taken place on that day. On Saturday the 21st I waited on Mr. *Strong*, who told me that he had been present at such second disinterment, [F2/37] and that he had sent for an experienced Surgeon of the neighbourhood, who upon inspection and examination of the corpse, had pronounced it to be that of a man. I was also informed on that day, the 21st, by a principal person of the parish, whose veracity no one can doubt, and whose information cannot be suspected, that the parish-officers had agreed among themselves, that from my frequent visits and enquiries I must have intention of delivering some account of the transaction to the world; and that, therefore, [38] to stop the narrative from going forth, they must invent some story of a Surgeon's inspection on the 4th, and of his declaration that the corpse was that of a woman. From this information it was easy to judge what would be the fate of any personal application to the parish-officers, with intent to obtain a restitution of what had been taken from the coffin; I, therefore, on Wednesday the 25th, addressed the following letter to Mr. *Strong:*

"Dear Sir,
        The reflection of a few / moments, after I left you on Saturday, / clearly shewed me, that the probability / [39] of the coffin in question being *Milton's* was not at all weakened, ei- / ther by the dates, or the number of persons on the *Smith's* monument; / but that it was rather confirmed by the latter circumstance. By the evi- / dence, which you told me was given / by the Surgeon, called in on Tuesday / the 17th,[6] the corpse is that of a male: / it is certainly not that of a man of 85: / if, therefore, it be one of the earlier / buried *Smiths*, all the later coffins of that family should appear; but not one / of them is found. I, then, suppose / the monument to have been put there, / because the flat pillar, after the pulpit / was removed, offered a convenient / situation for it, and "near this place" / to [40] be open, as it is in almost every / case where it appears, to very liberal / interpretation.
        It is, therefore, to be believed, that / the unworthy treatment, on the 4th, / was offered to the corpse of *Milton*. / Knowing what I know, I must not be / silent. It is a very unpleasing story to / relate; but as it has fallen to my task, / I will not shrink from it. I respect / nothing in this world more than truth / and the memory of *Milton*; and to / swerve a tittle from the first would / offend the latter. I shall give the / plain and simple narrative, as deli- / vered by the parties themselves: if it / sit heavy on any of their shoulders, it / is [41] a burthen of their own taking up, / and their own backs must bear it. / They are all, as I find, very fond of deriving honor to themselves from *Milton,* as their parishioner, perhaps / the mode, which I have hinted, is the / only one, which they have now left / themselves, of proving an equal desire / to do honor to him. If I had thought / that in personally proposing to the parish-officers a general search for and / collection of all the spoils, and to put them, / together with the mangled / corpse and old coffin, into a new / leaden one, I should have been at- / tended to, I would have taken that / method; but when I found such im- / pertinent inventions, as setting-up a fabulous[7] [Gᵛ/42] / surgeon to creep-in at a win- / dow, practised, I felt that so low an attempt at derision would ensure that / whatever I should afterwards propose / would be equally derided, and I had / then left no other means than to call / in the public opinion in aid of my / own, and to hope that we should at / length see the bones of an honest / man, and the first scholar and poet / our country can boast, restored to / their sepulchre.
        The narrative will appear, I be- / lieve, either to-morrow, or on Friday: / whenever it

does, your withers are / unwrung, and Mr. *Cole* has shewn / himself an upright church-warden. / [G/43] I cannot conclude without return- / ing you many thanks for your great / civilities, and am, &c.

The corpse was found entirely mutilated, by those who disinterred it on the 17th; almost all the ribs, the lower jaw, and one of the hands gone. Of all those who saw the body, on Wednesday the 4th, and on Thursday the 5th, there is not one person, who discovered a single hair of any other color than light brown, although both Mr. *Laming* and Mr. *Ellis* lifted up the head, and although the considerable quantity of hair which Mr. *Taylor* took was from the top of the head, and that which *Ellis* took was from behind it; yet, from the accounts of [G2^v/44] those who saw it on the 17th, it appears, that the hair on the back of the head, was found of dark brown, nearly approaching to black, although the front hair remaining was of the same light brown as that taken on the 4th. It does not belong to me either to account for, or to prove this fact.

On Wednesday, September the 1st, I waited on Mr. Dyson, who was the gentlemen sent for on the 17th to examine the corpse. I asked him, simply, whether from what had then appeared before him, he judged it to be male or female? His answer was, that, having examined the pelvis and the skull, he judged the corpse to be that of a man. I asked what [G2/45] was the shape of the head? He said, that the forehead was high and erect, though the top of the head was flat: and added, that the skull was of that shape and flatness at the top, which, differing from those of blacks, is observed to be common, and almost peculiar, to persons of very comprehensive intellects. I am a stranger to this sort of knowledge; but the opinion is a strong confirmation, that, from all the premises before him, he judged the head to be that of *Milton*. On a paper, which he shewed me, enclosing a bit of the hair, he had written, *"Milton's* hair."

Mr. *Dyson* is a surgeon, who received his professional education under the late Dr. [46] *Hunter,* is in partnership with Mr. *Price,* in Fore-Street where the church stands, is of easy access, and his affability can be exceeded only by his skill in an extensive line of practice.

Mr. *Taylor,* too, who is a surgeon of considerable practice and eminence in his county, judged the corpse, on the 4th, to be that of a male.

A man also, who has for many years acted as grave-digger in that parish, and who was present on the 17th, decided, upon sight of the skull, that it was male: with as little hesitation he pronounced another, which had been thrown out of the ground in digging, to be that of [47] a woman. Decisions obviously the result of practical, rather than of scientific knowledge; for, being asked his reasons, he could give none, but that observation had taught him to distinguish such subjects. Yet this latter sort of evidence is not to be too hastily rejected: it may not be understood by every body; but, to any one acquainted with those who are eminently skilled in judging of the genuineness of ancient coins, it will be perfectly intelligible. In that difficult and useful art the eye of a proficient decides at once: a novice, however, who should enquire for the reasons of such decision, would seldom receive a further answer than that the decision itself is the result of experience and observation, and that [49] the eye can be instructed only by long familiarity with the subject: yet all numismatic knowledge rests upon this sort of judgment.

After these evidences, what proofs are there, or what probable presumptions, that the corpse is that of a woman?

It was necessary to relate these facts, not only as they belonged to the subject, but lest, from the reports and papers above-mentioned, I might, otherwise, seem to have given either an unfaithful or a partial statement of the evidences before me: whereas now it will clearly be seen, what facts appeared on the first disinterment, which preceded, and what are to be attributed to the second, which succeeded the date of the narrative.

I have now added every circumstance, which has hitherto come to my knowledge, relative to this extraordinary transaction; and conclude with this declaration, that I should be very glad if any person would, from facts, give me reason to believe, that the corpse in question is rather that of *Elizabeth Smith,* whose name I know only from her monument, than that of *John Milton.*

P.N.

F.I. [Furnival's Inn]
8th of Sept. 1790 [50]

NOTES

1. Fellow of the Antiquarian Society, as distinguished from Neve, who was merely an amateur antiquarian.

2. As the "old print" captioned "St. Giles' Church, Cripplegate, 1682–1790 (south-west aspect)" on page 33 of Sir John James Baddeley, *Account of the Church and Parish of St. Giles Without Cripplegate, in the City of London/compiled from various old authorities, including the churchwarden's accounts, and the vestry minute books of the parish* (London, 1888), indicates, St. Giles once had a proper cemetery where there is now only an asphalt-paved parking lot.

3. This was the portrait that George Vertue showed to Deborah Milton Clarke, which she with great delight affirmed to be her father's. See *Notes & Queries,* July 6, 1861, 2.

4. Anthony à Wood, historian of Oxford University, and author of *Fasti Oxoniensis* (1691), which contains one of the early lives of Milton.

5. The reference is to George Steevens's "MILTON. Reasons why it is improbable that the Coffin lately dug up in the Parish Church of St. Giles, Cripplegate, should contain the Reliques of Milton," which first appeared anonymously in the *St. James's Chronicle, Or British Evening Post,* 4 September 1790, no. 4583.

6. Theophilus Dyson, MRCS. See below.

7. That is, fictional.

APPENDIX B
MILTON. Reasons why it is improbable that the Coffin lately dug up in the Parish Church of St. Giles, Cripplegate, should contain the Reliques of MILTON.

04 September 1790, For the *St James's Chronicle*

First,—BECAUSE MILTON was buried in 1674, and this coffin was found in a situation previously allotted to a wealthy family, unconnected with his own.—See the mural monument of the *Smiths,* dated 1653, &c. immediately over the place of the supposed MILTON's interment.

Secondly—The hair of MILTON is uniformly described and represented as of a light hue; but far the greater part of the ornament of his pretended scull is of the darkest brown, without any mixture of grey.° This difference is irreconcilable to probability. Our hair, after childhood, is

First appeared anonymously in the *St. James's Chronicle, Or British Evening Post* on 4 September 1790 (no 4583), personal transcription from a photocopy of the microfilmed original, courtesy of *Eighteenth Century Research Publications.*

°*The few hairs of a lighter colour are supposed to have been such as had grown on the sides of the cheeks, after the corpse had been interred.*

rarely found to undergo a total change of color; and MILTON was 66 years old when he died, a period at which human locks, in a greater or less degree, are interspersed with white.

Thirdly,—Because the scull in question is remarkably flat and small, and with the lowest of all possible foreheads; whereas the head of MILTON was large, and his brow conspicuously high. See his portrait so often engraved by the accurate *Vertue,* who was completely satisfied with the authenticity of his original.

Fourthly,—Because the hands of MILTON were full of chalk-stones. Now it chances that his substitute's left hand had been undisturbed, and therefore was in a condition to be properly examined. No vestige, however, of cretaceous substances was visible on it, although they are of a lasting nature, and have been found on the fingers of a dead person almost coeval with MILTON.

Fifthly,—Because there is reason to believe that the aforesaid remains are those of a young female (one of the three Miss Smiths) for the bones are delicate, the teeth small, slightly inserted in the jaw, and perfectly white, even, and sound. From the corroded state of the Pelvis, nothing could, with certainty, be inferred.

Sixthly,—Because MILTON was not in affluence—expired in an emaciated state,—in a cold month, and was interred by direction of his widow. An expensive outward coffin of lead, therefore, was needed, and not likely to be provided by a rapacious woman, who oppressed her husband's children while he was living, and cheated them after he was dead.

Seventhly—Because it is improbable that the circumstance of MILTON's having been deposited under the desk, should, if true, have been so effectually concealed from the whole train of his Biographers. It was, nevertheless, produced as an ancient and well-known tradition, as soon as the parishioners of Cripplegate were aware that such an incident was gaped for by Antiquarian appetence, and would be swallowed by Antiquarian credulity. How happened it that Bishop *Newton,* who urged similar enquiries concerning MILTON, above thirty years ago, in the same parish, could obtain no such information?

Eighthly,—Because we have not been told by *Wood, Philip, Richardson, Toland,* &c. &c. that Nature, among her other partialities to Milton, had indulged him with an uncommon share of Teeth. And yet, above a hundred have been already told as the furniture of his mouth, by the conscientious worthies who assisted in the plunder of his supposed carcase and finally submitted it to every insult that brutal vulgarity could devise and express. Thanks to Fortune, however, his corpse has hitherto been violated but by proxy! May his genuine reliques (if ought of him remains unmingled with common earth) continue to elude research, at least while the present Overseers of the Poor of Cripplegate are in office! Hard indeed would have been the fate of the author of Paradise Lost to have received shelter in that chancel, that, a hundred and sixteen years after his interment, his *dominus ultima* might be ransacked by two of the lowest human beings, a Retailer of Spiritous Liquors, and a man who lends six-pences to beggars, on such despicable securities as tattered bed-gowns, cankered porridge-pots, and rusty gridirons †.—*Cape faxa manu, cape robora Pastor!*—But an ecclesiastical court may yet have cognizance of this more than savage transaction. It will then be determined whether our tombs are our own, or may be robbed with impunity by the little tyrants of a workhouse.

> "If charnel-houses, and our graves, must send
> "Those that we bury, back, our monuments
> "Shall be the maws of kites." [quotation marks in original]

It should be added, that our Pawnbroker, gin-seller, and Co., by deranging the contents of their ideal MILTON's Coffin,—by carrying away his lower jaw, ribs, and right hand,—by employing one bone as an instrument to batter the rest,—by tearing the shrowd and winding-sheet to pieces, &c. &c. had annihilated all such further evidence as might have been collected from a skilful and complete examination of these nameless fragments of mortality. So far indeed were they mutilated, that, had they been genuine, we could not have said, with Horace,

Invenies etiam disjecti membra Poetae.

Who, after a perusal of the foregoing remarks, (which are founded in circumstantial truth) will congratulate the Parishioners of St. Giles, Cripplegate, on their discovery and treatment of the imaginary dust of *Milton?*—His favourite, *Shakespeare,* most fortunately reposes at a secure distance from the paws of Messieurs *Laming* and *Fountain,* who, otherwise, might have provoked the vengeance imprecated by our great dramatick Poet on the removers of his bones.

From the preceding censures, however, Mr. *Cole* (Churchwarden) and Messieurs *Strong* and *Ascough,* (Verity and Parish Clerks) should, in the most distinguished manner, be exempted. Throughout the whole of this extraordinary business, they conducted themselves with the strictest decency and propriety.—It should also be confessed by those whom curiosity has since attracted to the place of *Milton's* supposed disinterment, that the politeness of the same Parish Officers could only be exceeded by their respect for our illustrious author's memory, and their concern at the complicated indignity which his nominal ashes have sustained.

†*Between the creditable trades of Pawn-broker and Dramseller there is a strict alliance. As* Hogarth *observes, the money lent by Mr.* Gripe, *is immediately conveyed to the shop of* Mr.Killman, *who, in return for the produce of rags, distributes poison under the specious name of* Cordials. *See Hogarth's celebrated Print entitled,* Gin-Lane.

APPENDIX C
Caveat Lector: *Errata in Howell's "Milton's Mortal Remains and Their Literary Echoes"*

Perhaps the most charitable caution one can give to modern scholars regarding Howell's 1963 article is that it is erratic. Though it contains many valuable references, the author admits that he has neither seen nor had access to either edition of Neve's *Narrative*—rather, he has "pieced [it] out" from a number of related documents in preparation for writing his article on the subject. As one might expect, Howell's accuracy suffers as a result. He begins by asserting that "the full story of what the churchwardens did has been told in a rare and curious pamphlet written by the antiquary, Philip Neve" (18); he does not mean the churchwardens (Benjamin Cole and Andrew Wright), who Neve affirms were not party to the desecration—he means the overseers, John Laming and Jonathan Fountain, and quite possibly the apothecary to the workhouse, Gabriel Taylor, who were the principal perpetrators. Similarly, he refers to Thomas Strong, Esq., FAS, as "the overseer" (19)—actually, he was the parish solicitor, and vestry clerk. John Laming becomes (consistently) John *Laning* (19ff); Howell indicates that Cole was "prevailed upon . . . to agree to open the coffin" (19), when in fact Cole (who was not present at the "merry-meeting") neither knew nor consented to what Laming, Fountain, and Taylor were planning to do, as Steevens affirms (appendix B, 2). Like Gould and Thompson, Howell repeats the quip about the rector suing the parish that appears in *St. James's Chronicle* report of 7 September 1790, no. 4584—see note 55 of my essay—when in truth the allegation is pure sardonic fantasy: George Watson Hand, the vicar at that time, had contemplated no such thing (20).Twice on page 22, Howell refers to Milton's nephews as "Philips" rather than "Phillips" (first to "John Philips," in numbered paragraph 6, then to Edward, in paragraph 9, following his source, John Ashton, who on page 72, note 2, makes "Edward Philips" interchangeable with "Edward Phillips"). On page 24, Howell omits the last line of the inscription on the Whitbread bust ("Samuel Whitbread posuit, 1793") as noted previously, and says that, "as a result of Neve's pamphlet, Samuel Whitbread, the reformer and political storm-center of his day, erected a memorial to the poet in the form of a marble"—an assertion of cause-and-effect relationship for which he has no substantiation. Later on the same page, he follows French (*Life Records,* 5:99) without citing him in claiming that "both [the Whitbread] bust with its [Woodthorpe] shrine, and the [Montford] statue outside the western door were destroyed by the bombings which all but obliterated this section of London" during World War II (24): yet Pecheux reported in 1981 that she had seen both bust and statue (though not the shrine) in 1981, and both Ruth Lu San and I saw and photographed the Whitbread bust (in October 1993, and December 1999, respectively). I also photographed the Montford statue inside the church on Easter Sunday, 15 April 2001. Lastly, Howell says he is "indebted for the final word on the [various] locks [purported to be] . . . Milton's hair to Professor J. M. French, who, in his *Life Records* (V, 135) has collected all the available information on the subject" of their provenance, but he misquotes his source at least twice, first asserting that the lock of hair now at the Milton cottage was the donation of a "Mrs. Borchard of Lee"; in *The Life Records,* it is "Mrs. Barchard of *the* Lee, co. Bucks [italics mine], who had it from her great-grandfather, Dr. George Gregory, lecturer at St. Giles Cripplegate" (5:135). It was, French tells us, "said to have been taken from Milton's head at the time of his disinterment"—he does not indicate by whom— but according to Howell's rendition of the story, the lock "belonged originally to a lecturer at St. Giles Cripplegate, who got it from the head of the poet when the grave was opened in 1790" (28)—quite a different assertion, and equally without basis in fact—though, interestingly in this context, we might recall that Cromwell's bride was Elizabeth Bouchard, who married him at Cripplegate. The reference that follows French's remarks (CM 18:583) leads only to Patterson's comment that "several locks of [Milton's] hair are known. That which inspired Keats to write his sonnet is now at the Keats memorial, at Hampstead"—though on what basis Patterson can be certain of that, he does not say. Patterson's assertion notwithstanding, both Cathy De 'Frietas, interpretation officer of the Keats house in Hampstead, and Catherine Payling, curator of the Keats-Shelley house in Rome, confirm that the Leigh Hunt lock is now part of the Keats-Shelley holdings, where it resides in a reliquary that originally belonged to Pope Pius V, along with a lock of Elizabeth Barrett Browning's hair. None of Milton's hair is included in the collection at Hampstead.